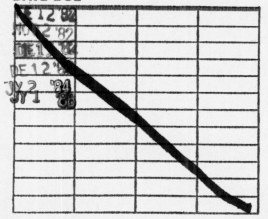

THE
FEDERAL SYSTEM
IN
CONSTITUTIONAL
LAW

C. HERMAN PRITCHETT

University of California, Santa Barbara

The Federal System in Constitutional Law

PRENTICE-HALL, INC., ENGLEWOOD CLIFFS, NEW JERSEY 07632

Library of Congress Cataloging in Publication Data

PRITCHETT, CHARLES HERMAN (date)
   The Federal system in constitutional law.

   Bibliography: p.
   Includes index.
   1. United States—Constitutional law—Cases.
2. Federal government—United States—Cases.   3. Separation of powers—United States—Cases.   I. Title.
KF4549.P756   342'.73'00264   77-13334
ISBN   0-13-308460-4

Printed in the United States of America

10 9 8 7 6 5 4 3 2 1

PRENTICE-HALL INTERNATIONAL, INC., *London*
PRENTICE-HALL OF AUSTRALIA PTY. LIMITED, *Sydney*
PRENTICE-HALL OF CANADA, LTD., *Toronto*
PRENTICE-HALL OF INDIA PRIVATE LIMITED, *New Delhi*
PRENTICE-HALL OF JAPAN, INC., *Tokyo*
PRENTICE-HALL OF SOUTHEAST ASIA PTE. LTD., *Singapore*
WHITEHALL BOOKS LIMITED, *Wellington, New Zealand*

CONTENTS

Twelve

THE COMMERCE POWER, 221

Thirteen

THE INVESTIGATORY POWER, 253

Part 2

THE FEDERAL SYSTEM

Fourteen

NATURE OF THE FEDERAL UNION, 271

Fifteen

JUDICIAL FEDERALISM, 298

PREFACE

The Constitution of the United States was drafted between May 14 and September 17, 1787, by 55 men meeting in the city of Philadelphia. The Constitutional Convention was assembled because it had become clear to the leaders of the new nation that the original governmental structure set up by the Articles of Confederation in 1781 was failing miserably. The Confederation in essence was not a government, but rather a league of friendship entered into by 13 sovereign states that yielded none of their sovereignty. Virtually all functions were concentrated in a single legislative chamber, the Congress. There was no separation of executive from legislative powers; Congress appointed such committees and civil officers as were needed to carry on executive functions. There was no judicial branch. The authority of Congress rested on the state legislatures that had created it. Each state legislature chose and paid its delegates to Congress, and each state had one vote. A two-thirds vote of the state delegations was required for the adoption of important measures, and amendments to the Articles required the unanimous consent of the states.

The powers essential to an effective government were denied to the Confederation. Congress had no direct authority over citizens. It could not levy taxes; it could only requisition funds from the states. It could not regulate commerce among the states or enforce commercial treaties with foreign countries. The public finances were in a hopeless state, and inflation led to the issuance of paper money by the states and forcible resistance to the collection of debts.

Responsible leaders saw the necessity for a stronger government. After several state legislatures took the initiative toward calling for a new constitution, Congress itself recommended that a convention meet in 1787 for the "sole and express purpose of revising the Articles of Confederation." When the Convention met on May 14, a plan for this limited purpose was submitted by the New Jersey delegation. It would simply have amended the Articles, maintaining the form of a confederation but one with substantially greater powers. The Virginia delegation, however, contended that nothing short of a national government would meet the needs of the country, and the New Jersey plan won the votes of only three states.

Acceptance of the national principle meant that the government would operate directly upon the people. It meant that the central government would have power to collect its own taxes, to make laws, and to enforce them in its own courts. Over each citizen there would be two governments—national and state—both deriving from the people and to both of which their citizens would owe obedience.

The new Constitution was signed by the delegates to the Convention on September 17, 1787. The campaign over ratification was intense and bitter. One of its legacies was the most famous commentary on American government, *The Federalist.* These essays were newspaper articles written to influence the vote in the doubtful state of New York by James Madison, Alexander Hamilton, and John Jay. The Constitution was submitted for ratification to conventions specially elected for that purpose in the states. It became effective when ratified by the ninth state, New Hampshire, on June 21, 1788.

There were two basic organizing principles in the new government set up by the Constitution—*separation of powers* and *federalism.* In this book Part 1 deals with the constitutional position of the three branches of the federal government and their interrelationships, each chapter providing a brief statement of principles and commentary, followed by illustrative Supreme Court decisions or other authoritative interpretations. In like fashion Part 2 examines the constitutional relationships between the federal government and the states. In the selection of cases the intention has been, within the inevitable space limitations, to include both representative historical interpretations and decisions dealing with current constitutional issues.

THE
FEDERAL SYSTEM
IN
CONSTITUTIONAL
LAW

Part 1

THE
SEPARATED
POWERS

Chapter One

THE INTENTION
OF THE
FRAMERS

INTRODUCTION

Under the Articles of Confederation the only governmental institution was Congress, but with a national government came the necessity of adding executive and judicial institutions and of relating them to each other. The preeminent authority on this subject was the Frenchman Baron de Montesquieu, who in his *Spirit of the Laws* (1748) had distinguished the three powers and had made their rigid separation the condition of liberty. While his work was known in America at that time and was referred to by James Madison in *No. 47* of *The Federalist*, it was probably not too influential in the decisions of the delegates. The division of authority was not established to fit any theoretical models but to handle the very practical problems which the Convention faced.

The Founding Fathers were still so close to George III that dread of a strong executive was very real to them. Their experience with state legislatures, on the other hand, had led them to fear the domination of an overweening Congress. Their experience with "paper money" democracy as practiced in some states had left them wary of putting too much power in the hands of the people. The solution to this dilemma was to set up a system of checks and balances which would blunt the drive of official power and popular emotion, providing, in Madison's words, by a "distribution and organization" of governmental powers, "better guards than are found in any other popular government against interested combinations of a majority against the rights of a minority." In *The Federalist,* particularly *Nos. 47, 48,* and *51,* Madison provided the classic explanation and defense of the constitutional arrangements for the separation of powers.

Actually, "separation of powers" is not a very exact description of the constitutional system in operation. A more accurate characterization would be "a system of separated institutions sharing powers." In the almost 200 years of experience under the Constitution, there have been periods of dominance by one or another of the three branches; but most government action requires the cooperative efforts of at least two, if not all three, of the separated institutions. As a result, competition and tension among the institutions and levels of government are inevitable, guaranteeing, as Justice Louis D. Brandeis wrote in *Myers* v. *United States* (1926), the frictions that would "preclude the exercise of arbitrary power." The purpose of the Framers, he continued, "was not to avoid friction, but, by means of the inevitable friction incident to the distribution of governmental powers among three departments, to save the people from autocracy."

THE FEDERALIST NO. 47

James Madison

One of the principal objections inculcated by the more respectable adversaries to the Constitution is its supposed violation of the political maxim that the legislative, executive, and judiciary departments ought to be separate and distinct. In the structure of the federal government no regard, it is said, seems to have been paid to this essential precaution in favor of liberty. The several departments of power are distributed and blended in such a manner as at once to destroy all symmetry and beauty of form, and to expose some of the essential parts of the edifice to the danger of being crushed by the disproportionate weight of other parts.

No political truth is certainly of greater intrinsic value, or is stamped with the authority of more enlightened patrons of liberty than that on which the objection is founded. The accumulation of all powers, legislative, executive, and judiciary, in the same hands, whether of one, a few, or many, and whether hereditary, self-appointed, or elective, may justly be pronounced the very definition of tyranny. Were the federal Constitution, therefore, really chargeable with this accumulation of power, or with a mixture of powers, having a dangerous tendency to such an accumulation, no further arguments would be necessary to inspire a universal reprobation of the system. I persuade myself, however, that it will be made apparent to everyone that the charge cannot be supported, and that the maxim on which it relies has been totally misconceived and misapplied. In order to form correct ideas on this important subject it will be proper to investigate the sense in which the preservation of liberty requires that the three great departments of power should be separate and distinct.

The oracle who is always consulted and cited on this subject is the celebrated Montesquieu. If he be not the author of this invaluable precept in the science of politics, he has the merit at least of displaying and recommending it most effectually to the attention of mankind. Let us endeavor, in the first place, to ascertain his meaning on this point.

The British Constitution was to Montesquieu what Homer has been to the didactic writers on epic poetry. As the latter have considered the work of the immortal bard as the perfect model from which the principles and rules of the epic art were to be drawn, and by which all similar works were to be judged, so this great political critic appears to have viewed the Constitution of England as the standard, or to use his own expression, as the mirror of political liberty; and to have delivered, in the form of elementary truths, the several characteristic principles of that particular system. That we may be sure, then, not to mistake his meaning in this case, let us recur to the source from which the maxim was drawn.

On the slightest view of the British Constitution, we must perceive that the legislative, executive, and judiciary departments are by no means totally separate and distinct from each other. The executive magistrate forms an integral part of the legislative authority. He alone has the prerogative of making treaties with foreign sovereigns which, when made, have, under certain limitations, the force of legislative acts. All the members of the judiciary department are appointed by him, can be removed by him on the address of the two Houses of Parliament, and form, when he pleases to consult them, one of his constitutional councils. One branch of the legislative department forms also a great constitutional council to the executive chief, as, on another hand, it is the sole depositary of judicial power in cases of impeachment, and is invested with the supreme appellate jurisdiction in all other cases. The judges, again, are so far connected with the legislative department as often to attend and participate in its deliberations, though not admitted to a legislative vote.

From these facts, by which Montesquieu was guided, it may clearly be inferred that in saying "There can be no liberty where the legislative and executive powers are united in the same person, or body of magistrates," or, "if the power of judging be not separated from the legislative and executive powers," he did not mean that these departments ought to have no *partial agency* in, or no *control* over, the acts of each other. His meaning, as his own words import, and still more conclusively as illustrated by the example in his eye, can amount to no more than this, that where the *whole* power of one department is exercised by the same hands which possess the *whole* power of another department, the fundamental principles of a free constitution are subverted.

THE FEDERALIST NO. 48

James Madison

It was shown in the last paper that the political apothegm there examined does not require that the legislative, executive, and judiciary departments should be wholly unconnected with each other. I shall undertake, in the next place, to show that unless these departments be so far connected and blended as to give to each a constitutional control over the others, the degree of separation which the maxim requires, as essential to a free government, can never in practice be duly maintained.

It is agreed on all sides that the powers properly belonging to one of the departments ought not to be directly and completely administered by either of the other departments. It is equally evident that none of them ought to possess, directly or indirectly, an overruling influence over the others in the administration of their respective powers. It will not be denied that power is of an encroaching nature and that it ought to be effectually restrained from passing the limits assigned to it. After discriminating, therefore, in theory, the several classes of power, as they may in their nature be legislative, executive, or judiciary, the next and most difficult task is to provide some practical security for each, against the invasion of the others. What this security ought to be is the great problem to be solved.

Will it be sufficient to mark, with precision, the boundaries of these departments in the constitution of the government, and to trust to these parchment barriers against the encroaching spirit of power? This is the security which appears to have been principally relied on by the compilers of most of the American constitutions. But experience assures us that the efficacy of the provision has been greatly overrated; and that some more adequate defense is indispensably necessary for the more feeble against the more powerful members of the government. The legislative department is everywhere extending the sphere of its activity and drawing all power into its impetuous vortex.

The founders of our republics have so much merit for the wisdom which they have displayed that no task can be less pleasing than that of pointing out the errors into which they have fallen. A respect for truth, however, obliges us to remark that they seem never for a moment to have turned their eyes from the danger, to liberty, from the overgrown and all-grasping prerogative of an hereditary magistrate, supported and fortified by an hereditary branch of the legislative authority. They seem never to have recollected the danger from legislative usurpations, which, by assembling all power in the same hands, must lead to the same tyranny as is threatened by executive usurpations.

In a government where numerous and extensive prerogatives are placed in the hands of an hereditary monarch, the executive department is very justly regarded as the source of danger, and watched with all the jealousy which a zeal for liberty ought to inspire. In a democracy, where a multitude of people exercise in person the legislative functions and are continually exposed, by their incapacity for regular deliberation and concerted measures, to the ambitious intrigues of their executive magistrates, tyranny may well be apprehended, on some favorable emergency, to start up in the same quarter. But in a representative republic where the executive magistracy is carefully limited, both in the extent and the duration of its power; and where the legislative power is exercised by an assembly, which is inspired by a supposed influence over the people with an intrepid confidence in its own strength; which is sufficiently numerous to feel all the passions which actuate a multitude, yet not so numerous as to be incapable of pursuing the objects of its passions by means which reason prescribes; it is against the enterprising ambition of this department that the people ought to indulge all their jealousy and exhaust all their precautions.

The legislative department derives a superiority in our governments from other circumstances. Its constitutional powers being at once more extensive, and less susceptible of precise limits, it can, with the greater facility, mask, under complicated and indirect measures, the encroachments which it makes on the co-ordinate departments. It is not unfrequently a question of real nicety in legislative bodies whether the operation of a particular measure will, or will not, extend beyond the legislative sphere. On the other side, the executive power being restrained within a narrower compass and being more simple in its nature, and the judiciary being described by landmarks still less uncertain, projects of usurpation by either of these departments would immediately betray and defeat themselves. Nor is this all: as the legislative department alone has access to the pockets of the people, and has in some constitutions full discretion, and in all a prevailing influence, over the pecuniary rewards of those who fill the other departments, a dependence is thus created in the latter, which gives still greater facility to encroachments of the former.

James Madison

To what expedient, then, shall we finally resort, for maintaining in practice the necessary partition of power among the several departments as laid down in the Constitution? The only answer that can be given is that as all these exterior provisions are found to be inadequate the defect must be supplied, by so contriving the interior structure of the government as that its several constituent parts may, by their mutual relations, be the means of keeping each other in their proper places. Without presuming to undertake a full development of this important idea I will hazard a few general observations which may perhaps place it in a clearer light, and enable us to form a more correct judgment of the principles and structure of the government planned by the convention.

In order to lay a due foundation for that separate and distinct exercise of the different powers of government, which to a certain extent is admitted on all hands to be essential to the preservation of liberty, it is evident that each department should have a will of its own; and consequently should be so constituted that the members of each should have as little agency as possible in the appointment of the members of the others. Were this principle rigorously adhered to, it would require that all the appointments for the supreme executive, legislative, and judiciary magistracies should be drawn from the same fountain of authority, the people, through channels having no communication whatever with one another. Perhaps such a plan of constructing the several departments would be less difficult in practice than it may in contemplation appear. Some difficulties, however, and some additional expense would attend the execution of it. Some deviations, therefore, from the principle must be admitted. In the constitution of the judiciary department in particular, it might be inexpedient to insist rigorously on the principle: first, because peculiar qualifications being essential in the members, the primary consideration ought to be to select that mode of choice which best secures these qualifications; second, because the permanent tenure by which the appointments are held in that department must soon destroy all sense of dependence on the authority conferring them.

It is equally evident that the members of each department should be as little dependent as possible on those of the others for the emoluments annexed to their offices. Were the executive magistrate, or the judges, not independent of the legislature in this particular, their independence in every other would be merely nominal.

But the great security against a gradual concentration of the several powers in the same department consists in giving to those who administer each department the necessary constitutional means and personal motives to resist encroachments of the others. The provision for defense must in this, as in all other cases, be made commensurate to the danger of attack. Ambition must be made to counteract ambition. The interest of the man must be connected with the constitutional rights of the place. It may be a reflection on human nature that such devices should be necessary to control the abuses of government. But what is government itself but the greatest of all reflections on human nature? If men were angels, no government would be necessary. If angels were to govern men, neither external nor internal controls on government would be necessary. In framing a government which is to be administered by men over men, the great difficulty lies in this: you must first enable the government to control the governed; and in the next place oblige it to control itself. A dependence on the people is, no doubt, the primary control on the government; but experience has taught mankind the necessity of auxiliary precautions.

This policy of supplying, by opposite and rival interests, the defect of better motives, might be traced through the whole system of human affairs, private as well as public. We see it particularly displayed in all the subordinate distributions of power, where the constant aim is to divide and arrange the several offices in such a manner as that each may be a check on the other—that the private interest of every individual may be a sentinel over the public rights. These inventions of prudence cannot be less requisite in the distribution of the supreme powers of the State.

Chapter Two

THE
FEDERAL COURT
SYSTEM

INTRODUCTION

In *No. 78* of *The Federalist* Alexander Hamilton forecast that the federal judiciary would be the weakest of the three departments of government. "The Executive not only dispenses the honours, but holds the sword of the community. The legislature not only commands the purse, but prescribes the rules by which the duties and rights of every citizen are to be regulated. The judiciary, on the contrary . . . may truly be said to have neither force nor will, but merely judgment." Nevertheless, the power of "judgment" as exercised by the Supreme Court has proved to be so effective that both the executive and the legislature have accepted judicial interpretations of their powers and position in the federal system.

Judicial Organization

The Supreme Court was created directly by Article III, section 1, of the Constitution. The members of the Constitutional Convention were clear that there had to be a top-level federal court, but they were less certain regarding whether a system of lower federal courts was needed. Consequently, Article III simply provided for "such inferior courts as the

Congress may, from time to time, ordain and establish." It was argued by some that the state courts could be authorized to try federal cases, subject to review by the Supreme Court. However, in the Judiciary Act of 1789 the advocates of a complete and separate system of federal courts were successful.

The Judiciary Act established a district court in each state, and grouped the districts into circuits, with a circuit court for each. The district courts were given jurisdiction over admiralty proceedings, and over lesser federal civil and criminal cases in general. District court decisions could be appealed to the circuit courts, which were also the courts of first instance for trial of all major civil and criminal cases coming within federal jurisdiction.

The 1789 statute did not provide for any circuit court judges as such. The circuit courts were to be held by a Supreme Court justice and the district judge of the particular district, sitting together. This arrangement required Supreme Court justices to spend much of the year traveling by coach or on horseback, or perhaps by ship along the coast, from district to district and back to the capital. As the size of the country and the volume of litigation increased, it became less and less practical for a Supreme Court justice to attend to his duties both on circuit and in Washington.

Judges were finally appointed for the circuit courts in 1869, but circuit riding was not completely abandoned until a new level of appellate courts, called circuit courts of appeal, was established in 1891. Even today, each Supreme Court justice is assigned as "circuit justice" for one of the 11 circuits, for purposes of certain paper work, and is entitled to sit on its court of appeals. The old circuit courts were finally combined with the district courts in 1911, and since 1948 the circuit courts of appeals have been designated simply as courts of appeals for the appropriate circuit.

The federal judicial system thus consists of three levels. There are 93 district courts—at least one in each state—staffed by some 400 district judges. Trials are held in the district courts before a single judge (certain statutes do require the impanelling of a three-judge district court). At the intermediate level are the courts of appeals for each of the ten circuits into which the country is divided, plus the District of Columbia. There are approximately 100 judges on the courts of appeals, and they review decisions of the district courts and also those of some federal administrative agencies. Each appeal is heard by a panel of three judges, although it is possible to request that all the judges in a circuit sit *en banc* on a case. The Supreme Court, headed by the Chief Justice of the United States and with eight Associate Justices, completes the federal judicial hierarchy.

The jurisdiction of the federal courts (i.e., their authority to decide cases) is defined by Article III on two different bases—subject matter and nature of the parties involved. The subject matter classifications are all cases in law and equity arising (1) under the Constitution, (2) under laws of the United States, and (3) under treaties made under the authority of the United States; an additional classification includes all cases of admiralty and maritime jurisdiction. Any case falling in one of these four fields can be brought in the federal courts regardless of who the parties to the controversy may be.

Issues arising under the first three of these headings are referred to generally as "federal questions." Such a case arises wherever an interpretation or application of the Constitution or a federal statute or treaty is essential to a judicial decision. A plaintiff seeking to bring a case in the federal courts on one of these grounds must set forth on the face of his complaint a substantial claim as to the *federal* question involved.

The second basis for federal court jurisdiction regards the parties involved. Article III extends federal jurisdiction to controversies (1) in which the United States is a party; (2) between two or more states; (3) between a state and citizens of another state; (4) between citizens of different states; (5) between a state, or the citizens thereof, and foreign states' citizens or subjects; and (6) to all cases affecting ambassadors, other public ministers, and consuls. Issues involving these classes of parties can be brought in the federal courts, no matter what the subject matter.

Of these classes, the first and the fourth are by far the most important in the generation of litigation. The United States enters federal courts as a party plaintiff in a great number of civil and criminal suits every year, and it can also be haled into court as a defendant in situations where it has waived its sovereign immunity and given its consent to be sued. When no consent to sue the government has been given, it may be possible to sue officials acting for the government, particularly if they are alleged to be acting beyond their statutory authority or under an unconstitutional statute.

Suits between citizens of different states are commonly referred to as "diversity of citizenship" cases. The purpose of opening the federal courts to such cases was originally to provide a neutral forum for the two parties, since the state courts might be biased in favor of their citizens. Today there is less likelihood of such bias, and abolition of this class of federal jurisdiction, or its substantial limitation, has been proposed.

The issues involved in diversity cases arise out of state law, but initially the Supreme Court held that federal judges were free to ignore state law and apply general legal principles in their settlement. However, in *Erie* v. *Tompkins* (1938) the Court reversed this century-old practice and ruled that federal judges in diversity cases must apply state law as declared by state courts or legislatures.

The provision extending federal jurisdiction to suits between a state and citizens of another state was the source of a controversy which resulted in adoption of the Eleventh Amendment. In *Chisholm* v. *Georgia* (1793) the Supreme Court ruled that this language, which had been generally understood to be an authorization to each state to sue citizens of other states, also permitted citizens to sue a state other than their own. This judicial misreading of constitutional intent aroused a storm in the states, and Congress promptly responded by initiating the Eleventh Amendment to reverse the ruling.

Suits falling under federal jurisdiction can also be brought in state courts, except in those areas—such as federal criminal, admiralty, patent, and bankruptcy cases—where Congress has given the federal courts exclusive jurisdiction. Where state courts *do* exercise federal jurisdiction, they are bound by the "supremacy clause" of the Constitution, Article VI, which, after making the Constitution, laws, and treaties of the United States "the supreme law of the land," continues: ". . . and the judges in every state shall be bound thereby, any thing in the Constitution or laws of any state to the contrary notwithstanding." Cases decided in state courts which raise a "federal question" are subject to review by the Supreme Court after they have progressed through the highest state court to which appeal is possible, although such review is by no means guaranteed.

The Federal Judiciary

As with other high level federal officials, federal judges are appointed by the President by and with the advice and consent of the Senate. This is frankly and entirely a political process. With few exceptions the President limits his choices to members of his own party. District judgeships are filled primarily on the recommendation of the senator for the state, if there is one from the President's party, or of prominent state party members. The nominees thus suggested are checked by the Department of Justice, the FBI, and the American Bar Association's Committee on the Federal Judiciary. Vacancies on the courts of appeals are sometimes filled by promotion of a district judge; the senators or state party organizations are still important, although not quite so dominant at this level.

For the Supreme Court, the President receives suggestions from many sources, particularly from his Attorney General, but he makes his own decision. Often he has his own ideas on the subject—either about specific persons or about the qualifications he seeks. In 1969 President Nixon announced that he would appoint only "strict constructionists" to the Supreme Court.

The senate confirmation stage also affords an opportunity for the political views of the nominee to be considered. The nomination of Louis D. Brandeis was resisted by senate conservatives in 1916, and senate liberals sought to prevent confirmation of Charles Evans Hughes as Chief Justice in 1930, but both efforts were unsuccessful. However, the nomination of John J. Parker was defeated in 1930 by senate liberals. President Johnson's effort to elevate Associate Justice Abe Fortas to the Chief Justiceship in 1968 was thwarted by a Republican filibuster. President Nixon was consequently able to name Warren Burger to succeed Earl Warren as Chief Justice in 1969, but Nixon's next two conservative nominees, Clement F. Haynsworth and G. Harrold Carswell, were rejected by the Democratic majority in the Senate.

Appointment of federal judges for "good behavior" is one of the great pillars of judicial independence. A federal judge can be removed from office only by conviction on impeachment. Only one Supreme Court justice has ever been subjected to impeachment proceedings; he was Samuel Chase, whose judicial conduct was marked by gross Federalist partisanship. In 1804 the Jeffersonians sought to impeach Chase, but failed to secure a conviction. Right-wing groups during the 1960s carried on a campaign to "impeach Earl Warren," and in 1970 Gerald Ford, then minority leader in the House of Representatives, proposed impeachment proceedings against the liberal William O. Douglas, but both efforts failed. Eight lower federal court judges have been impeached, four of whom were convicted.

The absence or inadequacy of retirement allowances has in the past been responsible for some judges retaining their posts long after they were physically or mentally incapable of continuing the work. But in 1937 Congress passed a liberalized retirement act which permits Supreme Court justices to retire after age 70 on full pay without resigning, remaining thereafter subject to recall for further judicial duty in the lower courts. The issue of judicial inability was raised in 1975 when Justice Douglas undertook to resume his Court duties after suffering a stroke; as his incapacity became clear, however, he retired.

The Supreme Court and Its Operation

The Supreme Court was originally composed of six justices, but its size was subsequently both reduced and increased by Congress, usually for political reasons. Since 1869 the number has been fixed at nine members. In 1937, after a number of President Franklin D. Roosevelt's New Deal measures had been declared unconstitutional by the Court, the President asked Congress to authorize six new seats on the Court, to which he could appoint favorable justices. The public regarded this as "court-packing," and the plan was defeated in Congress.

The Court is headed by the Chief Justice of the United States. His formal authority consists primarily of his role as presiding officer in court and in the conference and of his power to assign the writing of opinions. But he also has a significant symbolic role, as well as important administrative duties as head of the federal judicial system.

While the Supreme Court is primarily an appellate court, the Constitution does define two categories of cases which can be heard in the Court's *original jurisdiction,* i.e., without prior consideration by any other court. These are the cases in which a state is a party, and those cases affecting ambassadors, public ministers, and consuls. However, the Court generally does *not* have to accept a suit invoking its original jurisdiction unless there is some compelling issue of public policy involved.

All the remaining business of the Supreme Court comes to it in its *appellate jurisdiction,* which it exercises, as the Constitution says, ". . . with such exceptions, and under such regulations as the Congress shall make." In the post-Civil War period Congress used this authority over the Court's appellate jurisdiction to withdraw from its consideration a politically embarrassing case in which the Court had already heard argument. In **Ex parte McCardle** (1869) the Court agreed that such action was within congressional power and dismissed the case. On several subsequent occasions congressmen hostile to Court decisions have attempted to strip the Court of some of its appellate jurisdiction, but never successfully. It appears probable that the Court would declare any legislation of this sort unconstitutional as a violation of the separation of powers and as an attack on the status and independence of the nation's highest judicial tribunal.

Most of the cases the Supreme Court decides are brought up to it by the writ of *certiorari.* This is a discretionary writ; that is, the Supreme Court does not have to grant a petition for certiorari and in the very great majority of cases does not do so. For example, in the 1975 term only 136 petitions from federal courts of appeals were granted out of 2,412 filed, or 5.4 percent. Rule 14 of the Rules of the Supreme Court specifies that review on certiorari will be granted "only where there are special and important reasons therefor." Certiorari is granted on the vote of four of the nine justices. Exercise of the Court's discretion in deciding whether to grant certiorari may involve as much judicial statesmanship as the decision of a case on its merits.

In addition to certiorari, cases may come to the Supreme Court on the writ of *appeal,* which unlike certiorari is a matter of right. The decisions of three-judge district courts, required to sit in certain civil rights cases and prior to 1976 in suits challenging the constitutionality of federal or state statutes, go directly to the Supreme Court on appeal. Also, Congress has provided for review by appeal of state court decisions denying a litigant's claim of federal constitutional right. Technically the Court has no choice but to accept these cases, though in fact it often does not do so. The appellant is required to file a preliminary "jurisdictional statement," which the Court tends to treat as something like a petition for certiorari. If the Court decides to hear the case, probable jurisdiction is noted and the case set down for hearing; or the state court decision may be affirmed without hearing. But more often the Court will refuse review "for want of a substantial federal question."

The Supreme Court meets for business in October of every year, and this "October term" continues until the following June. The usual pattern of the Court's operation is to hear arguments of the counsel in the cases before it for two weeks at a time and then to recess for two weeks or so to study the cases and write opinions.

On Fridays during the term, the justices meet in conference to discuss and decide pending cases. At the conference the Chief Justice presents each case along with his views, and discussion then moves to the associate justices in order of seniority. When the vote is taken, the order is reversed, the most recent appointees to the Court voting first, and the Chief Justice last. Following the vote, the Chief Justice assigns the writing of the Court's opinion to himself or to one of his colleagues. If the decision was not unanimous and the Chief Justice voted in the minority, the senior Associate Justice in the majority controls the assignment of the decision. Drafts of opinions are circulated among the justices, and the author may revise the final opinion on the basis of comments by his colleagues. Concurring opinions are written by justices who agree with the ruling but not necessarily with all the reasoning in the majority opinion, while dissenting opinions are written by justices who reject both the decision *and* the reasoning. Since about 1940 the majority of the Court's decisions have been nonunanimous.

It is a fundamental principle of American and English jurisprudence that a decision by the highest court in a jurisdiction is a binding precedent on the questions of law involved in the case. The court making the decision and all of the courts subordinate to it are expected to follow the precedent and to give similar answers to similar questions whenever they arise thereafter. The Latin label for this rule is *stare decisis*, "to stand by the things decided." Although *stare decisis* is a fundamental principle, the Supreme Court does not always follow it. Particularly in constitutional cases, the Court may find it necessary to disregard or overrule its own prior decisions. Thus, when the Court declared racial segregation in the public schools unconstitutional in **Brown v. Board of Education** (1954), it had to reverse the principle of "separate but equal" treatment of the races that it had approved in *Plessy* v. *Ferguson* (1896).

Instruments of Judicial Power

The coercive powers of the federal courts (as well as state courts) are exercised primarily through a variety of writs inherited from the English common law and equity courts. Our consideration may be limited to two of the most important, the writs of *injunction* and of *habeas corpus.*

INJUNCTIONS. Originated by the English equity courts, the writ of injunction forbids, or in some instances commands the performance of, certain specific acts. Under the traditional rules of equity, to obtain an injunction a litigant must show that he has a legal right at stake, that he is suffering or is about to suffer "irreparable injury," and that there is no action at law that offers an adequate remedy (that is, the injury is of a type that cannot be compensated for by a monetary award).

The injunction fulfills a very important function for public policy since it is the principal instrument available to private persons for testing the legality of official action or for restraining other private parties from committing allegedly illegal acts. The injunction is also widely used by law officers to compel compliance with the law.

The extraordinary effectiveness of injunctions is largely due to the fact that violation of their terms is punishable as contempt of court. An unconstitutional statute can be violated with impunity, provided that its invalidity is established when a prosecution is brought. But, as the case of **Walker v. Birmingham** (1967) demonstrates, an injunction, even though it palpably infringes on constitutional rights, must be obeyed until its invalidity is established on appeal to a higher court.

HABEAS CORPUS. Called by Blackstone the "great writ of liberty," habeas corpus is an order from a judge directing an official who has custody of a prisoner to bring that prisoner into court so that the judge may determine the legality of the detention. Article I, section 9, provides that the privilege of the writ of habeas corpus may not be suspended "unless when in cases of rebellion or invasion the public safety may require it." In fact, Lincoln did suspend the writ during the Civil War.

Until 1867 the writ was not available against any sentence imposed by a court of competent jurisdiction. But in that year Congress, anticipating Southern resistance to new civil rights legislation, conferred on federal courts broad authorization to issue writs of habeas corpus to prisoners in custody "in violation of the Constitution or of any treaty or law of the United States."

THE CONTEMPT POWER. The contempt power provides a judge with the means to protect the dignity of the court and to punish disobedience of court orders. Contempts are civil or criminal. The aim of criminal contempt is to punish disrespect to the court, and imprisonment is for a specified period of time. Civil contempt is to protect the rights of one of the litigants or to compel performance of certain actions; the imprisonment is for an indeterminate period, that is, until the prisoner obeys the court order.

Disturbances within the courtroom and in the presence of the judge are called *direct contempts,* and can be prosecuted immediately without notice or hearing. This feature of the contempt power was subjected to a scathing attack by Justice Black in *Green* v. *United States* (1958), and subsequent developments have provided greater procedural protections in some contempt situations. Thus, if the judge postpones punishment of the disrespect until the end of the trial, then, according to **Mayberry v. Pennsylvania** (1971), the contempt must be tried by a different judge with notice, hearing, and representation by counsel.

Disobedience of a judicial order occurring outside the courtroom is an *indirect contempt,* and under the federal rules of criminal procedure can be prosecuted only after notice, with representation by counsel and trial by a different judge if the alleged contempt involved disrespect to or criticism of the judge.

Historically there has been no right to jury trial in contempt cases, but in *Cheff* v. *Schnackenberg* (1966) the Supreme Court held that contempt sentences of over six months could not be imposed without a jury trial. Refusal to testify before a grand jury may also be punished as civil contempt after a judicial order requiring the testimony has been secured.

THE FEDERALIST NO. 78

Alexander Hamilton

In unfolding the defects of the existing Confederation, the utility and necessity of a federal judicature have been clearly pointed out. It is the less necessary to recapitulate the considerations there urged as the propriety of the institution in the abstract is not disputed; the only questions which have been raised being relative to the manner of constituting it, and to its extent. To these points, therefore, our observations shall be confined.

According to the plan of the convention, all judges who may be appointed by the United States are to hold their offices *during good behavior;* which is conformable to the most approved of the State constitutions, and among the rest, of that of this State. Its propriety having been drawn into question by the adversaries of that plan is no light symptom of the rage for objection which disorders their imaginations and judgments. The standard of good behavior for the continuance in office of the judicial magistracy is certainly one of the most valuable of the modern improvements in the practice of government. In a monarchy it is an excellent barrier to the despotism of the prince; in a republic it is a no less excellent barrier to the encroachments and oppressions of the representative body. And it is the best expedient which can be devised in any government to secure a steady, upright, and impartial administration of the laws.

Whoever attentively considers the different departments of power must perceive that, in a government in which they are separated from each other, the judiciary, from the nature of its functions, will always be the least dangerous to the political rights of the Constitution; because it will be least in a capacity to annoy or injure them. The executive not only dispenses the honors but holds the sword of the community. The legislature not only commands the purse but prescribes the rules by which the duties and rights of every citizen are to be regulated. The judiciary, on the contrary, has no influence over either the sword or the purse; no direction either of the strength or of the wealth of the society, and can take no active resolution whatever. It may truly be said to have neither FORCE nor WILL but merely judgment; and must ultimately depend upon the aid of the executive arm even for the efficacy of its judgments.

This simple view of the matter suggests several important consequences. It proves incontestably that the judiciary is beyond comparison the weakest of the three departments of power;[1] that it can never attack with success either of the other two; and that all possible care is requisite to enable it to defend itself against their attacks. It equally proves that though individual oppression may now and then proceed from the courts of justice, the general liberty of the people can never be endangered from that quarter; I mean so long as the judiciary remains truly distinct from both the legislature and the executive. For I agree that "there is no liberty if the power of judging be not separated from the legislative and executive powers."[2] And it proves, in the last place, that as liberty can have nothing to fear from the judiciary alone, but would have everything to fear from its union with either of the other departments; that as all the effects of such a union must ensue from a dependence of the former on the latter, notwithstanding a nominal and apparent separation; that as, from the natural feebleness of the judiciary, it is in continual jeopardy of being overpowered, awed, or influenced by its co-ordinate branches; and that as nothing can contribute so much to its firmness and independence as permanency in office, this quality may therefore be justly regarded as

---

[1] The celebrated Montesquieu, speaking of them, says: "Of the three powers above mentioned, the JUDICIARY is next to nothing."—*Spirit of Laws*, Vol. I, page 186.

[2] *Idem*, page 181.

an indispensable ingredient in its constitution, and, in a great measure, as the citadel of the public justice and the public security. . . .

If, then, the courts of justice are to be considered as the bulwarks of a limited Constitution against legislative encroachments, this consideration will afford a strong argument for the permanent tenure of judicial offices, since nothing will contribute so much as this to that independent spirit in the judges which must be essential to the faithful performance of so arduous a duty. . . .

EX PARTE MC CARDLE

7 Wallace 506, 19 L. Ed. 264 (1869)

In the post-Civil War period, a Reconstruction program was enforced upon southern whites by the radical Republicans in Congress. An opponent of Reconstruction, William McCardle, a Mississippi editor, was held for trial before a military commission. He sought habeas corpus from the Supreme Court under an 1867 statute. Republican leaders in Congress feared that the Supreme Court, which had shown hostility to the Reconstruction program, would use the *McCardle* case to hold much of the legislation unconstitutional. Consequently Congress, over President Johnson's veto, repealed the 1867 act on which McCardle's appeal was founded. The case had already been argued before the Court before the repeal, but the decision had not been announced.

The CHIEF JUSTICE [CHASE] delivered the opinion of the court. . . .

The first question necessarily is that of jurisdiction; for, if the act of March, 1868, takes away the jurisdiction defined by the act of February, 1867, it is useless, if not improper, to enter into any discussion of other questions.

It is quite true, as was argued by the counsel for the petitioner, that the appellate jurisdiction of this court is not derived from acts of Congress. It is, strictly speaking, conferred by the Constitution. But it is conferred "with such exceptions and under such regulations as Congress shall make.". . .

The source of that jurisdiction, and the limitations of it by the Constitution and by statute, have been on several occasions subjects of consideration here. In the case of *Durousseau* v. *United States,* particularly, the whole matter was carefully examined, and the court held, that while "the appellate powers of this court are not given by the judicial act, but are given by the Constitution," they are, nevertheless, "limited and regulated by that act, and by such other acts as have been passed on the subject." The court said, further, that the judicial act was an exercise of the power given by the Constitution to Congress "of making exceptions to the

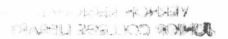

appellate jurisdiction of the Supreme Court." "They have described affirmatively," said the court, "its jurisdiction, and this affirmative description has been understood to imply a negation of the exercise of such appellate power as is not comprehended with it."

The principle that the affirmation of appellate jurisdiction implies the negation of all such jurisdiction not affirmed having been thus established, it was an almost necessary consequence that acts of Congress, providing for the exercise of jurisdiction, should come to be spoken of as acts granting jurisdiction, and not as acts making exceptions to the constitutional grant of it.

The exception to appellate jurisdiction in the case before us, however, is not an inference from the affirmation of other appellate jurisdiction. . . . The provision of the act of 1867, affirming the appellate jurisdiction of this court in cases of *habeas corpus* is expressly repealed. It is hardly possible to imagine a plainer instance of positive exception.

We are not at liberty to inquire into the motives of the legislature. We can only examine into its power under the Constitution; and the power to make exceptions to the appellate jurisdiction of this court is given by express words.

What, then, is the effect of the repealing act upon the case before us? We cannot doubt as to this. Without jurisdiction the court cannot proceed at all in any cause. Jurisdiction is power to declare the law, and when it ceases to exist, the only function remaining to the court is that of announcing the fact and dismissing the cause. And this is not less clear upon authority than upon principle. . . .

It is quite clear, therefore, that this court cannot proceed to pronounce judgment in this case, for it has no longer jurisdiction of the appeal; and judicial duty is not less fitly performed by declining ungranted jurisdiction than in exercising firmly that which the Constitution and the laws confer. . . .

The appeal of the petitioner in this case must be

Dismissed for want of jurisdiction. [3]

---

[3] In *Glidden* v. *Zdanok* (1962) Justice Douglas wrote, "There is a serious question whether the McCardle case could command a majority view today."

BROWN V. BOARD OF EDUCATION OF TOPEKA

347 U.S. 483, 74 S. Ct. 686, 98 L. Ed. 873 (1954)

MR. CHIEF JUSTICE WARREN delivered the opinion of the Court. . . .

These cases come to us from the States of Kansas, South Carolina, Virginia, and Delaware. They are premised on different facts and different local conditions, but a common legal question justifies their consideration together in this consolidated opinion. . . .

In each of the cases, minors of the Negro race, through their legal representatives, seek the aid of the courts in obtaining admission to the public schools of their community on a nonsegregated basis. In each instance, they had been denied admission to schools attended by white children under laws requiring or permitting segregation according to race. This segregation was alleged to deprive the plaintiffs of the equal protection of the laws under the Fourteenth Amendment. In each of the cases other than the Delaware case, a three-judge federal district court denied relief to the plaintiffs on the so-called "separate but equal" doctrine announced by this Court in *Plessy* v. *Ferguson.* . . . Under that doctrine, equality of treatment is accorded when the races are provided substantially equal facilities, even though these facilities be separate. . . .

In the first cases in this Court construing the Fourteenth Amendment, decided shortly after its adoption, the Court interpreted it as proscribing all state-imposed discriminations against the Negro race. The doctrine of "separate but equal" did not make its appearance in this Court until 1896 in the case of *Plessy* v. *Ferguson, supra,* involving not education but transportation. American courts have since labored with the doctrine for over half a century. In this Court, there have been six cases involving the "separate but equal" doctrine in the field of public education. In *Cumming* v. *County Board of Education.* . . . and *Gong Lum* v. *Rice.* . . . the validity of the doctrine itself was not challenged. In more recent cases, all on the graduate school level, inequality was found in that specific benefits enjoyed by white students were denied to Negro students of the same educational qualifications. *Missouri ex rel. Gaines* v. *Canada.* . . .; *Sipuel* v. *Oklahoma.* . . .; *Sweatt* v. *Painter.* . . .; *McLaurin* v. *Oklahoma State Regents.* . . . In none of these cases was it necessary to re-examine the doctrine to grant relief to the Negro plaintiff. And in *Sweatt* v. *Painter, supra,* the Court expressly reserved decision on the question whether *Plessy* v. *Ferguson* should be held inapplicable to public education.

In the instant cases, that question is directly presented. Here, unlike *Sweatt* v. *Painter,* there are findings below that the Negro and white schools involved have been equalized, or are being equalized, with respect to buildings, curricula, qualifications and salaries of teachers, and other "tangible" factors. Our decision, therefore, cannot turn on merely a comparison of these tangible factors in the Negro and white schools involved in each of the cases. We must look instead to the effect of segregation itself on public education.

In approaching this problem, we cannot turn the clock back to 1868 when the Amendment was adopted or even to 1896 when *Plessy* v. *Ferguson* was written. We must consider public education in the light of its full development and its present place in American life throughout the Nation. Only in this way can it be determined if segregation in public schools deprives these plaintiffs of the equal protection of the laws.

Today, education is perhaps the most important function of state and local governments. Compulsory school attendance laws and the great expenditures for education both demonstrate our recognition of the importance of education to our democratic society. It is required in the performance of our most basic public responsibilities, even service in the armed forces. It is the very foundation of good citizenship. Today it is a principal instrument in awakening the child to cultural values, in preparing him to adjust normally to his environment. In these days, it is doubtful that any child may reasonably be expected to succeed in life if he is denied the opportunity of an education. Such an opportunity, where the state has undertaken to provide it, is a right which must be made available to all on equal terms.

We come then to the question presented: Does segregation of children in public schools solely on the basis of race, even though the physical facilities and other "tangible" factors may be equal, deprive the children of the minority group of equal educational opportunities? We believe that it does.

In *Sweatt* v. *Painter, supra,* finding that a segregated law school for Negroes could not provide them equal educational opportunities, this Court relied in large part on "those qualities which are incapable of objective measurement but which make for greatness in a law school." In *McLaurin* v. *Oklahoma State Regents, supra,* the Court, in requiring that a Negro admitted to a white graduate school be treated like all other students, again resorted to intangible considerations: ". . . his ability to study, to engage in discussions and exchange views with other students, and, in general, to learn his profession." Such considerations apply with added force to children in grade and high schools. To separate them from others of similar age and qualifications solely because of their race generates a feeling of inferiority as to their status in the community that may affect their hearts and minds in a way unlikely ever to be undone. The effect of this separation on their educational opportunities was well stated by a finding in the Kansas case by a court which nevertheless felt compelled to rule against the Negro plaintiffs:

> Segregation of white and colored children in public schools has a detrimental effect upon the colored children. The impact is greater when it has the sanction of the law; for the policy of separating the races is usually interpreted as denoting the inferiority of the negro group. A sense of inferiority affects the motivation of a child to learn. Segregation with the sanction of law, therefore, has a tendency to [retard] the educational and mental development of negro children and to deprive them of some of the benefits they would receive in a racial[ly] integrated school system.

Whatever may have been the extent of psychological knowledge at the time of *Plessy* v. *Ferguson,* this finding is amply supported by modern authority. Any language in *Plessy* v. *Ferguson* contrary to this finding is rejected.

We conclude that in the field of public education the doctrine of "separate but equal" has no place. Separate educational facilities are inherently unequal. Therefore, we hold that the plaintiffs and others similarly situated for whom the actions have been brought are, by reason of the segregation complained of, deprived of the equal protection of the laws guaranteed by the Fourteenth Amendment. . . .

WALKER V. CITY OF BIRMINGHAM

388 U.S. 307, 87 S. Ct. 1824, 18 L. Ed. 2d 1210 (1967)

Peaceful demonstrations to protest racial discrimination in Birmingham were planned for Good Friday and Easter Sunday, 1963, by Martin Luther King, Jr., and other black ministers. Their applications for parade permits were denied, under an ordinance which authorized refusal of permits when required by considerations of "public welfare, peace, safety, health, decency, good order, morals or convenience. . . ." Learning that the ministers were proceeding with their plans despite the denial of a permit, city officials secured an ex parte injunction from a state court forbidding the demonstration, and copies were served on the ministers. Ignoring the injunction, King and his group carried out their planned program, which occasioned minor violence. The day after Easter the judge who had issued the injunction found the ministers in contempt of court.

MR. JUSTICE STEWART delivered the opinion of the court. . . .

In the present case . . . we are . . . asked to say that the Constitution compelled Alabama to allow the petitioners to violate this injunction, to organize and engage in these mass street parades and demonstrations, without any previous effort on their part to have the injunction dissolved or modified, or any attempt to secure a parade permit in accordance with its terms. . . . we cannot accept the petitioners' contentions in the circumstances of this case.

Without question the state court that issued the injunction had, as a court of equity, jurisdiction over the petitioners and over the subject matter of the controversy. And this is not a case where the injunction was transparently invalid or had only a frivolous pretense to validity. We have consistently recognized the strong interest of state and local governments in regulating the use of their streets and other public places. . . .

When protest takes the form of mass demonstrations, parades, or picketing on public streets and sidewalks, the free passage of traffic and the prevention of public disorder and violence become important objects of legitimate state concern. . . .

The generality of the language contained in the Birmingham parade ordinance upon which the injunction was based would unquestionably raise substantial constitutional issues concerning some of its provisions. . . . The petitioners, however, did not even attempt to apply to the Alabama courts for an authoritative construction of the ordinance. Had they done so, those courts might have given the licensing authority granted in the ordinance a narrow and precise scope. . . . it could not be assumed that this ordinance was void on its face.

The breadth and vagueness of the injunction itself would also unquestionably be subject to substantial constitutional question. But the way to raise that question was to apply to the Alabama courts to have the injunction modified or dissolved. The injunction in all events clearly prohibited mass parading without a permit, and the evidence shows that the petitioners fully understood that prohibition when they violated it.

The petitioners also claim that they were free to disobey the injunction because the parade ordinance on which it was based had been administered in the past in an arbitrary and discriminatory fashion. In support of this claim they sought to introduce evidence that, a few days before the injunction issued, requests for permits to picket had been made to a member of the city commission. One request had been rudely rebuffed, and this same official had later made clear that he was without power to grant the permit alone, since the issuance of such permits was the responsibility of the entire city commission. Assuming the truth of this proferred evidence, it does not follow that the parade ordinance was void on its face. The petitioners, moreover, did not apply for a permit either to the commission itself or to any commissioner after the injunction issued. Had they done so, and had the permit been refused, it is clear that their claim of arbitrary or discriminatory administration of the ordinance would have been considered by the state circuit court upon a motion to dissolve the injunction.

This case would arise in quite a different constitutional posture if the petitioners, before disobeying the injunction, had challenged it in the Alabama courts, and had been met with delay or frustration of their constitutional claims. But there is no showing that such would have been the fate of a timely motion to modify or dissolve the injunction. . . .

The rule of law that Alabama followed in this case reflects a belief that in the fair administration of justice no man can be judge in his own case, however exalted his station, however righteous his motives, and irrespective of his race, color, politics, or religion. This Court cannot hold that the petitioners were constitutionally free to ignore all the procedures of the law and carry their battle to the streets. One may sympathize with the petitioners' impatient commitment to their cause. But respect for judicial process is a small price to pay for the civilizing hand of law, which alone can give abiding meaning to constitutional freedom.

Affirmed.

MR. CHIEF JUSTICE WARREN, whom MR. JUSTICE BRENNAN and MR. JUSTICE FORTAS join, dissenting. . . .

MAYBERRY V. PENNSYLVANIA

400 U.S. 455, 91 S. Ct. 499, 27 L. Ed. 2d 532 (1971)

MR. JUSTICE DOUGLAS delivered the opinion of the Court. . . .

Petitioner and two codefendants were tried in a state court for prison breach and holding hostages in a penal institution. While they had appointed counsel as advisers, they represented themselves. The trial ended with a jury verdict of guilty of both charges on the 21st day, which was a Friday. The defendants were brought in for sentencing on the following Monday. Before imposing sentence on the verdicts the judge pronounced them guilty of criminal contempt. He found that petitioner had committed one or more contempts on 11 of the 21 days of trial and sentenced him to not less than one nor more than two years for each of the 11 contempts or a total of 11 to 22 years. . . .

Petitioner's conduct at the trial comes as a shock to those raised in the Western tradition that considers a courtroom a hallowed place of quiet dignity as far removed as possible from the emotions of the street.

On the first day of the trial petitioner came to the side bar to make suggestions and obtain rulings on trial procedures. Petitioner said: "It seems like the court has the intentions of railroading us" and moved to disqualify the judge. The motion was denied. Petitioner's other motions, including his request that the deputy sheriffs in the courtroom be dressed as civilians, were also denied. Then came the following colloquy:

Mr. Mayberry: I would like to have a fair trial of this case and like to be granted a fair trial under the Sixth Amendment.

The Court: You will get a fair trial.

Mr. Mayberry: It doesn't appear that I am going to get one the way you are overruling all our motions and that, and being like a hatchet man for the State.

The Court: This side bar is over.

Mr. Mayberry: Wait a minute, Your Honor.

The Court: It is over.

Mr. Mayberry: You dirty sonofabitch. . . .

The fifth charge relates to a protest which the defendants made that at the end of each trial day they were denied access to their legal documents —a condition which the trial judge shortly remedied. The following ensued:

Mr. Mayberry: You're a judge first. What are you working for? The prison authorities, you bum?

Mr. Livingston: I have a motion pending before Your Honor.

The Court: I would suggest—

Mr. Mayberry: Go to hell. I don't give a good God damn what you suggest, you stumbling dog.

Meanwhile one defendant told the judge if he did not get access to his papers at night he'd "blow your head off." Another defendant said he would not sit still and be "kowtowed and be railroaded into a life imprisonment." Then the following transpired:

Mr. Mayberry: You started all this bullshit in the beginning.

The Court: You keep quiet.

Mr. Mayberry: Wait a minute.

The Court: You keep quiet.

Mr. Mayberry: I am my own counsel.

The Court: You keep quiet.

Mr. Mayberry: Are you going to gag me?

The Court: Take these prisoners out of here. We will take a ten minute recess, members of the jury. . . .

As the court prepared to charge the jury, petitioner said:

Before Your Honor begins the charge to the jury defendant Mayberry wishes to place his objection on the record to the charge and to the whole proceedings from now on, and he wishes to make it known to the Court now that he has no intention of remaining silent while the Court charges the jury, and that he is going to continually object to the charge of the Court to the jury throughout the entire charge, and he is not going to remain silent. He is going to disrupt the proceedings verbally throughout the entire charge of the Court, and also he is going to be objecting to being forced to terminate his defense before he was finished.

The court thereupon had petitioner removed from the courtroom and later returned gagged. But petitioner caused such a commotion under gag that the court had him removed to an adjacent room where a loudspeaker system made the courtroom proceedings audible. The court phrased this contempt charge as follows:

On December 9, 1966, you have constantly, boisterously, and insolently interrupted the Court during its attempts to charge the jury, thereby creating an atmosphere of utter confusion and chaos.

These brazen efforts to denounce, insult, and slander the court and to paralyze the trial are at war with the concept of justice under law. Laymen, foolishly trying to defend themselves, may understandably create awkward and embarrassing scenes. Yet that is not the character of the record revealed here. We have here downright insults of a trial judge, and tactics taken from street brawls and transported to the courtroom. This is conduct not "befitting an American courtroom," as we said in Illinois v. Allen . . . and criminal contempt is one appropriate remedy. . . .

As these separate acts or outbursts took place, the arsenal of authority described in *Allen* was available to the trial judge to keep order in the courtroom. He could, with propriety, have instantly acted, holding petitioner in contempt, or excluding him from the courtroom, or otherwise insulating his vulgarity from the courtroom. . . . Where, however, he does not act the instant the contempt is committed, but waits until the end of the trial, on balance, it is generally wise where the marks of the unseemly conduct have left personal stings to ask a fellow judge to take his place. . . . a judge, vilified as was this Pennsylvania judge, necessarily becomes embroiled in a running, bitter controversy. No one so cruelly slandered is likely to maintain that calm detachment necessary for fair adjudication. . . .

Many of the words leveled at the judge in the instant case were highly personal aspersions, even "fighting words"—"dirty sonofabitch," "dirty tyrannical old dog," "stumbling dog," and "fool." He was charged with running a Spanish Inquisition and told to "Go to hell" and "Keep your mouth shut." Insults of that kind are apt to strike "at the most vulnerable and human qualities of a judge's temperament." Bloom v. Illinois. . . .

Our conclusion is that by reason of the Due Process Clause of the Fourteenth Amendment a defendant in criminal contempt proceedings should be given a public trial before a judge other than the one reviled by the contemnor. . . . In the present case that requirement can be satisfied only if the judgment of contempt is vacated so that on remand another judge, not bearing the sting of these slanderous remarks and having the impersonal authority of the law, sits in judgment on the conduct of petitioner as shown by the record.

Vacated and remanded.

Chapter Three

JUDICIAL
REVIEW

INTRODUCTION

American courts, both federal and state, possess the power of "judicial review," i.e., the power to invalidate legislative statutes and executive or administrative actions contrary to the Constitution. The basic theory on which the American practice of judicial review is based may be summarized as follows. The written Constitution is a superior law, subject to change only by an extraordinary legislative process, and as such it is superior to common and statutory law. The powers of the several departments of government are limited by the terms of the Constitution. Judges are expected to enforce the provisions of the Constitution as the highest law and to refuse to give effect to any legislative act or executive order in conflict therewith.

Curiously, there is nothing about this in the Constitution itself. The immediate source of the doctrine is the decision of Chief Justice John Marshall in the case of **Marbury** v. **Madison** (1803). Marshall's logic, which drew heavily on the argument of Alexander Hamilton in **Federalist No. 78,** was not unassailable. In fact, a powerful opposing view was stated by Justice Gibson of the Pennsylvania supreme court in the case of **Eakin v. Raub** (1825). But *Marbury* v. *Madison* has been ratified by time and practice and is a cornerstone of the American political system.

The Supreme Court has used its power of judicial review extensively. From 1789 to 1970 the Court declared unconstitutional 97 federal statutes, 737 state laws, and about 90 municipal ordinances. Exercise of this power and presidential or congressional resistance to its use have led to some of the classic battles in American history. Considering its formidable position, the Supreme Court is vulnerable in important respects; the President can change its constitutional views by nomination of persons having different ideas when vacancies occur, as President Nixon did in transforming the Warren Court into the Burger Court. When no vacancies occurred during President Roosevelt's first term, he proposed that Congress increase the size of the Court. The President can organize public opinion against the Court, as Roosevelt did against the "horse-and-buggy" decisions of the "nine old men" or as Nixon did in his "law-and-order" speeches during the 1968 campaign. Congress can threaten to limit the appellate jurisdiction of the Supreme Court, and it also controls the jurisdiction of the entire federal judicial system. The Senate can refuse to confirm nominees to the Court; and in considering nominations, the Senate can in effect conduct inquiries into the current state of judicial thinking. The ultimate method of "correcting" Supreme Court decisions is by constitutional amendment.

When judges hold the responsibility for interpreting the basic rules of the political system, and when they face the real possibility of retaliation and retribution if the executive or the legislature or the people disagree with judicial action, they must consider carefully how actively they should become involved in the legal aspects of controversial public policies. There are two general schools of thought among judges as to what their policy should be in this respect: activism and self-restraint.

Advocates of self-restraint stress the dangers to judicial prestige and the damage to the judicial image if judges become entangled in debate over proper public policies. The continued acceptance of judicial authority, it is argued, depends on the maintenance of a mystique of judicial aloofness and noninvolvement in political matters. Problems of policy are for politicians, not judges, to decide. The restrained judge submerges himself in the judicial tradition and thinks of himself as dominated by a role with tightly prescribed limitations and expectations.

The activist judge, on the other hand, may be described as goal oriented. His prime interest is in achieving the "right" result in the controversies that come before him. His tests for "rightness" are whether the decision is politically and morally acceptable and whether its effects will be beneficial to society. Since he views law as one form of social control, he will be more creative in developing new legal doctrines to support his conclusions about public policy and more willing to overrule precedents that stand in the way of the desired result. He is less hesitant to challenge the political branches and less fearful of becoming involved in controversy.

Activist judges may have either liberal or conservative political, economic, or social goals. The property-oriented Court of the late nineteenth century and of the first third of the twentieth century had no hesitation in striking down legislation which offended its economic biases. The decision in **Lochner v. New York** (1905) offered a classic confrontation between the conservative activism of Justice Peckham and the judicial restraint of Justice Holmes, who contended that the Court must accept any legislation for which there was a "reasonable" case. Three decades later a comparable clash occurred between Justices Roberts and Stone in **United States v. Butler** (1936).

But *Butler* was almost the last of the Court's efforts to second-guess legislatures on economic regulations. The Roosevelt Court, under the leadership of Justice Black, abandoned the due process test for economic legislation, holding that legislative "errors" were subject to correction by the people, not the courts. **Ferguson v. Skrupa** (1963) was a classic Black obituary for economic due process.

The concern of the Roosevelt Court shifted from economic freedom to political and civil liberties. A famous footnote in Justice Stone's opinion in an otherwise unimportant case, **United States v. Carolene Products Co.** (1938), outlined a justification for judicial activism where civil liberties infringements were involved. This rather tentative suggestion was picked up by Justices Black and Douglas and developed into the doctrine that First Amendment freedoms occupy a "preferred position" in the constitutional scheme of values, deserving all-out judicial protection. While the "preferred freedoms" idea won some victories in the 1940s, it was ineffective against the pressures of the Cold War. In **Dennis v. United States** (1951) Justice Frankfurter used judicial restraint, and in *Barenblatt* v. *United States* (1959) Justice Harlan used the "balancing" technique to uphold legislative action against communists (see Chapter 13).

Judicial activism was of course characteristic of the Warren Court, particularly in the 1960s, but it also survived on the Burger Court, as shown by the decisions limiting state abortion laws and in **Furman v. Georgia** (1972), which declared capital punishment to be cruel and unusual. Justice Rehnquist's dissent in *Furman* effectively restated the case for conservative judicial restraint, yet in fact his record on the Court showed him to be a consistent advocate of his ideological commitments.[1]

[1]See David L. Shapiro, "Mr. Justice Rehnquist: A Preliminary View," *Harvard Law Review*, 90, 293 (1976).

Alexander Hamilton

The complete independence of the courts of justice is peculiarly essential in a limited Constitution. By a limited Constitution, I understand one which contains certain specified exceptions to the legislative authority; such, for instance, as that it shall pass no bills of attainder, no *ex post facto* laws, and the like. Limitations of this kind can be preserved in practice no other way than through the medium of courts of justice, whose duty it must be to declare all acts contrary to the manifest tenor of the Constitution void. Without this, all the reservations of particular rights or privileges would amount to nothing.

Some perplexity respecting the rights of the courts to pronounce legislative acts void, because contrary to the Constitution, has arisen from an imagination that the doctrine would imply a superiority of the judiciary to the legislative power. It is urged that the authority which can declare the acts of another void must necessarily be superior to the one whose acts may be declared void. As this doctrine is of great importance in all the American constitutions, a brief discussion of the grounds on which it rests cannot be unacceptable.

There is no position which depends on clearer principles than that every act of a delegated authority, contrary to the tenor of the commission under which it is exercised, is void. No legislative act, therefore, contrary to the Constitution, can be valid. To deny this would be to affirm that the deputy is greater than his principal; that the servant is above his master; that the representatives of the people are superior to the people themselves; that men acting by virtue of powers may do not only what their powers do not authorize, but what they forbid.

If it be said that the legislative body are themselves the constitutional judges of their own powers and that the construction they put upon them is conclusive upon the other departments it may be answered that this cannot be the natural presumption where it is not to be collected from any particular provisions in the Constitution. It is not otherwise to be supposed that the Constitution could intend to enable the representatives of the people to substitute their *will* to that of their constituents. It is far more rational to suppose that the courts were designed to be an intermediate body between the people and the legislature in order, among other things, to keep the latter within the limits assigned to their authority. The interpretation of the laws is the proper and peculiar province of the courts. A constitution is, in fact, and must be regarded by the judges as, a fundamental law. It therefore belongs to them to ascertain its meaning as well as the meaning of any particular act proceeding from the legislative body. If there should happen to be an irreconcilable variance between the two, that which has the superior obligation and validity ought, of course, to be preferred; or, in other words, the Constitution ought to be preferred to the statute, the intention of the people to the intention of their agents.

Nor does this conclusion by any means suppose a superiority of the judicial to the legislative power. It only supposes that the power of the people is superior to both, and that where the will of the legislature, declared in its statutes, stands in opposition to that of the people, declared in the Constitution, the judges ought to be governed by the latter rather than the former. They ought to regulate their decisions by the fundamental laws rather than by those which are not fundamental. . . .

MARBURY V. MADISON

1 Cranch 137, 2 L. Ed. 60 (1803)

Before yielding control of the government in 1801, the Federalist majority in Congress created a number of new judicial posts, to which President John Adams nominated members of the Federalist party. John Marshall had already been appointed by Adams as Chief Justice, but he was also serving as Secretary of State. The commissions for the new judges were in his office, but he neglected to deliver them by midnight of March 3. James Madison, taking office as Jefferson's Secretary of State on March 4, found the commissions and declined to deliver them. One of the appointees, William Marbury, brought suit in the Supreme Court to compel delivery of his commission, relying on a provision of the Judiciary Act of 1789 which he claimed gave the Supreme Court original jurisdiction in such a case.

Marshall, writing the opinion in spite of his own involvement in the affair, contended that Marbury *was* entitled to his commission. But realizing that Jefferson would instruct Madison to ignore any court order for delivery of the commission, he avoided such a confrontation and at the same time claimed a far greater power for the Court by asserting that the act of 1789 had enlarged the original jurisdiction of the Supreme Court beyond that authorized by the Constitution and that consequently the Court must declare the statutory provision unconstitutional.

MR. CHIEF JUSTICE MARSHALL delivered the opinion of the Court. . . .

The question whether an act, repugnant to the constitution, can become the law of the land, is a question deeply interesting to the United States; but, happily, not of an intricacy proportioned to its interest. It seems only necessary to recognize certain principles, supposed to have been long and well established, to decide it. That the people have an original right to establish for their future government, such principles as, in their opinion, shall most conduce to their own happiness, is the basis on which the whole American fabric has been erected. The exercise of this original right is a very great exertion; nor can it, nor ought it, to be frequently repeated. The principles, therefore, so established, are deemed fundamental; and as the authority from which they proceed is supreme, and can seldom act, they are designed to be permanent.

This original and supreme will organizes the government, and assigns to different departments their respective powers. It may either stop here, or establish certain limits not to be transcended by those departments. The government of the United States is of the latter description. The powers of the legislature are defined and limited; and that those limits may not be mistaken, or forgotten, the constitution is written. To what purpose are powers limited, and to what purpose is that limitation committed to writing, if these limits may, at any time, be passed by those intended to be restrained? The distinction between a government with limited and unlimited powers is abolished, if those limits do not confine the persons on whom they are imposed, and if acts prohibited and acts allowed, are of equal obligation. It is a proposition too plain to be contested, that the constitution controls any legislative act repugnant to it; or that the legislature may alter the constitution by an ordinary act.

Between these alternatives, there is no middle ground. The constitution is either a superior paramount law, unchangeable by ordinary means, or it is on a level with ordinary legislative acts, and, like other acts, is alterable when the legislature shall please to alter it. If the former part of the alternative be true, then a legislative act, contrary to the constitution, is not law; if the latter part be true, then written constitutions are absurd attempts, on the part of the people, to limit a power, in its own nature, illimitable.

Certainly, all those who have framed written constitutions contemplate them as forming the fundamental and paramount law of the nation, and consequently, the theory of every such government must be, that an act of the legislature repugnant to the constitution is void. This theory is essentially attached to a written constitution, and is, consequently, to be considered, by this court, as one of the fundamental principles of our society. It is not, therefore, to be lost sight of, in the further consideration of this subject.

If an act of the legislature, repugnant to the constitution, is void, does it, not withstanding its invalidity, bind the courts, and oblige them to give it effect? Or, in other words, though it not be law, does it constitute a rule as operative as if it was a law? This would be to overthrow, in fact, what was established in theory; and would seem, at first view, an absurdity too gross to be insisted on. It shall, however, receive a more attentive consideration.

It is, emphatically, the province and duty of the judicial department, to say what the law is. Those who apply the rule to particular cases, must of necessity expound and interpret that rule. If two laws conflict with each other, the courts must decide on the operation of each. So, if a law be in opposition to the constitution; if both the law and the constitution apply to a particular case, so that the court must either decide that case, conformably to the law, disregarding the constitution; or conformably to the constitution, disregarding the law; the court must determine which of these conflicting rules governs the case: this is of the very essence of judicial duty. If then, the courts are to regard the constitution, and the constitution is superior to any ordinary act of the legislature, the constitution, and not such ordinary act, must govern the case to which they both apply.

Those, then, who controvert the principle that the constitution is to be considered, in court, as a paramount law, are reduced to the necessity of maintaining that courts must close their eyes on the constitution, and see only the law. This doctrine would subvert the very foundation of all written constitutions. . . . It would declare, that if the legislature shall do that which is expressly forbidden, such act, notwithstanding the express prohibition, is in reality effectual. It would be giving to the legislature a practical and real omnipotence, with the same breath which professes to restrict their powers within narrow limits. . . .

The judicial power of the United States is extended to all cases arising under the constitution. Could it be the intention of those who gave this power, to say, that in using it, the constitution should not be looked into? That a case arising under the constitution should be decided, without examining the instrument under which it arises? This is too extravagant to be maintained. In some cases, then, the constitution must be looked into by the judges. And if they can open it at all, what part of it are they forbidden to read or to obey?

There are many other parts of the constitution which serve to illustrate this subject. It is declared that "no tax or duty shall be laid on articles exported from any state." Suppose, a duty on the export of cotton, of tobacco, or of flour; and a suit intended to recover it. Ought judgment to be rendered in such a case? ought the judges to close their eyes on the constitution, and only see the law?

The constitution declares "that no bill of attainder or *ex post facto* law shall be passed." If, however, such a bill should be passed, and a person should be prosecuted under it; must the court condemn to death those victims whom the constitution endeavors to preserve?

"No person," says the constitution, "shall be convicted of treason, unless on the testimony of two witnesses to the same overt act, or on confession in open court." Here, the language of the constitution is addressed especially to the courts. It prescribes, directly for them, a rule of evidence not to be departed from. If the legislature should change that rule, and declare one witness, or a confession out of court, sufficient for conviction, must the constitutional principle yield to the legislative act?

From these, and many other selections which might be made, it is apparent that the framers of the constitution contemplated that instrument as a rule for the government of courts, as well as of the legislature. Why otherwise does it direct the judges to take an oath to support it? This oath certainly applies, in an especial manner, to their conduct in their official character. How immoral to impose it on them, if they were to be used as the instruments, and the knowing instruments, for violating what they swear to support! . . . Why does a judge swear to discharge his duties agreeably to the constitution of the United States, if that constitution forms no rule for his government? if it is closed upon him, and cannot be inspected by him? If such be the real state of things, this is worse than solemn mockery. To prescribe, or to take the oath, becomes equally a crime.

It is also not entirely unworthy of observation, that in declaring what shall be the supreme law of the land, the constitution itself is first mentioned; and not the laws of the United States, generally, but those only which shall be made in pursuance of the constitution, have that rank.

Thus, the particular phraseology of the constitution of the United States confirms and strengthens the principle, supposed to be essential to all written constitutions, that a law repugnant to the constitution is void; and that courts, as well as other departments, are bound by that instrument.

The rule must be discharged.

EAKIN V. RAUB

12 Sergeant & Rawle 330 (1825)

In this otherwise unimportant case, Justice Gibson of the Pennsylvania supreme court effectively stated the opposite side of the argument made by Marshall in *Marbury* v. *Madison.*

GIBSON, J. . . .

. . . Our judiciary is constructed on the principles of the common law, which enters so essentially into the composition of our social institutions as to be inseparable from them, and to be, in fact, the basis of the whole scheme of our civil and political liberty. In adopting any organ or instrument of the common law, we take it with just such powers and capacities as were incident to it at the common law, except where these are expressly, or by necessary implication, abridged or enlarged in the act of adoption; and, that such act is a written instrument, cannot vary its consequences or construction. . . . Now, what are the powers of the judiciary at the common law? They are those that necessarily arise out of its immediate business; and they are therefore, commensurate only with the judicial execution of the municipal law, or, in other words, with the administration of distributive justice, without extending to anything of a political cast whatever. . . . With us, although the legislature be the depository of only so much of the sovereignty as the people have thought fit to impart, it is nevertheless sovereign within the limit of its powers, and

may relatively claim the same pre-eminence here that it may claim elsewhere. It will be conceded, then, that the ordinary and essential powers
of the judiciary do not extend to the annulling of an act of the legislature. . . .

The constitution of *Pennsylvania* contains no express grant of political
powers to the judiciary. But, to establish a grant by implication, the
constitution is said to be a law of superior obligation; and, consequently,
that if it were to come into collision with an act of the legislature, the latter
would have to give way. This is conceded. But it is a fallacy, to suppose
that they can come into collision *before the judiciary*. . . .

The constitution and the right of the legislature to pass the act, may
be in collision. But is that a legitimate subject for judicial determination?
If it be, the judiciary must be a peculiar organ, to revise the proceedings
of the legislature, and to correct its mistakes; and in what part of the
constitution are we to look for this proud pre-eminence? Viewing the
matter in the opposite direction, what would be thought of an act of
assembly in which it should be declared that the Supreme Court had, in
a particular case, put a wrong construction on the constitution of the
United States, and that the judgment should therefore be reversed? It
would doubtless be thought a usurpation of judicial power. But it is by
no means clear, that to declare a law void which has been enacted according to the forms prescribed in the constitution, is not a usurpation of
legislative power. . . .

But it has been said to be emphatically the business of the judiciary,
to ascertain and pronounce what the law is; and that this necessarily
involves a consideration of the constitution. It does so; but how far? If
the judiciary will inquire into anything besides the form of enactment,
where shall it stop? There must be some point of limitation to such an
inquiry; for no one will pretend that a judge would be justifiable in calling
for the election returns, or scrutinizing the qualifications of those who
composed the legislature. . . .

. . . In theory, all the organs of the government are of equal capacity;
or, if not equal, each must be supposed to have superior capacity only for
those things which peculiarly belong to it; and, as legislation peculiarly
involves the consideration of those limitations which are put on the
law-making power, and the interpretation of the laws when made, involves only the construction of the laws themselves, it follows that the
construction of the constitution in this particular belongs to the legislature, which ought therefore to be taken to have superior capacity to judge
of the constitutionality of its own acts. But suppose all to be of equal
capacity in every respect, why should one exercise a controlling power
over the rest? That the judiciary is of superior rank, has never been
pretended, although it has been said to be coordinate. It is not easy,
however, to comprehend how the power which gives law to all the rest,
can be of no more than equal rank with one which receives it, and is
answerable to the former for the observance of its statutes. Legislation
is essentially an act of sovereign power; but the execution of the laws by

instruments that are governed by prescribed rules and exercise no power of volition, is essentially otherwise. . . .

. . . had it been intended to interpose the judiciary as an additional barrier, the matter would surely not have been left in doubt. The judges would not have been left to stand on the insecure and ever shifting ground of public opinion as to constructive powers; they would have been placed on the impregnable ground of an express grant. They would not have been compelled to resort to the debates in the convention, or the opinion that was generally entertained at the time. . . . The grant of a power so extraordinary ought to appear so plain, that he who should run might read. . . .

What I have in view in this inquiry, is the supposed right of the judiciary to interfere, in cases where the constitution is to be carried into effect through the instrumentality of the legislature, and where that organ must necessarily first decide on the constitutionality of its own act. The oath to support the constitution is not peculiar to the judges, but is taken indiscriminately by every officer of the government, and is designed rather as a test of the political principles of the man, than to bind the officer in the discharge of his duty: otherwise it is difficult to determine what operation it is to have in the case of a recorder of deeds, for instance, who, in the execution of his office, has nothing to do with the constitution. But granting it to relate to the official conduct of the judge, as well as every other officer, and not to his political principles, still it must be understood in reference to supporting the constitution, *only as far as that may be involved in his official duty:* and, consequently, if his official duty does not comprehend an inquiry into the authority of the legislature, neither does his oath. . . .

But do not the judges do a positive act in violation of the constitution, when they give effect to an unconstitutional law? Not if the law has been passed according to the forms established in the constitution. The fallacy of the question is, in supposing that the judiciary adopts the acts of the legislature as its own; whereas the enactment of a law and the interpretation of it are not concurrent acts, and as the judiciary is not required to concur in the enactment, neither is it in the breach of the constitution which may be the consequence of the enactment. The fault is imputable to the legislature, and on it the responsibility exclusively rests. . . .

But it has been said, that this construction would deprive the citizen of the advantages which are peculiar to a written constitution, by at once declaring the power of the legislature in practice to be illimitable. . . . But there is no magic or inherent power in parchment and ink, to command respect and protect principles from violation. In the business of government a recurrence to first principles answers the end of an observation at sea with a view to correct the dead reckoning; and for this purpose, a written constitution is an instrument of inestimable value. It is of inestimable value, also, in rendering its first principles familiar to the mass of people; for, after all, there is no effectual guard against legislative usurpation but public opinion, the force of which, in this country is inconceivably great. . . . Once let public opinion be so corrupt as to sanction every misconstruction of the constitution and abuse of power which the temptation of the moment may dictate, and the party which may happen to be predominant, will laugh at the puny efforts of a dependent power to arrest it in its course.

For these reasons, I am of opinion that it rests with the people, in whom full and absolute sovereign power resides, to correct abuses in legislation, by instructing their representatives to repeal the obnoxious act. . . . On the other hand, the judiciary is not infallible; and an error by it would admit of no remedy but a more distinct expression of the public will, through the extraordinary medium of a convention; whereas, an error by the legislature admits of a remedy by an exertion of the same will, in the ordinary exercise of the right of suffrage.—a mode better calculated to attain the end, without popular excitement.

LOCHNER V. NEW YORK

198 U.S. 45, 25 S. Ct. 539, 49 L. Ed. 937 (1905)

A New York law limited the hours of employment in bakeries to ten hours a day or sixty hours a week. Lochner, a bakery owner, was convicted of violating the law.

MR. JUSTICE PECKHAM . . . delivered the opinion of the Court. . . .

In every case that comes before this court, where legislation of this character is concerned, and where the protection of the federal Constitution is sought, the question necessarily arises: Is this a fair, reasonable, and appropriate exercise of the police power of the state, or is it an unreasonable, unnecessary, and arbitrary interference with the right of the individual to his personal liberty, or to enter into those contracts in relation to labor which may seem to him appropriate or necessary for the support of himself and his family? . . .

This is not a question of substituting the judgment of the court for that of the legislature. If the act be within the power of the state it is valid, although the judgment of the court might be totally opposed to the enactment of such a law. But the question would still remain: Is it within the police power of the state? and that question must be answered by the court.

The question whether this act is valid as a labor law, pure and simple, may be dismissed in a few words. There is no reasonable ground for interfering with the liberty of person or the right of free contract, by determining the hours of labor, in the occupation of a baker. There is no contention that bakers as a class are not equal in intelligence and capacity to men in other trades or manual occupations, or that they are not able to assert their rights and care for themselves without the protecting arm of the state, interfering with their independence of judgment and of action. They are in no sense wards of the state. Viewed in the light of a purely labor law, with no reference whatever to the question of health, we think that a law like the one before us involves neither the safety, the morals, nor the welfare, of the public, and that the interest of the public is not in the slightest degree affected by such an act. The law must be upheld, if at all, as a law pertaining to the health of the individual engaged in the occupation of a baker. . . .

. . . . The act is not, within any fair meaning of the term, a health law, but is an illegal interference with the rights of individuals, both employers and employés, to make contracts regarding labor upon such terms as they may think best, or which they may agree upon with the other parties to such contracts.

Statutes of the nature of that under review, limiting the hours in which grown and intelligent man may labor to earn their living, are mere meddlesome interferences with the rights of the individual, and they are not saved from condemnation by the claim that they are passed in the exercise of the police power. . . .

MR. JUSTICE HOLMES, dissenting. . . .

This case is decided upon an economic theory which a large part of the country does not entertain. If it were a question whether I agreed with that theory, I should desire to study it further and long before making up my mind. But I do not conceive that to be my duty, because I strongly believe that my agreement or disagreement has nothing to do with the right of a majority to embody their opinions in law. It is settled by various decisions of this court that state Constitutions and state laws may regulate life in many ways which we as legislators might think as injudicious, or if you like as tyrannical as this. . . .

The fourteenth amendment does not enact Mr. Herbert Spencer's Social Statics. . . .

. . . a Constitution is not intended to embody a particular economic theory, whether of paternalism and the organic relation of the citizen to the state or of *laissez faire.* It is made for people of fundamentally differing views, and the accident of our finding certain opinions natural and familiar, or novel, and even shocking, ought not to conclude our judgment upon the question whether statutes embodying them conflict with the Constitution of the United States.

General propositions do not decide concrete cases. The decision will depend on a judgment or intuition more subtle than any articulate major premise. But I think that the proposition just stated, if it is accepted, will carry us far toward the end. Every opinion tends to become a law. I think that the word "liberty," in the Fourteenth Amendment, is perverted when it is held to prevent the natural outcome of a dominant opinion, unless it can be said that a rational and fair man necessarily would admit that the statute proposed would infringe fundamental principles as they have been understood by the traditions of our people and our law. It does not need research to show that no such sweeping condemnation can be passed upon the statute before us. A reasonable man might think it a proper measure on the score of health. Men whom I certainly could not pronounce unreasonable would uphold it as a first instalment of a general regulation of the hours of work. . . .

UNITED STATES V. BUTLER

297 U.S. 1, 56 S. Ct. 312, 80 L. Ed. 477 (1936)

In this decision, which held unconstitutional a processing tax on farm commodities enacted by Congress in the Agricultural Adjustment Act of 1933 on the ground that it was an abuse of congressional spending power, Justice Roberts wrote a classic and often quoted defense of the judicial power to declare acts of Congress unconstitutional and denying that such action involved any judicial discretion. In reply, Justice Stone wrote an equally classic warning against judicial activism.

MR. JUSTICE ROBERTS delivered the opinion of the Court. . . .

There should be no misunderstanding as to the function of this court in such a case. It is sometimes said that the court assumes a power to overrule or control the action of the people's representatives. This is a misconception. The Constitution is the supreme law of the land ordained and established by the people. All legislation must conform to the principles it lays down. When an act of Congress is appropriately challenged in the courts as not conforming to the constitutional mandate the judicial branch of the Government has only one duty,—to lay the article of the Constitution which is invoked beside the statute which is challenged and to decide whether the latter squares with the former. All the court does, or can do, is to announce its considered judgment upon the question. The only power it has, if such it may be called, is the power of judgment. This court neither approves nor condemns any legislative policy. Its delicate and difficult office is to ascertain and declare whether the legislation is in accordance with, or in contravention of, the provisions of the Constitution; and having done that, its duty ends. . . .

MR. JUSTICE STONE, dissenting. . . .

1. The power of courts to declare a statute unconstitutional is subject to two guiding principles of decision which ought never to be absent from judicial consciousness. One is that courts are concerned only with the power to enact statutes, not with their wisdom. The other is that while unconstitutional exercise of power by the executive and legislative branches of the government is subject to judicial restraint, the only check

upon our own exercise of power is our own sense of self-restraint. For the removal of unwise laws from the statute books appeal lies not to the courts but to the ballot and to the processes of democratic government. . . .

That the governmental power of the purse is a great one is not now for the first time announced. Every student of the history of government and economics is aware of its magnitude and of its existence in every civilized government. Both were well understood by the framers of the Constitution when they sanctioned the grant of the spending power to the federal government, and both were recognized by Hamilton and Story, whose views of the spending power as standing on a parity with the other powers specifically granted, have hitherto been generally accepted.

The suggestion that it must now be curtailed by judicial fiat because it may be abused by unwise use hardly rises to the dignity of the argument. So may judicial power be abused. "The power to tax is the power to destroy," but we do not, for that reason, doubt its existence, or hold that its efficacy is to be restricted by its incidental or collateral effects upon the states. . . . The power to tax and spend is not without constitutional restraints. One restriction is that the purpose must be truly national. Another is that it may not be used to coerce action left to state control. Another is the conscience and patriotism of Congress and the Executive. "It must be remembered that legislators are the ultimate guardians of the liberties and welfare of the people in quite as great a degree as the courts." Justice Holmes, in *Missouri, Kansas & Texas Ry. Co. v. May.* . . .

A tortured construction of the Constitution is not to be justified by recourse to extreme examples of reckless congressional spending which might occur if courts could not prevent expenditures which, even if they could be thought to effect any national purpose, would be possible only by action of a legislature lost to all sense of public responsibility. Such suppositions are addressed to the mind accustomed to believe that it is the business of courts to sit in judgment on the wisdom of legislative action. Courts are not the only agency of government that must be assumed to have capacity to govern. Congress and the courts both unhappily may falter or be mistaken in the performance of their constitutional duty. But interpretation of our great charter of government which proceeds on any assumption that the responsibility for the preservation of our institutions is the exclusive concern of any one of the three branches of government, or that it alone can save them from destruction is far more likely, in the long run, "to obliterate the constituent members" of "an indestructible union of indestructible states" than the frank recognition that language, even of a constitution, may mean what it says: that the power to tax and spend includes the power to relieve a nationwide economic maladjustment by conditional gifts of money.

MR. JUSTICE BRANDEIS and MR. JUSTICE CARDOZO joined in this opinion.

FERGUSON V. SKRUPA

372 U.S. 726, 83 S. Ct. 1028, 10 L. Ed. 2d 93 (1963)

A Kansas statute made it a misdemeanor for any person to engage in the business of debt adjusting except as an incident to the practice of law. A federal district court held the law in violation of the Fourteenth Amendment due process clause and enjoined its enforcement.

MR. JUSTICE BLACK delivered the opinion of the Court. . . .

The only case discussed by the court below as support for its invalidation of the statute was *Commonwealth* v. *Stone* . . . (1959), in which the Superior Court of Pennsylvania struck down a statute almost identical to the Kansas act involved here. . . . In doing so, the Pennsylvania court relied heavily on *Adams* v. *Tanner* . . . (1917), which held that the Due Process Clause forbids a State to prohibit a business which is "useful" and not "inherently immoral or dangerous to public welfare."

Both the District Court in the present case and the Pennsylvania court in Stone adopted the philosophy of *Adams* v. *Tanner,* and cases like it, that it is the province of courts to draw on their own views as to the morality, legitimacy, and usefulness of a particular business in order to decide whether a statute bears too heavily upon that business and by so doing violates due process. Under the system of government created by our Constitution, it is up to legislatures, not courts, to decide on the wisdom and utility of legislation. There was a time when the Due Process Clause was used by this Court to strike down laws which were thought unreasonable, that is, unwise or incompatible with some particular economic or social philosophy. In this manner the Due Process Clause was used, for example, to nullify laws prescribing maximum hours for work in bakeries, *Lochner* v. *New York* . . . (1905), outlawing "yellow dog" contracts, *Coppage* v. *Kansas* . . . (1915), setting minimum wages for women, *Adkins* v. *Children's Hospital* . . . (1923), and fixing the weight of loaves of bread, *Jay Burns Baking Co.* v. *Bryan* . . . (1924). . . .

The doctrine that prevailed in *Lochner, Coppage, Adkins, Burns,* and like cases . . . has long since been discarded. We have returned to the original constitutional proposition that courts do not substitute their social and economic beliefs for the judgment of legislative bodies, who are elected to pass laws. . . . We refuse to sit as a "superlegislature to weigh the wisdom of legislation," and we emphatically refuse to go back to the time when courts used the Due Process Clause "to strike down state laws, regulatory of business and industrial conditions, because they may be unwise, improvident, or out of harmony with a particular school of thought." Nor are we able or willing to draw lines by calling a law "prohibitory" or "regulatory." Whether the legislature takes for its textbook Adam Smith, Herbert Spencer, Lord Keynes, or some other is no concern of ours. The Kansas debt adjustment statute may be wise or unwise. But relief, if any be needed, lies not with us but with the body constituted to pass laws for the State of Kansas. . . .

Reversed.

UNITED STATES V.
CAROLENE PRODUCTS CO.

304 U.S. 144, 58 S. Ct. 778, 82 L. Ed. 1234 (1938)

In this otherwise unimportant case, Justice Stone suggested in a famous footnote the justification for more activist judicial review in certain situations.

MR. JUSTICE STONE delivered the opinion of the Court. . . .

Regulatory legislation affecting ordinary commercial transactions is not to be pronounced unconstitutional unless in the light of the facts made known or generally assumed it is of such a character as to preclude the assumption that it rests upon some rational basis within the knowledge and experience of the legislators.[4]

[4]There may be narrower scope for operation of the presumption of constitutionality when legislation appears on its face to be within a specific prohibition of the Constitution, such as those of the first ten amendments, which are deemed equally specific when held to be embraced within the Fourteenth.

It is unnecessary to consider now whether legislation which restricts those political processes which can ordinarily be expected to bring about repeal of undesirable legislation, is to be subjected to more exacting judicial scrutiny under the general prohibitions of the Fourteenth Amendment than are most other types of legislation. . . .

Nor need we enquire whether similar considerations enter into the review of statutes directed at particular religious . . . or national . . . or racial minorities . . . whether prejudice against discrete and insular minorities may be a special condition, which tends seriously to curtail the operation of those political processes ordinarily to be relied upon to protect minorities, and which may call for a correspondingly more searching judicial inquiry.

DENNIS V. UNITED STATES

341 U.S. 494, 71 S. Ct. 857, 95 L. Ed. 1137 (1951)

The Smith Act makes it a crime to advocate, or conspire to advocate, the overthrow of the government by force or violence. Eleven leaders of the American Communist party were convicted under the act after a tumultous trial in New York in 1949. The Supreme Court granted certiorari after the conviction had been upheld by the court of appeals, but limited its review to the issue of the constitutionality of the Smith Act. The Court voted six to two that the act was constitutional; Justices Frankfurter and Jackson, while concurring with the majority, wrote separate opinions. Justices Black and Douglas were the dissenters.

MR. JUSTICE FRANKFURTER, concurring in affirmance of the judgment. . . .

. . . The demands of free speech in a democratic society as well as the interest in national security are better served by candid and informed weighing of the competing interests, within the confines of the judicial process, than by announcing dogmas too inflexible for the non-Euclidian problems to be solved.

But how are competing interests to be assessed? Since they are not subject to quantitative ascertainment, the issue necessarily resolves itself into asking, who is to make the adjustment?—who is to balance the relevant factors and ascertain which interest is in the circumstances to prevail? Full responsibility for the choice cannot be given to tbe courts. Courts are not representative bodies. They are not designed to be a good reflex of a democratic society. Their judgment is best informed, and therefore most dependable, within narrow limits. Their essential quality is detachment, founded on independence. History teaches that the independence of the judiciary is jeopardized when courts become embroiled in the passions of the day and assume primary responsibility in choosing between competing political, economic and social pressures.

Primary responsibility for adjusting the interests which compete in the situation before us of necessity belongs to the Congress. The nature of the power to be exercised by this Court has been delineated in decisions not charged with the emotional appeal of situations such as that now before us. We are to set aside the judgment of those whose duty it is to legislate only if there is no reasonable basis for it.

We must assure fairness of procedure, allowing full scope of governmental discretion but mindful of its impact on individuals in the context of the problem involved. And, of course, the proceedings in a particular case before us must have the warrant of substantial proof. Beyond these powers we must not go; we must scrupulously observe the narrow limits of judicial authority even though self-restraint is alone set over us. Above all we must remember that this Court's power of judicial review is not "an exercise of the powers of a superlegislature."

. . . Free-speech cases are not an exception to the principle that we are not legislators, that direct policy-making is not our province. How best to reconcile competing interests is the business of legislatures, and the balance they strike is a judgment not to be displaced by ours, but to be respected unless outside the pale of fair judgment.

On occasion we have strained to interpret legislation in order to limit its effect on interests protected by the First Amendment. . . . But in no case has a majority of this Court held that a legislative judgment, even as to freedom of utterance, may be overturned merely because the Court would have made a different choice between the competing interests had the initial legislative judgment been for it to make. . . .

It is not for us to decide how we would adjust the clash of interests which this case presents were the primary responsibility for reconciling it ours. Congress has determined that the danger created by advocacy of overthrow justifies the ensuing restriction on freedom of speech. The determination was made after due deliberation, and the seriousness of the congressional purpose is attested by the volume of legislation passed to effectuate the same ends.

Can we then say that the judgment Congress exercised was denied it by the Constitution? Can we establish a constitutional doctrine which forbids the elected representatives of the people to make this choice? Can we hold that the First Amendment deprives Congress of what it deemed necessary for the Government's protection?

To make validity of legislation depend on judicial reading of events still in the womb of time—a forecast, that is, of the outcome of forces at best appreciated only with knowledge of the topmost secrets of nations —is to charge the judiciary with duties beyond its equipment. . . .

Mr. Justice Black, dissenting. . . .

Mr. Justice Douglas, dissenting. . . .

The First Amendment provides that "Congress shall make no law . . . abridging the freedom of speech." The Constitution provides no exception. This does not mean, however, that the Nation need hold its hand until it is in such weakened condition that there is no time to protect itself from incitement to revolution. Seditious conduct can always be punished. But the command of the First Amendment is so clear that we should not allow Congress to call a halt to free speech except in the extreme case of peril from the speech itself. The First Amendment makes confidence in the common sense of our people and in their maturity of judgment the great postulate of our democracy. Its philosophy is that violence is rarely, if ever, stopped by denying civil liberties to those advocating resort to force. The First Amendment reflects the philosophy of Jefferson "that it is time enough for the rightful purposes of civil government for its officers to interfere when principles break out into overt acts against peace and good order." The political censor has no place in our public debates.

Unless and until extreme and necessitous circumstances are shown our aim should be to keep speech unfettered and to allow the processes of law to be invoked only when the provocateurs among us move from speech to action.

FURMAN V. GEORGIA

408 U.S. 238, 92 S. Ct. 2726, 33 L. Ed. 2d 346 (1972)

In this case a five-judge majority held that the death penalty as administered by American courts was imposed so arbitrarily and capriciously that it violated the constitutional ban on cruel and unusual punishment.

MR. JUSTICE REHNQUIST, with whom THE CHIEF JUSTICE [BURGER], MR. JUSTICE BLACKMUN, and MR. JUSTICE POWELL join, dissenting. . . .
. . . Whatever its precise rationale, today's holding necessarily brings into sharp relief the fundamental question of the role of judicial review in a democratic society. How can government by the elected representatives of the people co-exist with the power of the federal judiciary, whose members are constitutionally insulated from responsiveness to the popular will, to declare invalid laws duly enacted by the popular branches of government?

The answer, of course, is found in Hamilton's Federalist Paper No. 78 and in Chief Justice Marshall's classic opinion in *Marbury* v. *Madison*. . . . Sovereignty resides ultimately in the people as a whole, and by adopting through their States a written Constitution for the Nation, and subsequently adding amendments to that instrument, they have both granted certain powers to the national Government, and denied other powers to the national and the state governments. Courts are exercising no more than the judicial function conferred upon them by Art. III of the Constitution when they assess, in a case before them, whether or not a particular legislative enactment is within the authority granted by the Constitution to the enacting body, and whether it runs afoul of some limitation placed by the Constitution on the authority of that body. For the theory is that the people themselves have spoken in the Constitution, and therefore its commands are superior to the commands of the legislature, which is merely an agent of the people.

The Founding Fathers thus widely sought to have the best of both worlds, the undeniable benefits of both democratic self-government and individual rights protected against possible excesses of that form of government.

The courts in cases properly before them have been entrusted under the Constitution with the last word, short of constitutional amendment, as to whether a law passed by the legislature conforms to the Constitution. But just because courts in general, and this Court in particular, do have the last word, the admonition of Mr. Justice Stone in *United States* v. *Butler* must be constantly borne in mind:

> [W]hile unconstitutional exercise of power by the executive and legislative branches of the government is subject to judicial restraint, the only check upon our own exercise of power is our own sense of self-restraint. . . .

Rigorous attention to the limits of this Court's authority is likewise enjoined because of the natural desire that beguiles judges along with other human beings into imposing their own views of goodness, truth, and justice upon others. Judges differ only in that they have the power, if not the authority, to enforce their desires. This is doubtless why nearly two centuries of judicial precedent from this Court counsel the sparing use of that power. The most expansive reading of the leading constitutional cases does not remotely suggest that this Court has been granted a roving commission, either by the Founding Fathers or by the framers of the Fourteenth Amendment, to strike down laws that are based upon notions of policy or morality suddenly found unacceptable by a majority of this Court. . . .

A separate reason for deference to the legislative judgment is the consequence of human error on the part of the judiciary. . . . Human error there is bound to be, judges being men and women, and men and women being what they are. But an error in mistakenly sustaining the constitutionality of a particular enactment, while wrongfully depriving the individual of a right secured to him by the Constitution, nonetheless does so by simply letting stand a duly enacted law of a democratically chosen legislative body. The error resulting from a mistaken upholding of an individual constitutional claim against the validity of a legislative enactment is a good deal more serious. For the result in such a case is not to leave standing a law duly enacted by a representative assembly, but to impose upon the Nation the judicial fiat of a majority of a court of judges whose connection with the popular will is remote at best.

The task of judging constitutional cases imposed by Art. III cannot for this reason be avoided, but it must surely be approached with the deepest humility and genuine deference to legislative judgment. Today's decision to invalidate capital punishment is, I respectfully submit, significantly lacking in those attributes. For the reasons well stated in the opinions of The Chief Justice, Mr. Justice Powell, and Mr. Justice Blackmun, I conclude that this decision holding unconstitutional capital punishment is not an act of judgment, but rather an act of will. . . .

If there can be said to be one dominant theme in the Constitution, perhaps more fully articulated in The Federalist Papers than in the instrument itself, it is the notion of checks and balances. The Framers were well aware of the natural desire of office holders as well as others to seek to expand the scope and authority of their particular office at the expense of others. They sought to provide against success in such efforts by erecting adequate checks and balances in the form of grants of authority to each branch of the government in order to counteract and prevent usurpation on the part of the others.

This philosophy of the Framers is best described by one of the ablest and greatest of their number, James Madison, in Federalist No. 51:

> In framing a government which is to be administered by men over men, the great difficulty lies in this: you must first enable the government to control the governed; and in the next place oblige it to control itself.

Madison's observation applies to the Judicial Branch with at least as much force as to the Legislative and Executive Branches. While overreaching by the Legislative and Executive Branches may result in the sacrifice of individual protections that the Constitution was designed to secure against action of the State, judicial overreaching may result in sacrifice of the equally important right of the people to govern themselves. . . .

The very nature of judicial review, as pointed out by Justice Stone in his dissent in the *Butler* case, makes the courts the least subject to Madisonian check in the event that they shall, for the best of motives, expand judicial authority beyond the limits contemplated by the Framers. It is for this reason that judicial self-restraint is surely an implied, if not an expressed, condition of the grant of authority of judicial review. The Court's holding in these cases has been reached, I believe, in complete disregard of that implied condition.[2]

---

[2]Four years after this decision, in *Gregg* v. *Georgia* (1976), the Burger Court modified the position taken in *Furman* and by a vote of seven to two upheld capital punishment when imposed under state statutes requiring sentencing judges and juries to consider certain specified aggravating or mitigating circumstances of the crime and the offender. Such procedures were thought to reduce the arbitrariness and possible racial prejudice denounced in *Furman.* But state laws making the death penalty mandatory for certain specified offenses were at the same time declared unconstitutional in *Woodson* v. *North Carolina* (1976) by a vote of five to four, with Justice Rehnquist again protesting the Court's substitution of its own judgment for that of the legislature.

Chapter Four

JUSTICIABLE
QUESTIONS

INTRODUCTION

The judicial power given by the Constitution to the federal courts is the power to determine "cases" and "controversies" of the types specified in Article III. What is a case or controversy? Not every argument or dispute presented in the form of a lawsuit will qualify. To have a case or controversy in the constitutional sense there must be (1) adverse parties (2) who have a substantial legal interest (3) in a dispute arising out of facts, not hypothetical but real, (4) in which there can be an enforceable determination of the rights of the parties. A "justiciable" case is one which fulfills these requirements. Normally there is no difficulty in meeting the requirements, but occasionally the Supreme Court falls back on the case or controversy limitation to avoid passing on some broad or troublesome public issue.

A lawsuit must involve a genuine contest over substantial rights and interests because judges rely on the litigants and their counsel to inform the court fully, to explore all the issues of law and fact, and to explain and justify the result they wish the court to reach. The fact that the parties are in opposition and that opposing counsel can be relied on to point out each other's errors and omissions protects the court from acting without full understanding and consideration.

One reason the Supreme Court has refused to give advisory opinions is that it would not have the benefit of this complete exploration of all the issues in passing on a hypothetical question. For the same reason, it seeks to detect and to refuse to rule on made-up cases which are in reality nothing but attempts to obtain a court ruling on abstract questions of law.

An additional danger formerly involved in "friendly" lawsuits has now been eliminated by statute. Generally only the parties of record have a right to be heard in a case. Constitutional cases usually present important questions of policy in which the public has an interest, but prior to 1937 if a case started out as one between private persons, there was no provision for participation by any public agency. If the suit was a friendly one, both parties might in fact be seeking the same result—for instance, to get a statute declared unconstitutional. In such a situation, there would be no one before the court presenting the case *for* the statute.

In 1895, for example, the federal income tax was declared unconstitutional in a suit brought by a corporate stockholder against the corporation, to prevent it from paying the tax. It seems unlikely that the corporation fought very hard to uphold its obligation to pay the tax. This particular decision was in effect overruled by the Sixteenth Amendment, but the problem of representation of the public interest in constitutional litigation was not dealt with until 1937, when Congress provided that the United States must be joined as a party in any case in which the constitutionality of a federal statute is questioned.

An important element of justiciability is "standing to sue." Not everyone with enough money to bring a lawsuit is entitled to litigate the constitutionality or legality of government action in the federal courts. To have the standing necessary to maintain such an action, the plaintiff must show sufficiency of interest in the controversy, and this means satisfying the courts on two main issues: (1) that the interest is one that is peculiar and personal to the plaintiff and not one shared with all other citizens generally; and (2) that the interest defended is a legally recognized and protected right immediately threatened by some government action.

The first of the above principles is well demonstrated by the case of **Frothingham v. Mellon** (1923), in which the Supreme Court denied standing to a federal taxpayer who sought to have a congressional spending statute declared unconstitutional. Though taxpayer suits are common in state litigation, Justice Sutherland contended that the interest of any one federal taxpayer in the moneys of the Treasury was so miniscule as to afford no basis for a lawsuit. For almost 50 years this decision stood as a barrier to federal taxpayers' suits, but eventually **Flast v. Cohen** (1968) modified *Frothingham* to establish that at least some First Amendment issues could be brought by federal taxpayers.

The *Flast* decision was part of a general trend toward recognizing the right of litigants to bring "public actions" seeking to vindicate public rights, in which the plaintiff's interest is not purely personal but is shared with a wider public. In the *Flast* case Justice Harlan popularized the phrase "non-Hohfeldian plaintiff" to describe the public interest litigant. In **United States v. SCRAP** (1973) the Court likewise stressed that standing was not to be denied simply because many people suffered the same injury. However, public interest lawsuits still run the risk that they will be denied adjudication for lack of standing, as is demonstrated by **Laird v. Tatum** (1972) and **Warth v. Seldin** (1975).

Justiciability may also be denied on the ground that the controversy has not yet reached the stage where judicial action is timely or effective. In this situation the suit is held to lack "ripeness"; see the questionable majority decision of the Supreme Court in **Poe v. Ullman** (1961). Conversely, events may have proceeded since the filing of the suit to a point where judicial action is no longer needed or cannot provide the relief requested. Here the situation has become "moot." In **Roe v. Wade** (1973) a strict application of the mootness doctrine to a woman whose standing was based on her pregnancy would have produced a Catch-22 situation. But in *DeFunis v. Odegaard* (1974) the Court did resort to a mootness holding to avoid passing on a difficult case. A white law school applicant who had been rejected for admission contended that less qualified minority applicants had been accepted under an affirmative action program, and the trial judge ordered his admission. The university appealed, but by the time the case reached the Supreme Court DeFunis was in his third year of law school and guaranteed graduation. By a five to four vote the Court, while recognizing that the same issue would be raised in subsequent suits, held this proceeding moot.

Public actions often take the form of "class suits," which are brought by one or several persons in their own behalf and in behalf "of all others similarly situated." Rule 23 of the Federal Rules of Civil Procedure authorizes class actions where a number of persons have a common legal right and the group is "so numerous as to make it impractical to bring them all before the court." The class action lightens the load on the courts since they have to make only one decision to settle the rights of perhaps thousands of persons; from the viewpoint of the interest group it also saves time and money. If, for instance, one black voter were to institute a class action against state officials and could prove that they were refusing to permit qualified blacks to vote, the injunction would require that the officials cease discrimination against all black voters. Rule 23 requires notification to class members of the filing of the lawsuit. However, in **Eisen v. Carlisle & Jacquelin** (1974) notification proved impossible because of the number of persons (over two million) in the class. A lower court judge called the *Eisen* case "a Frankenstein monster posing as a class action," and the Supreme Court dismissed the suit.

FROTHINGHAM V. MELLON

282 U.S. 447, 43 S. Ct. 597, 67 L. Ed. 1078 (1923)

The Maternity Act of 1921 provided for grants from the U.S. Treasury to states that agreed to set up, under federal supervision, programs for the care of mothers and infants. A private citizen, Mrs. Frothingham, brought suit as a federal taxpayer, alleging that this expenditure of federal funds was unconstitutional.

MR. JUSTICE SUTHERLAND delivered the opinion of the Court. . . .

. . . [T]his plaintiff alleges . . . that she is a taxpayer of the United States; and her contention, though not clear, seems to be that the effect of the appropriations complained of will be to increase the burden of future taxation and thereby take her property without due process of law. The right of a taxpayer to enjoin the execution of a federal appropriation act, on the ground that it is invalid and will result in taxation for illegal purposes, has never been passed upon by this court. In cases where it was presented, the question has either been allowed to pass sub silentio or the determination of it expressly withheld. . . . The interest of a taxpayer of a municipality in the application of its moneys is direct and immediate and the remedy by injunction to prevent their misuse is not inappropriate. It is upheld by a large number of state cases and is the rule of this court. . . . But the relation of a taxpayer of the United States to the federal government is very different. His interest in the moneys of the treasury —partly realized from taxation and partly from other sources—is shared with millions of others, is comparatively minute and indeterminable, and the effect upon future taxation, of any payment out of the funds, so remote, fluctuating and uncertain, that no basis is afforded for an appeal to the preventive powers of a court of equity.

. . . We have no power per se to review and annul acts of Congress on the ground that they are unconstitutional. That question may be considered only when the justification for some direct injury suffered or threatened, presenting a justiciable issue, is made to rest upon such an act. Then the power exercised is that of ascertaining and declaring the law applicable to the controversy. It amounts to little more than the negative power to disregard an unconstitutional enactment, which otherwise would stand in the way of the enforcement of a legal right. The party who invokes the power must be able to show, not only that the statute is invalid, but that he has sustained or is immediately in danger of sustaining some direct injury as the result of its enforcement, and not merely that he suffers in some indefinite way in common with people generally. If a case for preventive relief be presented, the court enjoins, in effect, not the execution of the statute, but the acts of the official, the statute notwithstanding. Here the parties plaintiff have no such case. Looking through forms of words to the substance of their complaint, it is merely that officials of the executive department of the government are executing and will execute an act of Congress asserted to be unconstitutional; and this we are asked to prevent. To do so would be, not to decide a judicial controversy, but to assume a position of authority over the governmental acts of another and coequal department, an authority which plainly we do not possess. . . .

FLAST V. COHEN

392 U.S. 83, 88 S. Ct. 1942, 20 L. Ed. 2d 947 (1968)

Suit was filed in federal district court to enjoin the expenditure of federal funds under the Elementary and Secondary Education Act of 1965, some of which went to finance instruction in reading, arithmetic, and other subjects in religious schools, and to purchase textbooks and other instructional materials in such schools. The contention was that these expenditures promoted religious programs in violation of the Establishment Clause of the First Amendment. The district court, on the authority of the *Frothingham* case, held that the plaintiffs, who sued as federal taxpayers, lacked standing.

MR. CHIEF JUSTICE WARREN delivered the opinion of the Court. . . .
This Court first faced squarely the question whether a litigant asserting only his status as a taxpayer has standing to maintain a suit in a federal court in *Frothingham* v. *Mellon* . . . and that decision must be the starting point for analysis in this case. . . .
Although the barrier *Frothingham* erected against federal taxpayer suits has never been breached, the decision has been the source of some confusion and the object of considerable criticism. The confusion has developed as commentators have tried to determine whether *Frothingham* establishes a constitutional bar to taxpayer suits or whether the Court was simply imposing a rule of self-restraint which was not constitutionally compelled. The conflicting viewpoints are reflected in the arguments made to this Court by the parties in this case. The Government has pressed upon us the view that *Frothingham* announced a constitutional rule, compelled by the Article III limitations on federal court jurisdiction and grounded in considerations of the doctrine of separation of powers. Appellants, however, insist that *Frothingham* expressed no more than a

policy of judicial self-restraint which can be disregarded when compelling reasons for assuming jurisdiction over a taxpayer's suit exist. The opinion delivered in *Frothingham* can be read to support either position. . . .

The jurisdiction of federal courts is defined and limited by Article III of the Constitution. In terms relevant to the question for decision in this case, the judicial power of federal courts is constitutionally restricted to "cases" and "controversies." As is so often the situation in constitutional adjudication, those two words have an iceberg quality, containing beneath their surface simplicity submerged complexities which go to the very heart of our constitutional form of government. Embodied in the words "cases" and "controversies" are two complementary but somewhat different limitations. In part those words limit the business of federal courts to questions presented in an adversary context and in a form historically viewed as capable of resolution through the judicial process. And in part those words define the role assigned to the judiciary in a tripartite allocation of power to assure that the federal courts will not intrude into areas committed to the other branches of government. Justiciability is the term of art employed to give expression to this dual limitation placed upon federal courts by the case-and-controversy doctrine.

Justiciability is itself a concept of uncertain meaning and scope. Its reach is illustrated by the various grounds upon which questions sought to be adjudicated in federal courts have been held not to be justiciable. Thus, no justiciable controversy is presented when the parties seek adjudication of only a political question, when the parties are asking for an advisory opinion, when the question sought to be adjudicated has been mooted by subsequent developments, and when there is no standing to maintain the action. Yet it remains true that "[j]usticiability is . . . not a legal concept with a fixed content or susceptible of scientific verification. Its utilization is the resultant of many subtle pressures. . . ." *Poe* v. *Ullman*. . . .

. . . As we understand it, the Government's position is that the constitutional scheme of separation of powers, and the deference owed by the federal judiciary to the other two branches of government within that scheme, presents an absolute bar to taxpayer suits challenging the validity of federal spending programs. The Government views such suits as involving no more than the mere disagreement by the taxpayer "with the uses to which tax money is put." According to the Government, the resolution of such disagreements is committed to other branches of the Federal Government and not to the judiciary. Consequently, the Government contends that, under no circumstances, should standing be conferred on federal taxpayers to challenge a federal taxing or spending program. An analysis of the function served by standing limitations compels a rejection of the Government's position.

Standing is an aspect of justiciability and as such, the problem of standing is surrounded by the same complexities and vagaries that inhere in justiciability. . . . The "gist of the question of standing" is whether the party seeking relief has "alleged such a personal stake in the outcome of the controversy as to assure that concrete adverseness which sharpens the presentation of issues upon which the court so largely depends for illumination of difficult constitutional questions." *Baker* v. *Carr.* . . . In other words, when standing is placed in issue in a case, the question is whether the person whose standing is challenged is a proper party to request an adjudication of a particular issue and not whether the issue itself is justiciable. . . .

. . . A taxpayer may or may not have the requisite personal stake in the outcome, depending upon the circumstances of the particular case. Therefore, we find no absolute bar in Article III to suits by federal taxpayers challenging allegedly unconstitutional federal taxing and spending programs. There remains, however, the problem of determining the circumstances under which a federal taxpayer will be deemed to have the personal stake and interest that imparts the necessary concrete adverseness to such litigation so that standing can be conferred on the taxpayer *qua* taxpayer consistent with the constitutional limitations of Article III. . . . Whether such individuals have standing to maintain that form of action turns on whether they can demonstrate the necessary stake as taxpayers in the outcome of the litigation to satisfy Article III requirements.

The nexus demanded of federal taxpayers has two aspects to it. First, the taxpayer must establish a logical link between that status and the type of legislative enactment attacked. Thus, a taxpayer will be a proper party to allege the unconstitutionality only of exercises of congressional power under the taxing and spending clause of Art. I, § 8, of the Constitution. It will not be sufficient to allege an incidental expenditure of tax funds in the administration of an essentially regulatory statute. Secondly the taxpayer must establish a nexus between that status and the precise nature of the constitutional infringement alleged. Under this requirement, the taxpayer must show that the challenged enactment exceeds specific constitutional limitations imposed upon the exercise of the congressional taxing and spending power and not simply that the enactment is generaly beyond the powers delegated to Congress by Art. I, § 8. When both nexuses are established, the litigant will have shown a taxpayer's stake in the outcome of the controversy and will be a proper and appropriate party to invoke a federal court's jurisdiction. . . .

The taxpayer-appellants in this case have satisfied both nexuses to support their claim of standing under the test we announce today. Their constitutional challenge is made to an exercise by Congress of its power under Art. I, § 8, to spend for the general welfare, and the challenged program involves a substantial expenditure of federal tax funds. In addition, appellants have alleged that the challenged expenditures violate the Establishment and Free Exercise Clauses of the First Amendment. . . .

Reversed.

Mr. Justice Douglas, concurring. . . .

Mr. Justice Harlan, dissenting. . . .

The complaint in this case, unlike that in *Frothingham,* contains no allegation that the contested expenditures will in any fashion affect the amount of these taxpayers' own existing or foreseeable tax obligations. Even in cases in which such an allegation is made, the suit cannot result in an adjudication either of the plaintiff's tax liabilities or of the propriety of any particular level of taxation. The relief available to such a plaintiff consists entirely of the vindication of rights held in common by all citizens. . . .

Surely it is plain that the rights and interests of taxpayers who contest the constitutionality of public expenditures are markedly different from those of "Hohfeldian" plaintiffs, including those taxpayer-plaintiffs who challenge the validity of their own tax liabilities. We must recognize that these non-Hohfeldian plaintiffs complain, just as the petitioner in *Frothingham* sought to complain, not as taxpayers, but as "private attorneys-general." The interests they represent, and the rights they espouse, are bereft of any personal or proprietary coloration. They are, as litigants, indistinguishable from any group selected at random from among the general population, taxpayers and nontaxpayers alike. These are and must be, to adopt Professor Jaffe's useful phrase, "public actions" brought to vindicate public rights.

It does not, however, follow that suits brought by non-Hohfeldian plaintiffs are excluded by the "case or controversy" clause of Article III of the Constitution from the jurisdiction of the federal courts. This and other federal courts have repeatedly held that individual litigants, acting as private attorneys-general, may have standing as "representatives of the public interest." . . . non-Hohfeldian plaintiffs as such are not *constitutionally* excluded from the federal courts. The problem ultimately presented by this case is, in my view, therefore to determine in what circumstances, consonant with the character and proper functioning of the federal courts, such suits should be permitted. . . .

It seems to me clear that public actions, whatever the constitutional provisions on which they are premised, may involve important hazards for the continued effectiveness of the federal judiciary. Although I believe such actions to be within the jurisdiction conferred upon the federal courts by Article III of the Constitution, there surely can be little doubt that they strain the judicial function and press to the limit judicial authority. There is every reason to fear that unrestricted public actions might well alter the allocation of authority among the three branches of the Federal Government. . . . [But] there is available a resolution of this problem that entirely satisfies the demands of the principle of separation of powers. This Court has previously held that individual litigants have standing to represent the public interest, despite their lack of economic or other personal interests, if Congress has appropriately authorized such suits. . . . I would adhere to that principle. . . .

UNITED STATES V. STUDENTS CHALLENGING REGULATORY AGENCY PROCEDURES (SCRAP)

412 U.S. 669, 93 S. Ct. 2405, 37 L. Ed. 2d 254 (1973)

A small environmental group sought to enjoin enforcement of Interstate Commerce Commission orders allowing railroads to collect surcharges on goods being transported for purposes of recycling. In an earlier environmental case, *Sierra Club* v. *Morton* (1972), the Supreme Court had denied standing to the Sierra Club, which was suing to prevent the construction of a ski development in the Sequoia National Forest, on the ground that the Club had failed to allege that the development would directly harm its members.

MR. JUSTICE STEWART delivered the opinion of the Court. . . .

The appellants challenge the appellees' standing to sue, arguing that the allegations in the pleadings as to standing were vague, unsubstantiated and insufficient under our recent decision in *Sierra Club* v. *Morton*. . . . The appellees respond that unlike the petitioner in *Sierra Club,* their pleadings sufficiently alleged that they were "adversely affected" or "aggrieved" within the meaning of section 10 of the Administrative Procedure Act . . . and they point specifically to the allegations that their members used the forests, streams, mountains, and other resources in the Washington Metropolitan Area for camping, hiking, fishing, and sightseeing, and that this use was disturbed by the adverse environmental impact caused by the nonuse of recyclable goods brought about by a rate increase on those commodities. . . .

In *Sierra Club* . . . we . . . stress[ed] the importance of demonstrating that the party seeking review be himself among the injured, for it is this requirement that gives a litigant a direct stake in the controversy and prevents the judicial process from becoming no more than a vehicle for the vindication of the value interests of concerned bystanders. . . .

Unlike the specific and geographically limited federal action of which the petitioner complained in *Sierra Club,* the challenged agency action in this case is applicable to substantially all of the Nation's railroads and thus allegedly has an adverse environmental impact on all the natural resources of the country. Rather than a limited group of persons who used a picturesque valley in California, all persons who utilize the scenic resources of the country, and indeed all who breathe its air, could claim harm similar to that alleged by the environmental groups here. But we have already made it clear that standing is not to be denied simply because many people suffer the same injury. . . . To deny standing to persons who are in fact injured simply because many others are also injured, would mean that the most injurious and widespread Government actions could be questioned by nobody. We cannot accept that conclusion.

But the injury alleged here is also very different from that at issue in

Sierra Club because here the alleged injury to the environment is far less direct and perceptible. The petitioner there complained about the construction of a specific project that would directly affect the Mineral King Valley. Here, the Court was asked to follow a far more attenuated line of causation to the eventual injury of which the appellees complained—a general rate increase would allegedly cause increased use of nonrecyclable commodities as compared to recyclable goods, some of which resources might be taken from the Washington area, and resulting in more refuse that might be discarded in national parks in the Washington area. The railroads protest that the appellees could never prove that a general increase in rates would have this effect, and they contend that these allegations were a ploy to avoid the need to show some injury in fact.

Of course, pleadings must be something more than an ingenious academic exercise in the conceivable. A plaintiff must allege that he has been or will in fact be perceptibly harmed by the challenged agency action, not that he can imagine circumstances in which he could be affected by the agency's action. And it is equally clear that the allegations must be true and capable of proof at trial. But we deal here simply with the pleadings in which the appellees alleged a specific and perceptible harm that distinguished them from other citizens who had not used the natural resources that were claimed to be affected. If, as the railroads now assert, these allegations were in fact untrue, then the appellants should have moved for summary judgment on the standing issue and demonstrated to the District Court that the allegations were sham and raised no genuine issue of fact. We cannot say on these pleadings that the appellees could not prove their allegations which, if proved, would place them squarely among those persons injured in fact by the Commission's action, and entitled under the clear import of *Sierra Club* to seek review. The District Court was correct in denying the appellants' motion to dismiss the complaint for failure to allege sufficient standing to bring this lawsuit.

[On the issue of standing, CHIEF JUSTICE BURGER and JUSTICES WHITE and REHNQUIST dissented.]

LAIRD V. TATUM

408 U.S. 1, 92 S. Ct. 2318, 33 L. Ed. 2d 154 (1972)

In 1970 press reports and hearings before-the Subcommittee on Constitutional Rights of the Senate Judiciary Committee revealed that some 1,000 Army intelligence agents in 300 offices across the country had collected information on such diverse civilian activities as civil rights groups, community action organizations, church groups, and Earth Day observances. The Army's explanation was that the surveillance had been begun after the Army had been called in to help deal with urban unrest, and they believed it necessary to compile files of potential trouble-makers. After the activity was publicized, Secretary of Defense Laird ordered Army agents to cut back their surveillance to matters clearly bearing on the Army's mission and to destroy many of the dossiers it had collected on civilian activity.

This response was challenged as insufficient in a suit filed, with ACLU support, by the executive director of the Central Committee for Conscientious Objectors and 12 other individuals or groups who said they were targets of the surveillance. The district court dismissed the suit, but on appeal the Court of Appeals for the District of Columbia ruled two to one that there should be a trial on the plaintiffs' assertions.

MR. CHIEF JUSTICE BURGER delivered the opinion of the Court.

Respondents brought this class action in the District Court seeking declaratory and injunctive relief on their claim that their rights were being invaded by the Army's alleged "surveillance of lawful civilian political activity." The petitioners in response describe the activity as "gathering by lawful means, . . . [and] maintaining and using in their intelligence activities, . . . information relating to potential or actual civil disturbances [or] street demonstrations." . . . We granted certiorari to consider whether, as the Court of Appeals held, respondents presented a justiciable controversy in complaining of a "chilling" effect on the exercise of their First Amendment rights where such effect is allegedly caused, not by any "specific action of the Army against them, [but] only [by] the existence and operation of the intelligence gathering and distributing system, which is confined to the Army and related civilian investigative agencies." . . .

In recent years this Court has found in a number of cases that constitutional violations may arise from the deterrent, or "chilling," effect of governmental regulations that fall short of a direct prohibition against the exercise of First Amendment rights. . . . In none of these cases, however, did the chilling effect arise merely from the individual's knowledge that a governmental agency was engaged in certain activities or from the individual's concomitant fear that, armed with the fruits of those activities, the agency might in the future take some *other* and additional action detrimental to that individual. Rather, in each of these cases, the challenged exercise of governmental power was regulatory, proscriptive, or compulsory in nature, and the complainant was either presently or prospectively subject to the regulations, proscriptions, or compulsions that he was challenging. . . .

The decisions in these cases fully recognize that governmental action may be subject to constitutional challenge even though it has only an indirect effect on the exercise of First Amendment rights. At the same time, however, these decisions have in no way eroded the

"established principle that to entitle a private individual to invoke the judicial power to determine the validity of executive or legislative action he must show that he has sustained, or is immediately in danger of sustaining, a direct injury as the result of that action. . . ." Ex parte Levitt. . . . (1937).

The respondents do not meet this test; their claim, simply stated, is that they disagree with the judgments made by the Executive Branch with respect to the type and amount of information the Army needs and that the very existence of the Army's data-gathering system produces a constitutionally impermissible chilling effect upon the exercise of their First Amendment rights. That alleged "chilling" effect may perhaps be seen as arising from respondents' very perception of the system as inappropriate to the Army's role under our form of government, or as arising from respondents' beliefs that it is inherently dangerous for the military to be concerned with activities in the civilian sector, or as arising from respondents' less generalized yet speculative apprehensiveness that the Army may at some future date misuse the information in some way that would cause direct harm to respondents. Allegations of a subjective "chill" are not an adequate substitute for a claim of specific present objective harm or a threat of specific future harm; "the federal courts established pursuant to Article III of the Constitution do not render advisory opinions." United Public Workers of America (C.I.O.) v. Mitchell . . . (1947).

Stripped to its essentials, what respondents appear to be seeking is a broad scale investigation conducted by themselves as private parties armed with the subpoena power of a federal district court and the power of cross-examination to probe into the Army's intelligence-gathering activities, with the district court determining at the conclusion of that investigation the extent to which those activities may or may not be appropriate to the Army's mission. . . .

Carried to its logical end, this approach would have the federal courts as virtually continuing monitors of the wisdom and soundness of Executive action; such a role is appropriate for the Congress acting through its committees and the "power of the purse"; it is not the role of the judiciary, absent actual present or immediately threatened injury resulting from unlawful governmental action. . . .

Reversed.

MR. JUSTICE DOUGLAS, with whom MR. JUSTICE MARSHALL concurs, dissenting. . . .

The claim that respondents have no standing to challenge the Army's surveillance of them and the other members of the class they seek to represent is too transparent for serious argument. The surveillance of the Army over the civilian sector—a part of society hitherto immune from their control—is a serious charge. It is alleged that the Army maintains files on the membership, ideology, programs, and practices of virtually every activist political group in the country. . . . The Army uses undercover agents to infiltrate these civilian groups and to reach into confidential files of students and other groups. The Army moves as a secret group among civilian audiences, using cameras and an electronic ear for surveillance. The data it collects are distributed to civilian officials in state, federal, and local governments and to each military intelligence unit and troop command under the Army's jurisdiction (both here and abroad); and these data are stored in one or more data banks.

Those are the allegations; and the charge is that the purpose and effect of the system of surveillance is to harass and intimidate the respondents and to deter them from exercising their rights of political expression, protest, and dissent "by invading their privacy, damaging their reputations, adversely affecting their employment and their opportunities for employment and in other ways." Their fear is that "permanent reports of their activities will be maintained in the Army's data bank, and their 'profiles' will appear in the so-called 'Blacklist' and that all of this information will be released to numerous federal and state agencies upon request." . . .

One need not wait to sue until he loses his job or until his reputation is defamed. To withhold standing to sue until that time arrives would in practical effect immunize from judicial scrutiny all surveillance activities regardless of their misuse and their deterrent effect. . . .

Surveillance of civilians is none of the Army's constitutional business. . . .

MR. JUSTICE BRENNAN, with whom MR. JUSTICE STEWART and MR. JUSTICE MARSHALL join, dissent. . . .

WARTH V. SELDIN

422 U.S. 490, 95 S. Ct. 2197, 45 L. Ed. 2d 343 (1975)

Various organizations and individuals resident in the Rochester, New York, metropolitan area brought suit against Penfield, a suburb adjacent to Rochester, claiming that town's zoning ordinance effectively excluded persons of low and moderate income from living in the town. In the lower federal courts the complaint was dismissed for lack of standing. The plaintiffs were (1) Rochester residents of low or moderate income who were also members of minority racial and ethnic groups allegedly excluded from living in Penfield by the unavailability of housing they could afford; (2) Rochester taxpayers allegedly required to pay heavier taxes to provide public housing in Rochester because of Penfield's exclusionary zoning; and (3) civic, housing, and home building organizations.

MR. JUSTICE POWELL delivered the opinion of the Court. . . .

The rules of standing, whether as aspects of the Art. III case or controversy requirement or as reflections of prudential considerations defining and limiting the role of the courts, are threshold determinants of the

propriety of judicial intervention. It is the responsibility of the complainant clearly to allege facts demonstrating that he is a proper party to
invoke judicial resolution of the dispute and the exercise of the court's
remedial powers. We agree with the District Court and the Court of
Appeals that none of the petitioners here has met this threshold requirement. Accordingly, the judgment of the Court of Appeals is

Affirmed.

MR. JUSTICE DOUGLAS, dissenting. . . .

With all respect, I think that the Court reads the complaint and the
record with antagonistic eyes. There are in the background of this case
continuing strong tides of opinion touching on very sensitive matters,
some of which involve race, some class distinctions based on wealth. . . .

Standing has become a barrier to access to the federal courts, just as
"the political question" was in earlier decades. The mounting caseload
of federal courts is well known. But cases such as this one reflect festering
sores in our society; and the American dream teaches that if one reaches
high enough and persists there is a forum where justice is dispensed. I
would lower the technical barriers and let the courts serve that ancient
need. They can in time be curbed by legislative or constitutional restraints if an emergency arises. . . .

MR. JUSTICE BRENNAN, with whom MR. JUSTICE WHITE and MR.
JUSTICE MARSHALL join, dissenting.

In this case, a wide range of plaintiffs, alleging various kinds of injuries,
claimed to have been affected by the Penfield zoning ordinance, on its
face and as applied, and by other practices of the defendant officials of
Penfield. Alleging that as a result of these laws and practices low- and
moderate-income and minority people have been excluded from Penfield, and that this exclusion is unconstitutional, plaintiffs sought injunctive, declaratory, and monetary relief. The Court today, in an opinion that
purports to be a "standing" opinion but that actually, I believe, has
overtones of outmoded notions of pleading and of justiciability, refuses
to find that any of the variously situated plaintiffs can clear numerous
hurdles, some constructed here for the first time, necessary to establish
"standing." While the Court gives lip-service to the principle, oft-
repeated in recent years, that "standing in no way depends on the merits
of the plaintiff's contention that particular conduct is illegal," . . . in fact
the opinion, which tosses out of court almost every conceivable kind of
plaintiff who could be injured by the activity claimed to be unconstitutional, can be explained only by an indefensible hostility to the claim on
the merits. I can appreciate the Court's reluctance to adjudicate the
complex and difficult legal questions involved in determining the constitutionality of practices which assertedly limit residence in a particular
municipality to those who are white and relatively well-off, and I also
understand that the merits of this case could involve grave sociological
and political ramifications. But courts cannot refuse to hear a case on the
merits merely because they would prefer not to, and it is quite clear, when
the record is viewed with dispassion, that at least three of the groups of

plaintiffs have made allegations, and supported them with affidavits and documentary evidence, sufficient to survive a motion to dismiss for lack of standing. . . .

POE V. ULLMAN

367 U.S. 497, 81 S. Ct. 1752, 6 L. Ed. 2d 989 (1961)

A Connecticut statute, passed in 1879, prohibited the use of drugs or instruments to prevent conception, or the giving of assistance or counsel in their use. Periodic efforts to repeal the statute having failed, the Connecticut Planned Parenthood League resorted to the courts. A physician, alleging that the statute prevented his giving professional advice concerning contraceptives to patients whose lives would be endangered by child-bearing, sought a declaratory judgment that the statute was unconstitutional. In *Tileston* v. *Ullman* (1943) the Supreme Court in a *per curiam* opinion held that the physician lacked standing to bring the suit, since his own life was not in danger and the patients whose lives he was seeking to protect were not parties to the suit.

Following this failure, the next test case was brought by a physician and two of his patients, both of whom had had difficult and dangerous pregnancies, and who alleged that the state law threatened their health and lives by preventing the doctor from giving them birth control advice and treatment.

MR. JUSTICE FRANKFURTER announced the judgment of the Court in an opinion which the CHIEF JUSTICE, MR. JUSTICE CLARK, and MR. JUSTICE WHITTAKER join. . . .

Appellants' complaints in these declaratory judgment proceedings do not clearly, and certainly do not in terms, allege that appellee Ullman threatens to prosecute them for use of, or for giving advice concerning, contraceptive devices. The allegations are merely that, in the course of his public duty, he intends to prosecute any offenses against Connecticut law, and that he claims that use of and advice concerning contraceptives would constitute offenses. . . .

The Connecticut law prohibiting the use of contraceptives has been on the State's books since 1879. . . . During the more than three-quarters of a century since its enactment, a prosecution for its violation seems never to have been initiated, save in State v. Nelson. . . . The circumstances of that case, decided in 1940, only prove the abstract character of what is before us. There, a test case was brought to determine the constitutionality of the Act as applied against two doctors and a nurse who had allegedly disseminated contraceptive information. After the Supreme Court of Errors sustained the legislation on appeal from a demurrer to the information, the State moved to dismiss the information. Neither counsel nor our

own researches have discovered any other attempt to enforce the prohibition of distribution or use of contraceptive devices by criminal process.
The unreality of these law suits is illumined by another circumstance. We
were advised by counsel for appellants that contraceptives are commonly
and notoriously sold in Connecticut drug stores. Yet no prosecutions are
recorded; and certainly such ubiquitous, open, public sales would more
quickly invite attention of enforcement officials than the conduct in which
the present appellants wish to engage—the giving of private medical
advice by a doctor to his individual patients, and their private use of the
devices prescribed. The undeviating policy of nullification by Connecticut of its anti-contraceptive laws throughout all the long years that they
have been on the statute books bespeaks more than prosecutorial paral-
ysis. . . .

. . . with due regard to Dr. Buxton's standing as a physician and to his
personal sensitiveness, we cannot accept, as the basis of constitutional
adjudication, other than as chimerical the fear of enforcement of provisions that have during so many years gone uniformly and without exception unenforced. . . .

Dismissed.

MR. JUSTICE BLACK dissents because he believes that the constitutional
questions should be reached and decided.

MR. JUSTICE BRENNAN, concurring in the judgment. . . .

MR. JUSTICE DOUGLAS, dissenting. . . .

These cases are dismissed because a majority of the members of this
Court conclude, for varying reasons, that this controversy does not
present a justiciable question. That conclusion is too transparent to require an extended reply. . . .

Plaintiffs in No. 60 are two sets of husband and wife. One wife is
pathetically ill, having delivered a stillborn fetus. If she becomes pregnant again, her life will be gravely jeopardized. This couple have been
unable to get medical advice concerning the "best and safest" means to
avoid pregnancy from their physician, plaintiff in No. 61, because if he
gave it he would commit a crime. The use of contraceptive devices would
also constitute a crime. And it is alleged—and admitted by the State—that
the State's Attorney intends to enforce the law by prosecuting offenses
under the laws.

A public clinic dispensing birth-control information has indeed been
closed by the State. Doctors and a nurse working in that clinic were
arrested by the police and charged with advising married women on the
use of contraceptives. That litigation produced State v. Nelson . . . which
upheld these statutes. . . .

The Court refers to the Nelson prosecution as a "test case" and implies that it had little impact. Yet its impact was described differently by
a contemporary observer who concluded his comment with this sentence:
"This serious setback to the birth control movement [the Nelson case] led
to the closing of all the clinics in the state, just as they had been previously
closed in the state of Massachusetts." At oral argument, counsel for

appellants confirmed that the clinics are still closed. In response to a question from the bench, he affirmed that "no public or private clinic" has dared gave birthcontrol advice since the decision in the Nelson case.

These, then, are the circumstances in which the Court feels that it can, contrary to every principle of American or English common law, go outside the record to conclude that there exists a "tacit agreement" that these statutes will not be enforced. No lawyer, I think, would advise his clients to rely on that "tacit agreement." No police official, I think, would feel himself bound by that "tacit agreement." . . .

When the court goes outside the record to determine that Connecticut has adopted "The undeviating policy of nullification . . . of its anti-contraceptive laws," it selects a particularly poor case in which to exercise such a novel power. This is not a law which is a dead letter. Twice since 1940, Connecticut has reenacted these laws as part of general statutory revisions. Consistently, bills to remove the statutes from the books have been rejected by the legislature. In short, the statutes—far from being the accidental left-overs of another era—are the center of a continuing controversy in the State. . . .

Again, the Court relies on the inability of counsel to show any attempts, other than the Nelson case "to enforce the prohibition of distribution or use of contraceptive devices by criminal process." Yet, on oral argument, counsel for the appellee stated on his own knowledge that several proprietors had been prosecuted in the "minor police courts of Connecticut" after they had been "picked up" for selling contraceptives. The enforcement of criminal laws in minor courts has just as much impact as in those cases where appellate courts are resorted to. . . .

What are these people—doctor and patients—to do? Flout the law and go to prison? Violate the law surreptitiously and hope they will not get caught? By today's decision we leave them no other alternatives. It is not the choice they need have under the regime of the declaratory judgment and our constitutional system. It is not the choice worthy of a civilized society. A sick wife, a concerned husband, a conscientious doctor seek a dignified, discrete, orderly answer to the critical problem confronting them. We should not turn them away and make them flout the law and get arrested to have their constitutional rights determined. . . .

MR. JUSTICE HARLAN, dissenting. . . .

MR. JUSTICE STEWART, dissenting. . . .

ROE V. WADE

410 U.S. 113, 93 S. Ct. 705, 35 L. Ed. 2d 147 (1973)

The Texas criminal abortion laws, which proscribe procuring or attempting an abortion except on medical advice for the purpose of saving the mother's life, were challenged by a pregnant single woman.

MR. JUSTICE BLACKMUN delivered the opinion of the Court. . . .

Jane Roe, a single woman who was residing in Dallas County, Texas, instituted this federal action in March 1970 against the District Attorney of the county. She sought a declaratory judgment that the Texas criminal abortion statutes were unconstitutional on their face, and an injunction restraining the defendant from enforcing the statutes.

Roe alleged that she was unmarried and pregnant; that she wished to terminate her pregnancy by an abortion "performed by a competent, licensed physician, under safe, clinical conditions"; that she was unable to get a "legal" abortion in Texas because her life did not appear to be threatened by the continuation of her pregnancy; and that she could not afford to travel to another jurisdiction in order to secure a legal abortion under safe conditions. She claimed that the Texas statutes were unconstitutionally vague and that they abridged her right of personal privacy, protected by the First, Fourth, Fifth, Ninth, and Fourteenth Amendments. By an amendment to her complaint Roe purported to sue "on behalf of herself and all other women" similarly situated.

We are confronted with issues of justiciability, standing, and abstention. [Has Roe] established that "personal stake in the outcome of the controversy," *Baker* v. *Carr* . . . that insures that "the dispute sought to be adjudicated will be presented in an adversary context and in a form historically viewed as capable of judicial resolution," *Flast* v. *Cohen* . . . and *Sierra Club* v. *Morton?* . . .

A. *Jane Roe.* Despite the use of the pseudonym no suggestion is made that Roe is a fictitious person. For purposes of her case, we accept as true and as established, her existence; her pregnant state, as of the inception of her suit in March 1970 and as late as May 21 of that year when she filed an alias affidavit with the District Court; and her inability to obtain a legal abortion in Texas.

Viewing Roe's case as of the time of its filing and thereafter until as late as May, there can be little dispute that it then presented a case or controversy and that, wholly apart from the class aspects, she, as a pregnant single woman thwarted by the Texas criminal abortion laws, had standing to challenge those statutes. . . . Indeed we do not read the appellee's brief as really asserting anything to the contrary. The "logical nexus between the status asserted and claim sought to be adjudicated," *Flast* v.

Cohen . . . and the necessary degree of contentiousness, *Golden* v. *Zwickler* . . . are both present.

The appellee notes, however, that the record does not disclose that Roe was pregnant at the time of the District Court hearing on May 22, 1970, or on the following June 17 when the court's opinion and judgment were filed. And he suggests that Roe's case must now be moot because she and all other members of her class are no longer subject to any 1970 pregnancy.

The usual rule in federal cases is that an actual controversy must exist at stages of appellate or certiorari review, and not simply at the date the action is initiated. . . .

But when, as here, pregnancy is a significant fact in the litigation, the normal 266-day human gestation period is so short that the pregnancy will come to term before the usual appellate process is complete. If that termination makes a case moot, pregnancy litigation seldom will survive much beyond the trial stage, and appellate review will be effectively denied. Our law should not be that rigid. Pregnancy often comes more than once to the same woman, and in the general population, if man is to survive, it will always be with us. Pregnancy provides a classic justification for a conclusion of nonmootness. It truly could be "capable of repetition yet evading review." . . .

We therefore agree with the District Court that Jane Roe had standing to undertake this litigation, that she presented a judiciable controversy, and that the termination of her 1970 pregnancy has not rendered her case moot.

EISEN V. CARLISLE & JACQUELIN

417 U.S. 156, 94 S. Ct. 2140, 40 L. Ed. 2d 732 (1974)

Eisen brought a class action on behalf of himself and all other odd-lot traders on the New York Stock Exchange over a four-year period against brokerage firms handling 99 percent of the Exchange's odd-lot business, charging violation of the antitrust and securities laws. The federal district court decided that the suit could be maintained as a class action, that two and a quarter million members of the class could be identified by name and address, and that it would cost $225,000 to send individual notices to them. The judge proposed instead that only a limited number be notified individually, with notification by publication to the remainder. He also held that the brokerage firms should pay 90 percent of the costs of notification.

The Supreme Court, in an opinion by Mr. Justice Powell, held that the requirement of individual notification could not be dispensed with, and directed that the class action be dismissed.

Mr. Justice Douglas, with whom Mr. Justice Brennan and Mr. Justice Marshall concur, dissenting in part. . . .

I think in our society that is growing in complexity there are bound to be innumerable people in common disasters, calamities, or ventures who would go begging for justice without the class action but who could with all regard to due process be protected. Some of these are consumers whose claims may seem *de minimis* but who alone have no practical recourse for either remuneration or injunctive relief. Some may be environmentalists who have no photographic development plant about to be ruined because of air pollution by radiation but who suffer perceptibly by smoke, noxious gases, or radiation. Or the unnamed individual may be only a ratepayer being excessively charged by a utility or a homeowner whose assessment is slowly rising beyond his ability to pay.

The class action is one of the few legal remedies the small claimant has against those who command the status quo. I would strengthen his hand with the view of creating a system of law that dispenses justice to the lowly as well as to those liberally endowed with power and wealth.

Chapter Five

POLITICAL
QUESTIONS

INTRODUCTION

Controversies which meet the test of justiciability are nevertheless occasionally refused adjudication by the Supreme Court on the ground that they involve "political questions." Like justiciability, the political questions doctrine is a manifestation of the general principle of judicial self-restraint. It is based in part on constitutional doubts about the scope of judicial power and in part on a prudent awareness of the practical limitations of courts and judges. The constitutional element in determining justiciability is the extent of judicial power under Article III; the constitutional element in the political questions doctrine is the separation of powers. Consideration is given, in other words, not only to the proper scope of the judicial power but also to the powers and duties assigned to the legislative and executive branches.

Where the authority to make a certain decision appears to have been assigned by the Constitution exclusively to the Congress or to the President, the courts will refuse to interfere, although the case may be otherwise justiciable. The conclusion that the Constitution assigns authority to solve a particular problem to the two political branches of government is usually supported by practical considerations. Either the matter is not one suitable for handling by the judicial methods of taking evidence and hearing legal arguments, or enforcement of a court order would require an undesirable degree of interference in the affairs of other government agencies or for other reasons be unusually difficult. Sometimes, it must be admitted, these two factors, the theoretical and the practical, appear to be two different ways of saying the same thing—that judicial review in a particular case is simply not wise.

The first explicit application of the political question doctrine was in the case of *Luther* v. *Borden* (1849). The case arose out of efforts in 1841 to reform the government of Rhode Island, which was still operating largely under its 1663 charter. Liberal elements in the state joined in a rebellion led by Thomas Dorr, and for a time two rival governments coexisted, although not too peacefully. The lawsuit originated as a complaint by a private citizen against an official of the charter government for trespassing on his property. In his defense the official claimed that he was executing the command of the lawful government.

A decision would have hinged on the question of which government was the legitimate one; but the Supreme Court refused to decide this issue, which as a practical matter had long been decided by the time the case reached Washington. Congress had already seated representatives elected under the authority of the charter government, and the President had likewise recognized it as the legal government. These decisions by the political branches of the government, Chief Justice Taney held, were within their constitutional power to make and beyond the competence of the courts to review.

Out of the decision in *Luther* v. *Borden* evolved the doctrine that the guaranty of a "republican form of government" to every state in Article IV, section 4, is judicially unenforceable. In *Pacific States Telephone & Telegraph Co.* v. *Oregon* (1912) the Court refused to decide whether a provision for the initiative and referendum in the Oregon constitution deprived that state of a republican form of government. The Court confirmed its refusal to enforce the republican guaranty in the famous Tennessee legislative apportionment case, *Baker* v. *Carr* (1962).

The process of amending the Constitution has generally been regarded as a political matter entrusted to Congress and subject to very little in the way of judicial supervision or control. Until 1939, however, the Court was willing to pass on procedural problems relating to the adoption of amendments. When the Eighteenth Amendment was proposed by Congress, it specified a period of seven years within which ratification had to be effected by three-fourths of the states. In *Dillon* v. *Gloss* (1921) the Supreme Court ruled that Congress had a right to fix a definite period for ratification, "within reasonable limits," and that seven years was a reasonable length of time. The implication of this ruling seemed to be that an amendment could not be adopted if it had been before the country for more than a reasonable time. Consequently, when the child labor amendment, which Congress had proposed in 1924 with no time limit specified, was ratified by Kansas and Kentucky in 1937, efforts were made to get a judicial ruling that because of the lapse of time the amendment was no longer open for ratification.

In *Coleman* v. *Miller* (1939), however, the Court refused to take responsibility for deciding what was a "reasonable" period for ratification. That was essentially a political question, which Congress would have to determine. Four members of the Court went further to hold that the Court's assertion in *Dillon* v. *Gloss* that amendments must be ratified within a reasonable period was entirely unauthorized, and nothing more than an "admonition to Congress in the nature of an advisory opinion." Their view was that the entire process of amendment was political and "not subject to judicial guidance, control or interference at any point."

It is generally agreed that the Constitution gives the President primary authority over American relations with foreign governments. It follows, and the courts agree, that a question related to the conduct of foreign affairs is likely to be a political question with which the judiciary should not meddle. Court decisions to this effect will be examined in Chapters Eight and Nine.

The Supreme Court had great difficulty in deciding whether state apportionment of seats in state legislatures and the national House of Representatives constituted a political question. For sixteen years the rule was that stated in ***Colegrove* v. *Green*** (1946), where the Court in a four to three decision held itself unable to act against Illinois congressional districts grossly unequal in population due to failure to redistrict the state since 1901. However, in the 1962 case of ***Baker* v. *Carr*** the Court reversed this position and directed a federal court in Tennessee, where the state legislature had not been reapportioned since 1901, to hear a case challenging the unequal districts as unconstitutional under the equal protection clause of the Fourteenth Amendment. Justice Brennan's opinion in *Baker* v. *Carr* is now the authoritative statement of the political question doctrine.

COLEGROVE V. GREEN

328 U.S. 549, 66 S. Ct. 1198, 90 L. Ed. 1432 (1946)

The Illinois legislature, dominated by rural legislators, had not redrawn the district lines for congressional elections since 1901. The result was that there were wide disparities in population among the districts, with some having nine times the population of others. Three college professors in the Chicago area sought to force reapportionment by bringing suit to enjoin state election officials from holding the 1946 congressional elections. A three-judge court dismissed the case, and an appeal was taken to the Supreme Court, which at the time was composed of only seven members. Chief Justice Stone had just died, and Justice Jackson was absent for the entire term acting as chief American prosecutor at the Nuremberg war crimes trial.

MR. JUSTICE FRANKFURTER announced the judgment of the Court and an opinion in which MR. JUSTICE REED and MR. JUSTICE BURTON concur. . . .

We are of opinion that the petitioners ask of this Court what is beyond its competence to grant. This is one of those demands on judicial power which cannot be met by verbal fencing about "jurisdiction." It must be resolved by considerations on the basis of which this Court, from time to time, has refused to intervene in controversies. It has refused to do so because due regard for the effective working of our Government revealed this issue to be of a peculiarly political nature and therefore not meet for judicial determination.

This is not an action to recover for damage because of the discriminatory exclusion of a plaintiff from rights enjoyed by other citizens. The basis for the suit is not a private wrong, but a wrong suffered by Illinois as a polity. . . . In effect this is an appeal to the federal courts to reconstruct the electoral process of Illinois in order that it may be adequately represented in the councils of the Nation. Because the Illinois legislature has failed to revise its Congressional Representative districts in order to reflect great changes, during more than a generation, in the distribution of its population, we are asked to do this, as it were, for Illinois.

Of course no court can affirmatively remap the Illinois districts so as to bring them more in conformity with the standards of fairness for a representative system. At best we could only declare the existing electoral system invalid. The result would be to leave Illinois undistricted and to bring into operation, if the Illinois legislature chose not to act, the choice of members for the House of Representatives on a state-wide ticket. The last stage may be worse than the first. The upshot of judicial action may defeat the vital political principle which led Congress, more than a hundred years ago, to require districting. . . . Assuming acquiescence on the part of the authorities of Illinois in the selection of its Representatives by a mode that defies the direction of Congress for selection by districts, the House of Representatives may not acquiesce. In the exercise of its power to judge the qualifications of its own members, the House may reject a delegation of Representatives-at-large. . . . Nothing is clearer than that this controversy concerns matters that bring courts into immediate and active relations with party contests. From the determination of such issues this Court has traditionally held aloof. It is hostile to a democratic system to involve the judiciary in the politics of the people. And it is not less pernicious if such judicial intervention in an essentially political contest be dressed up in the abstract phrases of the law.

The appellants urge with great zeal that the conditions of which they complain are grave evils and offend public morality. The Constitution of the United States gives ample power to provide against these evils. But due regard for the Constitution as a viable system precludes judicial correction. Authority for dealing with such problems resides elsewhere. Article I, section 4 of the Constitution provides that "The Times, Places and Manner of holding Elections for . . . Representatives, shall be prescribed in each State by the Legislature thereof; but the Congress may at any time by Law make or alter such Regulations . . ." The short of it is that the Constitution has conferred upon Congress exclusive authority to secure fair representation by the States in the popular House and left to that House determination whether States have fulfilled their responsibility. If Congress failed in exercising its powers, whereby standards of fairness are offended, the remedy ultimately lies with the people. Whether Congress faithfully discharges its duty or not, the subject has been committed to the exclusive control of Congress. An aspect of government from which the judiciary, in view of what is involved, has been excluded by the clear intention of the Constitution cannot be entered by the federal courts because Congress may have been in default in exacting from States obedience to its mandate. . . .

To sustain this action would cut very deeply into the very being of Congress. Courts ought not to enter this political thicket. The remedy for unfairness in districting is to secure State legislatures that will apportion properly, or to invoke the ample powers of Congress. The Constitution has many commands that are not enforceable by courts because they clearly fall outside the conditions and purposes that circumscribe judicial action. Thus, "on Demand of the executive Authority," Art. IV, § 2, of a State it is the duty of a sister State to deliver up a fugitive from justice. But the fulfillment of this duty cannot be judicially enforced. Commonwealth of Kentucky v. Dennison. . . . The duty to see to it that the laws are faithfully executed cannot be brought under legal compulsion. State of Mississippi v. Johnson. . . . Violation of the great guaranty of a republican form of government in States cannot be challenged in the courts. Pacific States Telephone & Telegraph Co. v. Oregon. . . . The Constitution has left the performance of many duties in our governmental scheme to depend on the fidelity of the executive and legislative action and, ultimately, on the vigilance of the people in exercising their political rights. Dismissal of the complaint is affirmed.

[JUSTICE RUTLEGE concurred in the result. JUSTICES BLACK, DOUGLAS, and MURPHY dissented.]

BAKER V. CARR

369 U.S. 186, 82 S. Ct. 691, 7 L. Ed. 2d 663 (1962)

The *Colegrove* ruling that legislative reapportionment was a political question was undisturbed for 16 years. But its authority was questioned by the Court's 1960 decision in *Gomillion* v. *Lightfoot,* which declared unconstitutional an Alabama statute changing the boundaries of the city of Tuskegee in a way that excluded almost all the black residents from the city. *Baker* v. *Carr* was begun in Tennessee to challenge the failure of that state's legislature to reapportion election districts since 1901. A three-judge court, relying on *Colegrove,* dismissed the suit, and an appeal was taken to the Supreme Court.

MR. JUSTICE BRENNAN delivered the opinion of the Court. . . .

In holding that the subject matter of this suit was not justiciable, the District Court relied on *Colegrove* v. *Green,* . . . and subsequent *per curiam* cases. . . . We understand the District Court to have read the cited cases as compelling the conclusion that since the appellants sought to have a legislative apportionment held unconstitutional, their suit presented a "political question" and was therefore nonjusticiable. We hold that this challenge to an apportionment presents no nonjusticiable "political question. . . ."

Of course the mere fact that the suit seeks protection of a political right does not mean it presents a political question. Such an objection "is little more than a play upon words." *Nixon* v. *Herndon.* . . . Rather, it is argued that apportionment cases, whatever the actual wording of the complaint, can involve no federal constitutional right except one resting on the guaranty of a republican form of government, and that complaints based on that clause have been held to present political questions which are nonjusticiable.

We hold that the claim pleaded here neither rests upon nor implicates the Guaranty Clause and that its justiciability is therefore not foreclosed by our decisions of cases involving that clause. . . . Our discussion . . . requires review of a number of political question cases in order to expose the attributes of the doctrine—attributes which, in various settings, diverge, combine, appear, and disappear in seeming disorderliness. . . . That review reveals that in the Guaranty Clause cases and in the other "political question" cases, it is the relationship between the judiciary and the coordinate branches of the Federal government, and not the federal judiciary's relationship to the States, which gives rise to the "political questions."

We have said that "in determining whether a question falls within [the political question] category, appropriateness under our system of government of attributing finality to the action of the political departments and also the lack of satisfactory criteria for a judicial determination are dominant considerations." *Coleman* v. *Miller*. . . . The nonjusticiability of a political question is primarily a function of the separation of powers. Much confusion results from the capacity of the "political question" label to obscure the need for case-by-case inquiry. Deciding whether a matter has in any measure been committed by the Constitution to another branch of government, or whether the action of that branch exceeds whatever authority has been committed, is itself a delicate exercise in constitutional interpretation, and is a responsibility of this Court as ultimate interpreter of the Constitution. To demonstrate this requires no less than to analyze representative cases and to infer from them the analytical threads that make up the political question doctrine. We shall then show that none of those threads catches this case.

FOREIGN RELATIONS. There are sweeping statements to the effect that all questions touching foreign relations are political questions. Not only does resolution of such issues frequently turn on standards that defy judicial application, or involve the exercise of a discretion demonstrably committed to the executive or legislature; but many such questions uniquely demand single-voiced statement of the Government's views. Yet it is error to suppose that every case or controversy which touches foreign relations lies beyond judicial cognizance. Our cases in this field seem invariably to show a discriminating analysis of the particular question posed, in terms of the history of its management by the political branches, of its susceptibility to judicial handling in the light of its nature and posture in the specific case, and of the possible consequences of judicial action. . . .

DATES OF DURATION OF HOSTILITIES. Though it has been stated broadly that "the power which declared the necessity is the power to declare its cessation, and what the cessation requires," . . . here too analysis reveals isolable reasons for the presence of political questions. underlying this Court's refusal to review the political departments' determination of when or whether a war has ended. Dominant is the need for finality in the political determination. . . .

VALIDITY OF ENACTMENTS. In *Coleman* v. *Miller* . . . this Court held that the questions of how long a proposed amendment to the Federal Constitution remained open to ratification, and what effect a prior rejection had on a subsequent ratification, were committed to congressional resolution and involved criteria of decision that necessarily escaped the judicial grasp. . . .

THE STATUS OF INDIAN TRIBES. This Court's deference to the political departments in determining whether Indians are recognized as a tribe while it reflects familiar attributes of political questions . . . also has a unique element in that "the relation of the Indians to the United States is marked by peculiar and cardinal distinctions which exist no where else. . . ."

It is apparent that several formulations which vary slightly according to the settings in which the questions arise may describe a political question, although each has one or more elements which identifies it as essentially a function of the separation of powers. Prominent on the surface of any case held to involve a political question is found a textually demonstrable constitutional commitment of the issue to a coordinate political department; or a lack of judicially discoverable and manageable standards for resolving it; or the impossibility of deciding without an initial policy determination of a kind clearly for nonjudicial discretion; or the impossibility of a court's undertaking independent resolution without expressing lack of the respect due coordinate branches of government; or an unusual need for unquestioning adherence to a political decision already made; or the potentiality of embarrassment from multifarious pronouncements by various departments on one question.

Unless one of these formulations is inextricable from the case at bar, there should be no dismissal for nonjusticiability on the ground of a political question's presence. The doctrine of which we treat is one of "political questions," not one of "political cases." The courts cannot reject as "no law suit" a bona fide controversy as to whether some action denominated "political" exceeds constitutional authority. . . .

But it is argued that this case shares the characteristics of decisions that constitute a category not yet considered, cases concerning the Constitution's guaranty, in Art. IV, § 4, of a republican form of government. A conclusion as to whether the case at bar does present a political question cannot be confidently reached until we have considered those cases with special care. We shall discover that Guaranty Clause claims involve those elements which define a "political question," and for that reason and no other, they are nonjusticiable. In particular we shall discover that the nonjusticiability of such claims has nothing to do with their touching upon matters of state governmental organization. . . .

[The opinion then reviews at length *Luther v. Borden* (1849) and other cases involving the "republican form of government" issue.]

We come finally to the ultimate inquiry whether our precedents as to what constitutes a nonjusticiable "political question" bring the case before us under the umbrella of that doctrine. A natural beginning is to note whether any of the common characteristics which we have been able to identify and label descriptively are present. We find none: The question here is the consistency of state action with the Federal Constitution. We have no question decided, or to be decided, by a political branch of government coequal with this Court. Nor do we risk embarrassment of our government abroad or grave disturbance at home if we take issue with Tennessee as to the constitutionality of her action here challenged. Nor need the appellants, in order to succeed in this action, ask the Court to enter upon policy determinations for which judicially manageable standards are lacking. Judicial standards under the Equal Protection Clause are well developed and familiar and it has been open to courts since the enactment of the Fourteenth Amendment to determine, if on the particular facts they must, that a discrimination reflects *no* policy, but simply arbitrary and capricious action. . . .

Reversed and remanded.

MR. JUSTICE WHITTAKER did not participate in the decision of this case.

MR. JUSTICE DOUGLAS, concurring. . . .

MR. JUSTICE CLARK, concurring. . . .

MR. JUSTICE STEWART, concurring. . . .

MR. JUSTICE FRANKFURTER, whom MR. JUSTICE HARLAN joins, dissenting. . . .

In sustaining appellants' claim . . . this Court's uniform course of decision over the years is overruled or disregarded. . . .

The *Colegrove* doctrine, in the form in which repeated decisions have settled it, was not an innovation. It represents long judicial thought and experience. From its earliest opinions this Court has consistently recognized a class of controversies which do not lend themselves to judicial standards and judicial remedies. . . .

1. The cases concerning war or foreign affairs, for example, are usually explained by the necessity of the country's speaking with one voice in such matters. While this concern alone undoubtedly accounts for many of the decisions, others do not fit the pattern. . . . A controlling factor in such cases is that, decision respecting these kinds of complex matters of policy being traditionally committed not to courts but to the political agencies of government for determination by criteria of political expediency, there exists no standard ascertainable by settled judicial experience or process by reference to which a political decision affecting the question at issue between the parties can be judged. . . .

2. The Court has been particularly unwilling to intervene in matters concerning the structure and organization of the political institutions of the States. The abstention from judicial entry into such areas has been greater even than that which marks the Court's ordinary approach to issues of state power challenged under broad federal guarantees. . . .

3. The cases involving Negro disfranchisement are no exception to the principle. . . . For here the controlling command of Supreme Law is plain and unequivocal. An end of discrimination against the Negro was the compelling motive of the Civil War Amendments. . . .

4. The Court has refused to exercise its jurisdiction to pass on "abstract questions of political power, of sovereignty, of government." *Massachusetts v. Mellon*. . . . The crux of the matter is that courts are not fit instruments of decision where what is essentially at stake is the composition of those large contests of policy traditionally fought out in nonjudicial forums, by which governments and the actions of governments are made and unmade. . . .

5. The influence of these converging considerations—the caution not to undertake decision where standards meet for judicial judgment are lacking, the reluctance to interfere with matters of state government in the absence of an unquestionable and effectively enforceable mandate, the unwillingness to make courts arbiters of the broad issues of political organization historically committed to other institutions and for whose adjustment the judicial process is ill-adapted—has been decisive of the settled line of cases, reaching back more than a century, which holds that Art. IV, § 4, of the Constitution, guaranteeing to the States "a Republican Form of Government," is not enforceable through the courts. . . .

The present case involves all of the elements that have made the Guarantee Clause cases non-justiciable. It is in effect a Guarantee Clause claim masquerading under a different label. But it cannot make the case more fit for judicial action that appellants invoke the Fourteenth Amendment rather than Art. IV, § 4, where, in fact, the gist of their complaint is the same. . . .

Here appellants attack "the State as a State. . . ." Their complaint is that the basis of representation of the Tennessee Legislature hurts them. They assert that "a minority now rules in Tennessee," that the apportionment statute results in a "distortion of the constitutional system," that the General Assembly is no longer "a body representative of the people of the State of Tennessee," all "contrary to the basic principle of representative government. . . ." Accepting appellants' own formulation of the issue, one can know this handsaw from a hawk. Such a claim would be nonjusticiable not merely under Art. IV, § 4, but under any clause of the Constitution by virtue of the very fact that a federal court is not a forum for political debate. . . .

But appellants, of course, do not rest on this claim *simpliciter*. In invoking the Equal Protection Clause, they assert that the distortion of representative government complained of is produced by systematic discrimination against them by way of "a debasement of their votes. . . ."

Appellants invoke the right to vote and to have their votes counted. But they are permitted to vote and their votes are counted. They go to the polls, they cast their ballots, they send their representatives to the state councils. Their complaint is simply that the representatives are not sufficiently numerous or powerful—in short, that Tennessee has adopted a basis of representation with whith they are dissatisfied. . . . What is actually asked of the Court in this case is to choose among competing bases of representation—ultimately, really, among competing theories of political philosophy—in order to establish an appropriate frame of government for the State of Tennessee and thereby for all the States of the Union.

. . . This is not a case in which a State has, through a device however oblique and sophisticated, denied Negroes or Jews or red-headed persons a vote or given them only a third or a sixth of a vote. That was *Gomillion v. Lightfoot*. . . . What Tennessee illustrates is an old and still widespread method of representaion—representation by local geographical division, only in part respective of population—in preference to others, others, forsooth, more appealing. Appellants contest this choice and seek to make this Court the arbiter of the disagreement. They would make the Equal Protection Clause the charter of adjudication, asserting that the equality which it guarantees comports, if not the assurance of equal weight to every voter's vote, at least the basic conception that representation ought to be proportionate to population, a standard by reference to which the reasonableness of apportionment plans may be judged.

To find such a political conception legally enforceable in the broad and unspecific guarantee of equal protection is to rewrite the Constitution. . . .

Dissenting opinion of MR. JUSTICE HARLAN, whom MR. JUSTICE FRANKFURTER joins. . . .

Chapter Six

PRESIDENTIAL POWERS

INTRODUCTION

The establishment of a strong single-headed executive was one of the surprises of the Constitutional Convention. During the period immediately preceding the Revolution, the executive power, represented by royal governors had been far from popular, and when control passed into the hands of the states the first impulse was to slash away at the executive and exalt the legislatures. This distrust of the executive was also present at Philadelphia in 1787, and proposals were heard that the executive branch be headed by a committee of three, for fear that a single official might develop monarchical powers. Again, it was argued that if a single executive were set up, he should be encumbered by a council. But these views were defeated by those who had seen the fumbling and the weakness of a headless government under the Articles of Confederation. Experience in the states had shown that an unchecked legislature could be as dangerous as a tyrannical executive. In *No. 70* of *The Federalist* Hamilton gave a classic statement of the case for "a vigorous executive."

The development of presidential power since 1789 has occurred for the most part quite independently of judicial aid or assistance. The Supreme Court has only infrequently been called on to resolve the constitutional issues of the Presidency. On the basic problem of filling the presidential office, for example, none of the issues has been suitable for judicial consideration. But when executive action has impinged on private rights, or occasionally in cases of conflict between the President and Congress, judicial intervention to define the constitutional situation has been successfully invoked.

Sources and Limits of Presidential Power

Article II begins with the statement that "The executive power shall be vested in a President of the United States of America" and then continues with a number of more or less specific authorizations, such as the power to grant pardons, to receive ambassadors, to make appointments, and to see that the laws are faithfully executed. The executive power of the President is grounded in these provisions, but it may also derive on occasion from the very character of the executive function, which John Locke referred to as "residual." The executive is always in session, always capable of moving quickly, and therefore available to fill in gaps and meet emergencies. In contrast, as Locke says, "the law making power is not always in being, and is usually too numerous and so too slow for the dispatch requisite to execution."

The great controversies about executive power have consequently tended to be concerned with the latitude which the President may claim in meeting crises calling for the use of powers not specified in the law or in the Constitution. In general, there have been two views on this subject. One is well summarized by the "stewardship" conception of the office asserted by Theodore Roosevelt. In his *Autobiography* he set forth his belief that:

> The executive power was limited only by specific restrictions and prohibitions appearing in the Constitution or imposed by the Congress under its Constitutional powers. . . . I declined to adopt the view that what was imperatively necessary for the Nation could not be done by the President unless he could find some specific authorization to do it. My belief was that it was not only his right but his duty to do anything that the needs of the Nation demanded unless such action was forbidden by the Constitution or by the laws.[1]

On the other hand, William Howard Taft took a more cautious and limited view of the President's powers, saying:

> The true view of the Executive function is, as I conceive it, that the President can exercise no power which cannot be fairly and reason-

[1]Theodore Roosevelt, *Autobiography* (New York: The Macmillan Company, 1913), pp. 388–89.

ably traced to some specific grant of power or justly implied and included within such express grant as proper and necessary to its exercise. Such specific grant must be either in the Federal Constitution or in an act of Congress passed in pursuance thereof. There is no undefined residuum of power which he can exercise because it seems to him to be in the public interest.[2]

The issue that emerges from these conflicting statements is whether the President must always be able to cite a "law" of the United States or a specific constitutional authorization in support of his actions, or whether the broad "executive power" with which he is vested justifies any actions he conceives as being in the public interest, as long as there is no conflict with existing legislation or constitutional provisions. Locke put this issue in its classic form. Pointing to the relative characteristics of executive and legislature already mentioned, he concluded that the executive must always be equipped with discretionary and prerogative powers:

> For the legislators not being able to foresee and provide by laws for all that may be useful to the community, the executor of the laws, having the power in his hands, has by the common law of Nature a right to make use of it for the good of society, in many cases where the municipal law has given no direction, till the legislative can conveniently be assembled to provide for it. Many things there are which the law can by no means provide for, and those must necessarily be left to the discretion of him that has the executive power in his hands, to be ordered by him as the public good and advantage shall require; nay, it is fit that the laws themselves should in some cases give way to the executive power, or rather to this fundamental law of Nature and government—viz., that, as much as may be, all the members of the society are to be preserved.[3]

The Supreme Court found it necessary to take a position on this issue in the case of *In re Neagle* (1890). It lined up with Locke, holding that the President's duty to see that the laws are faithfully executed is not "limited to the enforcement of acts of Congress ... according to their express terms," but includes also "the rights, duties and obligations growing out of the Constitution itself, our international relations, and all the protection implied by the nature of the government under the Constitution."

[2]William Howard Taft, *Our Chief Magistrate and His Powers* (New York: Columbia University Press, 1916), pp. 139–40.
[3]John Locke, *Of Civil Government*, Book 2, Chapter 14.

The Court took a similar position five years later in the case of *In re Debs* (1895). President Cleveland had sent troops to Chicago to deal with a railroad strike and had his Attorney General secure a federal court injunction against the strikers. There was no explicit statutory basis for the injunction, but the Court ruled that the government had the right of self-preservation, whether claimed by statute or not, and that the executive was constitutionally entitled to act in such cases.

The more recent judicial view on implied powers of the executive has been less permissive. The Steel Seizure case, **Youngstown Sheet & Tube Co. v. Sawyer** (1952), was occasioned by President Truman's seizure of the nation's steel mills to prevent a threatened strike that would have cut off the supply of munitions to United States troops in Korea. The federal district judge who granted an injunction against the seizure specifically dismissed Roosevelt's stewardship theory as one that does not "comport with our recognized theory of government," and the Supreme Court majority held that in seizing the steel mills Truman had exercised an authority that Congress had definitely concluded the President should *not* have.

The decision in **New York Times Co. v. United States** (1971) was similar. The Nixon administration had applied to the federal courts for injunctions to prevent publication of the so-called "Pentagon Papers," a 47-volume study by a private research organization of the circumstances under which the United States became involved in the Vietnam War. The government's allegation was that publication would be harmful to the national security. But again the Court majority found no statutory authorization for such an injunction, which would so flagrantly challenge the First Amendment right of freedom of the press.

In the Crime Control Act of 1968 Congress provided for a system of judicially approved wiretapping for certain classes of crime on the request and approval of the Attorney General. The Nixon administration contended that this act did not interfere with the implied power of the President to order wiretapping in national security investigations, citing a provision in the statute that nothing contained therein should "be deemed to limit the constitutional power of the President" to protect the United States. However, in *United States v. United States District Court* (1972) the Supreme Court held that this language was not a grant of power and that, as far as domestic security measures were concerned, the prior judicial warrant procedures had to be followed. A later lower court decision, which the Supreme Court declined to review [*Barrett v. Zweibon* (1976)] held that wiretapping in the field of foreign affairs should also require prior judicial approval. Attorneys General Edward Levi and Griffin Bell announced that they would permit no warrantless wiretaps of

American citizens, and President Carter proposed legislation to this effect in 1977.[4]

The Appointing Power

Generally speaking, the President's appointing power has occasioned little constitutional litigation. Standing as one of the most important executive prerogatives, it is firmly grounded in the provisions of Article II, section 2, though with the important restriction that senatorial confirmation is required for all appointees except "inferior officers."

One of the few judicial statements on the appointing power occurred in **Buckley** v. **Valeo** (1976). When setting up the new plan for financing presidential elections in the Federal Election Campaign Act of 1974, Congress unwisely sought to share in the power of appointing the members of the commission which was to administer the statute. The six voting members were to be appointed, two by the President, two by the Speaker of the House, and two by the President Pro Tem of the Senate, appointments to be evenly divided between the two parties. The Supreme Court ruled that the members of the Federal Election Commission were "officers of the United States," not congressional staff members, and consequently could be appointed only by the President. The statute was promptly amended to this effect.

The Removal Power

The removal power has occasioned more serious constitutional problems. Impeachment is the only method of removal from office specified in the Constitution. There is no language pertaining to the President's power to remove or declaring whether officers appointed with the confirmation of the Senate can be removed by the President without Senate approval.

Varying opinions have been held on this question. In No. 77 of *The Federalist* Hamilton argued that the Senate was associated with the President in exercise of the removal power. However, in the debate on establishment of the State Department in the First Congress, Madison contended successfully for the position that the Secretary of State was removable by the President alone. The act as passed provided that the Department's chief clerk should act as Secretary if the latter was "removed from office by the President." This important decision, which

---

[4]In 1977 a federal district judge ruled that former President Nixon and two members of his administration had deprived Morton Halperin and his family of their constitutional rights by having their home telephone tapped for 21 months and ordered the payment of $5 in damages.

seemed to confirm the proposition that the President's removal power was conferred on him directly by the Constitution, and in which many of the drafters of the Constitution participated, has been called "the decision of 1789."

In accordance with this view, the President's sole control of the removal power was practically unquestioned until the Civil War, even with respect to appointments for which Congress had specified a fixed term of years. But in the bitter feud between President Andrew Johnson and the Congress after the Civil War, Congress sought to recapture a share in the removal power. The Tenure of Office Act passed in 1867 denied the President the power to remove the heads of executive departments without the advice and consent of the Senate. A violation of this act, which Johnson contended was unconstitutional, was one of the charges on which he was impeached. The act was repealed in 1887 without ever having been subjected to a definitive constitutional test.

In 1876 Congress passed an act providing for Senate participation in the removal of postmasters. Litigation arising under this statute resulted in 1926 in a long-delayed vindication of Johnson's position. The case was **Myers** v. **United States**, involving a postmaster who was removed by President Wilson before the expiration of his four-year term without securing Senate consent. Chief Justice Taft's opinion asserted that the President's removal power was constitutionally unlimited. Even though the decision could be determinative only for the type of position actually involved, Taft contended that the principle would apply generally, even in the case of executive officers to whom Congress had given "duties of a quasi-judicial character . . . and members of executive tribunals."

Nine years later the Court had to pass on a case of precisely this character involving a member of the Federal Trade Commission who had been removed by President Roosevelt without any showing of cause, although the statute specified "inefficiency, neglect of duty, or malfeasance in office" as grounds for presidential removal. In **Humphrey's Executor** v. **United States** (1935) the Court unanimously reversed Taft's dictum and held this language to be a valid restriction on the removal power. In *Wiener* v. *United States* (1958) the Court extended the *Humphrey* principle to cover a quasi-judicial officer where there had been no specific statutory language protecting against removal.

The Power to Pardon

Article II, section 2, provides that the President "shall have power to grant reprieves and pardons for offenses against the United States, except in cases of impeachment." A pardon is an act of grace intended to correct a conviction or sentence which seems mistaken, harsh, or disproportionate to the crime. However, Presidents have on numerous occasions used the pardoning power to grant amnesty to an entire group.

The effect of a pardon is to grant exemption from the punishment the law inflicts for a crime. It frees a convicted criminal from serving any uncompleted term of imprisonment, from paying any unpaid fine, and it restores any civil or political rights that may have been lost as a result of the conviction. A pardon must be accepted to be valid.

The power of the President to attach conditions to a pardon was upheld in *Schick* v. *Reed* (1974). On review of a soldier's murder conviction and death sentence imposed by court-martial, President Eisenhower had commuted the sentence to life imprisonment, with the condition that the prisoner would never be eligible for parole. After the Supreme Court declared the death sentence unconstitutional in 1972, the prisoner brought suit contending that since his original sentence had been invalid, the condition attached to the pardon was also invalid and that he was entitled to parole. The Court majority rejected these claims.

President Ford's pardon of Richard Nixon one month after Nixon's resignation as President in 1974 raised several constitutional questions. First, it was alleged that the pardon violated the spirit of the constitutional ban on pardons in cases of impeachment, since impeachment proceedings were under way in Congress at the time. Second, the timing and scope of the pardon were questioned. The pardon guaranteed Nixon absolute immunity from federal criminal prosecution at a time when possible criminal acts on his part were still actively under investigation. The pardon prevented any judicial determination as to whether in fact any criminal acts had occurred. President Carter's mass pardon for violators of the Selective Service Act during the Vietnam War, granted on the second day of his term in 1977, aroused considerable controversy but presented no constitutional questions.

The Power to Impound Appropriated Funds

A congressional appropriation has generally been regarded by the executive as merely an authorization to spend. Consequently Presidents have on numerous occasions placed part of an appropriation in "reserves" or have "impounded" some or all of the funds. Minor controversies between the two branches have resulted, but it was not until President Nixon undertook to impound appropriated funds on a massive scale, usually on the justification of holding down expenditures to control inflation, that the issue reached constitutional proportions. In the Congressional Budget and Impoundment Control Act of 1974 Congress recognized the power of the President to impound, but provided procedures for Congress to override such action. In *Train* v. *City of New York* (1975), where the impoundment occurred prior to passage of the 1974 act, the Supreme Court held that an appropriation which specified that certain sums "shall be allotted" did not permit any impoundment by the administration.

THE FEDERALIST NO. 70

Alexander Hamilton

There is an idea, which is not without its advocates, that a vigorous executive is inconsistent with the genius of republican government. The enlightened well-wishers to this species of government must at least hope that the supposition is destitute of foundation; since they can never admit its truth, without at the same time admitting the condemnation of their own principles. Energy in the executive is a leading character in the definition of good government. It is essential to the protection of the community against foreign attacks; it is not less essential to the steady administration of the laws; to the protection of property against those irregular and high-handed combinations which sometimes interrupt the ordinary course of justice; to the security of liberty against the enterprises and assaults of ambition, of faction, and of anarchy. Every man the least conversant in Roman history knows how often that republic was obliged to take refuge in the absolute power of a single man, under the formidable title of dictator, as well against the intrigues of ambitious individuals who aspired to the tyranny, and the seditions of whole classes of the community whose conduct threatened the existence of all government, as against the invasions of external enemies who menaced the conquest and destruction of Rome.

There can be no need, however, to multiply arguments or examples on this head. A feeble executive implies a feeble execution of the government. A feeble execution is but another phrase for a bad execution; and a government ill executed, whatever it may be in theory, must be, in practice, a bad government. . . .

IN RE NEAGLE

135 U.S. 1, 10 S. Ct. 658, 34 L. Ed. 55 (1890)

Supreme Court Justice Field, whose judicial circuit included California, had had his life threatened by a disappointed litigant named Terry, and the Attorney General assigned a United States marshal to protect Field while he was riding circuit in that state. When Terry appeared about to make a physical attack on Field in a California railroad station, the marshal, Neagle, shot and killed him. State authorities arrested Neagle and held him on a charge of murder. The United States sought Neagle's release on habeas corpus under a federal statute making the writ available to a person "in custody for an act done or omitted in pursuance of a law of the United States." Congress, however, had enacted no *law* authorizing the President or the Attorney General to assign marshals as bodyguards to Supreme Court Justices.

MR. JUSTICE MILLER delivered the opinion of the Court. . . .

We have no doubt that Mr. Justice Field when attacked by Terry was engaged in the discharge of his duties as circuit justice of the ninth circuit, and was entitled to all the protection under those circumstances which the law could give him.

It is urged, however, that there exists no statute authorizing any such protection as that which Neagle was instructed to give Judge Field in the present case, and indeed no protection whatever against a vindictive or malicious assault growing out of the faithful discharge of his official duties; and that the language of section 753 of the Revised Statutes, that the party seeking the benefit of the writ of habeas corpus must in this connection show that he is "in custody for an act done or omitted in pursuance of a law of the United States," makes it necessary that upon this occasion it should be shown that the act for which Neagle is imprisoned was done by virtue of an act of Congress. It is not supposed that any special act of Congress exists which authorizes the marshals or deputy marshals of the United States in express terms to accompany the judges of the Supreme Court through their circuits, and act as a bodyguard to them, to defend them against malicious assaults against their persons. But we are of opinion that this view of the statute is an unwarranted restriction of the meaning of a law designed to extend in a liberal manner the benefit of the writ of habeas corpus to persons imprisoned for the performance of their duty. And we are satisfied that if it was the duty of Neagle, under the circumstances, a duty which could only arise under the laws of the United States, to defend Mr. Justice Field from a murderous attack upon him, he brings himself within the meaning of the section we have recited. . . .

In the view we take of the Constitution of the United States, any obligation fairly and properly inferable from that instrument, or any duty of the marshal to be derived from the general scope of his duties under the laws of the United States, is "a law" within the meaning of this phrase. It would be a great reproach to the system of government of the United States, declared to be within its sphere sovereign and supreme, if there is to be found within the domain of its powers no means of protecting the judges, in the conscientious and faithful discharge of their duties, from the malice and hatred of those upon whom their judgments may operate unfavorably. . . .

Where, then, are we to look for the protection which we have shown Judge Field was entitled to when engaged in the discharge of his official duties? Not to the courts of the United States; because, as has been more than once said in this Court, in the division of the powers of government between the three great departments, executive, legislative and judicial, the judicial is the weakest for the purposes of self-protection and for the enforcement of the powers which it exercises. The ministerial officers through whom its command must be executed are marshals of the United States, and belong emphatically to the executive department of the government. They are appointed by the President, with the advice and consent of the Senate. They are removable from office at his pleasure. They are subjected by act of Congress to the supervision and control of the Department of Justice, in the hands of one of the cabinet officers of the President, and their compensation is provided by acts of Congress. The same may be said of the district attorneys of the United States, who prosecute and defend the claims of the government in the courts.

The legislative branch of the government can only protect the judicial officers by the enactment of laws for that purpose, and the argument we are now combating assumes that no such law has been passed by Congress.

If we turn to the executive department of the government, we find a very different condition of affairs. The Constitution, section 3, Article II, declares that the President "shall take care that the laws be faithfully executed," and he is provided with the means of fulfilling this obligation by his authority to commission all the officers of the United States, and, by and with the advice and consent of the Senate, to appoint the most important of them and to fill vacancies. He is declared to be commander-in-chief of the army and navy of the United States. The duties which are thus imposed upon him he is further enabled to perform by the recognition in the Constitution, and the creation by acts of Congress, of executive departments, which have varied in number from four or five to seven or eight, the heads of which are familiarly called cabinet ministers. These aid him in the performance of the great duties of his office, and represent him in a thousand acts to which it can hardly be supposed his personal attention is called, and thus he is enabled to fulfill the duty of his great department, expressed in the phrase that "he shall take care that the laws be faithfully executed."

Is this duty limited to the enforcement of acts of Congress or of treaties of the United States according to their express terms, or does it include the rights, duties and obligations growing out of the Constitution itself, our international relations, and all the protection implied by the nature of the government under the Constitution? . . .

We cannot doubt the power of the President to take measures for the protection of a judge of one of the courts of the United States, who, while in the discharge of the duties of his office, is threatened with a personal attack which may probably result in his death, and we think it clear that where this protection is to be afforded through the civil power, the Department of Justice is the proper one to set in motion the necessary means of protection. . . .

We therefore affirm the judgment of the circuit court authorizing his discharge from the custody of the sheriff of San Joaquin County.

MR. JUSTICE LAMAR delivered a dissenting opinion in which MR. CHIEF JUSTICE FULLER concurred.

YOUNGSTOWN SHEET & TUBE CO. V. SAWYER

343 U.S. 579, 72 S. Ct. 863, 96 L. Ed. 1153 (1952)

A few hours before a nationwide steel strike was to begin on April 9, 1952, President Truman, contending that the work stoppage would imperil American troops in Korea by cutting off munitions and supplies, issued an executive order directing the Secretary of Commerce to take possession of and operate the nation's steel mills. There was no statutory authorization for the seizure. When adopting the Taft-Hartley Act to deal with nationwide strikes in 1947, Congress had considered giving the President seizure power, but had not done so. However, the act did not forbid presidential seizure. The steel companies obeyed the Secretary's orders under protest and secured an injunction against the seizure in federal district court. The case went to the Supreme Court with unprecedented speed, and on June 2 the Court held by a six to three vote that the President had exceeded his constitutional powers.

MR. JUSTICE BLACK delivered the opinion of the Court. . . .

We are asked to decide whether the President was acting within his constitutional power when he issued an order directing the Secretary of Commerce to take possession of and operate most of the Nation's steel mills. The mill owners argue that the President's order amounts to lawmaking, a legislative function which the Constitution has expressly confided to the Congress and not to the President. The Government's position is that the order was made on findings of the President that his action was necessary to avert a national catastrophe which would inevitably result from a stoppage of steel production, and that in meeting this grave emergency the President was acting within the aggregate of his constitutional powers as the Nation's Chief Executive and the Commander in Chief of the Armed Forces of the United States. . . .

The President's power, if any, to issue the order must stem either from an act of Congress or from the Constitution itself. There is no statute that expressly authorizes the President to take possession of property as he did here. Nor is there any act of Congress to which our attention has been directed from which such a power can fairly be implied. Indeed, we do not understand the Government to rely on statutory authorization for this seizure. . . .

Moreover, the use of the seizure technique to solve labor disputes in order to prevent work stoppages was not only unauthorized by any congressional enactment; prior to this controversy, Congress had refused to adopt that method of settling labor disputes. When the Taft-Hartley Act was under consideration in 1947, Congress rejected an amendment which would have authorized such governmental seizures in cases of emergency. . . .

It is clear that if the President had authority to issue the order he did, it must be found in some provisions of the Constitution. And it is not claimed that express constitutional language grants this power to the President. The contention is that presidential power should be implied from the aggregate of his powers under the Constitution. Particular reliance is placed on provisions in Article II which say that "the executive Power shall be vested in a President . . ."; that "he shall take Care that the Laws be faithfully executed"; and that he "shall be Commander in Chief of the Army and Navy of the United States."

The order cannot properly be sustained as an exercise of the President's military power as Commander in Chief of the Armed Forces. The Government attempts to do so by citing a number of cases upholding broad powers in military commanders engaged in day-to-day fighting in a theater of war. Such cases need not concern us here. Even though "theater of war" be an expanding concept, we cannot with faithfulness to our constitutional system hold that the Commander in Chief of the Armed Forces has the ultimate power as such to take possession of private property in order to keep labor disputes from stopping production. This is a job for the Nation's lawmakers, not for its military authorities.

Nor can the seizure order be sustained because of the several constitutional provisions that grant executive power to the President. In the framework of our Constitution, the President's power to see that the laws are faithfully executed refutes the idea that he is to be a lawmaker. The Constitution limits his functions in the lawmaking process to the recommending of laws he thinks wise and the vetoing of laws he thinks bad. . . .

It is said that other Presidents without congressional authority have taken possession of private business enterprises in order to settle labor disputes. But even if this be true, Congress has not thereby lost its exclusive constitutional authority to make laws necessary and proper to carry out the powers vested by the Constitution "in the Government of the United States, or any Department or Officer thereof."

The Founders of this Nation entrusted the lawmaking power to the Congress alone in both good and bad times. It would do no good to recall the historical events, the fears of power and the hopes for freedom that lay behind their choice. Such a review would but confirm our holding that this seizure order cannot stand.

The judgment of the District Court is

Affirmed.

MR. JUSTICE FRANKFURTER, concurring. . . .

Although the considerations relevant to the legal enforcement of the principle of separation of powers seem to me more complicated and flexible than may appear from what Mr. Justice Black has written, I join his opinion because I thoroughly agree with the application of the principle to the circumstances of this case. . . .

The issue before us can be met, and therefore should be, without attempting to define the President's powers comprehensively. . . .

We must . . . put to one side consideration of what powers the President would have had if there had been no legislation whatever bearing on the authority asserted by the seizure, or if the seizure had been only for a short, explicitly temporary period, to be determined automatically unless Congressional approval were given. These and other questions, like or unlike, are not now here. I would exceed my authority were I to say anything about them. . . .

In adopting the provisions which it did, by the Labor Management Relations Act of 1947, for dealing with a "national emergency" arising out of a breakdown in peaceful industrial relations, Congress was very familiar with Government seizure as a protective measure. On a balance of considerations Congress chose not to lodge this power in the President. . . .

It cannot be contended that the President would have had power to issue this order had Congress explicitly negated such authority in formal legislation. Congress has expressed its will to withhold this power from the President as though it had said so in so many words. The authoritatively expressed purpose of Congress to disallow such power to the President and to require him, when in his mind the occasion arose for such a seizure, to put the matter to Congress and ask for specific authority from it, could not be more decisive if it had been written into §§ 206–210 of the Labor Management Relations Act of 1947. . . .

Apart from his vast share of responsibility for the conduct of our foreign relations, the embracing function of the President is that "he shall take Care that the Laws be faithfully executed." . . . Art. II, § 3. The nature of that authority has for me been comprehensively indicated by Mr. Justice Holmes. "The duty of the President to see that the laws be executed is a duty that does not go beyond the laws or require him to achieve more than Congress sees fit to leave within his power." *Myers* v.

United States. . . . The powers of the President are not as particularized as are those of Congress. But unenumerated powers do not mean undefined powers. The separation of powers built into our Constitution gives essential content to undefined provisions in the frame of our government. . . .

A scheme of government like ours no doubt at times feels the lack of power to act with complete, all-embracing, swiftly moving authority. No doubt a government with distributed authority, subject to be challenged in the courts of law, at least long enough to consider and adjudicate the challenge, labors under restrictions from which other governments are free. It has not been our tradition to envy such governments. In any event our government was designed to have such restrictions. The price was deemed not too high in view of the safeguards which these restrictions afford. . . .

MR. JUSTICE DOUGLAS, concurring. . . .

MR. JUSTICE JACKSON, concurring in the judgment and opinion of the Court. . . .

We may well begin by a somewhat over-simplified grouping of practical situations in which a President may doubt, or others may challenge, his powers, and by distinguishing roughly the legal consequences of this factor of relativity.

1. When the President acts pursuant to an express or implied authorization of Congress, his authority is at its maximum, for it includes all that he possesses in his own right plus all that Congress can delegate. In these circumstances, and in these only, may he be said (for what it may be worth), to personify the federal sovereignty. If his act is held unconstitutional under these circumstances, it usually means that the Federal Government as an undivided whole lacks power. A seizure executed by the President pursuant to an Act of Congress would be supported by the strongest of presumptions and the widest latitude of judicial interpretation, and the burden of persuasion would rest heavily upon any who might attack it.

2. When the President acts in absence of either a congressional grant or denial of authority, he can only rely upon his own independent powers, but there is a zone of twilight in which he and Congress may have concurrent authority, or in which its distribution is uncertain. Therefore, congressional inertia, indifference or quiescence may sometimes, at least as a practical matter, enable, if not invite, measures on independent presidential responsibility. In this area, any actual test of power is likely to depend on the imperatives of events and contemporary imponderables rather than on abstract theories of law.

3. When the President takes measures incompatible with the expressed or implied will of Congress, his power is at its lowest ebb, for then he can rely only upon his own constitutional powers minus any constitutional powers of Congress over the matter. Courts can sustain exclusive Presidential control in such a case only by disabling the Congress from acting upon the subject. Presidential claim to a power at once so conclusive and preclusive must be scrutinized with caution, for what is at stake is the equilibrium established by our constitutional system.

Into which of these classifications does this executive seizure of the steel industry fit? It is eliminated from the first by admission, for it is conceded that no congressional authorization exists for this seizure. . . .

Can it then be defended upon flexible tests available to the second category? It seems clearly eliminated from that class because Congress has not left seizure of private property an open field but has covered it by three statutory policies inconsistent with this seizure. . . . None of these were invoked. In choosing a different and inconsistent way of his own, the President cannot claim that it is necessitated or invited by failure of Congress to legislate upon the occasions, grounds and methods for seizure of industrial properties.

This leaves the current seizure to be justified only by the severe tests under the third grouping, where it can be supported only by any remainder of executive power after subtraction of such powers as Congress may have over the subject. In short, we can sustain the President only by holding that seizure of such strike-bound industries is within his domain and beyond control by Congress. Thus, this Court's first review of such seizures occurs under circumstances which leave Presidential power most vulnerable to attack and in the least favorable of possible constitutional postures. . . .

The Solicitor General seeks the power of seizure in three clauses of the Executive Article, the first reading, "The executive Power shall be vested in a President of the United States of America." Lest I be thought to exaggerate, I quote the interpretation which his brief puts upon it: "In our view, this clause constitutes a grant of all the executive powers of which the Government is capable." If that be true, it is difficult to see why the forefathers bothered to add several specific items, including some trifling ones. . . . I cannot accept the view that this clause is a grant in bulk of all conceivable executive power but regard it as an allocation to the presidential office of the generic powers thereafter stated.

The clause on which the Government next relies is that "The President shall be Commander in Chief of the Army and Navy of the United States." . . . These cryptic words have given rise to some of the most persistent controversies in our constitutional history. Of course, they imply something more than an empty title. But just what authority goes with the name has plagued Presidential advisers who would not waive or narrow it by nonassertion yet cannot say where it begins or ends. It undoubtedly puts the Nation's armed forces under Presidential command. Hence, this loose appellation is sometimes advanced as support for any Presidential action, internal or external, involving use of force, the idea being that it vests power to do anything, anywhere, that can be done with an army or navy. . . .

We should not use this occasion to circumscribe, much less to contract, the lawful role of the President as Commander-in-Chief. I should indulge the widest latitude of interpretation to sustain his exclusive function to command the instruments of national force, at least when turned against the outside world for the security of our society. But, when it is turned inward, not because of rebellion but because of lawful economic struggle between industry and labor, it should have no such indulgence. His command power is not such an absolute as might be implied from that office in a militaristic system but is subject to limitations consistent with a constitutional Republic whose law and policy-making branch is a representative Congress. The purpose of lodging dual titles in one man was to insure that the civilian would control the military, not to enable the military to subordinate the presidential office. No penance would ever expiate the sin against free government of holding that a President can escape control of executive powers by law through assuming his military role. What the power of command may include I do not try to envision, but I think it is not a military prerogative, without support of law, to seize persons or property because they are important or even essential for the military and naval establishment.

The third clause in which the Solicitor General finds seizure powers is that "he shall take Care that the Laws be faithfully executed." . . . That authority must be matched against words of the Fifth Amendment that "No person shall be . . . deprived of life, liberty or property, without due process of law. . . ." One gives a governmental authority that reaches so far as there is law, the other gives a private right that authority shall go no farther. These signify about all there is of the principle that ours is a government of laws, not of men, and that we submit ourselves to rulers only if under rules.

The Solicitor General lastly grounds support of the seizure upon nebulous, inherent powers never expressly granted but said to have accrued to the office from the customs and claims of preceding administrations. The plea is for a resulting power to deal with a crisis or an emergency according to the necessities of the case, the unarticulated assumption being that necessity knows no law. . . .

The appeal . . . that we declare the existence of inherent powers *ex necessitate* to meet an emergency asks us to do what many think would be wise, although it is something the forefathers omitted. . . . I do not think we rightfully may so amend their work, and, if we could, I am not convinced it would be wise to do so, although many modern nations have forthrightly recognized that war and economic crises may upset the normal balance between liberty and authority. . . .

In the practical working of our Government we already have evolved a technique within the framework of the Constitution by which normal executive powers may be considerably expanded to meet an emergency. Congress may and has granted extraordinary authorities which lie dormant in normal times but may be called into play by the Executive in war or upon proclamation of a national emergency.

In view of the ease, expedition and safety with which Congress can grant and has granted large emergency powers, certainly ample to embrace this crisis, I am quite unimpressed with the argument that we should affirm possession of them without statute. . . .

MR. JUSTICE BURTON, concurring in both the opinion and judgment of the Court. . . .

MR. JUSTICE CLARK, concurring in the judgment of the Court. . . .

I conclude that where Congress has laid down specific procedures to deal with the type of crisis confronting the President, he must follow those procedures in meeting the crisis; but that in the absence of such action by Congress, the President's independent power to act depends upon the gravity of the situation confronting the nation. I cannot sustain the seizure in question because here . . . Congress had prescribed methods to be followed by the President in meeting the emergency at hand.

MR. CHIEF JUSTICE VINSON, with whom MR. JUSTICE REED and MR. JUSTICE MINTON join, dissenting. . . .

Those who suggest that this is a case involving extraordinary powers should be mindful that these are extraordinary times. A world not yet recovered from the devastation of World War II has been forced to face the threat of another and more terrifying global conflict. . . .

One is not here called upon even to consider the possibility of executive seizure of a farm, a corner grocery store or even a single industrial plant. Such considerations arise only when one ignores the central fact of this case—that the Nation's entire basic steel production would have shut down completely if there had been no Government seizure. Even ignoring for the moment whatever confidential information the President may possess as "the Nation's organ for foreign affairs," the uncontroverted affidavits in this record amply support the finding that "a work stoppage would immediately jeopardize and imperil our national defense."

Plaintiffs do not remotely suggest any basis for rejecting the President's finding that *any* stoppage of steel production would immediately place the Nation in peril. Moreover, even self-generated doubts that *any* stoppage of steel production constitutes an emergency are of little comfort here. The Union and the plaintiffs bargained for 6 months with over 100 issues in dispute—issues not limited to wage demands but including the union shop and other matters of principle between the parties. At the time of seizure there was not, and there is not now, the slightest evidence to justify the belief that any strike will be of short duration. The Union and the steel companies may well engage in a lengthy struggle. Plaintiff's counsel tells us that "sooner or later" the mills will operate again. That may satisfy the steel companies and, perhaps, the Union. But our soldiers and our allies will hardly be cheered with the assurance that the ammunition upon which their lives depend will be forthcoming—"sooner or later," or, in other words, "too little and too late."

Accordingly, if the President has any power under the Constitution to meet a critical situation in the absence of express statutory authorization, there is no basis whatever for criticizing the exercise of such power in this case. . . .

A review of executive action demonstrates that our Presidents have on many occasions exhibited the leadership contemplated by the Framers when they made the President Commander in Chief, and imposed upon him the trust to "take Care that the Laws be faithfully executed." With or without explicit statutory authorization, Presidents have at such times dealt with national emergencies by acting promptly and resolutely to enforce legislative programs, at least to save those programs until Congress could act. Congress and the courts have responded to such executive initiative with consistent approval. . . .

The President reported to Congress the morning after the seizure that he acted because a work stoppage in steel production would immediately imperil the safety of the Nation by preventing execution of the legislative programs for procurement of military equipment. And, while a shutdown could be averted by granting the price concessions requested by plaintiffs, granting such concessions would disrupt the price stabilization program also enacted by Congress. Rather than fail to execute either legislative program, the President acted to execute both. . . .

The absence of a specific statute authorizing seizure of the steel mills as a mode of executing the laws—both the military procurement program and the anti-inflation program—has not until today been thought to prevent the President from executing the laws. Unlike an administrative commission confined to the enforcement of the statute under which it was created, or the head of a department when administering a particular statute, the President is a constitutional officer charged with taking care that a "mass of legislation" be executed. Flexibility as to mode of execution to meet critical situations is a matter of practical necessity. . . .

There is no statute prohibiting seizure as a method of enforcing legislative programs. Congress has in no wise indicated that its legislation is not to be executed by the taking of private property (subject of course to the payment of just compensation) if its legislation cannot otherwise be executed. . . .

Whatever the extent of Presidential power on more tranquil occasions, and whatever the right of the President to execute legislative programs as he sees fit without reporting the mode of execution to Congress, the single Presidential purpose disclosed on this record is to faithfully execute the laws by acting in an emergency to maintain the status quo, thereby preventing collapse of the legislative programs until Congress could act. The President's action served the same purposes as a judicial stay entered to maintain the status quo in order to preserve the jurisdiction of a court. In his Message to Congress immediately following the seizure, the President explained the necessity of his action in executing the military procurement and anti-inflation legislative programs and expressed his desire to cooperate with any legislative proposals approving, regulating or rejecting the seizure of the steel mills. Consequently, there is no evidence whatever of any Presidential purpose to defy Congress or act in any way inconsistent with the legislative will. . . .

As the District Judge stated, this is no time for "timorous" judicial action. But neither is this a time for timorous executive action. . . .

NEW YORK TIMES COMPANY V. UNITED STATES

403 U.S. 713, 91 S. Ct. 2140, 29 L. Ed. 2d 822 (1971)

In June, 1971, the *New York Times*, *Washington Post*, and certain other newspapers began to print excerpts from a 47-volume study of the origins and conduct of the Vietnam War which had been made under the auspices of the Defense Department and were classified as secret. The newspapers received the study from Daniel Ellsberg, who had access to the material as an employee of the Rand Corporation and who, contrary to regulations, had made copies of the study. The Attorney General secured injunctions to stop the publication from federal courts in New York and Washington. Both the newspapers and the government appealed to the Supreme Court, and by a vote of six to three the Court dissolved the injunctions, a brief per curiam opinion simply saying that the government had not overcome the heavy constitutional presumption against prior restraint of the press. Each of the justices wrote a separate opinion.

Per Curiam.

We granted certiorari . . . in these cases in which the United States seeks to enjoin the *New York Times* and the *Washington Post* from publishing the contents of a classified study entitled "History of U. S. Decision-Making Process on Viet Nam Policy."

"Any system of prior restraints of expression comes to this Court bearing a heavy presumption against its constitutional validity." *Bantam Books, Inc.* v. *Sullivan* . . . (1963); see also *Near* v. *Minnesota* . . . (1931). The Government "thus carries a heavy burden of showing justification for the imposition of such a restraint." *Organization for a Better Austin* v. *Keefe* . . . (1971). The District Court for the Southern District of New York in the *New York Times* case . . . and the District Court for the District of Columbia and the Court of Appeals for the District of Columbia Circuit . . . in the *Washington Post* case held that the Government had not met that burden. We agree. . . .

MR. JUSTICE BLACK, with whom MR. JUSTICE DOUGLAS joins, concurring. . . .

I adhere to the view that the Government's case against the Washington Post should have been dismissed and that the injunction against the New York Times should have been vacated without oral argument when the cases were first presented to this Court. I believe that every moment's continuance of the injunctions against these newspapers amounts to a flagrant, indefensible, and continuing violation of the First Amendment. . . . The Government does not even attempt to rely on any act of Congress. Instead it makes the bold and dangerously far-reaching contention that the courts should take it upon themselves to "make" a law abridging freedom of the press in the name of equity, presidential power and national security, even when the representatives of the people in

Congress have adhered to the command of the First Amendment and refused to make such a law. . . . To find that the President has "inherent power" to halt the publication of news by resort to the courts would wipe out the First Amendment and destroy the fundamental liberty and security of the very people the Government hopes to make "secure." No one can read the history of the adoption of the First Amendment without being convinced beyond any doubt that it was injunctions like those sought here that Madison and his collaborators intended to outlaw in this Nation for all time. . . .

MR. JUSTICE DOUGLAS, with whom MR. JUSTICE BLACK joins, concurring. . . .

MR. JUSTICE STEWART, with whom MR. JUSTICE WHITE joins, concurring. . . .

In the governmental structure created by our Constitution, the Executive is endowed with enormous power in the two related areas of national defense and international relations. This power, largely unchecked by the Legislative and Judicial branches, has been pressed to the very hilt since the advent of the nuclear missile age. For better or for worse, the simple fact is that a President of the United States possesses vastly greater constitutional independence in these two vital areas of power than does, say, a prime minister of a country with a parliamentary form of government.

In the absence of the governmental checks and balances present in other areas of our national life, the only effective restraint upon executive policy and power in the areas of national defense and international affairs may lie in an enlightened citizenry—in an informed and critical public opinion which alone can here protect the values of democratic government. For this reason, it is perhaps here that a press that is alert, aware, and free most vitally serves the basic purpose of the First Amendment. For without an informed and free press there cannot be an enlightened people.

Yet it is elementary that the successful conduct of international diplomacy and the maintenance of an effective national defense require both confidentiality and secrecy. Other nations can hardly deal with this Nation in an atmosphere of mutual trust unless they can be assured that their confidences will be kept. And within our own executive departments, the development of considered and intelligent international policies would be impossible if those charged with their formulation could not communicate with each other freely, frankly, and in confidence. In the area of basic national defense the frequent need for absolute secrecy is, of course, self-evident.

I think there can be but one answer to this dilemma, if dilemma it be. The responsibility must be where the power is. If the Constitution gives the Executive a large degree of unshared power in the conduct of foreign affairs and the maintenance of our national defense, then under the Constitution the Executive must have the largely unshared duty to determine and preserve the degree of internal security necessary to exercise that power successfully. It is an awesome responsibility, requiring judgment and wisdom of a high order. I should suppose that moral, political, and practical considerations would dictate that a very first principle of that wisdom would be an insistence upon avoiding secrecy for its own sake. For when everything is classified, then nothing is classified, and the system becomes one to be disregarded by the cynical or the careless, and to be manipulated by those intent on self-protection or self-promotion. I should suppose, in short, that the hallmark of a truly effective internal security system would be the maximum possible disclosure, recognizing that secrecy can best be preserved only when credibility is truly maintained. But be that as it may, it is clear to me that it is the constitutional duty of the Executive—as a matter of sovereign prerogative and not as a matter of law as the courts know law—through the promulgation and enforcement of executive regulations, to protect the confidentiality necessary to carry out its responsibilities in the fields of international relations and national defense.

This is not to say that Congress and the courts have no role to play. Undoubtedly Congress has the power to enact specific and appropriate criminal laws to protect government property and preserve government secrets. Congress has passed such laws, and several of them are of very colorable relevance to the apparent circumstances of these cases. And if a criminal prosecution is instituted, it will be the responsibility of the courts to decide the applicability of the criminal law under which the charge is brought. Moreover, if Congress should pass a specific law authorizing civil proceedings in this field, the courts would likewise have the duty to decide the constitutionality of such a law as well as its applicability to the facts proved.

But in the cases before us we are asked neither to construe specific regulations nor to apply specific laws. We are asked, instead, to perform a function that the Constitution gave to the Executive, not the Judiciary. We are asked, quite simply, to prevent the publication by two newspapers of material that the Executive Branch insists should not, in the national interest, be published. I am convinced that the Executive is correct with respect to some of the documents involved. But I cannot say that disclosure of any of them will surely result in direct, immediate, and irreparable damage to our Nation or its people. That being so, there can under the First Amendment be but one judicial resolution of the issues before us. I join the judgments of the Court.

MR. JUSTICE WHITE, with whom MR. JUSTICE STEWART joins, concurring. . . .

MR. JUSTICE MARSHALL, concurring. . . .

MR. CHIEF JUSTICE BURGER, dissenting. . . .

. . . To me it is hardly believable that a newspaper long regarded as a great institution in American life would fail to perform one of the basic and simple duties of every citizen with respect to the discovery or possession of stolen property or secret government documents. That duty, I had thought—perhaps naively—was to report forthwith, to responsible public officers. This duty rests on taxi drivers, Justices, and the New York Times. The course followed by the Times, whether so calculated or not, removed any possibility of orderly litigation of the issues. If the action of the judges up to now has been correct, that result is sheer happenstance.

MR. JUSTICE HARLAN, with whom THE CHIEF JUSTICE and MR. JUSTICE BLACKMUN join, dissenting. . . .

It is plain to me that the scope of the judicial function in passing upon the activities of the Executive Branch of the Government in the field of foreign affairs is very narrowly restricted. This view is, I think, dictated by the concept of separation of powers upon which our constitutional system rests. . . .

I can see no indication in the opinions of either the District Court or the Court of Appeals in the *Post* litigation that the conclusions of the Executive were given even the deference owing to an administrative agency, much less that owing to a co-equal branch of the Government operating within the field of its constitutional prerogative.

Accordingly, I would vacate the judgment of the Court of Appeals for the District of Columbia Circuit on this ground and remand the case for further proceedings in the District Court. Before the commencement of such further proceedings, due opportunity should be afforded the Government for procuring from the Secretary of State or the Secretary of Defense or both an expression of their views on the issue of national security. The ensuing review by the District Court should be in accordance with the views expressed in this opinion. And for the reasons stated above I would affirm the judgment of the Court of Appeals for the Second Circuit.

MR. JUSTICE BLACKMUN, dissenting. . . .

The First Amendment, after all, is only one part of an entire Constitution. Article II of the great document vests in the Executive Branch primary power over the conduct of foreign affairs and places in that branch the responsibility for the Nation's safety. Each provision of the Constitution is important, and I cannot subscribe to a doctrine of unlimited absolutism for the First Amendment at the cost of downgrading other provisions. . . .

I strongly urge, and sincerely hope, that these two newspapers will be fully aware of their ultimate responsibilities to the United States of America. Judge Wilkey, dissenting in the District of Columbia case, after a review of only the affidavits before his court (the basic papers had not then been made available by either party), concluded that there were a number of examples of documents that, if in the possession of the Post, and if published, "could clearly result in great harm to the nation," and he defined "harm" to mean "the death of soldiers, the destruction of alliances, the greatly increased difficulty of negotiation with our enemies, the inability of our diplomats to negotiate * * *." I, for one, have now been able to give at least some cursory study not only to the affidavits, but to the material itself. I regret to say that from this examination I fear that Judge Wilkey's statements have possible foundation. I therefore share his concern. I hope that damage has not already been done. If, however, damage has been done, and if, with the Court's action today, these newspapers proceed to publish the critical documents and there results therefrom "the death of soldiers, the destruction of alliances, the greatly increased difficulty of negotiation with our enemies, the inability of our diplomats to negotiate," to which list I might add the factors of prolongation of the war and of further delay in the freeing of United States prisoners, then the Nation's people will know where the responsibility for these sad consequences rests.

BUCKLEY V. VALEO

424 U.S. 1, 96 S. Ct. 612, 46 L. Ed. 2d. 659 (1976)

The Federal Election Campaign Act of 1974 was a complex and novel statute providing for public financing of presidential primary and election campaigns and limitation on campaign contributions and expenditures. The act was to be administered by a Federal Election Commission composed of six voting and two nonvoting members. Two of the six voting members were to be appointed by the President, with confirmation by both the House and Senate; two were to be appointed by the Speaker of the House, and two by the President pro tempore of the Senate. In this suit Senator James L. Buckley and others challenged the constitutionality of the act in its entirety. The following excerpt deals only with the challenge to the method of appointing the members of the Commission.

Per Curiam....
Appellants urge that since Congress has given the Commission wide-ranging rule-making and enforcement powers with respect to the substantive provisions of the Act, Congress is precluded under the principle of separation of powers from vesting in itself the authority to appoint those who will exercise such authority. Their argument is based on the language of Art. II, sec. 2, cl. 2, of the Constitution, which provides in pertinent part as follows:

"[The President] shall nominate, and by and with the Advice and Consent of the Senate, shall appoint Ambassadors, other public Ministers and Consuls, Judges of the supreme Court, and all other Officers of the United States, whose Appointments are not herein otherwise provided for, and which shall be established by Law: but the Congress may by Law vest the Appointment of such inferior Officers, as they think proper, in the President alone, in the Courts of Law, or in the Heads of Departments." ...

We think that the term "Officers of the United States" as used in Art. II, defined to include "all persons who can be said to hold an office under the government" in *United States* v. *Germaine* . . . is a term intended to have substantive meaning. We think its fair import is that any appointee exercising significant authority pursuant to the laws of the United States is an Officer of the United States, and must, therefore, be appointed in the manner prescribed by § 2, cl. 2 of that Article. . . .

Although two members of the Commission are initially selected by the President, his nominations are subject to confirmation not merely by the Senate, but by the House of Representatives as well. The remaining four voting members of the Commission were appointed by the President *pro tempore* of the Senate and by the Speaker of the House. While the second part of the Clause authorizes Congress to vest the appointment of the officers described in that part in "the Courts of Law, or in the Heads of Departments," neither the Speaker of the House nor the President *pro tempore* of the Senate comes within this language. . . .

Thus with respect to four of the six voting members of the Commission, neither the President, the head of any department, nor the judiciary has any voice in their selection.

The Appointments Clause specifies the method of appointment only for "Officers of the United States" whose appointment is not "otherwise provided for" in the Constitution. But there is no provision of the Constitution remotely providing any alternative means for the selection of the members of the Commission or for anybody like them. Appellee Commission has argued, and the Court of Appeals agreed, that the Appointments Clause of Art. II should not be read to exclude the "inherent power of Congress" to appoint its own officers to perform functions necessary to that body as an institution. But . . . nothing in our holding with respect to Art. II, § 2, cl. 2, will deny to Congress "all power to appoint its own inferior officers to carry out appropriate legislative functions." . . .

Appellee Commission and *amici* contend somewhat obliquely that because the Framers had no intention of relegating Congress to a position below that of the coequal Judicial and Executive Branches of the National Government, the Appointments Clause must somehow be read to include Congress or its officers as among those in whom the appointment power may be vested. But the debates of the Constitutional Convention, and the Federalist Papers, are replete with expressions of fear that the Legislative Branch of the National Government will aggrandize itself at the expense of the other two branches. The debates during the Convention, and the evolution of the draft version of the Constitution, seem to us to lend considerable support to our reading of the language of the Appointments Clause itself. . . .

Appellee Commission and *amici* urge that because of what they conceive to be the extraordinary authority reposed in Congress to regulate elections, this case stands on a different footing than if Congress had exercised its legislative authority in another field. There is of course no doubt that Congress has express authority to regulate congressional elections, by virtue of the power conferred in Art. I, § 4. This Court has also held that it has very broad authority to prevent corruption in national

Presidential elections. *Burroughs* v. *United States* . . . (1934). But Congress has plenary authority in all areas in which it has substantive legislative jurisdiction, *McCulloch* v. *Maryland* . . . (1819), so long as the exercise of that authority does not offend some other constitutional restriction. We see no reason to believe that the authority of Congress over federal election practices is of such a wholly different nature from the other grants of authority to Congress that it may be employed in such a manner as to offend well established constitutional restrictions stemming from the separation of powers.

The position that because Congress has been given explicit and plenary authority to regulate a field of activity, it must therefore have the power to appoint those who are to administer the regulatory statute is both novel and contrary to the language of the Appointments Clause. Unless their selection is elsewhere provided for, *all* Officers of the United States are to be appointed in accordance with the Clause. Principal officers are selected by the President with the advice and consent of the Senate. Inferior officers Congress may allow to be appointed by the President alone, by the heads of departments, or by the judiciary. No class or type of officer is excluded because of its special functions. The President appoints judicial as well as executive officers. Neither has it been disputed—and apparently it is not now disputed—that the Clause controls the appointment of the members of a typical administrative agency even though its functions, as this Court recognized in *Humphrey's Executor* v. *United States* . . . (1935), may be "predominantly quasijudicial and quasi-legislative" rather than executive. The Court in that case carefully emphasized that although the members of such agencies were to be independent of the executive in their day-to-day operations, the executive was not excluded from selecting them. . . .

We are also told by appellees and *amici* that Congress had good reason for not vesting in a Commission composed wholly of Presidential appointees the authority to administer the Act, since the administration of the Act would undoubtedly have a bearing on any incumbent President's campaign for re-election. While one cannot dispute the basis for this sentiment as a practical matter, it would seem that those who sought to challenge incumbent Congressmen might have equally good reason to fear a Commission which was unduly responsive to Members of Congress whom they were seeking to unseat. But such fears, however rational, do not by themselves warrant a distortion of the Framers' work.

Appellee Commission and *amici* finally contend, and the majority of the Court of Appeals agreed with them, that whatever shortcomings the provisions for the appointment of members of the Commission might have under Art. II, Congress had ample authority under the Necessary and Proper Clause of Art. I to effectuate this result. We do not agree. The proper inquiry when considering the Necessary and Proper Clause is not the authority of Congress to create an office or a commission, which is broad indeed, but rather its authority to provide that its own officers may appoint to such office or commission.

So framed, the claim that Congress may provide for this manner of appointment under the Necessary and Proper Clause of Art. I stands on no better footing than the claim that it may provide for such manner of appointment because of its substantive authority to regulate federal elections. Congress could not, merely because it concluded that such a measure was "necessary and proper" to the discharge of its substantive legislative authority, pass a bill of attainder or ex post facto law contrary to the prohibitions contained in § 9 of Art. I. No more may it vest in itself, or in its officers, the authority to appoint officers of the United States when the Appointments Clause by clear implication prohibits it from doing so. . . .

. . . we hold that most of the powers conferred by the Act upon the Federal Election Commission can be exercised only by "Officers of the United States," appointed in conformity with Art. II, sec. 2, cl. 2, of the Constitution, and therefore cannot be exercised by the Commission as presently constituted. . . .

MYERS V. UNITED STATES

272 U.S. 52, 47 S. Ct. 21, 71 L. Ed. 160 (1926)

MR. CHIEF JUSTICE TAFT delivered the opinion of the court.

This case presents the question whether under the Constitution the President has the exclusive power of removing executive officers of the United States whom he has appointed by and with the advice and consent of the Senate. . . .

By the 6th section of the Act of Congress of July 12, 1876 . . . under which Myers was appointed with the advice and consent of the Senate as a first-class postmaster, it is provided that:

"Postmasters of the first, second, and third classes shall be appointed and may be removed by the President by and with the advice and consent of the Senate, and shall hold their offices for four years unless sooner removed or suspended according to law."

The Senate did not consent to the President's removal of Myers during his term. If this statute in its requirement that his term should be four years unless sooner removed by the President by and with the consent of the Senate is valid, the appellant, Myers' administratrix, is entitled to recover his unpaid salary for his full term and the judgment of the Court of Claims must be reversed. The government maintains that the requirement is invalid, for the reason that under Article II of the Constitution the President's power of removal of executive officers appointed by him with the advice and consent of the Senate is full and complete without consent of the Senate. . . .

The question where the power of removal of executive officers appointed by the President by and with the advice and consent of the Senate was vested, was presented early in the first session of the First Congress. There is no express provision respecting removals in the Constitution, except as Section 4 of Article II . . . provides for removal from office by impeachment. The subject was not discussed in the Constitutional Convention. . . .

The vesting of the executive power in the President was essentially a grant of the power to execute the laws. But the President alone and unaided could not execute the laws. He must execute them by the assistance of subordinates. This view has since been repeatedly affirmed by this court.

. . . As he is charged specifically to take care that they be faithfully executed, the reasonable implication, even in the absence of express words, was that as part of his executive power he should select those who were to act for him under his direction in the execution of the laws. The further implication must be, in the absence of any express limitation respecting removals, that as his selection of administrative officers is essential to the execution of the laws by him, so must be his power of removing those for whom he cannot continue to be responsible. . . .

The power to prevent the removal of an officer who has served under the President is different from the authority to consent to or reject his appointment. When a nomination is made, it may be presumed that the Senate is, or may become, as well advised as to the fitness of the nominee as the President, but in the nature of things the defects in ability or intelligence or loyalty in the administration of the laws of one who has served as an officer under the President are facts as to which the President, or his trusted subordinates, must be better informed than the Senate, and the power to remove him may therefore be regarded as confined for very sound and practical reasons, to the governmental authority which has administrative control. The power of removal is incident to the power of appointment, not to the power of advising and consenting to appointment, and when the grant of the executive power is enforced by the express mandate to take care that the laws be faithfully executed, it emphasizes the necessity for including within the executive power as conferred the exclusive power of removal. . . .

Made responsible under the Constitution for the effective enforcement of the law, the President needs as an indispensable aid to meet it the disciplinary influence upon those who act under him of a reserve power of removal. . . .

In all such cases, the discretion to be exercised is that of the President in determining the national public interest and in directing the action to be taken by his executive subordinates to protect it. In this field his cabinet officers must do his will. He must place in each member of his official family, and his chief executive subordinates, implicit faith. The moment that he loses confidence in the intelligence, ability, judgment or loyalty of any one of them, he must have the power to remove him without delay. To require him to file charges and submit them to the consideration of the Senate might make impossible that unity and co-ordination in executive administration essential to effective action.

The duties of the heads of departments and bureaus in which the discretion of the President is exercised and which we have described, are the most important in the whole field of executive action of the government. There is nothing in the Constitution which permits a distinction between the removal of the head of a department or a bureau, when he discharges a political duty of the President or exercises his discretion, and the removal of executive officers engaged in the discharge of their other normal duties. The imperative reasons requiring an unrestricted power to remove the most important of his subordinates in their most important duties must, therefore, control the interpretation of the Constitution as to all appointed by him.

But this is not to say that there are not strong reasons why the President should have a like power to remove his appointees charged with other duties than those above described. The ordinary duties of officers prescribed by statute come under the general administrative control of the President by virtue of the general grant to him of the executive power, and he may properly supervise and guide their construction of the statutes under which they act in order to secure that unitary and uniform execution of the laws which Article 2 of the Constitution evidently contemplated in vesting general executive power in the President alone. Laws are often passed with specific provision for the adoption of regulations by a department or bureau head to make the law workable and effective. The ability and judgment manifested by the official thus empowered, as well as his energy and stimulation of his subordinates, are subjects which the President must consider and supervise in his administrative control. Finding such officers to be negligent and inefficient, the President should have the power to remove them. Of course there may be duties so peculiarly and specifically committed to the discretion of a particular officer as to raise a question whether the President may overrule or revise the officer's interpretation of his statutory duty in a particular instance. Then there may be duties of a quasi-judicial character imposed on executive officers and members of executive tribunals whose decisions after hearing affect interests of individuals, the discharge of which the President can not in a particular case properly influence or control. But even in such a case he may consider the decision after its rendition as a reason for removing the officer, on the ground that the discretion regularly entrusted to that officer by statute has not been on the whole intelligently or wisely exercised. Otherwise he does not discharge his own constitutional duty of seeing that the laws be faithfully executed.

For the reasons given, we must therefore hold that the provision of the law of 1876 by which the unrestricted power of removal of first-class postmasters is denied to the President is in violation of the Constitution and invalid. This leads to an affirmance of the judgment of the Court of Claims. . . .

Judgment affirmed.

MR. JUSTICE McREYNOLDS wrote a separate dissenting opinion.

MR. JUSTICE BRANDEIS, dissenting. . . .

. . . May the President, having acted under the statute in so far as it creates the office and authorizes the appointment, ignore, while the Senate is in session, the provision which prescribes the condition under which a removal may take place? . . .

. . . The argument is that appointment and removal of officials are executive prerogatives; that the grant to the President of "the executive Power" confers upon him, as inherent in the office, the power to exercise these two functions without restriction by Congress, except in so far as the power to restrict his exercise of them is expressly conferred upon Congress by the Constitution; that in respect to appointment certain restrictions of the executive power are so provided for; but that in respect to removal, there is no express grant to Congress of any power to limit the President's prerogative. The simple answer to the argument is this: The ability to remove a subordinate executive officer, being an essential of effective government, will, in the absence of express constitutional provision to the contrary, be deemed to have been vested in some person or body. . . . But it is not a power inherent in a chief executive. The President's power of removal from statutory civil inferior offices, like the power of appointment to them, comes immediately from Congress. It is true that the exercise of the power of removal is said to be an executive act; and that when the Senate grants or withholds consent to a removal by the President, it participates in an executive act. But the Constitution has confessedly granted to Congress the legislative power to create offices, and to prescribe the tenure thereof; and it has not in terms denied to Congress the power to control removals. To prescribe the tenure involves prescribing the conditions under which incumbency shall cease. For the possibility of removal is a condition or qualification of the tenure. When Congress provides that the incumbent shall hold the office for four years unless sooner removed with the consent of the Senate, it prescribes the term of the tenure. . . .

MR. JUSTICE HOLMES, dissenting. . . .

The arguments drawn from the executive power of the President, and from his duty to appoint officers of the United States (when Congress does not vest the appointment elsewhere), to take care that the laws be faithfully executed, and to commission all officers of the United States, seem to me spider's webs inadequate to control the dominant facts.

We have to deal with an office that owes its existence to Congress and that Congress may abolish tomorrow. Its duration and the pay attached to it while it lasts depend on Congress alone. Congress alone confers on the President the power to appoint to it and at any time may transfer the power to other hands. With such power over its own creation, I have no more trouble in believing that Congress has power to prescribe a term of life for it free from any interference than I have in accepting the undoubted power of Congress to decree its end. I have equally little trouble in accepting its power to prolong the tenure of an incumbent until Congress or the Senate shall have assented to his removal. The duty of the President to see that the laws be executed is a duty that does not go beyond the laws or require him to achieve more than Congress sees fit to leave within his power.

HUMPHREY'S EXECUTOR V. UNITED STATES

295 U.S. 602, 55 S. Ct. 869, 79 L. Ed. 1611 (1935)

The Federal Trade Commission Act provided that commissioners should be appointed by the President, with the advice and consent of the Senate, for seven-year terms and made them removable by the President for inefficiency, neglect of duty, or malfeasance in office. William Humphrey, whose term ran to 1938, was removed by President Roosevelt in 1933 because his views did not harmonize with those of the President.

MR. JUSTICE SUTHERLAND delivered the opinion of the Court. . . .

The commission is to be nonpartisan; and it must, from the very nature of its duties, act with entire impartiality. It is charged with the enforcement of no policy except the policy of the law. Its duties are neither political nor executive, but predominantly quasi-judicial and quasi-legislative. Like the Interstate Commerce Commission, its members are called upon to exercise the trained judgment of a body of experts "appointed by law and informed by experience." . . .

. . . the language of the act, the legislative reports, and the general purposes of the legislation as reflected by the debates, all combine to demonstrate the congressional intent to create a body of experts who shall gain experience by length of service; a body which shall be independent of executive authority, *except in its selection,* and free to exercise its judgment without the leave or hindrance of any other official or any department of the government. To the accomplishment of these purposes, it is clear that Congress was of opinion that length and certainty of tenure would vitally contribute. And to hold that, nevertheless, the members of the commission continue in office at the mere will of the President, might be to thwart, in large measure, the very ends which Congress sought to realize by definitely fixing the term of office.

We conclude that the intent of the act is to limit the executive power of removal to the causes enumerated, the existence of none of which is claimed here; and we pass to the second question.

To support its contention that the removal provision of § 1, as we have just construed it, is an unconstitutional interference with the executive power of the President, the government's chief reliance is *Myers* v. *United States.* . . . That case has been so recently decided, and the prevailing and dissenting opinions so fully review the general subject of the power of executive removal, that further discussion would add little of value to the wealth of material there collected. These opinions examine at length the historical, legislative and judicial data bearing upon the question, beginning with what is called "the decision of 1789" in the first Congress and coming down almost to the day when the opinions were delivered. They occupy 243 pages of the volume in which they are printed. Nevertheless, the narrow point actually decided was only that the President had power to remove a postmaster of the first class, without the advice and consent of the Senate as required by act of Congress. In the course of the opinion of the court, expressions occur which tend to sustain the government's contention, but these are beyond the point involved and, therefore, do not come within the rule of stare decisis. In so far as they are out of harmony with the views here set forth, these expressions are disapproved. . . .

The office of a postmaster is so essentially unlike the office now involved that the decision in the Myers case cannot be accepted as controlling our decision here. A postmaster is an executive officer restricted to the performance of executive functions. He is charged with no duty at all related to either the legislative or judicial power. The actual decision in the Myers case finds support in the theory that such an officer is merely one of the units in the executive department and, hence, inherently subject to the exclusive and illimitable power of removal by the Chief Executive, whose subordinate and aide he is. Putting aside dicta, which may be followed if sufficiently persuasive but which are not controlling, the necessary reach of the decision goes far enough to include all purely executive officers. It goes no farther; much less does it include an officer who occupies no place in the executive department and who exercises no part of the executive power vested by the Constitution in the President.

The Federal Trade Commission is an administrative body created by Congress to carry into effect legislative policies embodied in the statute in accordance with the legislative standard therein prescribed, and to perform other specified duties as a legislative or as a judicial aid. Such a body cannot in any proper sense be characterized as an arm or an eye of the executive. Its duties are performed without executive leave and, in the contemplation of the statute, must be free from executive control. In administering the provisions of the statute in respect of "unfair methods of competition," that is to say, in filling in and administering the details embodied by that general standard, the commission acts in part quasi-legislatively and in part quasi-judicially. . . .

If Congress is without authority to prescribe causes for removal of members of the trade commission and limit executive power of removal accordingly, that power at once becomes practically all-inclusive in respect of civil officers with the exception of the judiciary provided for by the Constitution. The Solicitor General, at the bar, apparently recognizing this to be true, with commendable candor, agreed that his view in respect of the removability of members of the Federal Trade Commission necessitated a like view in respect of the Interstate Commerce Commission and the Court of Claims. We are thus confronted with the serious question whether not only the members of these quasi-legislative and quasi-judicial bodies, but the judges of the legislative Court of Claims, exercising judicial power . . . continue in office only at the pleasure of the President.

We think it plain under the Constitution that illimitable power of removal is not possessed by the President in respect of officers of the character of those just named. The authority of Congress, in creating quasi-legislative or quasi-judicial agencies, to require them to act in discharge of their duties independently of executive control cannot well be doubted; and that authority includes, as an appropriate incident, power to fix the period during which they shall continue, and to forbid their removal except for cause in the meantime. For it is quite evident that one who holds his office only during the pleasure of another cannot be depended upon to maintain an attitude of independence against the latter's will.

The fundamental necessity of maintaining each of the three general departments of government entirely free from the control of coercive influence, direct or indirect, of either of the others, has often been stressed and is hardly open to serious question. So much is implied in the very fact of the separation of the powers of these departments by the Constitution; and in the rule which recognizes their essential coequality. The sound application of a principle that makes one master in his own house precludes him from imposing his control in the house of another who is master there. . . .

. . . Whether the power of the President to remove an officer shall prevail over the authority of Congress to condition the power by fixing a definite term and precluding a removal except for cause will depend upon the character of the office; the Myers decision, affirming the power of the President alone to make the removal, is confined to purely executive officers; and as to officers of the kind here under consideration, we hold that no removal can be made during the prescribed term for which the officer is appointed, except for one or more of the causes named in the applicable statute. . . .

Chapter Seven

PRESIDENTIAL
ACCOUNTABILITY

INTRODUCTION

The Constitution provides only one method of enforcing the responsibility of the President and that is by the process of impeachment. Article I even makes special provision that when the Senate sits in an impeachment proceeding against the President, the Chief Justice shall preside instead of the Vice President, who would have a personal interest in the outcome of the trial.

Impeachment

The first, and until 1973 the only, serious effort to impeach a President was that against Andrew Johnson in 1868. Conviction in the Senate failed by one vote, and the vindictive partisanship of the impeachment effort was so disgraceful that it was generally thought to have precluded any future effort to impeach a President. Consequently, as the possible implication of Richard Nixon in the Watergate scandals began to emerge in early 1973, initial suggestions of impeachment were not taken seriously. But the sensational televised hearings conducted by the Senate Select Committee on Watergate, chaired by Senator Sam Ervin; the revelation that White House conversations had been taped; the firing by the President of Special Prosecutor Archibald Cox; and all the other shattering events of that period resulted in the undertaking of an impeachment inquiry by the House Judiciary Committee, culminating in public hearings in July, 1974.

Two major constitutional issues were raised by these proceedings. First was the meaning of "high crimes and misdemeanors," which along with "treason" and "bribery" constitute grounds for impeachment. The phrase, which originated in English parliamentary impeachment practice, was subject to at least three possible interpretations. One was that offered by Gerald Ford when he was urging the impeachment of Justice Douglas in 1970:

> . . . an impeachable offense is whatever a majority of the House of Representatives considers it to be at a given moment in history; conviction results from whatever offense or offenses two-thirds of the other body considers to be sufficiently serious to require removal of the accused from office.

The second position went to the opposite extreme, asserting that impeachment was limited to serious, indictable crimes. As President Nixon's attorneys argued in their presentation to the House Judiciary Committee: "Not only do the words inherently require a criminal offense, but one of a very serious nature, committed in one's governmental capacity."

The third position, which falls between the other two, was that violation of a criminal statute was not a prerequisite for impeachment as long as the offense was a serious one. The staff lawyers for the Judiciary Committee concluded:

> To confine impeachable conduct to indictable offenses may well be to set a standard so restrictive as not to reach conduct that might adversely affect the system of government. Some of the most grievous offenses against our constitutional form of government may not entail violations of the criminal law.

The majority of the House Judiciary Committee adopted this middle position, which was also clearly the view of the academic community.[1] A minority on the Judiciary Committee, however, insisted that an indictable criminal offense must be proved—as the saying went, they insisted on finding a "smoking gun" at the scene of the crime.

With this division within the committee, it voted three articles of impeachment. The first, charging obstruction of justice by the President in

[1]See Raoul Berger, *Impeachment: The Constitutional Problems* (Cambridge: Harvard University Press, 1973); House Committee on the Judiciary, *Impeachment: Selected Materials* (Washington: Government Printing Office, 1973).

the Watergate cover-up, was adopted by a vote of 27 to 11 with 6 Republicans joining the 21 Democrats. The second alleged abuse of presidential power by misuse of the FBI, CIA, and other government agencies; it was adopted by a vote of 28 to 10. The third, charging Nixon with contempt of Congress by refusing to obey the committee's subpoenas, was more narrowly passed by 21 to 17. The committee refused to approve two additional articles dealing with Nixon's taxes and with the secret bombing of Cambodia.

Eventually the "smoking gun" was supplied by Nixon himself when on August 5, 1974, under pressure of the Supreme Court's unanimous opinion in *United States* v. *Nixon,* he released transcripts of tapes revealing that he had taken command of the cover-up only six days after the Watergate break-in and that he had kept this information from his staff and his counsel. With this damning evidence, the ten Republicans who had supported the President in the votes on all three articles came over to accept the obstruction of justice charge.

A second constitutional issue involved in the Nixon impeachment was whether there was any limit on the investigative powers of the House Judiciary Committee while conducting an impeachment inquiry. The argument for the committee was that the impeachment power of Congress is an intentional breach in the separation of powers principle, and that consequently Congress is the sole judge of what evidence is relevant and can compel its production by the executive. The President's position was that preservation of the integrity of the Presidency required that he decide what evidence was relevant to the investigation, and in fact he refused to obey subpoenas for tapes demanded by the committee. The committee did not seek to hold the President in contempt for his refusal. Instead, as just noted, the refusal to honor the committee's subpoenas was made the basis for the third article of impeachment. President Nixon's resignation, effective August 9, 1974, had the result of aborting the impeachment proceedings; the Judiciary Committee simply submitted a final report to the House.

Executive Privilege

President Nixon's involvement in the Watergate scandals provoked an unprecedented examination of the constitutional position of the office. Separation of powers problems that previously had been only subjects for speculation by constitutional scholars suddenly erupted in newspaper headlines and television commentaries. A major issue was the validity of the claim of "executive privilege," which Nixon had initially put forth to justify refusal to respond to congressional requests for information and which he subsequently raised in denying access to White House tapes and other records demanded by the congressional investigating committees, the Watergate special prosecutor, and the judges in several Watergate cases.

Nixon's position was that executive privilege had been asserted by all Presidents as far back as George Washington, that his discussions with members of the White House staff were protected by the necessity of confidentiality, and that the principle of separation of powers guarantees each of the branches of government the right to defend itself against incursions by the other branches.

While it is true that earlier Presidents had on occasion refused to submit information requested by Congress, the instances were considerably fewer than Nixon claimed, and the phrase "executive privilege" and the defense of confidentiality dated back only to the Eisenhower administration. As the Senate Watergate Committee began operations in 1973, Nixon forbade any of his White House aides to testify before it, a position from which he quickly withdrew under pressure, and in fact the Ervin Committee did hear testimony from all relevant White House aides.

The Subpoena Issue

Nixon also refused to submit White House tapes subpoenaed by both the Senate Committee and the House Judiciary Committee in its impeachment inquiry. Historically there had been some doubt regarding whether the President was subject to subpoena because of the obvious enforcement problem, if he chose to resist. The principal precedent was Chief Justice Marshall's subpoena to President Jefferson in the 1807 treason trial of Aaron Burr. While Marshall's opinion in **United States v. Burr** clearly rejected the contention that the President was immune from subpoena, later developments in the case were somewhat confused, leading to the mistaken impression that Jefferson had refused to respond to the subpoena. In **Mississippi v. Johnson** (1867) the Supreme Court declined to issue an injunction against the President, pointing out that if he refused obedience, the Court would be "without power to enforce its process."

The Ervin Committee's effort to enforce its subpoena was rejected for technical reasons, and the House Judiciary Committee did not go to court. But when Nixon refused the demand of the Watergate special prosecutor, Archibald Cox, to make tapes available to the Watergate grand jury, Cox did seek enforcement of the subpoena and was upheld by Judge John J. Sirica. The judge considered it immaterial that "the court has not the physical power to enforce its order to the President," and simply relied on "the good faith of the executive branch." Recognizing that there was some need to protect presidential confidentiality, Sirica indicated that he would himself review the subpoenaed materials to screen out any matter where executive privilege was validly invoked, and then pass the rest on to the grand jury. Sirica's ruling was upheld by the Court of Appeals for the District of Columbia in *Nixon v. Sirica* (1973), and Nixon chose to comply without carrying an appeal to the Supreme Court.

The Supreme Court's turn to speak on executive privilege came in 1974. Special Prosecutor Leon Jaworksi, who had replaced Cox after Cox had been fired in the "Saturday night massacre," demanded an additional 64 tapes for use by the grand jury in preparing its indictment against former Attorney General John N. Mitchell, H. R. Haldeman, John Ehrlichman, and other Watergate figures. Judge Sirica ordered compliance, and his decision was upheld by the Supreme Court in *United States* v. *Nixon* (1974). The Court unanimously denied the President's right to make a final unreviewable claim of executive privilege.

> Neither the doctrine of separation of powers, nor the need for confidentiality of high-level communications, without more, can sustain an absolute, unqualified, presidential privilege of immunity from judicial process under all circumstances.

The Court did grant that there was a limited executive privilege with a constitutional base—mentioning particularly the need to protect military, diplomatic, or sensitive national security secrets—and assured that the courts would recognize claims of confidentiality related to the President's ability to discharge his constitutional powers effectively. But no national security claims were involved here. There was only "the generalized assertion of privilege," which "must be considered in light of our historic commitment to the rule of law" and "must yield to the demonstrated specific need for evidence in a pending criminal trial."

Nixon's counsel had refused to give advance assurance that the President would obey a Supreme Court order upholding the subpoena, but in fact he did. It was generally agreed that if he had challenged the Supreme Court ruling, it would have been cause for immediate impeachment.

Other Constitutional Issues

Another issue presented by Watergate was whether or not a President is subject to criminal indictment while in office. The Watergate grand jury was convinced that Nixon had participated in the cover-up, and it wished to indict him along with the other principals. However, Special Prosecutor Jaworski told the grand jury that the President was constitutionally protected against indictment; consequently, the grand jury merely named Nixon as an "unindicted coconspirator." In accepting the case of *United States* v. *Nixon* the Supreme Court agreed to consider whether an incumbent President can be named in this manner; but after consideration, the justices ruled that the issue was irrelevant and so failed to express an opinion on it.

The Constitution makes it clear that after a President leaves office he can be prosecuted for criminal acts performed in office, even if he has already been convicted on impeachment for those acts (Article I, section 3). Nixon faced the prospect of various legal actions following his resignation. A proposal that Congress grant him immunity from criminal prosecution was dropped, and in any event it could have had no binding effect. President Ford's pardon foreclosed any federal criminal prosecutions, but Nixon remained liable to suit in civil cases.

Still another Watergate problem was that of ownership of presidential papers and records. Past practice proceeded on the assumption that Presidents own their papers and take them with them when they leave the White House. However, this practice developed when the Presidency was practically a personal office, with only a few assistants and secretaries. Since 1939, when the Executive Office of the President was established, the Presidency has become institutionalized. It is difficult to conceive of the estimated 42 million pages generated in the Executive Office during Nixon's presidency as his "personal" papers.

Shortly after Nixon resigned as President, he made an agreement with the Administrator of General Services for storage near his California home of this mass of paper plus 880 tape recordings, to which he would have access with the consent of the Administrator. Nixon could withdraw any of the materials except the tapes after three years, and could order the tapes destroyed after five years. The tapes would be automatically destroyed after ten years or at Nixon's death.

Concerned about the possible destruction of presidential materials of broad public and historical interest, Congress passed the Presidential Recordings and Materials Preservation Act, directing the General Services Administration to take custody of the materials, return to Nixon those personal and private in nature, and adopt regulations governing eventual public access to those materials having historical value.

Nixon brought suit challenging the statute as violative of the separation of powers, the presidential privilege of confidentiality and right of privacy, his associational First Amendment rights, and the bill of attainder clause (which prohibits legislative punishment). In ***Nixon*** v. ***Administrator of General Services*** (1977) the Court majority rejected all these claims. On the bill of attainder issue, clearly Nixon had been singled out for treatment different from that accorded any other President, but the Court said that the circumstances were special; because of the threat of destruction of presidential materials Nixon "constituted a legitimate class of one." Chief Justice Burger, dissenting along with Rehnquist, contended that the holding was "a grave repudiation of nearly 200 years of judicial precedent and historical practice."

UNITED STATES V. BURR

25 F. Cas. 30, No. 14, 692 (C.C.D. Va. 1807)

In the preliminary stage of the treason prosecution of Aaron Burr in 1807, his counsel sought to procure as evidence a letter written by a General Wilkinson to President Jefferson, by means of a subpoena calling both for Jefferson's attendance and production of the letter *(subpoena duces tecum)*. Marshall ruled that any person charged with a crime in federal court had a right to process to compel the attendance of witnesses, even the President of the United States. There has been much confusion concerning Jefferson's reaction. Corwin says that Jefferson refused to respond to the subpoena. In fact, Jefferson's counsel admitted that the President might be summoned as a witness, but disputed issuance of a *subpoena duces tecum.* In a later misdemeanor proceeding against Burr a second letter was subpoenaed. Jefferson apparently submitted the latter with deletions of material irrelevant to the charge. Thus it is not correct to say that Jefferson denied the subpoena power of the Court. A portion of Marshall's opinion of June 13, 1807, follows.

. . . it remains to inquire whether a subpoena duces tecum can be directed to the president of the United States, and whether it ought to be directed in this case? This question originally consisted of two parts. It was at first doubted whether a subpoena could issue, in any case, to the chief magistrate of the nation; and if it could, whether that subpoena could do more than direct his personal attendance; whether it could direct him to bring with him a paper which was said to constitute the gist of his testimony. While the argument was opening, the attorney for the United States avowed his opinion that a general subpoena might issue to the president; but not a subpoena duces tecum. This terminated the argument on that part of the question.

The court, however, has thought it necessary to state briefly the foundation of its opinion, that such a subpoena may issue. In the provisions of the constitution, and of the statute, which give to the accused a right to the compulsory process of the court, there is no exception whatever. The obligation, therefore, of those provisions is general; and it would seem that no person could claim an exemption from them, but one who would not be a witness. At any rate, if an exception to the general principle exists, it must be looked for in the law of evidence. The exceptions furnished by the law of evidence (with only one reservation), so far as they are personal, are of those only whose testimony could not be received. The single reservation alluded to is the case of the king. Although he may, perhaps, give testimony, it is said to be incompatible with his dignity to appear under the process of the court.

Of the many points of difference which exist between the first magistrate in England and the first magistrate of the United States, in respect to the personal dignity conferred on them by their respective nations, the court will only select and mention two. It is a principle of the English constitution that the king can do no wrong, that no blame can be imputed to him, that he cannot be named in debate. By the constitution of the United States, the president, as well as any other officer of the government, may be impeached, and may be removed from office on high crimes and misdemeanors. By the constitution of Great Britain, the crown is hereditary, and the monarch can never be a subject. By that of the United States, the president is elected from the mass of the people, and, on the expiration of the time for which he is elected, returns to the mass of the people again. How essentially this difference of circumstances must vary the policy of the laws of the two countries, in reference to the personal dignity of the executive chief, will be perceived by every person. . . . If, in any court of the United States, it has ever been decided that a subpoena cannot issue to the president, that decision is unknown to this court.

If, upon any principle, the president could be construed to stand exempt from the general provisions of the constitution, it would be, because his duties as chief magistrate demand his whole time for national objects. But it is apparent that this demand is not unremitting; and, if it should exist at the time when his attendance on a court is required, it would be shown on the return of the subpoena, and would rather constitute a reason for not obeying the process of the court than a reason against its being issued. . . .

Much has been said about the disrespect to the chief magistrate, which is implied by this motion, and by such a decision of it as the law is believed to require. These observations will be very truly answered by the declaration that this court feels many, perhaps, peculiar motives for manifesting as guarded a respect for the chief magistrate of the Union as is compatible with its official duties. To go beyond these would exhibit a conduct which would deserve some other appellation than the term respect. It is not for the court to anticipate the event of the present prosecution. Should it terminate as is expected on the part of the United States, all those who are concerned in it should certainly regret that a paper which the accused believed to be essential to his defense, which may, for aught that now appears, be essential had been withheld from him. I will not say, that this circumstance would, in any degree, tarnish the reputation of the government; but I will say, that it would justly tarnish the reputation of the court which had given its sanction to its being withheld. . . .

A motion was made on behalf of the state of Mississippi in the original jurisdiction of the Supreme Court for an injunction against President Andrew Johnson to restrain him from executing the Reconstruction Acts of 1867.

The CHIEF JUSTICE [CHASE] delivered the opinion of the Court. . . .

. . . We shall limit our inquiry to the question . . . whether, in any case, the President of the United States may be required, by the process of this Court, to perform a purely ministerial act under a positive law, or may be held amenable, in any case, otherwise than by impeachment for crime.

The single point which requires consideration is this: Can the President be restrained by injunction from carrying into effect an act of Congress alleged to be unconstitutional?

It is assumed by the counsel for the state of Mississippi, that the President, in the execution of the Reconstruction Acts, is required to perform a mere ministerial duty. In this assumption there is, we think, a confounding of the terms ministerial and executive, which are by no means equivalent in import.

A ministerial duty, the performance of which may, in proper cases, be required of the head of a department, by judicial process, is one in respect to which nothing is left to discretion. It is a simple, definite duty, arising under conditions admitted or proved to exist, and imposed by law. . . .

Very different is the duty of the President in the exercise of the power to see that the laws are faithfully executed, and among these laws the acts named in the bill. By the first of these acts he is required to assign generals to command in the several military districts, and to detail sufficient military force to enable such officers to discharge their duties under the law. By the supplementary act, other duties are imposed on the several commanding generals, and these duties must necessarily be performed under the supervision of the President as commander-in-chief. The duty thus imposed on the President is in no just sense ministerial. It is purely executive and political.

An attempt on the part of the judicial department of the government to enforce the performance of such duties by the President might be justly characterized, in the language of Chief Justice Marshall, as "an absurd and excessive extravagance."

It is true that in the instance before us the interposition of the Court is not sought to enforce action by the Executive under constitutional legislation, but to restrain such action under legislation alleged to be unconstitutional. But we are unable to perceive that this circumstance takes the case out of the general principles which forbid judicial interference with the exercise of executive discretion. . . .

The impropriety of such interference will be clearly seen upon consideration of its possible consequences.

Suppose the bill filed and the injunction prayed for allowed. If the President refuse obedience, it is needless to observe that the Court is without power to enforce its process. If, on the other hand, the President complies with the order of the Court and refuses to execute the acts of Congress, is it not clear that a collision may occur between the executive and legislative departments of the government? May not the House of Representatives impeach the President for such refusal? And in that case could this Court interfere, in behalf of the President, thus endangered by compliance with its mandate, and restrain by injunction the Senate of the United States from sitting as a court of impeachment? Would the strange spectacle be offered to the public world of an attempt by this Court to arrest proceedings in that court?

These questions answer themselves.

It is true that a state may file an original bill in this Court. And it may be true, in some cases, that such a bill may be filed against the United States. But we are fully satisfied that this Court has no jurisdiction of a bill to enjoin the President in the performance of his official duties; and that no such bill ought to be received by us.

It has been suggested that the bill contains a prayer that, if the relief sought cannot be had against Andrew Johnson, as President, it may be granted against Andrew Johnson as a citizen of Tennessee. But it is plain that relief as against the execution of an act of Congress by Andrew Johnson, is relief against its execution by the President. A bill praying an injunction against the execution of an act of Congress by the incumbent of the presidential office cannot be received, whether it describes him as President or as a citizen of a state.

The motion for leave to file the bill is, therefore, denied.

NIXON V. SIRICA

U.S. Court of Appeals, District of Columbia
487 F. 2d 700 (1973)

On July 23, 1973, Watergate Special Prosecutor Archibald Cox, acting on behalf of the June, 1973, grand jury, caused to be issued a *subpoena duces tecum* to President Nixon, requiring him, or any appropriate subordinate official, to produce for the grand jury certain enumerated tape recordings and documents.

President Nixon complied with the subpoena insofar as it related to memoranda of two minor White House aides, but otherwise declined to follow the subpoena's directive. In a letter dated July 25, 1973, the President advised that the tape recordings would not be provided, and by way of explanation wrote:

United States District Court

For the District of Columbia

THE UNITED STATES
vs.

...... JOHN DOE . . ..

| REPORT TO UNITED STATES DISTRICT COURT HOUSE
Between 3d Street and John Marshall Place and on Constitution Avenue NW.
~~KXXXXXXXX~~ Grand Jury Room 3
Washington, D.C.

To:........Richard M. Nixon, The White House, Washington, D. C., or any

.... subordinate officer, official, or employee with custody or

.... control of the documents or objects hereinafter described on

.... the attached schedule.

You are hereby commanded to attend before the Grand Jury of said Court on .....Thursday............

the....26th. day of.... ......July............., 19.73., at......................10........o'clock...A..M., to testify ~~on behalf of the United States and not depart the Court without leave of the Court or District Attorney~~ and to bring with you the documents or objects listed on the attached sched- *WITNESS: The Honorable* John J. Sirica *Chief Judge of said Court, this* ule.

...... 23rd. . ... *day of*............July............., *19.73*

Archibald Cox

ARCHIBALD COX
Attorney for the United States

JAMES F. DAVEY, *Clerk.*

By *Robert L. Line*

Deputy Clerk.

Form No. USA-92-184 (Rev. 7-1-71)

... I follow the example of a long line of my predecessors as President of the United States who have consistently adhered to the position that the President is not subject to compulsory process from the courts. ...

The Special Prosecutor then applied to Judge John J. Sirica, Chief Judge of the U. S. District Court for the District of Columbia, for enforcement of the subpoena. On August 7, 1973, attorneys for President Nixon filed the following brief in support of the President's refusal to surrender the tape recordings of White House conversations and other documents to the Special Prosecutor.

SUMMARY OF ARGUMENT

The present proceeding, though a well-intentioned effort to obtain evidence for criminal prosecutions, represents a serious threat to the nature of the Presidency as it was created by the Constitution, as it has been sustained for years, and as it exists today.

If the special prosecutor should be successful in the attempt to compel disclosure of recordings of Presidential conversations, the damage to the institution of the Presidency will be severe and irreparable. The character of that office will be fundamentally altered and the total structure of government—dependent as it is upon a separation of powers—will be impaired.

The consequence of an order to disclose recordings or notes would be that no longer could a President speak in confidence with his close advisers on any subject. The threat of potential disclosure of any and all conversations would make it virtually impossible for President Nixon or his successors in that great office to function. Beyond that, a holding that the President is personally subject to the orders of a court would effectively destroy the status of the executive branch as an equal and coordinate element of government.

There is no precedent that can be said to justify or permit such a result. On the contrary, it is clear that while courts and their grand juries have the power to seek evidence of all persons, including the President, the President has the power and thus the privilege to withhold information if he concludes that disclosure would be contrary to the public interest.

Plea for Privacy

The breadth of this privilege is frequently debated. Whatever its boundaries it must obtain with respect to a President's private conversations with his advisers as well as to private conversations by judges and legislators with their advisers. These conversations reflect advisory opinions, recommendations, and deliberations that are an essential part of the process by which Presidential decisions and policies are formulated.

Presidential privacy must be protected, not for its own sake, but because of the paramount need for frank expression and discussion among the President and those consulted by him in the making of Presidential decisions.

The privilege with regard to recordings was not waived by the decision of the President, in the interest of having the truth about Watergate come out, to permit testimony about portions of those conversations by persons who participated in them. Testimony can be limited, as recordings cannot, to the particular area in which privilege is not being claimed.

Nor does the privilege vanish because there are claims that some of the statements made to the President by others in these conversations may have been pursuant to a criminal conspiracy by those other persons. That others may have acted in accordance with a criminal design does not alter the fact that the President's participation in these conversations was pursuant to his constitutional duty to see that the laws are faithfully executed and that he is entitled to claim executive privilege to preserve the confidentiality of private conversations he held in carrying out that duty.

In the exercise of his discretion to claim executive privilege the President is answerable to the Nation but not to the courts. The courts, a co-equal but not a superior branch of government, are not free to probe the mental processes and the private confidences of the President and his advisers. To do so would be a clear violation of the constitutional separation of powers. Under that doctrine the judicial branch lacks power to compel the President to produce information that he has determined it is not in the public interest to disclose.

The issue here is starkly simple: Will the Presidency be allowed to continue to function?

On August 29, 1973, Judge Sirica handed down his opinion *(In re Subpoena to Richard M. Nixon)* rejecting the President's contentions and ordering him to produce the subpoenaed documents "forthwith for the Court's examination *in camera.*" After judicial examination, any portion of the tapes not ruled by Sirica as subject to privilege would be forwarded to the grand jury. President Nixon's counsel appealed this ruling to the Court of Appeals for the District of Columbia, which heard the case *en banc.* On October 12 the Court of Appeals upheld Judge Sirica's decision. No appeal was taken to the Supreme Court, and the President complied with the subpoena.

Per Curiam. . . .
We deem it essential to emphasize the narrow contours of the problem that compels the Court to address the issues raised by this case. The central question before us is, in essence, whether the President may, in his sole discretion, withhold from a grand jury evidence in his possession that is relevant to the grand jury's investigations.

Counsel for the President contend on two grounds that Judge Sirica lacked jurisdiction to order submission of the tapes for inspection. Counsel argue, first, that, so long as he remains in office, the President is absolutely immune from the compulsory process of a court; and, second, that Executive privilege is absolute with respect to presidential communications, so that disclosure is at the sole discretion of the President. This immunity and this absolute privilege are said to arise from the doctrine of separation of powers and by implication from the Constitution itself. It is conceded that neither the immunity nor the privilege is express in the Constitution.

It is clear that the want of physical power to enforce its judgments does not prevent a court from deciding an otherwise justiciable case. Nevertheless, if it is true that the President is legally immune from court process, this case is at an end. The judiciary will not, indeed cannot, indulge in rendering an opinion to which the President has no legal duty to conform. We must, therefore, determine whether the President is *legally* bound to comply with an order enforcing a subpoena.

We note first that courts have assumed that they have the power to enter mandatory orders to Executive officials to compel production of evidence. While a claim of an absolute Executive immunity may not have been raised directly before these courts, there is no indication that they entertained any doubts of their power.

Youngstown Sheet & Tube Co.: v. *Sawyer* in which an injunction running against the Secretary of Commerce was affirmed, is only the most celebrated instance of the issuance of compulsory process against Executive officials.

There is not the slightest hint in any of the *Youngstown* opinions that the case would have been viewed differently if President Truman rather than Secretary Sawyer had been the named party. If *Youngstown* still stands, it must stand for the case where the President has himself taken possession and control of the property unconstitutionally seized, and the injunction would be framed accordingly. The practice of judicial review would be rendered capricious—and very likely impotent—if jurisdiction vanished whenever the President personally denoted an Executive action or omission as his own. This is not to say that the President should lightly be named as a party defendant. As a matter of comity, courts should normally direct legal process to a lower Executive official even though the effect of the process is to restrain or compel the President. Here, unfortunately, the court's order must run directly to the President, because he has taken the unusual step of assuming personal custody of the Government property sought by the subpoena.

The President also attempts to distinguish *United States* v. *Burr,* in which Chief Justice Marshall squarely ruled that a subpoena may be directed to the President. It is true that *Burr* recognized a distinction between the issuance of a subpoena and the ordering of compliance with that subpoena, but the distinction did not concern judicial power or jurisdiction. A subpoena *duces tecum* is an order to produce documents or to show cause why they need not be produced. An order to comply does not make the subpoena more compulsory; it simply maintains its original force. . . . A compliance order was, for Marshall, distinct from an order to show cause simply because compliance was not to be ordered before weighing the President's particular reasons for wishing the subpoenaed documents to remain secret. The court was to show respect for the President in weighing those reasons, but the ultimate decision remained with the court.

Thus, to find the President immune from judicial process, we must read out of *Burr* and *Youngstown* the underlying principles that the eminent jurists in each case thought they were establishing. The Constitution makes no mention of special presidential immunities. Indeed, the Executive Branch generally is afforded none. This silence cannot be ascribed to oversight. James Madison raised the question of Executive privileges during the Constitutional Convention, and Senators and Representatives enjoy an express, if limited, immunity from arrest, and an express privilege from inquiry concerning "Speech and Debate" on the floors of Congress. Lacking textual support, counsel for the President nonetheless would have us infer immunity from the President's political mandate, or from his vulnerability to impeachment, or from his broad discretionary powers. These are invitations to refashion the Constitution, and we reject them.

Though the President is elected by nationwide ballot, and is often said to represent all the people, he does not embody the nation's sovereignty. He is not above the law's commands: "With all its defects, delays and inconveniences, men have discovered no technique for long preserving free government except that the Executive be under the law * * *." Sovereignty remains at all times with the people, and they do not forfeit through elections the right to have the law construed against and applied to every citizen.

Nor does the Impeachment Clause imply immunity from routine court process. While the President argues that the Clause means that impeachability precludes criminal prosecution of an incumbent, we see no need to explore this question except to note its irrelevance to the case before us. The order entered below, and approved here in modified form, is not a form of criminal process. Nor does it compete with the impeachment device by working a constructive removal of the President from office. The subpoena names in the alternate "any subordinate officer," and the tasks of compliance may obviously be delegated in whole or in part so as not to interfere with the President's official responsibilities. By contemplating the possibility of post-impeachment trials for violations of law committed in office, the Impeachment Clause itself reveals that incumbency does not relieve the President of the routine legal obligations that confine all citizens. That the Impeachment Clause may qualify the court's power to sanction non-compliance with judicial orders is immaterial. Whatever the qualifications, they were equally present in *Youngstown:* Commerce Secretary Sawyer, the defendant there, was an impeachable "civil officer," but the injunction against him was nonetheless affirmed. The legality of judicial orders should not be confused with the legal consequences of their breach; for the courts in this country always assume that their orders will be obeyed, especially when addressed to responsible government officials. Indeed, the President has, in this case, expressly abjured the course of setting himself above the law.

Finally, the President reminds us that the landmark decisions recognizing judicial power to mandamus Executive compliance with "ministerial" duties also acknowledged that the Executive Branch enjoys an unreviewable discretion in many areas of "political" or "executive" administration. While true, this is irrelevant to the issue of presidential immunity from judicial process. The discretionary-ministerial distinction concerns the nature of the act or omission under review, not the official title of the defendant. No case holds that an act is discretionary merely because the President is the actor. If the Constitution or the laws of evidence confer upon the President the absolute discretion to withhold material subpoenaed by a grand jury, then of course we would vacate, rather than approve with modification, the order entered below. However, this would be because the order touched upon matters within the President's sole discretion, not because the President is immune from process generally. . . .

MACKINNON, CIRCUIT JUDGE, concurring in part and dissenting in part. . . .

WILKEY, CIRCUIT JUDGE, dissenting. . . .

UNITED STATES V. NIXON

418 U.S. 683, 94 S. Ct. 3090, 41 L. Ed. 2d 1039 (1974)

In preparation for the prosecution of former Attorney General John N. Mitchell, H. R. Haldeman, John Ehrlichman, and others for conspiracy to defraud the United States and to obstruct justice, Special Prosecutor Leon Jaworski caused a *subpoena duces tecum* to be issued on April 16, 1974, directing President Nixon to produce tape recordings and documents relating to conversations with certain of his aides and advisers. On May 20 United States District Judge John J. Sirica denied the President's motion to quash the subpoena. The President sought review by the Court of Appeals for the District of Columbia, but the special prosecutor filed in the Supreme Court a petition for writ of certiorari before judgment, which the Supreme Court granted. The case was argued on July 8, 1974, and decided on July 24. Justice Rehnquist did not participate.

MR. CHIEF JUSTICE BURGER delivered the opinion of the Court. . . .

. . . we turn to the claim that the subpoena should be quashed because it demands "confidential conversations between a President and his close advisors that it would be inconsistent with the public interest to produce." The first contention is a broad claim that the separation of powers doctrine precludes judicial review of a President's claim of privilege. The second contention is that if he does not prevail on the claim of absolute privilege, the court should hold as a matter of constitutional law that the privilege prevails over the subpoena *duces tecum.*

In the performance of assigned constitutional duties each branch of the Government must initially interpret the Constitution, and the interpretation of its powers by any branch is due great respect from the others. The President's counsel, as we have noted, reads the Constitution as providing an absolute privilege of confidentiality for all Presidential communications. Many decisions of this Court, however, have unequivocally reaffirmed the holding of Marbury v. Madison. . . . (1803), that "[i]t is emphatically the province and duty of the judicial department to say what the law is." . . .

. . . No holding of the Court had defined the scope of judicial power specifically relating to the enforcement of a subpoena for confidential Presidential communications for use in a criminal prosecution, but other exercises of power by the Executive Branch and the Legislative Branch have been found invalid as in conflict with the Constitution. Powell v. McCormack (1969); Youngstown, Sheet & Tube Co. v. Sawyer, . . . (1952). In a series of cases, the Court interpreted the explicit immunity conferred by express provisions of the Constitution on Members of the House and Senate by the Speech or Debate Clause, U.S. Const. Art. I, § 6. . . . Since this Court has consistently exercised the power to construe and delineate claims arising under express powers, it must follow that the

Court has authority to interpret claims with respect to powers alleged to derive from enumerated powers.

. . . Our System of government "requires that federal courts on occasion interpret the Constitution in a manner at variance with the construction given the document by another branch." Powell v. McCormack. . . . And in Baker v. Carr . . . the Court stated:

> "[D]eciding whether a matter has in any measure been committed by the Constitution to another branch of government, or whether the action of that branch exceeds whatever authority has been committed, is itself a delicate exercise in constitutional interpretation, and is a responsibility of this Court as ultimate interpreter of the Constitution."

Notwithstanding the deference each branch must accord the others, the "judicial Power of the United States" vested in the federal courts by Art. III, § 1, of the Constitution can no more be shared with the Executive Branch than the Chief Executive, for example, can share with the Judiciary the veto power, or the Congress share with the Judiciary the power to override a Presidential veto. Any other conclusion would be contrary to the basic concept of separation of powers and the checks and balances that flow from the scheme of a triparite government. . . . We therefore reaffirm that it is the province and duty of this Court "to say what the law is" with respect to the claim of privilege presented in this case. . . .

. . . In support of his claim of absolute privilege, the President's counsel urges two grounds, one of which is common to all governments and one of which is peculiar to our system of separation of powers. The first ground is the valid need for protection of communications between high Government officials and those who advise and assist them in the performance of their manifold duties; the importance of this confidentiality is too plain to require further discussion. Human experience teaches that those who expect public dissemination of their remarks may well temper candor with a concern for appearances and for their own interests to the detriment of the decisionmaking process. Whatever the nature of the privilege of confidentiality of Presidential communications in the exercise of Art. II powers, the privilege can be said to derive from the supremacy of each branch within its own assigned area of constitutional duties. Certain powers and privileges flow from the nature of enumerated powers; the protection of the confidentiality of Presidential communications has similar constitutional underpinnings.

The second ground asserted by the President's counsel in support of the claim of absolute privilege rests on the doctrine of separation of powers. Here it is argued that the independence of the Executive Branch within its own sphere, Humphrey's Executor v. United States . . . (1935); Kilbourn v. Thompson . . . (1881), insulates a President from a judicial subpoena in an ongoing criminal prosecution, and thereby protects confidential Presidential communications.

. . . However, neither the doctrine of separation of powers, nor the need for confidentiality of high-level communications, without more, can sustain an absolute, unqualified Presidential privilege of immunity from judicial process under all circumstances. The President's need for complete candor and objectivity from advisers calls for great deference from the courts. However, when the privilege depends solely on the broad, undifferentiated claim of public interest in the confidentiality of such conversations, a confrontation with other values arises. Absent a claim of need to protect military, diplomatic, or sensitive national security secrets, we find it difficult to accept the argument that even the very important interest in confidentiality of Presidential communications is significantly diminished by production of such material for *in camera* inspection with all the protection that a district court will be obliged to provide.

The impediment that an absolute, unqualified privilege would place in the way of the primary constitutional duty of the Judicial Branch to do justice in criminal prosecutions would plainly conflict with the function of the courts under Art. III. In designing the structure of our Government and dividing and allocating the sovereign power among three co-equal branches, the Framers of the Constitution sought to provide a comprehensive system, but the separate powers were not intended to operate with absolute independence. . . .

To read the Art. II powers of the President as providing an absolute privilege as against a subpoena essential to enforcement of criminal statutes on no more than a generalized claim of the public interest in confidentiality of nonmilitary and nondiplomatic discussions would upset the constitutional balance of "a workable government" and gravely impair the role of the courts under Art. III.

. . . Since we conclude that the legitimate needs of the judicial process may outweigh Presidential privilege, it is necessary to resolve those competing interests in a manner that preserves the essential functions of each branch. The right and indeed the duty to resolve that question does not free the Judiciary from according high respect to the representations made on behalf of the President. United States v. Burr. . . .

. . . The expectation of a President to the confidentiality of his conversations and correspondence, like the claim of confidentiality of judicial deliberations, for example, has all the values to which we accord deference for the privacy of all citizens and, added to those values, is the necessity for protection of the public interest in candid, objective, and even blunt or harsh opinions in Presidential decisionmaking. A President and those who assist him must be free to explore alternatives in the process of shaping policies and making decisions and to do so in a way many would be unwilling to express except privately. These are the considerations justifying a presumptive privilege for Presidential communications. The privilege is fundamental to the operation of Government and inextricably rooted in the separation of powers under the Constitution. In Nixon v. Sirica . . . (1973), the Court of Appeals held that such Presidential communications are "presumptively privileged," . . . and this position is accepted by both parties in the present litigation. We agree with Mr. Chief Justice Marshall's observation, therefore, that "[i]n no case of this kind would a court be required to proceed against the president as against an ordinary individual." United States v. Burr . . .

. . . But this presumptive privilege must be considered in light of our historic commitment to the rule of law. This is nowhere more profoundly manifest than in our view that "the two fold aim [of criminal justice] is that guilt shall not escape or innocence suffer." Berger v. United States. . . . We have elected to employ an adversary system of criminal justice in which the parties contest all issues before a court of law. The need to develop all relevant facts in the adversary system is both fundamental and comprehensive. The ends of criminal justice would be defeated if judgments were to be founded on a partial or speculative presentation of the facts. The very integrity of the judicial system and public confidence in the system depend on full disclosure of all the facts, within the framework of the rules of evidence. To ensure that justice is done, it is imperative to the function of courts that compulsory process be available for the production of evidence needed either by the prosecution or by the defense. . . .

. . . In this case the President challenges a subpoena served on him as a third party requiring the production of materials for use in a criminal prosecution; he does so on the claim that he has a privilege against disclosure of confidential communications. He does not place his claim of privilege on the ground they are military or diplomatic secrets. As to these areas of Art. II duties the courts have traditionally shown the utmost deference to Presidential responsibilities. . . .

No case of the Court, however, has extended this high degree of deference to a President's generalized interest in confidentiality. Nowhere in the Constitution, as we have noted earlier, is there any explicit reference to a privilege of confidentiality, yet to the extent this interest relates to the effective discharge of a President's powers, it is constitutionally based.

. . . The right to the production of all evidence at a criminal trial similarly has constitutional dimensions. The Sixth Amendment explicitly confers upon every defendant in a criminal trial the right "to be confronted with the witnesses against him" and "to have compulsory process for obtaining witnesses in his favor." Moreover, the Fifth Amendment also guarantees that no person shall be deprived of liberty without due process of law. It is the manifest duty of the courts to vindicate those guarantees, and to accomplish that it is essential that all relevant and admissible evidence be produced.

In this case we must weigh the importance of the general privilege of confidentiality of Presidential communications in performance of the President's responsibilities against the inroads of such a privilege on the fair administration of criminal justice. The interest in preserving confidentiality is weighty indeed and entitled to great respect. However, we cannot conclude that advisers will be moved to temper the candor of their remarks by the infrequent occasions of disclosure because of the possibility that such conversations will be called for in the context of a criminal prosecution.

On the other hand, the allowance of the privilege to withhold evidence that is demonstrably relevant in a criminal trial would cut deeply into the guarantee of due process of law and gravely impair the basic function of the courts. A President's acknowledged need for confidentiality in the communications of his office is general in nature, whereas the constitutional need for production of relevant evidence in a criminal proceeding is specific and central to the fair adjudication of a particular criminal case in the administration of justice. Without access to specific facts a criminal prosecution may be totally frustrated. The President's broad interest in confidentiality of communications will not be vitiated by disclosure of a limited number of conversations preliminarily shown to have some bearing on the pending criminal cases.

... We conclude that when the ground for asserting privilege as to subpoenaed materials sought for use in a criminal trial is based only on the generalized interest in confidentiality, it cannot prevail over the fundamental demands of due process of law in the fair administration of criminal justice. The generalized assertion of privilege must yield to the demonstrated, specific need for evidence in a pending criminal trial. . . .

NIXON V. ADMINISTRATOR OF GENERAL SERVICES

433 U.S. --, 97 S. Ct. 2777, 53 L. Ed. 2d 867 (1977)

After Richard Nixon resigned as President, he entered into an agreement with the Administrator of General Services providing for storage near Nixon's California home of presidential materials (estimated at 42 million documents and 880 tape recordings) accumulated during his terms of office. Under the agreement neither Nixon nor the Administrator could gain access to the materials without the other's consent. During the first three years Nixon could make and withdraw copies of documents. After three years he could withdraw the originals except for tape recordings, which could not be withdrawn for five years. Thereafter Nixon could direct destruction of any tapes, and all the tapes were to be destroyed after ten years or Nixon's death, whichever occurred first.

After public announcement of this agreement Congress undertook to abrogate it by passing the Presidential Recordings and Materials Preservation Act. Title I directed the Administrator to take custody of the materials and have them screened by government archivists in order to return to Nixon those personal and private in nature, and preserve those having historical value. The Administrator was to promulgate regulations governing eventual public access to the publicly-held materials. Nixon filed an action challenging the constitutionality of the act, which was upheld by a three-judge district court in the District of Columbia.

MR. JUSTICE BRENNAN delivered the opinion of the Court. . . .

SEPARATION OF POWERS

We reject at the outset appellant's argument that the Act's regulation of the disposition of Presidential materials within the Executive Branch constitutes, without more, a violation of the principle of separation of powers. Neither President Ford nor President Carter supports this claim. The Executive Branch became a party to the Act's regulation when President Ford signed the Act into law, and the administration of President Carter, acting through the Solicitor General, vigorously supports affirmance of the District Court's judgment sustaining its constitutionality. Moreover, the control over the materials remains in the Executive Branch. The Administrator of the General Services Administration, who must promulgate and administer the regulations that are the keystone of the statutory scheme, is himself an official of the Executive Branch, appointed by the President. The career archivists appointed to do the initial screening for the purpose of selecting out and returning to appellant his private and personal papers similarly are Executive Branch employees.

[In any event, appellant's argument, as the District Court found,] rests upon an "archaic view of the separation of powers as requiring three airtight departments of government." . . . Rather, in determining whether the Act disrupts the proper balance between the coordinate branches, the proper inquiry focuses on the extent to which it prevents the Executive Branch from accomplishing its constitutionally assigned functions. *United States v. Nixon.* . . . Only where the potential for disruption is present must we then determine whether that impact is justified by an overriding need to promote objectives within the constitutional authority of Congress. . . .

PRESIDENTIAL PRIVILEGE

Having concluded that the separation of powers principle is not necessarily violated by the Administrator's taking custody and screening appellant's papers, we next consider appellant's more narrowly defined claim that the Presidential privilege shields these records from archival scrutiny. . . .

The appellant bases his claim of Presidential privilege in this case on the assertion that the potential disclosure of communications given to the appellant in confidence would adversely affect the ability of future Presidents to obtain the candid advice necessary for effective decisionmaking. We are called upon to adjudicate that claim, however, only with respect to the process by which the materials will be screened and catalogued by professional archivists. . . .

The screening constitutes a very limited intrusion by personnel in the Executive Branch sensitive to executive concerns. These very personnel have performed the identical task in each of the Presidential libraries without any suggestion that such activity has in any way interfered with executive confidentiality. Indeed, in light of this consistent historical practice, past and present executive officials must be well aware of the possibility that, at some time in the future, their communications may be reviewed on a confidential basis by professional archivists. . . .

PRIVACY

. . . The overwhelming bulk of the 42 million documents and the 880 tape recordings pertain, not to appellant's private communications, but to the official conduct of his Presidency. Most of the 42 million papers were prepared and seen by others and were widely circulated within the Government. Appellant concedes that he saw no more than 200,000, and we do not understand him to suggest that his privacy claim extends to items he never saw. . . . Further, it is logical to assume that the tape recordings made in the Presidential offices primarily relate to the conduct and business of the Presidency. And, of course, appellant cannot assert any privacy claim as to the documents and tape recordings that he has already disclosed to the public. . . . Therefore appellant's privacy claim embracing, for example, "extremely private communications between [him] and, among others, his wife, his daughters, his physician, lawyer and clergyman, and his close friends as well as personal diary dictabelts and his wife's personal files," relates only to a very small fraction of the massive volume of official materials with which they are presently commingled. . . .

. . . appellant has a legitimate expectation of privacy in his personal communications. But the constitutionality of the Act must be viewed in the context of the limited intrusion of the screening process, of appellant's status as a public figure, of his lack of any expectation of privacy in the overwhelming majority of the materials, of the important public interest in preservation of the materials, and of the virtual impossibility of segregating the small quantity of private materials without comprehensive screening. When this is combined with the Act's sensitivity to appellant's legitimate privacy interests, the unblemished record of the archivists for discretion, and the likelihood that the regulations to be promulgated by the Administrator will further moot appellant's fears that his materials will be reviewed by "a host of persons," . . . we are compelled to agree with the District Court that appellant's privacy claim is without merit.

FIRST AMENDMENT

During his Presidency appellant served also as head of his national political party and spent a substantial portion of his working time on partisan political matters. Records arising from his political activities, like his private and personal records, are not segregated from the great mass of materials. He argues that the Act's archival screening process therefore necessarily entails invasion of his constitutionally protected rights of associational privacy and political speech. . . . [T]he District Court acknowledged that appellant "would appear to have a legitimate expectation that he would have an opportunity to remove some of the sensitive political documents before any government screening took place," [but found] no reason to believe that the mandated regulations when promulgated would not adequately protect against public access to materials implicating appellant's privacy in political association, and that "any burden arising solely from review by professional and discreet archivists is not significant." The court therefore held that the Act does not significantly interfere with or chill appellant's First Amendment rights. We agree. . . .

BILL OF ATTAINDER CLAUSE

Finally, we address appellant's argument that the Act constitutes a bill of attainder proscribed by Art. I, § 9 of the Constitution. His argument is that Congress acted on the premise that he had engaged in "misconduct," was an "unreliable custodian" of his own documents, and generally was deserving of a "legislative judgment of blameworthiness." . . . Thus, he argues, the Act is pervaded with the key features of a bill of attainder: a law that legislatively determines guilt and inflicts punishment without provision of the protections of a judicial trial. . . .

. . . in the present case, the Act's specificity—the fact that it refers to appellant by name—does not automatically offend the Bill of Attainder Clause. Indeed, viewed in context, the focus of the enactment can be fairly and rationally understood. It is true that Title I deals exclusively with appellant's papers. But Title II casts a wider net by establishing a special commission to study and recommend appropriate legislation regarding the preservation of the records of future Presidents and all other federal officials. In this light, Congress' action to preserve only appellant's records is easily explained by the fact that at the time of the Act's passage, only his materials demanded immediate attention. [H]e alone had entered into a depository agreement . . . which by terms called for the destruction of certain of the materials. . . . [In] short, appellant constituted a legitimate class of one, and this provides a basis for Congress' decision to proceed with dispatch with respect to his materials while accepting the status of his predecessors' papers and ordering the further consideration of generalized standards to govern his successors. . . .

We, of course, are not blind to appellant's plea that we recognize the social and political realities of 1974. It was a period of political turbulence unprecedented in our history. But this Court is not free to invalidate acts of Congress based upon inferences that we may be asked to draw from our personalized reading of the contemporary scene or recent history. In judging the constitutionality of the Act, we may only look to its terms, to the intent expressed by Members of Congress who voted its passage, and to the existence or nonexistence of legitimate explanations for its apparent effects. We are persuaded that none of these factors is suggestive that the Act is a punitive bill of attainder. . . .

Affirmed.

MR. JUSTICE WHITE, concurring. . . .

MR. JUSTICE STEVENS, concurring. . . .

The statute before the Court does not apply to all Presidents or former Presidents. It singles out one, by name, for special treatment. Unlike all other former Presidents in our history, he is denied custody of his own Presidential papers; he is subjected to the burden of prolonged litigation over the administration of the statute; and his most private papers and conversations are to be scrutinized by government archivists. The statute implicitly condemns him as an unreliable custodian of his papers. Legislation which subjects a named individual to this humilating treatment must raise serious questions under the Bill of Attainder Clause.

Bills of Attainder were typically directed at once powerful leaders of government. By special legislative acts, Parliament deprived one statesman after another of his reputation, his property, and his potential for future leadership. The motivation for such bills was as much political as it was punitive—and often the victims were those who had been the most relentless in attacking their political enemies at the height of their own power. In light of this history, legislation like that before us must be scrutinized with great care. . . .

Like the Court, however, I am persuaded that "appellant constituted a legitimate class of one." . . . The opinion of the Court leaves unmentioned the two facts which I consider decisive in this regard. Appellant resigned his office under unique circumstances and accepted a pardon for offenses committed while in office. By so doing, he placed himself in a different class from all other Presidents. . . . Even though unmentioned, it would be unrealistic to assume that historic facts of this consequence did not affect the legislative decision.

Since these facts provide a legitimate justification for the specificity of the statute, they also avoid the conclusion that this otherwise nonpunitive statute is made punitive by its specificity. If I did not consider it appropriate to take judicial notice of those facts, I would be unwilling to uphold the power of Congress to enact special legislation directed only at one former President at a time when his popularity was at its nadir. For even when it deals with Presidents or former Presidents, the legislative focus should be upon "the calling" rather than "the person." . . . In short, in my view, this case will not be a precedent for future legislation which relates, not to the Office of President, but just to one of its occupants.

Without imputing a similar reservation to the Court, I join its opinion with the qualification that these unmentioned facts have had a critical influence on my vote to affirm.

Mr. Justice Blackmun, concurring in part and concurring in the judgment. . . .

Mr. Justice Powell, concurring in part and concurring in the judgment. . . .

Mr. Chief Justice Burger, dissenting.

In my view, the Court's holding is a grave repudiation of nearly 200 years of judicial precedent and historical practice. That repudiation arises out of an Act of Congress passed in the aftermath of a great national crisis which culminated in the resignation of a President. The Act violates firmly established constitutional principles in several respects.

I find it very disturbing that fundamental principles of constitutional law are subordinated to what seem the needs of a particular situation. That moments of great national distress give rise to passions reminds us why the three Branches of government were created as separate and coequal, each intended as a check, in turn, on possible excesses by one or both of the others. The Court, however, has now joined a Congress, in haste to "do something," and has invaded historic, fundamental principles of the separate powers of coequal Branches of government. To "punish" one person, Congress—and now the Court—tears into the fabric of our constitutional framework. . . .

Mr. Justice Rehnquist, dissenting. . . .

[T]oday's decision countenances the power of any future Congress to seize the official papers of an out-going President as he leaves the inaugural stand. In so doing, it poses a real threat to the ability of future Presidents to receive candid advice and to give candid instructions. This result, so at odds with our previous case law on the separation of powers, will daily stand as a veritable sword of Damocles over every succeeding President and his advisors. . . . [T]he Act is a clear violation of the constitutional principle of separation of powers. . . .

Chapter Eight

THE
PRESIDENT
AND FOREIGN RELATIONS

INTRODUCTION

The provisions of the Constitution pertaining to foreign relations take the form of assignments of particular functions to the various branches of the government. They do not by any means cover the whole range of foreign affairs, and there is no grant of authority over foreign relations in broad terms comparable to the authorization to regulate commerce among the states and with foreign nations. However, such a grant is not necessary. Authority over foreign affairs is an inherent power, which attaches to the federal government as a sovereign entity and derives from the Constitution only as the Constitution is the creator of that sovereign entity. In *United States* v. *Curtiss-Wright Export Corp.* (1936) Justice Sutherland gave a classic explanation of the difference in the sources of the federal government's powers in the fields of domestic and foreign affairs.

Allocation of Powers

As for the location of the federal power to carry on the foreign relations of the United States, the principal theoretical writers on whom the Founders relied—Blackstone, Locke, and Montesquieu—were unanimous in contending that the responsibility must rest with the executive. Nevertheless, the Constitution allocated the power to declare war to Congress. It made the Senate's consent necessary to the ratification of treaties, and by a two-thirds vote. It made the Senate's advice and consent a condition to the appointment of ambassadors. When account is taken of the general law making and appropriating powers of Congress, the exercise of which is often essential to the formulation and execution of foreign policy decisions, it is clear that the Constitution, as Corwin has said, "considered only for its affirmative grants of powers capable of affecting the issue, is an invitation to struggle for the privilege of directing American foreign policy."[1]

For this struggle the President is powerfully equipped by the general characteristics of executive power already noted, by his constitutional authority as Commander in Chief, and by his recognized position as "the Nation's organ for foreign affairs." The Supreme Court has repeatedly recognized the President's primacy and special position in this area, as it did in the *Curtiss-Wright* case.

The powers which the President exercises as "sole organ" of foreign relations for the nation can be briefly indicated. He is the channel for communications to and from other nations, and conducts negotiations directly or through his appointed representatives. He has the power of recognizing foreign governments. He can use his control of the armed forces to implement his policies and to protect American rights or interests abroad. The Supreme Court has recognized that the President's preeminent position in the area of foreign relations largely precludes judicial review of his decisions. Justice Jackson made this point well in *Chicago & Southern Air Lines* v. *Waterman S. S. Corp.* (1948).

To a considerable degree the President's power as "sole organ" cancels out the most important grant of external authority to Congress—the power to declare war. For the President can, by his management of foreign affairs and his use of the armed forces, so shape the nation's policies and the development of events that he leaves Congress no choice. In any event, declarations of war have presumably become irrelevant in the age of nuclear warfare.

Treaties

On the other hand, the necessity of securing Senate consent by a two-thirds vote for the ratification of treaties has proved in practice to be a real limitation on executive policy making. Partly because of the hazards of Senate treaty approval, the President has made extensive use of "exec-

---

[1]Edward S. Corwin, *The President: Office and Powers, 1787–1957*, 4th rev. ed. (New York: New York University Press, 1957), p. 171.

utive agreements" with foreign countries, which do not require Senate assent. They may be employed for minor matters which it would be inappropriate to embody in a treaty, but often they deal with concerns of major importance. Unless such agreements are based on acts of Congress authorizing them, they are usually said to find their constitutional authority in the President's power as Commander-in-Chief or as the sole organ of international relations. Efforts to distinguish between the legal effects of treaties and executive agreements have generally been unsuccessful.

Article VI sets up treaties and acts of Congress on a par—both are "the supreme law of the land." In case of conflict between a treaty and a statute, the later in point of time generally supersedes the earlier. However, a non-self-executing treaty (i.e., one which requires congressional legislation to put it into effect) does not supersede an earlier conflicting act of Congress.

According to Article VI, laws must be made "in pursuance" of the Constitution in order to have status as supreme law of the land, but treaties need be made only "under the authority of the United States." Considerable effort has been made to conjure up from this difference in wording the bogey of a treaty power unlimited by the Constitution. Some substance may seem to be given to these fears by the fact that the Supreme Court has never held a treaty unconstitutional and by the circumstances of the Court's decision in *Missouri* v. *Holland* (1920).

Admittedly there is something startling about the holding in that case whereby ratification of a treaty gave Congress constitutional powers it did not possess in the absence of a treaty. But this result is an inevitable consequence of the plenary nature of federal power over foreign affairs. The incapacity of the states for foreign relationships requires that the federal government have authority to deal with all matters which are of legitimate concern to American foreign relations. This does not mean, however, that the treaty power can be used to amend the Constitution, nor does it open up constitutional rights to revision by treaties. Any doubt on this score was removed by the Supreme Court's decision in *Reid* v. *Covert* (1957) which declared that Article VI did not permit the United States "to exercise power under an international agreement without observing constitutional prohibitions."

Control over Passports

A passport is necessary in order for a citizen to leave or enter the United States, and consequently the power of the Secretary of State over the issuance of passports gives him the authority to control travel. During the 1950s the policy of the State Department to refuse passports to persons suspected of being Communists was subjected to attack in the courts. In *Kent* v. *Dulles* (1958) the Supreme Court held that "the right to travel is a part of the 'liberty' of which the citizen cannot be deprived without the due process of law of the Fifth Amendment." Having decided this much, the Court found it unnecessary to take up the difficult question of how far this liberty might be curtailed without infringing due process, because the majority concluded that Congress had *not* authorized the power to refuse passports that the State Department had been exercising.

The State Department then fell back on the passport provisions of the Internal Security Act of 1950, the registration provisions of which had been upheld by the Supreme Court in 1961. However, denial of passports to Communists under this statute was held unconstitutional by the Court in *Aptheker* v. *Secretary of State* (1964). Again the Court did not say that the right to travel was absolute. Rather it held that the statutory denial of passports to any member of a communist organization, regardless of degree of activity in the organization or the purposes of the travel, was unconstitutionally broad and indiscriminate in its scope.

In contrast to *Kent* and *Aptheker*, the Supreme Court in *Zemel* v. *Rusk* (1965) upheld the State Department's refusal to validate passports for travel to Communist Cuba. Unlike the denial of passports to individuals because of their views or affiliations, geographical area restrictions on travel were thought to be justified by considerations of national security and therefore raised no First or Fifth Amendment problems. However, subsequent judicial decisions rendered the area restriction policy unenforceable,[2] and in 1977 President Carter terminated foreign area travel restrictions.

UNITED STATES V. CURTISS-WRIGHT EXPORT CORP.

299 U.S. 304, 57 S. Ct. 216, 81 L. Ed. 255 (1936)

A joint resolution adopted by Congress in 1934 authorized the President by proclamation to prohibit the sale of arms within the United States to certain South American belligerent states. The President issued such a proclamation. A conviction for violation of the proclamation and joint resolution was attacked on the ground that the statute constituted an unlawful delegation of legislative power to the President. The Court had recently declared three congressional statutes unconstitutional on this ground in *Panama Refining Co.* v. *Ryan* (1935), *Schechter Poultry Corp.* v. *United States* (1935), and *Carter* v. *Carter Coal Co.*

---

[2] *United States* v. *Laub* (1967). *Travis* v. *United States* (1967), *Lynd* v. *Rusk* (1967).

(1936). All three of these cases, however, involved regulation of the nation's internal affairs.

MR. JUSTICE SUTHERLAND delivered the opinion of the Court. . . .

FIRST. It is contended that by the Joint Resolution the going into effect and continued operation of the resolution was conditioned (a) upon the President's judgment as to its beneficial effect upon the re-establishment of peace between the countries engaged in armed conflict in the Chaco; (b) upon the making of a proclamation, which was left to his unfettered discretion, thus constituting an attempted substitution of the President's will for that of Congress; (c) upon the making of a proclamation putting an end to the operation of the resolution, which again was left to the President's unfettered discretion; and (d) further, that the extent of its operation in particular cases was subject to limitation and exception by the President, controlled by no standard. In each of these particulars, appellees urge that Congress abdicated its essential functions and delegated them to the Executive.

Whether, if the Joint Resolution had related solely to internal affairs, it would be open to the challenge that it constituted an unlawful delegation of legislative power to the Executive, we find it unnecessary to determine. The whole aim of the resolution is to affect a situation entirely external to the United States, and falling within the category of foreign affairs. The determination which we are called to make, therefore, is whether the Joint Resolution, as applied to that situation, is vulnerable to attack under the rule that forbids a delegation of the lawmaking power. In other words, assuming (but not deciding) that the challenged delegation, if it were confined to internal affairs, would be invalid, may it nevertheless be sustained on the ground that its exclusive aim is to afford a remedy for a hurtful condition within foreign territory?

It will contribute to the elucidation of the question if we first consider the differences between the powers of the federal government in respect of foreign or external affairs and those in respect of domestic or internal affairs. That there are differences between them, and that these differences are fundamental, may not be doubted.

The two classes of powers are different, both in respect of their origin and their nature. The broad statement that the federal government can exercise no powers except those specifically enumerated in the Constitution, and such implied powers as are necessary and proper to carry into effect the enumerated powers, is categorically true only in respect of our internal affairs. In that field, the primary purpose of the Constitution was to carve from the general mass of legislative powers *then possessed by the states* such portions as it was thought desirable to vest in the federal government, leaving those not included in the enumeration still in the states. . . . That this doctrine applies only to powers which the states had is self-evident. And since the states severally never possessed international powers, such powers could not have been carved from the mass of state powers but obviously were transmitted to the United States from some other source. During the Colonial period, those powers were possessed exclusively by and were entirely under the control of the Crown. By the Declaration of Independence, "the Representatives of the United States of America" declared the United (not the several) Colonies to be free and independent states, and as such to have "full Power to levy War, conclude Peace, contract Alliances, establish Commerce and to do all other Acts and Things which Independent States may of right do."

As a result of the separation from Great Britain by the colonies, acting as a unit, the powers of external sovereignty passed from the Crown not to the colonies severally, but to the colonies in their collective and corporate capacity as the United States of America. Even before the Declaration, the colonies were a unit in foreign affairs, acting through a common agency—namely, the Continental Congress, composed of delegates from the thirteen colonies. That agency exercised the powers of war and peace, raised an army, created a navy, and finally adopted the Declaration of Independence. Rulers come and go; governments end and forms of government change; but sovereignty survives. A political society cannot endure without a supreme will somewhere. Sovereignty is never held in suspense. When, therefore, the external sovereignty of Great Britain in respect of the colonies ceased, it immediately passed to the Union. See *Penhallow* v. *Doane*. . . . That fact was given practical application almost at once. The treaty of peace, made on September 3, 1783, was concluded between his Britannic Majesty and the "United States of America." . . .

The Union existed before the Constitution, which was ordained and established among other things to form "a more perfect Union." Prior to that event, it is clear that the Union, declared by the Articles of Confederation to be "perpetual," was the sole possessor of external sovereignty, and in the Union it remained without change save in so far as the Constitution in express terms qualified its exercise. The Framers' Convention was called and exerted its powers upon the irrefutable postulate that though the states were several their people in respect of foreign affairs were one. . . .

It results that the investment of the federal government with the powers of external sovereignty did not depend upon the affirmative grants of the Constitution. The powers to declare and wage war, to conclude peace, to make treaties, to maintain diplomatic relations with other sovereignties, if they had never been mentioned in the Constitution, would have vested in the federal government as necessary concomitants of nationality. Neither the Constitution nor the laws passed in pursuance of it have any force in foreign territory unless in respect of our own citizens (see *American Banana Co.* v. *United Fruit Co.* . . . ; and operations of the nation in such territory must be governed by treaties, international understandings and compacts, and the principles of international law. As a member of the family of nations, the right and power of the United States in that field are equal to the right and power of the other members of the international family. Otherwise, the United States is not completely sovereign. . . .

Not only, as we have shown, is the federal power over external affairs in origin and essential character different from that over internal affairs, but participation in the exercise of the power is significantly limited. In this vast external realm, with its important, complicated, delicate and manifold problems, the President alone has the power to speak or listen as a representative of the nation. He *makes* treaties with the advice and consent of the Senate; but he alone negotiates. Into the field of negotiation the Senate cannot intrude; and Congress itself is powerless to invade it. . . .

It is important to bear in mind that we are here dealing not alone with an authority vested in the President by an exertion of legislative power, but with such an authority plus the very delicate, plenary and exclusive power of the President as the sole organ of the federal government in the field of international relations—a power which does not require as a basis for its exercise an act of Congress, but which, of course, like every other governmental power, must be exercised in subordination to the applicable provisions of the Constitution. It is quite apparent that if, in the maintenance of our international relations, embarrassment—perhaps serious embarrassment—is to be avoided and success for our aims achieved, congressional legislation which is to be made effective through negotiation and inquiry within the international field must often accord to the President a degree of discretion and freedom from statutory restriction which would not be admissible were domestic affairs alone involved. Moreover, he, not Congress, has the better opportunity of knowing the conditions which prevail in foreign countries, and especially is this true in time of war. He has his confidential sources of information. He has his agents in the form of diplomatic, consular and other officals. Secrecy in respect of information gathered by them may be highly necessary, and the premature disclosure of it productive of harmful results. Indeed, so clearly is this true that the first President refused to accede to a request to lay before the House of Representatives the instructions, correspondence and documents relating to the negotiation of the Jay Treaty—a refusal the wisdom of which was recognized by the House itself and has never been doubted.

The marked difference between foreign affairs and domestic affairs in this respect is recognized by both houses of Congress in the very form of their requisitions for information from the executive departments. In the case of every department except the Department of State, the resolution *directs* the official to furnish the information. In the case of the State Department dealing with foreign affairs, the President is *requested* to furnish the information "if not incompatible with the public interest." A statement that to furnish the information is not compatible with the public interest rarely, if ever, is questioned.

When the President is to be authorized by legislation to act in respect to a matter intended to affect a situation in foreign territory, the legislator properly bears in mind the important consideration that the form of the President's action—or, indeed, whether he shall act at all—may well depend, among other things, upon the nature of the confidential information which he has or may thereafter receive, or upon the effect which his action may have upon our foreign relations. This consideration, in connection with what we have already said on the subject, discloses the unwisdom of requiring Congress in this field of governmental power to lay down narrowly definite standards by which the President is to be governed. As this court said in *Mackenzie* v. *Hare,* ... "As a government, the United States is invested with all the attributes of sovereignty. As it has the character of nationality it has the powers of nationality, especially those which concern its relations and intercourse with other countries. *We should hesitate long before limiting or embarrassing such powers."* (Italics supplied.)

In the light of the foregoing observations, it is evident that this court should not be in haste to apply a general rule which will have the effect of condemning legislation like that under review as constituting an unlawful delegation of legislative power. The principles which justify such legislation find overwhelming support in the unbroken legislative practice which has prevailed almost from the inception of the national government to the present day. . . .

Practically every volume of the United States Statutes contains one or more acts or joint resolutions of Congress authorizing action by the President in respect of subjects affecting foreign relations, which either leave the exercise of the power to his unrestricted judgment, or provide a standard far more general than that which has always been considered requisite with regard to domestic affairs. . . .

The result of holding that the joint resolution here under attack is void and unenforceable as constituting an unlawful delegation of legislative power would be to stamp this multitude of comparable acts and resolutions as likewise invalid. And while this court may not, and should not, hesitate to declare acts of Congress, however many times repeated, to be unconstitutional if beyond all rational doubt it finds them to be so, an impressive array of legislation such as we have just set forth, enacted by nearly every Congress from the beginning of our national existence to the present day, must be given unusual weight in the process of reaching a correct determination of the problem. A legislative practice such as we have here, evidenced not by only occasional instances, but marked by the movement of a steady stream for a century and a half of time, goes a long way in the direction of proving the presence of unassailable ground for the constitutionality of the practice, to be found in the origin and history of the power involved, or in its nature, or in both combined. . . .

Both upon principle and in accordance with precedent, we conclude there is sufficient warrant for the broad discretion vested in the President to determine whether the enforcement of the statute will have a beneficial effect upon the reestablishment of peace in the affected countries; whether he shall make proclamation to bring the resolution into operation; whether and when the resolution shall cease to operate and to make proclamation accordingly; and to prescribe limitations and exceptions to which the enforcement of the resolution shall be subject. . . .

The judgment of the court below must be reversed and the cause remanded for further proceedings in accordance with the foregoing opinion.

Reversed.

MR. JUSTICE MCREYNOLDS does not agree. He is of opinion that the court below reached the right conclusion and its judgment ought to be affirmed.

MR. JUSTICE STONE took no part in the consideration or decision of this case.

CHICAGO & SOUTHERN AIR LINES V. WATERMAN S. S. CORP.

333 U.S. 103, 68 S. Ct. 431, 92 L. Ed. 568 (1948)

The Civil Aeronautics Act authorized judicial review of air route orders issued by the Civil Aeronautics Board. However, applications by citizen carriers to engage in overseas and foreign air transportation, unlike domestic route applications, were subject to approval by the President and did not become final until they had received his approval. The issue in this case was whether presidentially approved foreign route orders were subject to judicial review.

MR. JUSTICE JACKSON delivered the opinion of the Court. . . .

The court below considered, and we think quite rightly, that it could not review such provisions of the order as resulted from Presidential direction. The President, both as Commander-in-Chief and as the Nation's organ for foreign affairs, has available intelligence services whose reports neither are nor ought to be published to the world. It would be intolerable that courts, without the relevant information, should review and perhaps nullify actions of the Executive taken on information properly held secret. Nor can courts sit in camera in order to be taken into executive confidences. But even if courts could require full disclosure, the very nature of executive decisions as to foreign policy is political, not judicial. Such decisions are wholly confided by our Constitution to the political departments of the government, Executive and Legislative. They are delicate, complex, and involve large elements of prophecy. They are and should be undertaken only by those directly responsible to the people whose welfare they advance or imperil. They are decisions of a kind for which the Judiciary has neither aptitude, facilities nor responsibility and have long been held to belong in the domain of political power not subject to judicial intrusion or inquiry. . . . We therefore agree that whatever of this order emanates from the President is not susceptible of review by the Judicial Department. . . .

MISSOURI V. HOLLAND

252 U.S. 416, 40 S. Ct. 382, 64 L. Ed. 641 (1920)

A 1913 act of Congress strictly regulating the killing of migratory birds in the United States was declared unconstitutional by two lower federal courts as violating the rights of the states. These decisions were not appealed to the Supreme Court. Instead, the United States negotiated a treaty with Great Britain, declaring it the purpose of the United States and Canada to protect migratory birds and to enact legislation toward that end. Carrying out the treaty provisions and under their authority, Congress then adopted the Migratory Bird Act of 1918.

Mr. Justice Holmes delivered the opinion of the court. . . .
. . . The question raised is the general one whether the treaty and statute are void as an interference with the rights reserved to the States. To answer this question it is not enough to refer to the Tenth Amendment, reserving the powers not delegated to the United States, because by Article II, § 2, the power to make treaties is delegated expressly, and by Article VI treaties made under the authority of the United States, along with the Constitution and laws of the United States made in pursuance thereof, are declared the supreme law of the land. If the treaty is valid there can be no dispute about the validity of the statute under Article I, § 8, as a necessary and proper means to execute the powers of the Government. The language of the Constitution as to the supremacy of treaties being general, the question before us is narrowed to an inquiry into the ground upon which the present supposed exception is placed.

It is said that a treaty cannot be valid if it infringes the Constitution, that there are limits, therefore, to the treaty-making power, and that one such limit is that what an act of Congress could not do unaided, in derogation of the powers reserved to the States, a treaty cannot do. An earlier act of Congress that attempted by itself and not in pursuance of a treaty to regulate the killing of migratory birds within the States had been held bad in the District Court. *United States* v. *Shauver . . . United States* v. *McCullagh* . . . Those decisions were supported by arguments that migratory birds were owned by the States in their sovereign capacity for the benefit of their people, and that under cases like *Geer* v. *Connecticut,* . . . this control was one that congress had no power to displace. The same argument is supposed to apply now with equal force.

Whether the two cases cited were decided rightly or not they cannot be accepted as a test of the treaty power. Acts of Congress are the supreme law of the land only when made in pursuance of the Constitution, while treaties are declared to be so when made under the authority of the United States. It is open to question whether the authority of the United States means more than the formal acts prescribed to make the convention. We do not mean to imply that there are no qualifications to the treaty-making power; but they must be ascertained in a different way. It is obvious that there may be matters of the sharpest exigency for the national well being that an act of Congress could not deal with but that a treaty followed by such an act could, and it is not lightly to be assumed that, in matters requiring national action, "a power which must belong to and somewhere reside in every civilized government" is not to be found. *Andrews* v. *Andrews* . . . What was said in that case with regard to the powers of the States applies with equal force to the powers of the nation in cases where the States individually are incompetent to act. We are not yet discussing the particular case before us but only are considering the validity of the test proposed. With regard to that we may add that when we are dealing with words that also are a constituent act, like the Constitution of the United States, we must realize that they have called into life a being the development of which could not have been foreseen completely by the most gifted of its begetters. It was enough for them to realize or to hope that they had created an organism; it has taken a century and has cost their successors much sweat and blood to prove that they created a nation. The case before us must be considered in the light of our whole experience and not merely in that of what was said a hundred years ago. The treaty in question does not contravene any prohibitory words to be found in the Constitution. The only question is whether it is forbidden by some invisible radiation from the general terms of the Tenth Amendment. We must consider what this country has become in deciding what that Amendment has reserved.

The State as we have intimated founds its claim of exclusive authority upon an assertion of title to migratory birds, an assertion that is embodied in statute. No doubt it is true that as between a State and its inhabitants the State may regulate the killing and sale of such birds, but it does not follow that its authority is exclusive of paramount powers. To put the claim of the State upon title is to lean upon a slender reed. Wild birds are not in the possession of anyone; and possession is the beginning of ownership. The whole foundation of the State's rights is the presence within their jurisdiction of birds that yesterday had not arrived, tomorrow may be in another State and in a week a thousand miles away. If we are to be accurate we cannot put the case of the State upon higher ground than that the treaty deals with creatures that for the moment are within the State borders, that it must be carried out by officers of the United States within the same territory, and that but for the treaty the State would be free to regulate this subject itself. . . .

Here a national interest of very nearly the first magnitude is involved. It can be protected only by national action in concert with that of another power. The subject matter is only transitorily within the State and has no permanent habitat therein. But for the treaty and the statute there soon might be no birds for any powers to deal with. We see nothing in the Constitution that compels the Government to sit by while a food supply is cut off and the protectors of our forests and our crops are destroyed.

It is not sufficient to rely upon the States. The reliance is vain, and were it otherwise, the question is whether the United States is forbidden to act. We are of opinion that the treaty and statute must be upheld. . . .

Decree affirmed.

MR. JUSTICE VAN DEVANTER and MR. JUSTICE PITNEY dissent.

Chapter Nine

THE
PRESIDENT
AND THE WAR POWER

INTRODUCTION

The war power of Congress has seldom been subjected to judicial criticism or limitation. The reason, of course, is that the power to wage war must be the power to wage war successfully, and judges are unlikely to set their opinions over against those of the legislature as to the steps necessary for success in combat. Wartime legislation controlling economic freedom and the use of private property has with rare exceptions been supported. In upholding rent controls during World War II, Justice Douglas said in *Bowles* v. *Willingham* (1944), "A Nation which can demand the lives of its men and women in the waging of . . . war is under no constitutional necessity of providing a system of price control on the domestic front which will assure each landlord a 'fair return' on his property."

Extent of the War Power

The war power does not require the existence of a state of war for its exercise. It can be a justification of preparatory action before war starts, and for ameliorating action after war is over. The so-called Wartime Prohibition Act was passed in 1918 11 days after the armistice. The rent control act passed in 1947 was upheld in *Woods* v. *Miller Co.* (1948), the Court pointing out "that there has not yet been eliminated the deficit in housing which in considerable measure was caused by the heavy demobilization of veterans and by the cessation or reduction in residential construction during the period of hostilities."

Conscription during the First World War was upheld in the *Selective Draft Law Cases* (1918), against contentions that it amounted to involuntary servitude. Subsequently the Supreme Court did exercise some discretion in interpreting congressional legislation exempting conscientious objectors from military service. In *United States* v. *Seeger* (1965) and *Welsh* v. *United States* (1970) the Court rather clearly extended exemption beyond the congressional intention.

The Constitution is clear on how wars are declared but does not indicate how they are ended, and so the judicial response has been again to accept the political decisions. Termination of the legal state of war is effected normally by negotiation of a treaty, but there is American experience with other methods. The Civil War was ended by presidential proclamation, and World War I by a joint declaration of Congress. "Whatever the mode," the Supreme Court said in *Ludecke* v. *Watkins* (1948), termination of a state of war "is a political act."

The difficult constitutional issues concerning the extent of the war power have been raised by actions of the President rather than by congressional legislation. The President's tremendous executive authority is buttressed here by his status as Commander-in-Chief. In No. 69 of *The Federalist,* Hamilton thought that the President's role as Commander-in-Chief would amount "to nothing more than the supreme command and direction of the military and naval forces, as first general and admiral of the Confederacy," while the more significant powers of declaring war and raising and regulating fleets and armies would be exercised by Congress.

Actually this was an accurate enough forecast of the limited role of Commander in Chief from 1789 to 1861. It was President Lincoln who, in his resolve to save the Union, linked together the presidential power to take care that the laws be faithfully executed with that of Commander-in-Chief to yield a result approaching constitutional dictatorship. For ten weeks after the fall of Fort Sumter until he called Congress into special session, Lincoln met the emergency by a series of actions which were for the most part without statutory authorization, although they were subsequently ratified by Congress. He added 40,000 men to the Army and Navy, closed the Post Office to treasonable correspondence, paid out two million dollars from unappropriated funds in the Treasury, proclaimed a blockade of Southern ports, suspended the writ of habeas corpus in several areas, and caused the arrest and detention of persons suspected of treasonable practices. Lincoln's inauguration of military operations by instituting the blockade without authorization by Congress was narrowly upheld by the Supreme Court in the *Prize Cases* (1863), on the ground that the President was obligated to meet the emergency and to determine "what degree of force the crisis demands." But Lincoln's suspension of the writ of habeas corpus and establishment of military commissions to try persons charged with disloyalty were declared unconstitutional by the Court in *Ex parte Milligan* (1866).

Congress and the War Power

Though Congress has the power to declare war, the President's control over the armed forces and responsibility for the conduct of foreign relations, as pointed out in the preceding chapter, has made Congress a distinctly secondary participant in decisions on inauguration of military action. The most recent illustration was the disastrous American involvement in Indochina, which was accomplished by use of the Commander-in-Chief powers by four different Presidents. After the initial commitment of American advisers and a small number of troops in Vietnam by Presidents Eisenhower and Kennedy, President Johnson used the occasion of an alleged North Vietnamese torpedo boat attack on two United States destroyers in the Gulf of Tonkin to ask Congress for a joint resolution of support to strengthen his hand. Johnson subsequently relied on the Gulf of Tonkin Resolution as authorizing and justifying the tremendous escalation of military operations in Vietnam and the bombing of North Vietnam.

Efforts in Congress to recapture some control of the war making power were tremendously accelerated in 1970 by Nixon's precipitate expansion of military activities into Cambodia without any prior consultation with Congress, but they had only limited success. Various "end the war" and withdrawal resolutions failed, and an effort by a member of Congress to stop the bombing by court order failed in *Holtzman v. Schlesinger* (1973). But Congress did eventually order the bombing of Cambodia stopped by August 15, 1973. It is significant that the House Judiciary Committee, when considering the impeachment of President Nixon in 1974, rejected an article of impeachment condemning him for the secret bombing of Cambodia.

Congressional frustration over its impotence in control of the war power did produce the War Powers Resolution, passed in 1973 over President Nixon's veto. The law sets a 60-day limit on any presidential commitment of United States troops abroad without specific congressional authorization, with a 30-day extension if necessary for the safe withdrawal of the troops. The act requires presidential consultation with Congress in every possible instance before introducing armed forces into hostilities or into situations where imminent involvement in hostilities is clearly indicated. However, in 1975 President Ford undertook a sea and air rescue mission of the American merchant vessel *Mayaguez* after its seizure off Cambodia, including bombing of the Cambodian mainland and serious loss of life by the American forces, before notifying Congress of the operation.

Many efforts were made to secure judicial rulings that the Vietnam War was unconstitutional because there had been no declaration of war by Congress. They were all rejected, either directly or indirectly, on political question grounds. For example, *Sarnoff* v. *Shultz* (1972) was a suit brought against the Secretary of the Treasury to enjoin disbursements in aid of American military operations in Vietnam. The suit was dismissed in the trial court on the ground that it presented a political question beyond judicial cognizance, and the Supreme Court denied certiorari.

In an effort to force the Supreme Court to confront the Vietnam issue, the Massachusetts legislature in 1970 passed a law providing that Massachusetts servicemen could refuse to take part in armed hostilities in the absence of a declaration of war by Congress. The state attorney general was authorized to bring a suit in the name of the state in the original jurisdiction of the Supreme Court, seeking a declaration that the military action in Vietnam was unconstitutional and an injunction forbidding the Secretary of Defense to send any citizen of Massachusetts to Vietnam until Congress declared war. The Supreme Court in *Massachusetts* v. *Laird* (1970) denied the state's motion to file the suit.

The case was then filed in federal district court in Boston, but the district judge held that the Supreme Court's refusal of the case meant that Massachusetts lacked standing and that the controversy lacked justiciability. This decision was affirmed by the Court of Appeals for the First Circuit in **Massachusetts v. Laird** (1971).

Military Justice

The armed forces maintain a system of courts-martial for punishment of offenses by their members, under regulations prescribed by Congress. Articles of War were adopted for the Army by Congress in 1789 and for the Navy in 1800. In 1950 these two statutes, as amended, were replaced by the Uniform Code of Military Justice, setting up a single and modernized system for all the armed services.

Courts-martial are totally distinct from the civilian courts and exercise no part of the judicial power of the United States. The decision of a court-martial must be affirmed by the appropriate command officers, and a final appeal may be taken on matters of law to the Court of Military Appeals. This is a bench of three civilian judges set up by the Uniform

Code of Military Justice, appointed for 15-year terms by the President with the advice and consent of the Senate.

The right to indictment by grand jury is specifically made inapplicable by the Constitution to "cases arising in the land and naval forces," and of course there is no right to trial by jury. But the Court of Military Appeals has ruled that all of the other constitutional rights of criminal defendants in the civilian courts are to be honored in courts-martial "except insofar as they are made inapplicable either expressly or by necessary implication."

The principal objection to court-martial procedure has been "command influence." The commanding officer appoints the pretrial investigating officers, authorizes searches and arrests, convenes the court-martial, decides whether the accused shall remain in pretrial confinement, selects the prosecutor and often the defense counsel, chooses the members of the court, decides whether a sentence to confinement will be deferred pending appeal, and makes the initial review of the case.

The writ of habeas corpus furnishes a method whereby detention as a result of a court-martial decision can be reviewed by the civil courts. On occasion the Supreme Court has been critical of the court-martial system, comparing it unfavorably with the civil courts. This attitude motivated the Court in *United States ex rel. Toth* v. *Quarles* (1955) to deny the right of the Air Force to subject a civilian ex-serviceman to court-martial for a crime allegedly committed during his period of military service. The same inclination to limit the jurisdiction of courts-martial was even more evident in **O'Callahan** v. **Parker** (1969), where the Court held that there was no justification for trying a member of the armed forces by court-martial for a crime cognizable in a civilian court which had been committed off post and while on leave. However, in *Schlesinger* v. *Councilman* (1975) the Court upheld trial by general court-martial on a marijuana charge, and also rejected a challenge to the legitimacy of the entire military justice system as denying due process of law.

The unpopular Vietnam War, fought with a largely conscript army, created strains within the armed forces, resistance to military discipline, and new claims for First Amendment rights of criticism and free discussion. In **Parker v. Levy** (1974) the Court upheld the conviction by court-martial of a medical officer who talked against the war and urged enlisted personnel to refuse to obey orders that might send them into combat. He had contended that two articles of the Uniform Code which proscribed "conduct unbecoming an officer and a gentleman" and forbidding "all disorders and neglects to the prejudice of good order and discipline" were unconstitutional as infringing on rights of free speech and unduly vague in violation of the Fifth Amendment.

Wartime controls over the economy have generally raised no constitutional issues, as we have already seen. An exception was President Truman's seizure of the nation's steel mills in 1952, but this did not come in a period of declared war, and Justice Black's opinion for the Court in the *Steel Seizure Case* refused to give any consideration to claims that the action could be justified by his status as Commander in Chief.

The enforced evacuation of Japanese and Japanese-Americans from the West Coast early in World War II by combined executive–legislative action was, in spite of its subsequent ratification by the Supreme Court, one of the most disgraceful episodes in the long history of the war power under the Constitution. In *Hirabayashi* v. *United States* (1943) the Court limited its consideration to, and upheld, the curfew regulations that had preceded registration for evacuation. But ***Korematsu* v. *United States*** (1944) held that the military authorities were not unjustified in concluding that the Japanese residents of the coast area constituted a potentially grave danger to the public safety, a danger so pressing that there was no time to set up procedures for determining the loyalty or disloyalty of individual Japanese residents.

THE PRIZE CASES

2 Black 635, 17 L. Ed. 459 (1863)

President Lincoln declared a blockade of Confederate ports in April, 1861. This case concerned four vessels which had been captured as prizes by Union naval vessels.

MR. JUSTICE GRIER. . . .

The right of prize and capture has its origin in the *jus belli*, and is governed and adjudged under the law of nations. To legitimate the capture of a neutral vessel or property on the high seas, a war must exist *de facto*, and the neutral must have a knowledge or notice of the intention of one of the parties belligerent to use this mode of coercion against a port, city, or territory, in possession of the other.

Let us enquire whether, at the time this blockade was instituted, a state of war existed which would justify a resort to these means of subduing the hostile force.

War has been well defined to be, "That state in which a nation prosecutes its right by force."

The parties belligerent in a public war are independent nations. But it is not necessary to constitute war, that both parties should be acknowledged as independent nations or sovereign States. A war may exist where one of the belligerents claims sovereign rights as against the other.

Insurrection against a government may or may not culminate in an organized rebellion, but a civil war always begins by insurrection against the lawful authority of the Government. A civil war is never solemnly declared; it becomes such by its accidents—the number, power, and organization of the persons who originate and carry it on. . . .

As a civil war is never publicly proclaimed, *eo nomine* against insurgents, its actual existence is a fact in our domestic history which the Court is bound to notice and to know.

The true test of its existence, as found in the writing of the sages of the common law, may be thus summarily stated: "When the regular course of justice is interrupted by revolt, rebellion, or insurrection, so that the Courts of Justice cannot be kept open, *civil war exists* and hostilities may be prosecuted on the same footing as if those opposing the Government were foreign enemies invading the land."

By the Constitution, Congress alone has the power to declare a national or foreign war. It cannot declare war against a State, or any number of States, by virtue of any clause in the Constitution. The Constitution confers on the President the whole Executive power. He is bound to take care that the laws be faithfully executed. He is Commander-in-Chief of the Army and Navy of the United States, and of the militia of the several States when called into the actual service of the United States. He has no power to initiate or declare a war either against a foreign nation or a domestic State. But by the Acts of Congress of February 28, 1795, and 3rd of March, 1807, he is authorized to call out the militia and use the military and naval forces of the United States in case of invasion by foreign nations, and to suppress insurrection against the government of a State or of the United States.

If a war be made by invasion of a foreign nation, the President is not only authorized but bound to resist force by force. He does not initiate the war, but is bound to accept the challenge without waiting for any special legislative authority. And whether the hostile party be a foreign invader, or States organized in rebellion, it is none the less a war, although the declaration of it be "unilateral."

The law of nations is also called the law of nature; it is founded on the common consent as well as the common sense of the world. It contains no such anomalous doctrine as that which this court are now for the first time desired to pronounce, to wit: That insurgents who have risen in rebellion against their sovereign, expelled her court, established a revolutionary government, organized armies, and commenced hostilities are not *enemies* because they are *traitors;* and a war levied on the government by traitors in order to dismember and destroy it, it not a *war* because it is an "insurrection."

Whether the President in fulfilling his duties, as Commander-in-Chief, is suppressing an insurrection, has met with such armed hostile resistance, and a civil war of such alarming proportions as will compel him to accord to them the character of belligerents, is a question to be decided *by him,* and this court must be governed by the decisions and acts of the political department of the government to which this power was intrusted. "He must determine what degree of force the crisis demands." . . .

MR. JUSTICE NELSON, dissenting. . . .

This great and pervading change in the existing condition of a country, and in the relations of all her citizens or subjects, external and internal, from a state of peace, is the immediate effect and result of a state of war: and hence the same code which has annexed to the existence of a war all these distributing consequences has declared that the right of making war belongs exclusively to the supreme or sovereign power of the State.

This power in all civilized nations is regulated by the fundamental laws or municipal constitution of the country.

By our Constitution this power is lodged in Congress. . . . [B]efore this insurrection against the established Government can be dealt with on the footing of a civil war, within the meaning of the law of nations and the Constitution of the United States, and which will draw after it belligerent right, it must be recognized or declared by the war making power of the Government. No power short of this can change the legal status of the Government or the relations of its citizens from that of peace to a state of war, or bring into existence all those duties and obligations of neutral third parties growing out of a state of war, The war power of the Government must be exercised before this changed condition of the Government and people and of neutral third parties can be admitted. There is no difference in this respect between a civil or a public war. . . .

So the war carried on by the President against insurrectionary districts in the Southern States, as in the case of the King of Great Britain in the American Revolution, was a personal war against those in rebellion, and with encouragement and support of loyal citizens with a view to their co-operation and aid in suppressing the insurgents, with this difference, as the war making power belonged to the King, he might have recognized or declared the war at the beginning to be a civil war which would draw after it all the rights of a belligerent, but in the case of the President no such power existed: the war therefore from necessity was a personal war, until Congress assembled and acted upon this state of things. . . .

MR. CHIEF JUSTICE TANEY, MR. JUSTICE CATRON and MR. JUSTICE CLIFFORD concurred in the dissenting opinion of MR. JUSTICE NELSON.

EX PARTE MILLIGAN

4 Wall. 218, 18 L.Ed. 281 (1866)

President Lincoln, by proclamation of September 24, 1862, suspended the writ of habeas corpus and ordered that all persons "guilty of any disloyal practice affording aid and comfort to the rebels" should be liable to trial by courts-martial or military commissions. Congress by statute in 1863 authorized suspension of the writ. Milligan, a resident of Indiana and a Southern sympathizer not in the military forces, was seized and tried on charges of disloyalty by a military commission in Indiana. The civil courts were open and functioning in Indiana, and there was no military action there. Following his conviction, Milligan sought a writ of habeas corpus in the Circuit Court. The judges were divided, and they certified to the Supreme Court the questions raised by this case.

MR. JUSTICE DAVIS delivered the opinion of the court. . . .

The controlling question in the case is this: Upon the facts stated in Milligan's petition, and the exhibits filed, had the military commission mentioned in its jurisdiction, legally, to try and sentence him? Milligan, not a resident of one of the rebellious States, or a prisoner of war, but a citizen of Indiana for twenty years past, and never in the military or naval service, is while at his home, arrested by the military power of the United States, imprisoned, and, on certain criminal charges preferred against him, tried, convicted, and sentenced to be hanged by a military commission, organized under the direction of the military commander of the military district of Indiana. Had this tribunal the legal power and authority to try and punish this man? . . .

The Constitution of the United States is a law for rulers and people, equally in war and in peace, and covers with the shield of its protection all classes of men, at all times, and under all circumstances. No doctrine involving more pernicious consequences was ever invented by the wit of man than that any of its provisions can be suspended during any of the great exigencies of government. Such a doctrine leads directly to anarchy or despotism, but the theory of necessity on which it is based is false; for the government, within the Constitution, has all the powers granted to it which are necessary to preserve its existence; as has been happily proved by the result of the great effort to throw off its just authority.

Have any of the rights guaranteed by the Constitution been violated in the case of Milligan? and if so, what are they?

Every trial involves the exercise of judicial power; and from what source did the military commission that tried him derive their authority? Certainly no part of the judicial power of the country was conferred on them; because the Constitution expressly vests it "in one supreme court and such inferior courts as the Congress may from time to time ordain and establish," and it is not pretended that the commission was a court ordained and established by Congress. They cannot justify on the mandate of the President, because he is controlled by law, and has his appropriate sphere of duty, which is to execute, not to make, the laws; and there is "no unwritten criminal code to which resort can be had as a source of jurisdiction."

But it is said that the jurisdiction is complete under the "laws and usages of war."

It can serve no useful purpose to inquire what those laws and usages are, whence they originated, where found, and on whom they operate; they can never be applied to citizens in States which have upheld the authority of the government, and where the courts are open and their process unobstructed. This court has judicial knowledge that in Indiana the Federal authority was always unopposed, and its courts always open to hear criminal accusations and redress grievances; and no usage of war could sanction a military trial there for any offense whatever of a citizen in civil life, in nowise connected with the military service. Congress could grant no such power; and to the honor of our national legislature be it said, it has never been provoked by the state of the country even to attempt its exercise. One of the plainest constitutional provisions was, therefore, infringed when Milligan was tried by a court not ordained and established by Congress, and not composed of judges appointed during good behavior.

Why was he not delivered to the Circuit Court of Indiana to be proceeded against according to law? No reason of necessity could be urged against it; because Congress had declared penalties against the offenses charged, provided for their punishment, and directed that court to hear and determine them. And soon after this military tribunal was ended, the Circuit Court met, peacefully transacted its business, and adjourned. It needed no bayonets to protect it, and required no military aid to execute its judgments. It was held in a State, eminently distinguished for patriotism, by judges commissioned during the Rebellion, who were provided with juries, upright, intelligent, and selected by a marshal appointed by the President. The government had no right to conclude that Milligan, if guilty, would not receive in that court merited punishment; for its records disclose that it was constantly engaged in the trial of similar offenses, and was never interrupted in its administration of criminal justice. If it was dangerous, in the distracted condition of affairs, to leave Milligan unrestrained of his liberty, because he "conspired against the government, afforded aid and comfort to rebels, and incited the people to insurrection," the law said, arrest him, confine him closely, render him powerless to do further mischief; and then present his case to the grand jury of the district, with proofs of his guilt, and, if indicted, try him according to the course of the common law. If this had been done, the Constitution would have been vindicated, the law of 1863 enforced, and the securities for personal liberty preserved and defended.

Another guarantee of freedom was broken when Milligan was denied a trial by jury. The great minds of the country have differed on the correct interpretation to be given to the various provisions of the Federal Constitution; and judicial decision has been often invoked to settle their true meaning; but until recently no one ever doubted that the right of trial by jury was fortified in the organic law against the power of attack. It is now assailed; but if ideas can be expressed in words, and language has any meaning, this right—one of the most valuable in a free country—is preserved to every one accused of crime who is not attached to the army, or navy, or militia in actual service. The sixth amendment affirms that "in all criminal prosecutions the accused shall enjoy the right to a speedy and public trial by an impartial jury,"—language broad enough to embrace all persons and cases; but the fifth, recognizing the necessity of an indictment, or presentment, before anyone can be held to answer for high crimes, "except cases arising in the land or naval forces, or in the militia, when in actual service, in time of war or public danger;" and the framers of the Constitution, doubtless, meant to limit the right of trial of jury, in the sixth amendment, to those persons who were subject to indictment or presentment in the fifth.

The discipline necessary to the efficiency of the army and navy required other and swifter modes of trial than are furnished by the common-law courts; and in pursuance of the power conferred by the Constitution, Congress has declared the kinds of trial, and the manner in which they shall be conducted, for offenses committed while the party is in the military or naval service. Every one connected with these branches of the public service is amenable to the jurisdiction which Congress has created for their government, and, while thus serving, surrenders his right to be tried by the civil courts. All other persons, citizens of States where the courts are open, if charged with crime, are guaranteed the inestimable privilege of trial by jury. . . .

It is claimed that martial law covers with its broad mantle the proceedings of this military commission. The proposition is this: that in a time of war the commander of an armed force (if, in his opinion, the exigencies of the country demand it, and of which he is the judge) has the power, within the lines of his military district, to suspend all civil rights and their remedies, and subject citizens as well as soldiers to the rule of his will; and in the exercise of his lawful authority cannot be restrained, except by his superior officer or the President of the United States.

If this position is sound to the extent claimed, then when war exists, foreign or domestic, and the country is subdivided into military departments for mere convenience, the commander of one of them can, if he chooses, within his limits, on the plea of necessity, with the approval of the Executive, substitute military force for, and to the exclusion of, the laws, and punish all persons, as he thinks right and proper without fixed or certain rules.

The statement of this proposition shows its importance; for, if true, republican government is a failure, and there is an end of liberty regulated by law. Martial law, established on such a basis, destroys every guarantee of the Constitution, and effectually renders the "military independent of, and superior to, the civil power,"—the attempt to do which by the King of Great Britain was deemed by our fathers such an offense, that they assigned it to the world as one of the causes which impelled them to declare their independence. Civil liberty and this kind of martial law cannot endure together; the antagonism is irreconcilable; and, in the conflict, one or the other must perish. . . .

[CHIEF JUSTICE CHASE and JUSTICES WAYNE, SWAYNE, and MILLER agreed that the military commissions in Indiana were not authorized by Congress, but held that it would have been constitutional for Congress to do so.]

HOLTZMAN V. SCHLESINGER

414 U.S. 1304, 94 S. Ct. 1, 38 L. Ed. 2d 18 (1973)

The Supreme Court declined certiorari in all cases that would have required it to pass on the constitutionality of the Vietnam War. Several justices would have granted review to bring up such cases—Douglas alone in *Mitchell* v. *United States* (1967); Douglas and Stewart in *Mora* v. *McNamara* (1967); Douglas, Stewart, and Harlan in *Massachusetts* v. *Laird* (1970); and Douglas and Brennan in *Berk* v. *Laird* (1971) and *Sarnoff* v. *Shultz* (1972)—but the required four votes were never available. In *Holtzman* v. *Schlesinger* both Marshall and Douglas had an opportunity to express their individual views on the subject.

MR. JUSTICE MARSHALL, Circuit Justice.

This case is before me on an application to vacate a stay entered by a three-judge panel of the United States Court of Appeals for the Second Circuit. Petitioners, a Congresswoman from New York and several air force officers serving in Asia, brought this action to enjoin continued United States air operations over Cambodia. They argue that such military activity has not been authorized by Congress and that, absent such authorization, it violates Article I, § 8, cl. 11 of the Constitution. The United States District Court agreed and, on petitioners' motion for summary judgment, permanently enjoined respondents, the Secretary of Defense, the Acting Secretary of the Air Force, and the Deputy Secretary of Defense, from "participating in any way in military activities in or over Cambodia or releasing any bombs which may fall in Cambodia." However, the effective date of the injunction was delayed until July 27, 1973, in order to give respondents an opportunity to apply to the Court of Appeals for a stay pending appeal. Respondents promptly applied for such a stay, and the application was granted, without opinion, on July 27. Petitioners then filed this motion to vacate the stay. For the reasons stated below, I am unable to say that the Court of Appeals abused its discretion in staying the District Court's order. In view of the complexity and importance of the issues involved and the absence of authoritative precedent, it would be inappropriate for me, acting as a single Circuit Justice, to vacate the order of the Court of Appeals.

Since the facts of this dispute are on the public record and have been exhaustively canvassed in the District Court's opinion, it would serve no purpose to repeat them in detail here. It suffices to note that publicly acknowledged United States involvement in the Cambodian hostilities began with the President's announcement on April 30, 1970, that this country was launching attacks "to clean out major enemy sanctuaries on the Cambodian-Vietnam border," and that American military action in that country has since met with gradually increasing congressional resistance.

Although United States ground troops had been withdrawn from the Cambodian theater by June 30, 1970, in the summer of that year, Congress enacted the so called Fulbright Proviso prohibiting the use of funds for military support to Cambodia. The following winter, Congress reenacted the same limitation with the added proviso that "nothing contained in this section shall be construed to prohibit support of actions required to insure the safe and orderly withdrawal or disengagement of U. S. Forces from Southeast Asia, or to aid in the release of Americans held as prisoners of war." 84 Stat. 2037. These provisions have been attached to every subsequent military appropriations act. Moreover, in the Special Foreign Assistance Act of 1971, Congress prohibited the use of funds to support American ground combat troops in Cambodia under any circumstances and expressly provided that "[m]ilitary and economic assistance provided by the United States to Cambodia . . . shall not be construed as a commitment by the United States to Cambodia for its defense."

Congressional efforts to end American air activities in Cambodia intensified after the withdrawal of American ground troops from Vietnam and the return of American prisoners of war. On May 10, 1973, the House of Representatives refused an administration request to authorize the transfer of $175 million to cover the costs of the Cambodian bombing. . . . Shortly thereafter, both Houses of Congress adopted the socalled Eagleton Amendment prohibiting the use of any funds for Cambodian combat operations. Although this provision was vetoed by the President, an amendment to the Continuing Appropriations Resolution was ultimately adopted and signed by the President into law which stated:

> "Notwithstanding any other provision of law, on or after August 15, 1973, no funds herein or heretofore appropriated may be obligated or expended to finance directly or indirectly combat activities by United States military forces in or over or from off the shores of North Vietnam, Laos or Cambodia." . . . 87 Stat. 130.

Against this background, petitioners forcefully contend that continued United States military activity in Cambodia is illegal. Specifically, they argue that the President is constitutionally disabled in nonemergency situations from exercising the warmaking power in the absence of some affirmative action by Congress. . . . In light of the Fulbright Proviso, petitioners take the position that Congress has never given its assent for military activity in Cambodia once American ground troops and prisoners of war were extricated from Vietnam. . . .

In my judgment, petitioners' contentions in this case are far from frivolous and may well ultimately prevail. Although tactical decisions as to the conduct of an ongoing war may present political questions which the federal courts lack jurisdiction to decide, . . . and although the courts may lack the power to dictate the form which congressional assent to warmaking must take . . . there is a respectable and growing body of lower court opinion holding that Art. I, § 8, cl. 11, imposes some judicially manageable standards as to congressional authorization for warmaking, and that these standards are sufficient to make controversies concerning them justiciable. . . .

Similarly, as a matter of substantive constitutional law, it seems likely that the President may not wage war without some form of congressional approval—except, perhaps in the case of a pressing emergency or when the President is in the process of extricating himself from a war which Congress once authorized. At the very beginning of our history, Mr. Chief Justice Marshall wrote for a unanimous Court that

> "The whole powers of war being, by the Constitution of the United States, vested in Congress, the acts of that body can alone be resorted to as our guide in this inquiry. It is not denied . . . that Congress may authorize general hostilities, in which case the general laws of war apply in our situation, or partial hostilities, in which case the laws of war, so far as they may actually apply to our situation, must be noticed." Talbot v. Seeman . . . (1801).

In my judgment, nothing in the 172 years since those words were written alter[s] that fundamental constitutional postulate. . . .

. . . A fair reading of Congress' actions concerning the war in Cambodia may well indicate that the legislature has authorized only "partial hostilities"—that it has never given its approval to the war except to the extent that it was necessary to extricate American troops and prisoners from Vietnam. Certainly, this seems to be the thrust of the Fulbright Proviso. Moreover, this Court could easily conclude that after the Paris Peace Accords the Cambodian bombing is no longer justifiable as an extension of the war which Congress did authorize and that the bombing is not required by the type of pressing emergency which necessitates immediate presidential response.

. . . Thus, if the decision were mine alone, I might well conclude on the merits that continued American military operations in Cambodia are unconstitutional. But the Supreme Court is a collegial institution, and its decisions reflect the views of a majority of the sitting Justices. . . .

. . . In my judgment, I would exceed my legal authority were I, acting alone, to grant this application. The application to vacate the stay entered below must therefore be denied.

Application denied.

Opinion of MR. JUSTICE DOUGLAS.

My BROTHER MARSHALL, after a hearing, denied this application, . . . which in effect means that the decision of the District Court holding that the bombing of Cambodia is unconstitutional is stayed pending hearing on the merits before the Court of Appeals.

Application for stay denied by one Justice may be made to another. We do not, however, encourage the practice; and when the Term starts, the Justices all being in Washington, D. C., the practice is to refer the second application to the entire Court. That is the desirable practice to discourage "shopping around."

When the Court is in recess that practice cannot be followed, for the Justices are scattered. Yakima, Washington, where I have scheduled the hearing, is nearly 3,000 miles from Washington D. C. Group action by all Members is therefore impossible.

I approached this decision, however, with a feeling of great deference to the judgment of my BROTHER MARSHALL, realizing that while his decision is not binding on me it is one to which I pay the greatest deference.

My BROTHER MARSHALL accurately points out that if the foreign policy goals of this Government are to be weighed the Judiciary is probably the least qualified branch to weigh them. He also states that if stays by judicial officers in cases of this kind are to be vacated the circumstances must be "exceptional." I agree with those premises, and I respect the views of those who share my BROTHER MARSHALL's predilections.

But this case in its stark realities involves the grim consequences of a capital case. The classic capital case is whether Mr. Lew, Mr. Low, or Mr. Lucas should die. The present case involves whether Mr. X (an unknown person or persons) should die. No one knows who they are. They may be Cambodian farmers whose only "sin" is a desire for socialized medicine to alleviate the suffering of their families and neighbors. Mr. X may be the American pilot or navigator who drops a ton of bombs on a Cambodian village. The upshot is that we know that someone is about to die.

Since that is true I see no reason to balance the equities and consider the harm to our foreign policy if one or a thousand more bombs do not drop. The reason is that we live under the Constitution and in Art. I, § 8, it gives to Congress the power to "declare War." The basic question on the merits is whether Congress within the meaning of Art. I, § 8, has "declared war" on Cambodia.

It has become popular to think the President has that power to declare war. But there is not a word in the Constitution that grants that power to him. It runs only to Congress.

The Court in the *Prize Cases* said:

"By the Constitution, Congress alone has the power to declare a national or foreign war. . . . The Constitution confers on the President the whole Executive power. . . . He has no power to initiate or declare a war either against a foreign nation or a domestic State."

The question of justiciability does not seem substantial. In the *Prize Cases,* decided in 1863, the Court entertained a complaint raising the constitutionality of the Civil War. In my time we held that Truman in the undeclared Korean War . . . had no power to seize the steel mills in order to increase war production. The *Prize Cases* and the *Youngstown* case involved the seizure of property. But the Government conceded on oral argument that property is no more important than life under our Constitution. Our Fifth Amendment which curtails federal power under the Due Process Clause protects "life, liberty, and property" in that order. Property is important, but if Truman could not seize it in violation of the Constitution I do not see how any President can take "life" in violation of the Constitution.

When a stay in a capital case is before us, we do not rule on guilt or innocence. A decision on the merits follows and does not precede the stay. If there is doubt whether due process has been followed in the procedures, the stay is granted because death is irrevocable. By the same token I do not sit today to determine whether the bombing of Cambodia is constitutional. Some say it is merely an extension of the "war" in Vietnam, a "war" which the Second Circuit has held in Berk v. Laird. . . . to raise a "political" question, not a justiciable one. I have had serious doubts about the correctness of that decision, but our Court has never passed on the question authoritatively. I have expressed my doubts on the merits in various opinions dissenting from denial of certiorari. But if the "war" in Vietnam were assumed to be a constitutional one, the Cambodian bombing is quite a different affair. Certainly Congress did not in terms declare war against Cambodia and there is no one so reckless to say that the Cambodian forces are an imminent and perilous threat to our shores. The briefs are replete with references to recent acts of Congress which, to avoid a presidential veto, were passed to make clear—as I read them—that no bombing of Cambodia was to be financed by appropriated funds after August 15, 1973. Arguably that is quite different from saying that Congress has declared war on Cambodia for a limited purpose and only up to and not beyond August 15, 1973. If the acts in question are so construed the result would be, as the District Court said, that the number of votes needed to sustain a presidential veto—one-third plus one—would be all that was needed to bring into operation the new and awesome power of a President to declare war. The merits of the present controversy are therefore, to say the least, substantial, since denial of the application before me would catapult our airmen as well as Cambodian peasants into the death zone. I do what I think any judge would do in a capital case—vacate the stay entered by the Court of Appeals.

It is so ordered.

Stay vacated.

[Later the same day JUSTICE MARSHALL, having consulted his colleagues by telephone, set aside JUSTICE DOUGLAS' order and reentered the stay. Two days later, when the bomb load of an American B-52 fell short and struck the Cambodian town of Neak Luong, 137 Cambodian peasants were killed.]

MASSACHUSETTS V. LAIRD

U. S. Court of Appeals, First Circuit 451 F. 2d 26 (1971)

Before ALDRICH, CHIEF JUDGE, McENTEE and COFFIN, CIRCUIT JUDGES.

COFFIN, CIRCUIT JUDGE.

The question sought to be raised in this action is whether the United States involvement in Vietnam is unconstitutional, a war not having been declared or ratified by the Congress. . . .

While the challenge to the constitutionality of our participation in the Vietnam war is a large question, so also is the question whether such an issue is given to the courts to decide, under the circumstances of this case. The Supreme Court has thus far not ruled on the latter issue in this context. Other federal courts have differed in their rationales. Scholars have probed "the political question" and have found it just as much an impenetrable thicket as have the courts. . . .

In our own search for a principled resolution of the question of the appropriateness of our deciding the merits, we seek first to understand the theory of the complaint, then to identify the appropriate legal standard, and finally to apply that standard to the issue raised.

The Massachusetts statute, pursuant to which plaintiffs bring this action, is based on the simple proposition that participation by the United States in hostilities other than an emergency is unconstitutional unless "initially authorized or subsequently ratified by a congressional declaration of war according to the constitutionally established procedures in Article 1, Section 8 [Clause 11th], of the Constitution. . . ." The complaint expands this theory by recognizing that constitutionality could be achieved by a "constitutional equivalent" for a declaration of war or by specific ratification of executive actions.

In any event, despite some language charging the executive with exercising the "war-making powers" of Congress, the thrust of the complaint is not that the executive has usurped a power—the power to declare war —given to Congress. There is no claim that the executive has made any declaration. The charge is, rather, that since hostilities have long since transcended a response to an emergency, both Congress and the executive have acted unconstitutionally in sustaining the hostilities without a

Congressional declaration of war. In effect the relief sought by the complaint is to order the executive to "get out or get a declaration from Congress."

Plaintiffs have understandably devoted considerable attention to the criteria of justiciability catalogued in Baker v. Carr. . . . They assert that there are judicially discoverable standards for determining whether hostilities in Vietnam require a declaration of war; that no nonjudicial policy determination is required—only a determination of authority; that no lack of respect to coordinate branches will be shown, but, rather, respect for the Constitution; that circumstances do not require unquestioning adherence to a political decision already made; and that, with a court acting as final arbiter, there is no risk of embarrassment from multifarious pronouncements.

We are not so sanguine that these factors can be so easily disposed of. Perhaps they impose no insuperable obstacle to principled decision in the case of long-continued, large-scale hostilities. But, once given the principle that a plaintiff may challenge the constitutionality of undeclared military operations, a court must be prepared to adjudicate whether actions are justified as emergency ones needing no declaration, or have gone beyond this bound. In the latter event the court must adjudicate whether Congress has expressly or impliedly ratified them. Workable standards, fact finding, the prospect of conflicting inferior court decisions, and other factors might well give pause to the most intrepid court.

We do not, however, rely on these factors. Partly we feel that to base abstinence on such pragmatic, if realistic, considerations is not desirable unless so clearly dictated by circumstances that it cannot be mistaken as abdication. Moreover, on a question so dominant in the minds of so many, we deem it important to rule as a matter of constitutional interpretation if at all possible. Finally, and of course most pertinently, we derive recent guidance from the Supreme Court's approach in Powell v. McCormack . . . (1969), giving dominant consideration to the first decisional factor listed in Baker v. Carr, *supra*. This is the inquiry "whether there is a 'textually demonstrable constitutional commitment of the issue to a coordinate political department' of government and what is the scope of such commitment. . . ."

[After a detailed discussion of the constitutional issues the Court concluded:]

. . . we are inclined to believe that the Constitution, in giving some essential powers to Congress and others to the executive committed the matter to both branches, whose joint concord precludes the judiciary from measuring a specific executive action against any specific clause in isolation. . . .

We need not go so far as to say that in a situation of shared powers, the executive acting and the Congress silent, no constitutional issue arises. . . .

All we hold here is that in a situation of prolonged but undeclared hostilities, where the executive continues to act not only in the absence of any conflicting Congressional claim of authority but with steady Congressional support, the Constitution has not been breached. The war in Vietnam is a product of the jointly supportive actions of the two branches to whom the congeries of the war powers have been committed. Because the branches are not in opposition, there is no necessity of determining boundaries. Should either branch be opposed to the continuance of hostilities, however, and present the issue in clear terms, a court might well take a different view. This question we do not face. Nor does the prospect that such a question might be posed indicate a different answer in the present case.

Affirmed.

O'CALLAHAN V. PARKER

395 U.S. 258, 89 S. Ct. 1683, 23 L. Ed. 2d 291 (1969)

An army sergeant stationed in Hawaii, on an evening pass and in civilian clothes, broke into a room in a Honolulu hotel and attempted to rape a young woman. He was apprehended by city police, who turned him over to the military; he was tried by court-martial and convicted. He sought federal habeas corpus from a district court, alleging that the court-martial had no jurisdiction to try him for a nonmilitary offense committed off post.

MR. JUSTICE DOUGLAS delivered the opinion of the Court. . . .

If the case does not arise "in the land or naval forces," then the accused gets *first*, the benefit of an indictment by a grand jury and *second*, a trial by jury before a civilian court as guaranteed by the Sixth Amendment. . . .

Those civil rights are the constitutional stakes in the present litigation. . . .

A court-martial is tried, not by a jury of the defendant's peers which must decide unanimously, but by a panel of officers empowered to act by a two-thirds vote. The presiding officer at a court-martial is not a judge whose objectivity and independence are protected by tenure and undiminishable salary and nurtured by the judicial tradition, but is a military law officer. Substantially different rules of evidence and procedure apply in military trials. Apart from those differences, the suggestion of the possibility of influence on the actions of the court-martial by the officer who convenes it, selects its members and the counsel on both sides, and who usually has direct command authority over its members is a pervasive one in military law, despite strenuous efforts to eliminate the danger.

A court-martial is not yet an independent instrument of justice but remains to a significant degree a specialized part of the overall mechanism by which military discipline is preserved.

That a system of specialized military courts, proceeding by practices different from those obtaining in the regular courts and in general less favorable to defendants, is necessary to an effective national defense establishment, few would deny. But the justification for such a system rests on the special needs of the military, and history teaches that expansion of military discipline beyond its proper domain carries with it a threat to liberty. . . .

While the Court of Military Appeals takes cognizance of some constitutional rights of the accused who are court-martialed, courts-martial as an institution are singularly inept in dealing with the nice subleties of constitutional law. Article 134 . . . punishes as a crime "all disorders and neglects to the prejudice of good order and discipline in the armed forces." Does this satisfy the standards of vagueness as developed by the civil courts? It is not enough to say that a court-martial may be reversed on appeal. One of the benefits of a civilian trial is that the trap of Article 134 may be avoided by a declaratory judgment proceeding or otherwise. * * * A civilian trial, in other words, is held in an atmosphere conducive to the protection of individual rights, while a military trial is marked by the age-old manifest destiny of retributive justice. . . .

We have concluded that the crime to be under military jurisdiction must be service connected, lest "cases arising in the land or naval forces, or in the Militia, when in actual service in time of War or public danger," as used in the Fifth Amendment, be expanded to deprive every member of the armed services of the benefits of an indictment by a grand jury and a trial by a jury of his peers. The power of Congress to make "Rules for the Government and Regulation of the land and naval Forces," Art. I, § 8, cl. 14, need not be sparingly read in order to preserve those two important constitutional guarantees. For it is assumed that an express grant of general power to Congress is to be exercised in harmony with express guarantees of the Bill of Rights. We were advised on oral argument that Art. 134 is construed by the military to give it power to try a member of the armed services for income tax evasion. This article has been called "a catch-all" that "incorporates almost every Federal penal statute into the Uniform Code." R. Everett, Military Justice in the Armed Forces of the United States 68–69 (1956). The catalogue of cases put within reach of the military is indeed long; and we see no way of saving to servicemen and servicewomen in any case the benefits of indictment and of trial by jury, if we conclude that this petitioner was properly tried by court-martial.

In the present case petitioner was properly absent from his military base when he committed the crimes with which he is charged. There was no connection—not even the remotest one—between his military duties and the crimes in question. The crimes were not committed on a military post or enclave; nor was the person whom he attacked performing any duties relating to the military. Moreover, Hawaii, the situs of the crime, is not an armed camp under military control, as are some of our far-flung outposts.

Finally, we deal with peacetime offenses, not with authority stemming from the war power. Civil courts were open. The offenses were committed within our territorial limits, not in the occupied zone of a foreign country. The offenses did not involve any question of the flouting of military authority, the security of a military post, or the integrity of military property.

We have accordingly decided that since petitioner's crimes were not service connected, he could not be tried by court-martial but rather was entitled to trial by the civilian courts.

Reversed.

MR. JUSTICE HARLAN, whom MR. JUSTICE STEWART and MR. JUSTICE WHITE join, dissenting.

I consider that the terms of the Constitution and the precedents in this Court point clearly to sustaining court-martial jurisdiction in this instance. The Court's largely one-sided discussion of the competing individual and governmental interests at stake, and its reliance upon what are at best wholly inconclusive historical data, fall far short of supporting the contrary conclusion which the majority has reached. In sum, I think that the Court has grasped for itself the making of a determination which the Constitution has placed in the hands of the Congress, and that in so doing the Court has thrown the law in this realm into a demoralizing state of uncertainty. I must dissent. . . .

PARKER V. LEVY

417 U.S. 733, 94 S. Ct. 2547, 41 L. Ed. 2d 439 (1974)

Captain Howard B. Levy, a physician assigned to Fort Jackson, South Carolina, made public statements to enlisted men declaring his opposition to the Vietnam War, encouraging black servicemen not to go there, and characterizing Special Forces personnel as killers of peasants and murderers of women and children. He was convicted by court-martial for violation of Articles 133 and 134 of the Uniform Code of Military Justice, which punish, respectively, "conduct unbecoming an officer and a gentleman" and "all disorders and neglect to the prejudice of good order and discipline in the armed forces." On petition for habeas corpus the Court of Appeals reversed, finding Articles 133 and 134 void for vagueness.

MR. JUSTICE REHNQUIST delivered the opinion of the Court. . . .

This Court has long recognized that the military is, by necessity, a specialized society separate from civilian society. We have also recognized that the military has, again by necessity, developed laws and traditions of its own during its long history. The differences between the military and civilian communities result from the fact that "it is the primary business of armies and navies to fight or be ready to fight wars should the occasion arise." Toth v. Quarles . . . (1955). . . .

Just as military society has been a society apart from civilian society, so "[m]ilitary law * * * is a jurisprudence which exists separate and apart from the law which governs in our federal judicial establishment." Burns v. Wilson. . . . And to maintain the discipline essential to perform its mission effectively, the military has developed what "may not unfitly be called the customary military law" or "general usage of the military service." Martin v. Mott . . . (1827). . . .

The differences noted by this settled line of authority, first between the military community and the civilian community, and second between military law and civilian law, continue in the present day under the Uniform Code of Military Justice. That Code cannot be equated to a civilian criminal code. It, and the various versions of the Articles of War which have preceded it, regulate aspects of the conduct of members of the military which in the civilian sphere are left unregulated. While a civilian criminal code carves out a relatively small segment of potential conduct and declares it criminal, the Uniform Code of Military Justice essays more varied regulation of a much larger segment of the activities of the more tightly knit military community. In civilian life there is no legal sanction —civil or criminal—for failure to behave as an officer and a gentleman; in the military world, Art. 133 imposes such a sanction on a commissioned officer. The Code likewise imposes other sanctions for conduct that in civilian life is not subject to criminal penalties; disrespect towards superior commissioned officers . . . cruelty towards, or oppression or maltreatment of subordinates, . . . negligent damaging, destruction, or wrongful disposition of military property of the United States; improper hazarding of a vessel . . . drunkenness on duty . . . and malingering. . . .

But the other side of the coin is that the penalties provided in the Code vary from death and substantial penal confinement at one extreme to forms of administrative discipline which are below the threshold of what would normally be considered a criminal sanction at the other. . . .

In short, the Uniform Code of Military Justice regulates a far broader range of the conduct of military personnel than a typical state criminal code regulates of the conduct of civilians; but at the same time the enforcement of that code in the area of minor offenses is often by sanctions which are more akin to administrative or civil sanctions than to civilian criminal ones.

The availability of these lesser sanctions is not surprising in view of the different relationship of the Government to members of the military. It is not only that of law giver to citizen, but also that of employer to employee. Indeed, unlike the civilian situation, the Government is often employer, landlord, provisioner and law giver rolled into one. That relationship also reflects the different purposes of the two communities. As we observed in In re Grimley, . . . the military "is an executive arm" whose "law is that of obedience." While members of the military community enjoy many of the same rights and bear many of the same burdens as do members of the civilian community, within the military community there is simply not the same autonomy as there is in the larger civilian community. The military establishment is subject to the control of the civilian commander-in-chief and the civilian departmental heads under him, and its function is to carry out the policies made by those civilian superiors.

With these very significant differences between military law and civilian law and between the military community and the civilian community in mind, we turn to appellee's challenges to the constitutionality of Arts. 133 and 134.

Appellee urges that both Arts. 133 and 134 ("the General Article") are "void for vagueness" under the Due Process Clause of the Fifth Amendment and overbroad in violation of the First Amendment. . . . Each of these Articles has been construed by the United States Court of Military Appeals or by other military authorities in such a manner as to at least partially narrow its otherwise broad scope. . . .

The effect of the constructions of Arts. 133 and 134 by the Court of Military Appeals and by other military authorities has been twofold: It has narrowed the very broad reach of the literal language of the Articles, and at the same time has supplied considerable specificity by way of examples of the conduct which they cover. It would be idle to pretend that there are not areas within the general confines of the Articles' language which have been left vague despite these narrowing constructions. But even though sizable areas of uncertainty as to the coverage of the Articles may remain after their official interpretation by authoritative military sources, further content may be supplied even in these areas by less formalized custom and usage. . . . And there also cannot be the slightest doubt under the military precedents that there is a substantial range of conduct to which both Articles clearly apply without vagueness or imprecision. It is within that range that appellee's conduct squarely falls. . . .

Since appellee could have had no reasonable doubt that his published statements urging Negro enlisted men not to go to Vietnam if ordered to do so was both "unbecoming an officer and a gentleman," and "to the prejudice of good order and discipline in the armed forces," in violation of the provisions of Art. 133 and Art. 134, respectively, his challenge to them as unconstitutionally vague under the Due Process Clause of the Fifth Amendment must fail.

We likewise reject appellee's contention that Arts. 133 and 134 are facially invalid because of their "overbreadth." . . .

While the members of the military are not excluded from the protection granted by the First Amendment, the different character of the military community and of the military mission require a different application of those protections. The fundamental necessity for obedience, and the consequent necessity for imposition of discipline, may render permissible within the military that which would be constitutionally impermissible outside it. Doctrines of First Amendment overbreadth asserted in support of challenges to imprecise language like that contained in Arts. 133 and 134 are not exempt from the operation of these principles. . . .

There is a wide range of the conduct of military personnel to which the Arts. 133 and 134 may be applied without infringement of the First Amendment. While there may lurk at the fringes of the Articles, even in the light of their narrowing construction by the United States Court of Military Appeals, some possibility that conduct which would be ultimately held to be protected by First Amendment could be included within their prohibition, we deem this insufficient to invalidate either of them at the behest of appellee. His conduct, that of a commissioned officer publicly urging enlisted personnel to refuse to obey orders which might send them into combat, was unprotected under the most expansive notions of the First Amendment. Articles 133 and 134 may constitutionally prohibit that conduct, and a sufficiently large number of similar or related types of conduct so as to preclude their invalidation for overbreadth. . . .

Reversed.

MR. JUSTICE MARSHALL took no part in the consideration or decision of this case.

MR. JUSTICE BLACKMUN, with whom THE CHIEF JUSTICE [BURGER] joins, concurring. . . .

MR. JUSTICE DOUGLAS, dissenting. . . .

MR. JUSTICE STEWART, with whom MR. JUSTICE DOUGLAS and MR. JUSTICE BRENNAN join, dissenting.

. . . The Court today, reversing an unanimous judgment of the Court of Appeals, upholds the constitutionality of these statutes. I find it hard to imagine criminal statutes more patently unconstitutional than these vague and uncertain General Articles, and I would, accordingly, affirm the judgment before us. . . .

It is plain that Arts. 133 and 134 are vague on their face; indeed, the opinion of the Court does not seriously contend to the contrary. Men of common intelligence—including judges of both military and civil courts—must necessarily speculate as to what such terms as "conduct unbecoming an officer and a gentleman" and "conduct of a nature to bring discredit upon the armed forces" really mean. In the past, this Court has held unconstitutional statutes penalizing "misconduct," conduct that was "annoying," "reprehensible," or "prejudicial to the best interests" of a city, and it is significant that military courts have resorted to several of these very terms in describing the sort of acts proscribed by Arts. 133 and 134.

If there be any doubt as to the absence of truly limiting constructions of the General Articles, it is swiftly dispelled by even the most cursory review of convictions under them in the military courts. Article 133 has been recently employed to punish such widely disparate conduct as dishonorable failure to repay debts, selling whiskey at an unconscionable price to an enlisted man, cheating at cards, and having an extramarital affair. Article 134 has been given an even wider sweep, having been applied to sexual acts with a chicken, window peeping in a trailer park, and cheating while calling bingo numbers. Convictions such as these leave little doubt that "[a]n infinite variety of other conduct, limited only by the scope of a commander's creativity or spleen, can be made the subject of court-martial under these articles." . . .

In short, the General Articles are in practice as well as theory "catchalls," designed to allow prosecutions for practically any conduct that may offend the sensibilities of a military commander. . . .

It may be that military necessity justifies the promulgation of substantive rules of law that are wholly foreign to civilian life, but I fail to perceive how any legitimate military goal is served by enshrouding these rules in language so vague and uncertain as to be incomprehensible to the servicemen who are to be governed by them. Indeed, I should suppose that vague laws, with their serious capacity for arbitrary and discriminatory enforcement, can in the end only hamper the military's objectives of high morale and *esprit de corps*. . . .

KOREMATSU V. UNITED STATES

323 U.S. 214, 65 S. Ct. 193, 89 L. Ed. 194 (1944)

In 1942, by presidential and congressional action based on military recommendations, all persons of Japanese ancestry on the West Coast were subjected to curfew and were later ordered to leave their places of residence for internment in detention camps. The Supreme Court upheld the curfew in *Hirabayashi* v. *United States* (1943). Fred Korematsu, an American citizen, was convicted of failing to report for transfer to a detention camp, and he appealed to the Supreme Court.

MR. JUSTICE BLACK delivered the opinion of the Court. . . .

It should be noted, to begin with, that all legal restrictions which curtail the civil rights of a single racial group are immediately suspect. That is not to say that all such restrictions are unconstitutional. . . . Pressing public necessity may sometimes justify the existence of such restrictions; racial antagonism never can. . . .

The 1942 Act was attacked in the Hirabayashi Case. . . . We upheld the curfew order as an exercise of the power of the government to take steps necessary to prevent espionage and sabotage in an area threatened by Japanese attack.

In the light of the principles we announced in the Hirabayashi Case, we are unable to conclude that it was beyond the war power of Congress and the Executive to exclude those of Japanese ancestry from the West Coast war area at the time they did. True, exclusion from the area in which one's home is located is a far greater deprivation than constant confinement to the home from 8 p.m. to 6 a.m. Nothing short of apprehension by the proper military authorities of the gravest imminent danger to the public safety can constitutionally justify either. But exclusion from a threatened area, no less than curfew, has a definite and close relationship to the prevention of espionage and sabotage. The military authorities, charged with the primary responsibility of defending our shores, concluded that curfew provided inadequate protection and ordered exclusion. They did so, as pointed out in our Hirabayashi opinion, in accordance with congressional authority to the military to say who should, and who should not, remain in the threatened areas. . . .

Here, as in the Hirabayashi Case . . . "we cannot reject as unfounded the judgment of the military authorities and of Congress that there were disloyal members of that population, whose number and strength could not be precisely and quickly ascertained. . . ."

. . . It was because we could not reject the finding of the military authorities that it was impossible to bring about an immediate segregation of the disloyal from the loyal that we sustained the validity of the curfew order as applying to the whole group. In the instant case, temporary exclusion of the entire group was rested by the military on the same ground. The judgment that exclusion of the whole group was for the same reason a military imperative answers the contention that the exclusion was in the nature of group punishment based on antagonism to those of Japanese origin. That there were members of the group who retained loyalties to Japan has been confirmed by investigations made subsequent to the exclusion. Approximately five thousand American citizens of Japanese ancestry refused to swear unqualified allegiance to the United States and to renounce allegiance to the Japanese Emperor, and several thousand evacuees requested repatriation to Japan. . . .

. . . [W]e are not unmindful of the hardships imposed by it upon a large group of American citizens. . . . But hardships are part of war, and war is an aggregation of hardships. Compulsory exclusion of large groups of citizens from their homes, except under circumstances of direst emergency and peril, is inconsistent with our basic governmental institutions. But when under conditions of modern warfare our shores are threatened by hostile forces, the power to protect must be commensurate with the threatened danger. . . .

We are thus being asked to pass at this time upon the whole subsequent detention program in both assembly and relocation centers, although the only issues framed at the trial related to petitioner's remaining in the prohibited area in violation of the exclusion order. Had petitioner here left the prohibited area and gone to an assembly center we cannot say either as a matter of fact or law, that his presence in that center would have resulted in his detention in a relocation center. Some who did report to the assembly center were not sent to relocation centers, but were released upon condition that they remain outside the prohibited zone until the military orders were modified or lifted. This illustrates that they pose different problems and may be governed by different princi-ples. The lawfulness of one does not necessarily determine the lawfulness of the others. . . .

Since the petitioner has not been convicted of failing to report or to remain in an assembly or relocation center, we cannot in this case deter-mine the validity of those separate provisions of the order. . . . It will be time enough to decide the serious constitutional issues which petitioner seeks to raise when an assembly or relocation order is applied or is certain to be applied to him, and we have its terms before us.

Some of the members of the Court are of the view that evacuation and detention in an Assembly Center were inseparable. . . . The power to exclude includes the power to do it by force if necessary. And any forcible measure must necessarily entail some degree of detention or restraint whatever method of removal is selected. But whichever view is taken, it results in holding that the order under which petitioner was convicted was valid.

It is said that we are dealing here with the case of imprisonment of a citizen in a concentration camp solely because of his ancestry. . . . Our task would be simple, our duty clear, were this a case involving the imprisonment of a loyal citizen in a concentration camp because of racial prejudice. Regardless of the true nature of the assembly and relocation centers—and we deem it unjustifiable to call them concentration camps with all the ugly connotations that term implies—we are dealing specifi-cally with nothing but an exclusion order. To cast this case into outlines of racial prejudice, without reference to the real military dangers which were presented, merely confuses the issue. Korematsu was not excluded from the Military Area because of hostility to him or his race. He *was* excluded because we are at war with the Japanese Empire, because the properly constituted military authorities feared an invasion of our West Coast and felt constrained to take proper security measures, because they decided that the military urgency of the situation demanded that all citizens of Japanese ancestry be segregated from the West Coast tempo-rarily, and finally, because Congress, reposing its confidence in this time of war in our military leaders— as inevitably it must—determined that they should have the power to do just this. There was evidence of disloy-alty on the part of some, the military authorities considered that the need for action was great, and time was short. We cannot—by availing our-selves of the calm perspective of hindsight—now say that at that time these actions were unjustified.

Affirmed.

MR. JUSTICE FRANKFURTER, concurring . . .

The provisions of the Constitution which confer on the Congress and the President powers to enable this country to wage war are as much part of the Constitution as provisions looking to a nation at peace. And we have had recent occasion to quote approvingly the statement of former Chief Justice Hughes that the war power of the Government is "the power to wage war successfully." Hirabayashi v. United States. . . . Therefore, the validity of action under the war power must be judged wholly in the context of war. That action is not to be stigmatized as lawless because like action in times of peace would be lawless. . . . The respective spheres of action of military authorities and of judges are of course very different. But within their sphere, military authorities are no more outside the bounds of obedience to the Constitution than are judges within theirs. . . . To recognize that military orders are "reasonably expedient military precautions" in time of war and yet to deny them constitutional legitimacy makes of the Constitution an instrument for dialetic subtleties not reasonably to be attributed to the hard-headed Framers, of whom a majority had had actual participation in war. If a military order such as that under review does not transcend the means appropriate for conducting war, such action by the military is as constitutional as would be any authorized action by the Interstate Commerce Commission within the limits of the constitutional power to regulate commerce . . . I find nothing in the Constitution which denies to Congress the power to enforce such a valid military order by making its violation an offense triable in the civil courts. . . . To find that the Constitution does not forbid the military measures now complained of does not carry with it approval of that which Congress and the Executive did. That is their business, not ours.

MR. JUSTICE ROBERTS:

I dissent, because I think the indisputable facts exhibit a clear violation of Constitutional rights. . . .

MR. JUSTICE MURPHY, dissenting:

This exclusion . . . goes over "the very brink of constitutional Power" and falls into the ugly abyss of racism.

In dealing with matters relating to the prosecution and progress of a war, we must accord great respect and consideration to the judgments of the military authorities who are on the scene and who have full knowledge of the military facts. . . . And their judgments ought not to be overruled lightly by those whose training and duties ill-equip them to deal intelligently with matters so vital to the physical security of the nation.

At the same time, however, it is essential that there be definite limits to military discretion. . . . Thus, like other claims conflicting with the asserted constitutional rights of the individual, the military claim must subject itself to the judicial process of having its reasonableness determined and its conflicts with other interests reconciled. . . .

The judicial test of whether the Government, on a plea of military necessity, can validly deprive an individual of any of his constitutional rights is whether the deprivation is reasonably related to a public danger that is so "immediate, imminent, and impending" as not to admit of delay and not to permit the intervention of ordinary constitutional processes to alleviate the danger. . . . Civilian Exclusion Order No. 34, banishing from a prescribed area of the Pacific Coast "all persons of Japanese ancestry, both alien and non-alien," clearly does not meet that test. Being an obvious racial discrimination, the order deprives all those within its scope of the equal protection of the laws as guaranteed by the Fifth

Amendment. It further deprives these individuals of their constitutional rights to live and work where they will, to establish a home where they choose and to move about freely. In excommunicating them without benefit of hearings, this order also deprives them of all their constitutional rights to procedural due process. Yet no reasonable relation to an "immediate, imminent, and impending" public danger is evident to support this racial restriction. . . .

It must be conceded that the military and naval situation in the spring of 1942 was such as to generate a very real fear of invasion of the Pacific Coast, accompanied by fears of sabotage and espionage in that area. The military command was therefore justified in adopting all reasonable means necessary to combat these dangers. . . . But the exclusion, either temporarily or permanently, of all persons with Japanese blood in their veins has no such reasonable relation. And that relation is lacking because the exclusion order necessarily must rely for its reasonableness upon the assumption that *all* persons of Japanese ancestry may have a dangerous tendency to commit sabotage and espionage and to aid our Japanese enemy in other ways. . . .

That this forced exclusion was the result in good measure of this erroneous assumption of racial guilt rather than bona fide military necessity is evidenced by the Commanding General's Final Report on the evacuation from the Pacific Coast area. In it he refers to all individuals of Japanese descent as "subversive," as belonging to "an enemy race" whose "racial strains are undiluted," and as constituting "over 112,000 potential enemies . . . at large today" along the Pacific Coast. In support of this blanket condemnation of all persons of Japanese descent, however, no reliable evidence is cited. . . .

Justification for the exclusion is sought, instead, mainly upon questionable racial and sociological grounds not ordinarily within the realm of expert military judgment. Individuals of Japanese ancestry are condemned because they are said to be "a large, unassimilated, tightly knit racial group, bound to an enemy nation by strong ties of race, culture, custom and religion." They are claimed to be given to "emperor worshipping ceremonies" and to "dual citizenship." Japanese language schools and allegedly pro-Japanese organizations are cited as evidence of possible group disloyalty, together with facts as to certain persons being educated and residing at length in Japan. It is intimated that many of these individuals deliberately resided "adjacent to strategic points," thus enabling them "to carry into execution a tremendous program of sabotage on a mass scale should any considerable number of them have been inclined to do so." The need for protective custody is also asserted. The report refers without identity to "numerous incidents of violence" as well as to other admittedly unverified or cumulative incidents. From this, plus certain other events not shown to have been connected with the Japanese Americans, it is concluded that the "situation was fraught with danger to the Japanese population itself" and that the general public "was ready to take matters into its own hands." Finally, it is intimated, though not directly charged or proved, that persons of Japanese ancestry were responsible for three minor isolated shellings and bombings of the Pacific Coast area, as well as for unidentified radio transmissions and night signalling.

The main reasons appear . . . to be largely an accumulation of much of the misinformation, half-truths and insinuations that for years have been directed against Japanese Americans by people with racial and economic prejudices—the same people who have been among the foremost advocates of the evacuation. A military judgment based upon such racial and sociological considerations is not entitled to the great weight ordinarily given the judgments based upon strictly military considerations. Especially is this so when every charge relative to race, religion, culture, geographical location, and legal and economic status has been substantially discredited by independent studies made by experts in these matters. . . .

I dissent, therefore, from this legalization of racism. Racial discrimination in any form and in any degree has no justifiable part whatever in our democratic way of life. It is unattractive in any setting but it is utterly revolting among a free people who have embraced the principles set forth in the Constitution of the United States. . . .

MR. JUSTICE JACKSON, dissenting. . . .

A citizen's presence in the locality . . . was made a crime only if his parents were of Japanese birth. Had Korematsu been one of four—the others being, say, a German alien enemy, an Italian alien enemy, and a citizen of American-born ancestors, convicted of treason but out on parole—only Korematsu's presence would have violated the order. . . .

Now, if any fundamental assumption underlies our system, it is that guilt is personal and not inheritable. . . . But here is an attempt to make an otherwise innocent act a crime merely because this prisoner is the son of parents as to whom he had no choice, and belongs to a race from which there is no way to resign. . . .

But the "law" which this prisoner is convicted of disregarding is not found in an act of Congress, but in a military order. Neither the Act of Congress nor the Executive Order of the President, nor both together, would afford a basis for this conviction. It rests on the orders of General DeWitt. And it is said that if the military commander had reasonable military grounds for promulgating the orders, they are constitutional and become law, and the Court is required to enforce them. There are several reasons why I cannot subscribe to this doctrine.

It would be impracticable and dangerous idealism to expect or insist that each specific military command in an area of probable operations will conform to conventional tests of constitutionality. . . .

. . . The armed services must protect a society, not merely its Constitution. The very essence of the military job is to marshall physical force, to remove every obstacle to its effectiveness, to give it every strategic advantage. Defense measures will not, and often should not, be held within the limits that bind civil authority in peace. . . . But a commander in temporarily focusing the life of a community on defense is carrying out a military program; he is not making law in the sense the courts know the term. He issues orders, and they may have a certain authority as military commands, although they may be very bad as constitutional law.

But if we cannot confine military expedients by the Constitution, neither would I distort the Constitution to approve all that the military may deem expedient. . . . I cannot say, from any evidence before me, that the orders of General DeWitt were not reasonably expedient military precautions, nor could I say that they were. But even if they were permissible military procedures, I deny that it follows that they are constitutional. If, as the Court holds, it does follow, then we may as well say that any military order will be constitutional and have done with it. . . .

In the very nature of things military decisions are not susceptible of intelligent judicial appraisal. . . . Hence courts can never have any real alternative to accepting the mere declaration of the authority that issued the order that it was reasonably necessary from a military viewpoint.

Much is said of the danger to liberty from the Army program. . . . But a judicial construction of the due process clause that will sustain this order is a far more subtle blow to liberty than the promulgation of the order itself. A military order, however unconstitutional, is not apt to last longer than the military emergency. Even during that period a succeeding commander may revoke it all. But once a judicial opinion rationalizes such an order to show that it conforms to the Constitution or rather rationalizes the Constitution to show that the Constitution sanctions such an order, the Court for all time has validated the principle of racial discrimination in criminal procedure and of transplanting American citizens. The principle then lies about like a loaded weapon ready for the hand of any authority that can bring forward a plausible claim of an urgent need. . . .

I should hold that a civil court cannot be made to enforce an order which violates constitutional limitations even if it is a reasonable exercise of military authority. . . . I do not suggest that the courts should have attempted to interfere with the Army in carrying out its task. But I do not think they may be asked to execute a military expedient that has no place in law under the Constitution. I would reverse the judgment and discharge the prisoner.

Chapter Ten

MEMBERSHIP OF CONGRESS

INTRODUCTION

There was little doubt in the minds of the delegates to the Constitutional Convention that if a national government was to be established, there must be a two-house legislature. This was the practice in England and in almost all of the states. The New Jersey plan for revising the Articles retained a Congress of one house, but after it was defeated there was no further consideration of a unicameral legislature. In **Nos. 62** and **63** of *The Federalist,* Madison made an eloquent case for a second legislative body, contending that there was no historical example of a "long-lived republic" that did not have a senate.

The Senate

The two-house legislature of course made possible the compromise between large and small states without which probably no constitution could have been adopted. The Virginia plan had proposed that representation in the Senate, as well as in the House of Representatives, should be proportional to population, but the small states were implacably opposed. Early in the Convention Paterson of New Jersey warned that his state would never confederate on the Virginia principle, while Wilson of

Pennsylvania replied that his state would not confederate on the basis of the New Jersey plan. Ultimately equal representation in the Senate was adopted by a 5 to 4 vote. Madison, who had vigorously fought equal representation, in *The Federalist* **No. 62** undertook to find the merits inherent in the compromise.

Article I, section 3, provides for two senators from each state; with the admission of new states the size of the Senate has grown from its original 26 to the present 100. Article V guarantees that "no state, without its consent, shall be deprived of its equal suffrage in the Senate."

The Constitution originally provided that senators would be chosen from each state by its legislature. This arrangement gave effect to the idea that the Senate represented state *governments* rather than the *people* of the state. The movement for direct election of senators was motivated partly by the scandals and deadlocks which characterized legislative elections and partly by the development of a more progressive tone in the country. Eventually the Seventeenth Amendment was adopted, becoming effective in 1913, and providing for the election of senators by direct popular vote.

The House of Representatives

Representation in the House is based on population. For this purpose Article I provided for an "enumeration," or census, to be made within three years after the first meeting of Congress and every ten years thereafter. The apportionment of representatives among the states depends not only upon the decennial census, but also upon subsequent adoption of an apportionment plan that will give effect to the changes in state population patterns since the previous census. Because no state ever wished to see its representation reduced, the total number of seats in the House was increased until it reached the figure of 435 after the 1910 census.

Following the 1920 census Congress for the first time found itself unable to agree on an apportionment plan, because the alternatives were either to reduce the representation of eleven states or again increase the size of the House. Finally, in 1929 a permanent reapportionment statute was adopted which requires the Census Bureau to prepare tables showing allocation of representatives to each state under two alternative methods of handling population fractions left over after the state populations have been divided by the country-wide ratio. A reapportionment then goes into effect automatically on the basis of the plan used in the previous apportionment unless Congress itself enacts a different one.

Fixing the number of representatives from each state is only the first part of the election process. It is still necessary to divide the states into election districts (except for states with only one representative). The responsibility for districting is in general left to the states, under the provisions of Article I, section 4, that "the times, places, and manner of holding elections for Senators and Representatives shall be prescribed in each state by the legislature thereof."

However, the section goes on to provide that "the Congress may at any time by law make or alter such regulations. . . ." Beginning in 1842 Congress did make some effort to prohibit the practice of *gerrymandering*,[1] but the failure of Congress to renew any such restrictions in 1929 was construed by the Supreme Court in *Wood* v. *Broom* (1932) as repealing all the previous laws, leaving the states completely free in drawing district lines.

Following the census of 1910, which showed a shift of population to the cities, rurally-dominated legislatures in a number of states refused to redistrict at all, with the result that massive disparities in population among districts developed. In Illinois by 1940 district populations ranged from 112,000 to 914,000. As already noted in Chapter Five, the Supreme Court in *Colegrove* v. *Green* (1946) refused to take any remedial action on the ground that congressional districting was a "political question," and any remedies were a congressional responsibility. But, as we also know, in 1962 the decision in *Baker* v. *Carr* reversed *Colegrove* and opened the way for court tests of the constitutionality of unequal population districting.

In the first such case to reach the Supreme Court, *Gray* v. *Sanders* (1963), Justice Douglas announced the "one person, one vote" rule as the Court struck down the discriminatory Georgia county-unit system. The test of congressional districting came the following year in **Wesberry v. Sanders** (1964), where Justice Black derived the principle of equality of population in congressional districts from certain of Madison's statements at the Constitutional Convention, and more specifically from the language of Article I about choosing representatives "by the people of the several states."

Following *Wesberry* the process of congressional redistricting by the state legislatures went forward with remarkable speed. Initially the Court was rather rigid in enforcing the equal population rule. In *Kirkpatrick* v. *Preisler* (1969) and in *Wells* v. *Rockefeller* (1969), where the population variables were minimal, the apportionment plans were still invalidated because of failure to show that a "good-faith effort to achieve precise mathematical equality" had been made. Even many friends of the one-person, one-vote rule believed that this was an unrealistic standard, and the Court subsequently modified its position, although the principal

[1]Gerrymandering is the practice whereby the majority party in the state legislature draws district lines that will concentrate the strength of the opposition party into as few districts as possible and spread the strength of its own party over as many districts as possible. The usual result of gerrymandering is a number of odd-shaped districts.

cases involved state and local legislatures rather than congressional districts.

Equality of population is no guarantee against gerrymandering. In fact, to the degree that achievement of population equality requires disregarding local government boundaries, it makes gerrymandering easier. However, the Supreme Court has been reluctant to undertake the task of controlling gerrymanders unless there is an obvious racial motive involved. Even in *Wright* v. *Rockefeller* (1964), where there was a strong prima facie case that congressional district lines had been drawn with racial considerations in mind, the Court held that the evidence was still not compelling. As a matter of fact, the Supreme Court held in *United Jewish Organizations* v. *Carey* (1977) that states obligated by the Voting Rights Act of 1965 to increase the voting strength of nonwhites may properly use racial criteria in drawing state legislative districts. Here a reapportionment plan in New York City had been drawn with the purpose of spreading nonwhite strength through several legislative districts, but it split in half a tightly knit enclave of 30,000 ultra-orthodox Hasidic Jews. Their contention that using race to define electoral districts was illegal was denied by the Court, although Chief Justice Burger, dissenting, claimed this was a "racial gerrymander."

Members of Congress

Each house of Congress is authorized by Article I, section 5, to "be the judge of the elections, returns and qualifications of its own members." The "qualifications," it has been established by **Powell v. McCormack** (1969), are only those stated in the Constitution, namely, age, citizenship, and residence. Congressmen are not subject to impeachment, but each house may expel its members by a two-thirds vote, punish them for "disorderly behavior," or vote censure against them. Senator Joseph McCarthy was censured in 1954 for conduct "contrary to Senatorial traditions."

Article I, section 6, provides that "for any speech or debate in either house, [members of Congress] shall not be questioned in any other place." The purpose of such legislative immunity is to protect legislators from intimidation by the executive or to prevent holding them accountable before a possibly hostile judiciary. While legislators may abuse their freedom, the constitutional theory is that the public interest will be best served if they are free to criticize, investigate, or take unpopular positions.

The "speech or debate" clause means that congressmen cannot be sued for libel or slander or in any other way held legally accountable for statements made in their official capacity except by the House or Senate.

Not only words spoken on the floor of Congress but also written reports, resolutions offered, the act of voting, and all things "generally done in a session of the House by one of its members in relation to the business before it" are covered. However, *Gravel* v. *United States* (1972) interpreted legislative "business" rather strictly.

The Supreme Court has been somewhat uncertain about the effect of the speech or debate clause upon criminal prosecutions of congressmen. *United States* v. *Johnson* (1966) ruled that the clause prevented any judicial inquiry into the motivation of a congressman who had been charged with accepting money from private interests for giving a speech in the House. But *United States* v. *Brewster* (1972) held that acceptance of a bribe to influence a vote was not a legislative act and could be punished.

FEDERALIST NOS. 62, 63

James Madison

ON THE NECESSITY OF A SENATE

FIRST. It is a misfortune incident to republican government, though in a less degree than to other governments, that those who administer it may forget their obligations to their constituents and prove unfaithful to their important trust. In this point of view a senate, as a second branch of the legislative assembly distinct from and dividing the power with a first, must be in all cases a salutary check on the government. It doubles the security to the people by requiring the concurrence of two distinct bodies in schemes of usurpation or perfidy, where the ambition or corruption of one would otherwise be sufficient. This is a precaution founded on such clear principles, and now so well understood in the United States, that it would be more than superfluous to enlarge on it. I will barely remark that as the improbability of sinister combinations will be in proportion to the dissimilarity in the genius of the two bodies, it must be politic to distinguish them from each other by every circumstance which will consist with a due harmony in all proper measures, and with the genuine principles of republican government.

SECOND. The necessity of a senate is not less indicated by the propensity of all single and numerous assemblies to yield to the impulse of sudden and violent passions, and to be seduced by factious leaders to intemperate and pernicious resolutions. Examples on this subject might be cited without number; and from proceedings within the United States, as well as from the history of other nations. But a position that will not be contradicted need not be proved. All that need be remarked is that a body which is to correct this infirmity ought itself to be free from it, and consequently ought to be less numerous. It ought, moreover, to possess great firmness, and consequently ought to hold its authority by a tenure of considerable duration.

THIRD. Another defect to be supplied by a senate lies in a want of due acquaintance with the objects and principles of legislation. It is not possible that an assembly of men called for the most part from pursuits of a private nature continued in appointment for a short time and led by no permanent motive to devote the intervals of public occupation to a study of the laws, the affairs, and the comprehensive interests of their country, should, if left wholly to themselves, escape a variety of important errors in the exercise of their legislative trust. . . .

FOURTH. The mutability in the public councils arising from a rapid succession of new members, however qualified they may be, points out, in the strongest manner, the necessity of some stable institution in the government. Every new election in the States is found to change one half of the representatives. From this change of men must proceed a change of opinions; and from a change of opinions, a change of measures. But a continual change even of good measures is inconsistent with every rule of prudence and every prospect of success. . . .

In another point of view, great injury results from an unstable government. The want of confidence in the public councils damps every useful undertaking, the success and profit of which may depend on a continuance of existing arrangements. What prudent merchant will hazard his fortunes in any new branch of commerce when he knows not but that his plans may be rendered unlawful before they can be executed? What farmer or manufacturer will lay himself out for the encouragement given to any particular cultivation or establishment, when he can have no assurance that his preparatory labors and advances will not render him a victim to an inconstant government? In a word, no great improvement or laudable enterprise can go forward which requires the auspices of a steady system of national policy. . . .

A *fifth* desideratum, illustrating the utility of a senate, is the want of a due sense of national character. Without a select and stable member of the government, the esteem of foreign powers will not only be forfeited by an unenlightened and variable policy, proceeding from the causes already mentioned, but the national councils will not possess that sensibility to the opinion of the world which is perhaps not less necessary in order to merit than it is to obtain its respect and confidence. . . .

Yet however requisite a sense of national character may be, it is evident that it can never be sufficiently possessed by a numerous and changeable body. It can only be found in a number so small that a sensible degree of the praise and blame of public measures may be the portion of each individual; or in an assembly so durably invested with public trust that the pride and consequence of its members may be sensibly incorporated with the reputation and prosperity of the community. . . .

Thus far I have considered the circumstances which point out the necessity of a well-constructed Senate only as they relate to the representatives of the people. To a people as little blinded by prejudice or corrupted by flattery as those whom I address, I shall not scruple to add that such an institution may be sometimes necessary as a defense to the people against their own temporary errors and delusions. As the cool and deliberate sense of the community ought, in all governments, and actually will, in all free governments, ultimately prevail over the views of its rulers; so there are particular moments in public affairs when the people, stimulated by some irregular passion, or some illicit advantage, or misled by the artful misrepresentations of interested men, may call for measures which they themselves will afterwards be the most ready to lament and condemn. In these critical moments, how salutary will be the interference of some temperate and respectable body of citizens, in order to check the misguided career and to suspend the blow meditated by the people against themselves, until reason, justice, and truth can regain their authority over the public mind? What bitter anguish would not the people of Athens have often escaped if their government had contained so provident a safeguard against the tyranny of their own passions? Popular liberty might then have escaped the indelible reproach of decreeing to the same citizens the hemlock on one day and statues on the next. . . .

It adds no small weight to all these considerations to recollect that history informs us of no long-lived republic which had not a senate. . . .

In answer to all these arguments, suggested by reason, illustrated by examples, and enforced by our own experience, the jealous adversary of the Constitution will probably content himself with repeating that a senate appointed not immediately by the people, and for the term of six years, must gradually acquire a dangerous pre-eminence in the government and finally transform it into a tyrannical aristocracy.

To this general answer the general reply ought to be sufficient, that liberty may be endangered by the abuses of liberty as well as by the abuses of power; that there are numerous instances of the former, as well as of the latter, and that the former, rather than the latter, is apparently most to be apprehended by the United States. . . .

FEDERALIST NO. 62

James Madison

ON EQUALITY OF STATE REPRESENTATION IN THE SENATE

III. The equality of representation in the Senate is another point which, being evidently the result of compromise between the opposite pretensions of the large and the small States, does not call for much discussion. If indeed it be right that among a people thoroughly incorporated into one nation every district ought to have a *proportional* share in the government and that among independent and sovereign States, bound together by a simple league, the parties, however unequal in size, ought to have an *equal* share in the common councils, it does not appear to be without some reason that in a compound republic, partaking both of the national and federal character, the government ought to be founded on a mixture of the principles of proportional and equal representation. But it is superfluous to try, by the standard of theory, a part of the Constitution which is allowed on all hands to be the result, not of theory, but "of a spirit of amity, and that mutual deference and concession which the peculiarity of our political situation rendered indispensable." A common government, with powers equal to its objects, is called for by the voice, and still more loudly by the political situation, of America. A government founded on principles more consonant to the wishes of the larger States is not likely to be obtained from the smaller States. The only option, then, for the former lies between the proposed government and a government still more objectionable. Under this alternative, the advice of prudence must be to embrace the lesser evil; and instead of indulging a fruitless anticipation of the possible mischiefs which may ensue, to contemplate rather the advantageous consequences which may qualify the sacrifice.

In this spirit it may be remarked that the equal vote allowed to each State is at once a constitutional recognition of the portion of sovereignty remaining in the individual States and an instrument for preserving that residuary sovereignty. So far the equality ought to be no less acceptable to the large than to the small States; since they are not less solicitous to guard, by every possible expedient, against an improper consolidation of the States into one simple republic.

Another advantage accruing from this ingredient in the constitution of the Senate is the additional impediment it must prove against improper acts of legislation. No law or resolution can now be passed without the concurrence, first, of a majority of the people, and then of a majority of the States. It must be acknowledged that this complicated check on legislation may in some instances be injurious as well as beneficial; and that the peculiar defense which it involves in favor of the smaller States would be more rational if any interests common to them and distinct from those of the other States would otherwise be exposed to peculiar danger. But as the larger States will always be able, by their power over the supplies, to defeat unreasonable exertions of this prerogative of the lesser States, and as the facility and excess of lawmaking seem to be the diseases to which our governments are most liable, it is not impossible that this part of the Constitution may be more convenient in practice than it appears to many in contemplation. . . .

WESBERRY V. SANDERS

376 U.S. 1, 84 S. Ct. 526, 11 L. Ed. 2d 481 (1964)

On the basis of the 1960 census, the population in Georgia congressional districts varied from 824,000 to 272,000. A three-judge district court found that the apportionment was grossly discriminatory, but by a two to one vote held that *Colegrove* v. *Green* required that the suit be dismissed "for want of equity."

MR. JUSTICE BLACK delivered the opinion of the Court. . . .
[After holding that the lower court had erred in following *Colegrove* v. *Green* rather than *Baker* v. *Carr,* the opinion continued:]
This brings us to the merits. We agree with the District Court that the 1931 Georgia apportionment grossly discriminates against voters in the Fifth Congressional District. A single Congressman represents from two to three times as many Fifth District voters as are represented by each of the Congressmen from the other Georgia congressional districts. The apportionment statute thus contracts the value of some votes and expands that of others. If the Federal Constitution intends that when qualified voters elect members of Congress each vote be given as much weight as any other vote, then this statute cannot stand.
We hold that, construed in its historical context, the command of Art. I, § 2, that Representatives be chosen "by the People of the several States" means that as nearly as is practicable one man's vote in a congressional election is to be worth as much as another's. . . .
To say that a vote is worth more in one district than in another would not only run counter to our fundamental ideas of democratic government, it would cast aside the principle of a House of Representatives elected "by the People," a principle tenaciously fought for and established at the Constitutional Convention. The history of the Constitution, particularly that part of it relating to the adoption of Art. I, § 2, reveals that those who framed the Constitution meant that, no matter what the mechanics of an election, whether statewide or by districts, it was population which was to be the basis of the House of Representatives. . . .
The question of how the legislature should be constituted precipitated the most bitter controversy of the Convention. . . .
Some delegates opposed election by the people. The sharpest objection arose out of the fear on the part of small States like Delaware that if population were to be the only basis of representation the populous States like Virginia would elect a large enough number of representatives to wield overwhelming power in the National Government. . . .
The delegates who wanted every man's vote to count alike were sharp in their criticism of giving each State, regardless of population, the same voice in the National Legislature. Madison entreated the Convention "to renounce a principle wch. was confessedly unjust," and Rufus King of

Massachusetts "was prepared for every event, rather than sit down under a Govt. founded in a vicious principle of representation and which must be as shortlived as it would be unjust."

The dispute came near ending the Convention without a Constitution. Both sides seemed for a time to be hopelessly obstinate. Some delegations threatened to withdraw from the Convention if they did not get their way. . . .

The deadlock was finally broken when a majority of the States agreed to what has been called the Great Compromise, based on a proposal which had been repeatedly advanced by Roger Sherman and other delegates from Connecticut. It provided on the one hand that each State, including little Delaware and Rhode Island, was to have two Senators. As a further guarantee that these Senators would be considered state emissaries, they were to be elected by the state legislatures, Art. I, § 3, and it was specially provided in Article V that no State should ever be deprived of its equal representation in the Senate. The other side of the compromise was that, as provided in Art. I, § 2, members of the House of Representatives should be chosen "by the People of the several States" and should be "apportioned among the several States * * * according to their respective Numbers." . . .

The debates at the Convention make at least one fact abundantly clear: that when the delegates agreed that the House should represent "people" they intended that in allocating Congressmen the number assigned to each State should be determined solely by the number of the State's inhabitants. The Constitution embodied Edmund Randolph's proposal for a periodic census to ensure "fair representation of the people," an idea endorsed by Mason as assuring that "numbers of inhabitants" should always by the measure of representation in the House of Representatives. The Convention also overwhelmingly agreed to a resolution offered by Randolph to base future apportionment squarely on numbers and to delete any reference to wealth. And the delegates defeated a motion made by Elbridge Gerry to limit the number of Representatives from newer Western States so that it would never exceed the number from the original States.

It would defeat the principle solemnly embodied in the Great Compromise—equal representation in the House for equal numbers of people—for us to hold that, within the States, legislatures may draw the lines of congressional districts in such a way as to give some voters a greater voice in choosing a Congressman than others. The House of Representatives, the Convention agreed, was to represent the people as individuals, and on a basis of complete equality for each voter. The delegates were quite aware of what Madison called the "vicious representation" in Great Britain whereby "rotten boroughs" with few inhabitants were represented in Parliament on or almost on a par with cities of greater population. . . .

It is in the light of such history that we must construe Art. I, § 2, of the Constitution, which, carrying out the ideas of Madison and those of like views, provides that Representatives shall be chosen "by the People of the several States" and shall be "apportioned among the several States . . . according to their respective Numbers." . . .

While it may not be possible to draw congressional districts with mathematical precision, that is no excuse for ignoring our Constitution's plain objective of making equal representation for equal numbers of people the fundamental goal for the House of Representatives. That is the high standard of justice and common sense which the Founders set for us.

Reversed and remanded.

MR. JUSTICE HARLAN, dissenting. . . .

I had not expected to witness the day when the Supreme Court of the United States would render a decision which casts grave doubt on the constitutionality of the composition of the House of Representatives. It is not an exaggeration to say that such is the effect of today's decision. The Court's holding that the Constitution requires States to select Representatives either by elections at large or by elections in districts composed "as hearly as is practicable" of equal population places in jeopardy the seats of almost all the members of the present House of Representatives.

In the last congressional election, in 1962, Representatives from 42 States were elected from congressional districts. In all but five of those States, the difference between the populations of the largest and smallest districts exceeded 100,000 persons. A difference of this magnitude in the size of districts the average population of which in each State is less than 500,000 is presumably not equality among districts "as nearly as is practicable," although the Court does not reveal its definition of that phrase. Thus, today's decision impugns the validity of the election of 398 Representatives from 37 States, leaving a "constitutional" House of 37 members now sitting.

Only a demonstration which could not be avoided would justify this Court in rendering a decision the effect of which, inescapably as I see it, is to declare constitutionally defective the very composition of a coordinate branch of the Federal Government. The Court's opinion not only fails to make such a demonstration, it is unsound logically on its face and demonstrably unsound historically. . . .

POWELL V. MC CORMACK

395 U.S. 486, 89 S. Ct. 1944, 23 L. Ed. 2d 491 (1969)

Adam Clayton Powell, black congressman from New York and then the most influential member of his race in a public position, was reelected to Congress in November, 1966. There was a judgment of criminal contempt outstanding against him, and his conduct as chairman of the House Education and Labor Committee had been bizarre and irregular. When the House organized in January, 1967, Powell was not permitted to take his seat. After an inquiry the House in March, by a vote of 307 to 116, excluded Powell and declared his seat vacant.

Powell, charging that he had been unlawfully excluded because the only qualifications for membership are those listed in Article I, section 2, brought suit against the Speaker of the House and certain of its employees for payment of his salary. Two federal courts rejected his suit. In the meantime he was twice reelected, once in the special election to fill the vacancy, and again in the regular election in November, 1968. He was then seated but fined $25,000. The principal issue before the Supreme Court, which rejected the contention that the case was moot, was whether the judiciary had any constitutional right to review decisions by Congress on the qualifications of its members. In reading the opinion, it is important to understand that either house of Congress can expel a member by a two-thirds vote. The vote against Powell was by more than a two-thirds majority, but the vote was to exclude, not to expel.

MR. CHIEF JUSTICE WARREN delivered the opinion of the Court. . . .

III. SPEECH OR DEBATE CLAUSE

Respondents [McCormack et al.] assert that the Speech or Debate Clause of the Constitution, Art. I, sec. 6, is an absolute bar to petitioners' [Powell et al.] action. This Court has on four prior occasions—Dombrowski v. Eastland (1967); United States v. Johnson (1966); Tenney v. Brandhove (1951); and Kilbourn v. Thompson (1881)—been called upon to determine if allegedly unconstitutional action taken by legislators or legislative employees is insulated from judicial review by the Speech or Debate Clause. . . .

The Speech or Debate Clause, adopted by the Constitutional Convention without debate or opposition, finds its roots in the conflict between Parliament and the Crown culminating in the Glorious Revolution of 1688 and the English Bill of Rights of 1689. Drawing upon this history, we concluded in United States v. Johnson that the purpose of this clause was "to prevent intimidation [of legislators] by the executive and accountability before a possibly hostile judiciary." Although the clause sprung from a fear of seditious libel actions instituted by the Crown to punish unfavorable speeches made in Parliament, we have held that it would be a "narrow view" to confine the protection of the Speech or Debate Clause to words spoken in debate. Committee reports, resolutions, and the act of voting are equally covered, as are "things generally done in a session of the House by one of its members in relation to the business before it." Kilbourn v. Thompson. Furthermore, the clause provides not only a defense on the merits but also protects a legislator from the burden of defending himself. Dombrowski v. Eastland. . . .

Our cases make it clear that the legislative immunity created by the Speech or Debate Clause performs an important function in representative government. It insures that legislators are free to represent the interests of their constituents without fear that they will be later called to task in the courts for that representation. . . .

Legislative immunity does not, of course, bar all judicial review of legislative acts. That issue was settled by implication as early as 1803, see

Marbury v. Madison, and expressly in Kilbourn v. Thompson, the first of this Court's cases interpreting the reach of the Speech or Debate Clause. Challenged in Kilbourn was the constitutionality of a House resolution ordering the arrest and imprisonment of a recalcitrant witness who had refused to respond to a subpoena issued by a House investigating committee. While holding that the Speech or Debate Clause barred Kilbourn's action for false imprisonment brought against several members of the House, the Court nevertheless reached the merits of Kilbourn's attack and decided that, since the House had no power to punish for contempt, Kilbourn's imprisonment pursuant to the resolution was unconstitutional. It therefore allowed Kilbourn to bring his false imprisonment action against Thompson, the House's Sergeant-at-Arms, who had executed the warrant for Kilbourn's arrest.

The Court first articulated in Kilbourn and followed in Dombrowski v. Eastland the doctrine that, although an action against a Congressman may be barred by the Speech or Debate Clause, legislative employees who participated in the unconstitutional activity are responsible for their acts. . . . In Kilbourn and Dombrowski we thus dismissed the action against members of Congress but did not regard the Speech or Debate Clause as a bar to reviewing the merits of the challenged congressional action since congressional employees were also sued. Similarly, this action may be dismissed against the Congressmen since petitioners are entitled to maintain their action against House employees and to judicial review of the propriety of the decision to exclude Petitioner Powell.

IV. EXCLUSION OR EXPULSION

The resolution excluding Petitioner Powell was adopted by a vote in excess of two-thirds of the 434 Members of Congress—307 to 116. . . . Article I, § 5, grants the House authority to expel a member "with the Concurrence of two thirds." Respondents assert that the House may expel a member for any reason whatsoever and that, since a two-thirds vote was obtained, the procedure by which Powell was denied his seat in the 90th Congress should be regarded as an expulsion not an exclusion. Cautioning us not to exalt form over substance, respondents quote from the concurring opinion of Judge McGowan in the court below:

> "Appellant Powell's cause of action for a judicially compelled seating thus boils down, in my view, to the narrow issue of whether a member found by his colleagues . . . to have engaged in official misconduct must, because of the accidents of timing, be formally admitted before he can be either investigated or expelled. The sponsor of the motion to exclude stated on the floor that he was proceeding on the theory that the power to expel included the power to exclude, provided a ⅔ vote was forthcoming. It was. Therefore, success for Mr. Powell on the merits would mean that the District Court must admonish the House that it is form, not substance, that should govern in great affairs, and accordingly command the House members to act out a charade."

Although respondents repeatedly urge this Court not to speculate as to the reasons for Powell's exclusion, their attempt to equate exclusion with expulsion would require a similar speculation that the House would have voted to expel Powell had it been faced with that question. Powell had not been seated at the time House Resolution 278 was debated and passed. After a motion to bring the Select Committee's proposed resolution to an immediate vote had been defeated, an amendment was offered which mandated Powell's exclusion. Mr. Celler, chairman of the Select Committee, then posed a parliamentary inquiry to determine whether a two-thirds vote was necessary to pass the resolution if so amended "in the sense that it might amount to an expulsion." . . . The Speaker replied that "action by a majority vote would be in accordance with the rules." . . . Had the amendment been regarded as an attempt to expel Powell, a two-thirds vote would have been constitutionally required. The Speaker ruled that the House was voting to exclude Powell, and we will not speculate what the result might have been if Powell had been seated and expulsion proceedings subsequently instituted. . . .

Had the intent of the Framers emerged from these materials with less clarity, we would nevertheless have been compelled to resolve any ambiguity in favor of a narrow construction of the scope of Congress' power to exclude members-elect. A fundamental principle of our representative democracy is, in Hamilton's words, "that the people should choose whom they please to govern them." . . . As Madison pointed out at the Convention, this principle is undermined as much by limiting whom the people can select as by limiting the franchise itself. In apparent agreement with this basic philosophy, the Convention adopted his suggestion limiting the power to expel. To allow essentially that same power to be exercised under the guise of judging qualifications, would be to ignore Madison's warning . . . against "vesting an improper & dangerous power in the Legislature." . . . Moreover, it would effectively nullify the Convention's decision to require a two-third vote for expulsion. Unquestionably, Congress has an interest in preserving its institutional integrity, but in most cases that interest can be sufficiently safeguarded by the exercise of its power to punish its members for disorderly behavior and, in extreme cases, to expel a member with the concurrence of two-thirds. In short, both the intention of the Framers, to the extent it can be determined, and an examination of the basic principles of our democratic system persuade us that the Constitution does not vest in the Congress a discretionary power to deny membership by a majority vote.

VII. CONCLUSION

To summarize, we have determined . . . that in judging the qualifications of its members Congress is limited to the standing qualifications prescribed in the Constitution. Respondents concede that Powell met these. Thus, there is no need to remand this case to determine whether he was entitled to be seated in the 90th Congress. Therefore, we hold that, since Adam Clayton Powell, Jr., was duly elected by the voters of the 18th Congressional District of New York and was not ineligible to serve under any provision of the Constitution, the House was without power to exclude him from its membership. . . .

Mr. Justice Douglas [concurring]. . . .

Mr. Justice Stewart, dissenting.

I believe that events which have taken place since certiorari was granted in this case on November 18, 1968, have rendered it moot, and that the Court should therefore refrain from deciding the novel, difficult, and delicate constitutional questions which the case presented at its inception. . . .

GRAVEL V. UNITED STATES

408 U.S. 606, 92 S. Ct. 2614, 33 L. Ed. 2d 583 (1972)

During the national crisis resulting from newspaper publication of the Pentagon Papers (a classified 47-volume study made under the auspices of the Defense Department on the circumstances of American involvement in the Vietnam War), Senator Mike Gravel, Chairman of the Senate Subcommittee on Public Buildings and Grounds, convened the committee in a night session, proceeded to read aloud summaries of the Papers, and then introduced all 47 volumes into the record as an exhibit. Subsequently, he gave a copy of the Papers to the Beacon Press, publishing arm of the Unitarian Church in Boston, for publication.

A federal grand jury impaneled to investigate the release of the Papers to the publisher subpoenaed an aide of Senator Gravel, who intervened on the aide's behalf to quash the subpoena. The court of appeals ruled that the grand jury could not inquire into the action or motives of the senator or his aide. However, the publication itself was held not to be a legislative act, and while the case was on appeal to the Supreme Court, FBI agents demanded and secured bank records of the Beacon Press, including names of contributors to the Unitarian Church.

The Supreme Court by a vote of five to four agreed that both Gravel and his aide were protected by the Speech or Debate Clause in all respects except for the arrangements with the Beacon Press.

Opinion of the Court by Mr. Justice White, announced by Mr. Justice Blackmun. . . .

We are convinced . . . that the Court of Appeals correctly determined that Senator Gravel's alleged arrangement with Beacon Press to publish the Pentagon Papers was not protected speech or debate within the meaning of Art. I, sec. 6, cl. 1, of the Constitution. . . .

Prior cases have read the Speech or Debate Clause "broadly to effectuate its purposes" . . . and have included within its reach anything "generally done in a session of the House by one of its members in relation to the business before it." *Kilbourn v. Thompson.* . . .

But the clause has not been extended beyond the legislative sphere. . . . Legislative acts are not all-encompassing. The heart of the clause is speech or debate in either House, and insofar as the clause is construed to reach other matters, they must be an integral part of the deliberative and communicative processes by which Members participate in committee and House proceedings with respect to the consideration and passage or rejection of proposed legislation or with respect to other matters which the Constitution places within the jurisdiction of either House. . . . [T]he courts have extended the privilege to matters beyond pure speech or debate in either House, but only when necessary to prevent indirect impairment of such deliberations. . . .

Here private publication by Senator Gravel through the cooperation of Beacon Press was in no way essential to the deliberations of the House; nor does questioning as to private publication threaten the integrity or independence of the House by impermissibly exposing its deliberations to executive influence. The Senator had conducted his hearings, the record and any report that was forthcoming were available both to his committee and the House. Insofar as we are advised, neither Congress nor the full committee ordered or authorized the publication. We cannot but conclude that the Senator's arrangements with Beacon Press were not part and parcel of the legislative process. . . .

MR. JUSTICE DOUGLAS, dissenting. . . .

I would construe the Speech and Debate Clause to insulate Senator Gravel and his aides from inquiry concerning the Pentagon Papers, and Beacon Press from inquiry concerning publication of them, for that publication was but another way of informing the public as to what had gone on in the privacy of the Executive Branch concerning the conception and pursuit of the so-called 'war' in Vietnam. Alternatively, I would hold that Beacon Press is protected by the First Amendment from prosecution or investigations for publishing or undertaking to publish the Pentagon Papers. . . .

MR. JUSTICE BRENNAN, with whom MR. JUSTICE DOUGLAS, and MR. JUSTICE MARSHALL, join, dissenting. . . .

In holding that Senator Gravel's alleged arrangement with Beacon Press to publish the Pentagon Papers is not shielded from extrasenatorial inquiry by the Speech or Debate Clause, the Court adopts what for me is a far too narrow view of the legislative function. The Court seems to assume that words spoken in debate or written in congressional reports are protected by the Clause, so that if Senator Gravel had recited part of the Pentagon Papers on the Senate floor or copied them into a Senate report, those acts could not be questioned 'in any other place.' Yet because he sought a wider audience, to publicize information deemed relevant to matters pending before his own committee, the Senator suddenly loses his immunity and is exposed to grand jury investigation and possible prosecution for the publication. The explanation for this anomalous result is the Court's belief that 'Speech or Debate' encompasses only acts necessary to the internal deliberations of Congress concerning proposed legislation. . . .

Thus the Court excludes from the sphere of protected legislative activity a function that I had supposed lay at the heart of our democratic system. I speak, of course, of the legislator's duty to inform the public about matters affecting the administration of government. That this 'informing function' falls into the class of things 'generally done in a session of the House by one of its members in relation to the business before it,' *Kilbourn v. Thompson,* was explicitly acknowledged by the Court in *Watkins v. United States.* . . .

. . . It requires no citation of authority to state that public concern over current issues—the War, race relations, governmental invasions of privacy—has transformed itself in recent years into what many believe is a crisis of confidence, in our system of government and its capacity to meet the needs and reflect the wants of the American people. Communication between Congress and the electorate tends to alleviate that doubt by exposing and clarifying the workings of the political system, the policies underlying new laws and the role of the Executive in their administration. To the extent that the informing function succeeds in fostering public faith in the responsiveness of Government, it is not only an 'ordinary' task of the legislator but one that is essential to the continued vitality of our democratic institutions.

Unlike the Court, therefore, I think that the activities of Congressmen in communicating with the public are legislative acts protected by the Speech or Debate Clause. I agree with the Court that not every task performed by a legislator is privileged; intervention before Executive departments is one that is not. But the informing function carries a far more persuasive claim to the protections of the Clause. It has been recognized by this Court as something 'generally done' by Congressmen, the Congress itself has established special concessions designed to lower the cost of such communication, and, most important, the function furthers several well-recognized goals of representative government. To say in the face of these facts that the informing function is not privileged merely because it is not necessary to the internal deliberations of Congress is to give the Speech or Debate Clause an artificial and narrow reading unsupported by reason.

Whether the Speech or Debate Clause extends to the informing function is an issue whose importance goes beyond the fate of a single Senator or Congressman. What is at stake is the right of an elected representative to inform, and the public to be informed, about matters relating directly to the workings of our Government. The dialogue between Congress and people has been recognized, from the days of our founding, as one of the necessary elements of a representative system. We should not retreat from that view merely because, in the course of that dialogue, information may be revealed that is embarrassing to the other branches of government or violates their notions of necessary secrecy. A member of Congress who exceeds the bounds of propriety in performing this official task may be called to answer by the other members of his chamber. We do violence to the fundamental concepts of privilege, however, when we subject that same conduct to judicial scrutiny at the instance of the Executive. The threat of 'prosecution by an unfriendly executive and conviction by a hostile judiciary,' which the Clause was designed to avoid, can only lead to timidity in the performance of this vital function. The Nation as a whole benefits from the congressional investigation and exposure of official corruption and deceit. It likewise suffers when that exposure is replaced by muted criticism, carefully hushed behind congressional walls.

MR. JUSTICE STEWART, dissenting in part. . . .

UNITED STATES V. BREWSTER

408 U.S. 501, 92 S. Ct. 2531, 33 L. Ed. 2d 507 (1972)

Daniel Brewster, a former U.S. Senator, had been charged with accepting bribes in exchange for promises related to official acts while a member of Congress. The trial judge dismissed the indictment on the ground that Brewster was immune from prosecution because of the Speech or Debate Clause.

MR. CHIEF JUSTICE BURGER delivered the opinion of the Court. . . .

. . . The immunities of the Speech or Debate Clause were not written into the Constitution simply for the personal or private benefit of Members of Congress, but to protect the integrity of the legislative process by insuring the independence of individual legislators. The genesis of the Clause at common law is well known. In his opinion for the Court in United States v Johnson . . . (1966), Mr. Justice Harlan canvassed the history of the Clause and concluded that it "was the culmination of a long struggle for parliamentary supremacy. Behind these simple phrases lies a history of conflict between the Commons and the Tudor and Stuart monarchs during which successive monarchs utilized the criminal and civil law to suppress and intimidate critical legislators. Since the Glorious Revolution in Britain, and throughout United States history, the privilege has been recognized as an important protection of the independence and integrity of the legislature." . . .

. . . Although the Speech or Debate Clause's historic roots are in English history, it must be interpreted in light of the American experience and in the context of the American constitutional scheme of government rather than the English parliamentary system. We should bear in mind that the English system differs from ours in that their parliament is the supreme authority, not a coordinate branch. Our speech or debate privilege was designed to preserve legislative independence, not supremacy. Our task, therefore, is to apply the Clause in such a way as to insure the independence of the legislature without altering the historic balance of the three co-equal branches of Government.

. . . In United States v Johnson the Court reviewed the conviction of a former Representative on seven counts of violating the federal conflict of interest statute, and on one count of conspiracy to defraud the United States. . . .

In applying the Speech or Debate Clause, the Court focused on the specific facts of the Johnson prosecution. The conspiracy to defraud count alleged an agreement among Representative Johnson and three codefendants to obtain the dismissal of pending indictments against officials of savings and loan institutions. For these services, which included a speech made by Johnson on the House floor, the Government claimed Johnson was paid a bribe. The Court held that the use of evidence of a speech to support a count under a broad conspiracy statute was prohibited by the Speech or Debate Clause. The Government was, therefore, precluded from prosecuting the conspiracy count on retrial, insofar as it depended on inquiries into speeches made in the House. . . .

. . . The Court in Johnson emphasized that its decision did not affect a prosecution which, though founded on a criminal statute of general application, "does not draw in question the legislative acts of the defendant member of Congress or his motives for performing them." . . . The Court did not question the power of the United States to try Johnson on the conflict of interest counts, and it authorized a new trial on the conspiracy count, provided that all references to the making of the speech were eliminated. . . .

Johnson thus stands as a unanimous holding that a Member of Congress may be prosecuted under a criminal statute provided that the Government's case does not rely on legislative acts or the motivation for legislative acts. A legislative act has consistently been defined as an act generally done in Congress in relation to the business before it. In sum, the Speech or Debate Clause prohibits inquiry only into those things generally said or done in Congress in the performance of official duties and the motivation for those acts.

. . . It is well known, of course, that Members of the Congress engage in many activities other than the purely legislative activities protected by the Speech and Debate Clause. These include a wide range of legitimate "errands" performed for constituents, the making of appointments with government agencies, assistance in securing government contracts, preparing so-called "news letters" to constituents, news releases, speeches delivered outside the Congress. The range of these related activities has grown over the years. They are performed in part because they have come to be expected by constituents and because they are a means of developing continuing support for future elections. Although these are entirely legitimate activities, they are political in nature rather than legislative, in the sense that term has been used by the Court in prior cases. But it has never been seriously contended that these political matters, however appropriate, have the protection afforded by the Speech or Debate Clause. . . .

In no case has this Court ever treated the Clause as protecting all conduct *relating* to the legislative process. In every case thus far before this Court, the Speech or Debate Clause has been limited to an act which was clearly a part of the legislative process—the *due* functioning of the process. . . .

. . . Mr. Justice White suggests that permitting the Executive to initiate the prosecution of a Member of Congress for the specific crime of bribery is subject to serious potential abuse that might endanger the independence of the legislature—for example, a campaign contribution might be twisted by a ruthless prosecutor into a bribery indictment. But . . . the Executive is not alone in possessing power potentially subject to abuse; such possibilities are inherent in a system of government which delegates to each of the three branches separate and independent powers. . . .

. . . We do not discount entirely the possibility that an abuse might occur, but this possibility, which we consider remote, must be balanced against the potential danger flowing from either the absence of a bribery statute applicable to Members of Congress or a holding that the statute violates the Constitution. As we noted at the outset, the purpose of the Speech or Debate Clause is to protect the individual legislator, not simply for his own sake, but to preserve the independence and thereby the integrity of the legislative process. But financial abuses, by way of bribes, perhaps even more than Executive power, would gravely undermine legislative integrity and defeat the right of the public to honest representation. Depriving the Executive of the power to investigate and prosecute and the Judiciary of the power to punish bribery of Members of Congress is unlikely to enhance legislative independence. Given the disinclination and limitations of each House to police these matters, it is understandable that both Houses deliberately delegated this function to the courts, as they did with the power to punish persons committing contempts of Congress. . . .

. . . Taking a bribe is, obviously, no part of the legislative process or function; it is not a legislative act. It is not, by any conceivable interpretation, an act performed as a part of or even incidental to the role of a legislator. . . .

. . . The only reasonable reading of the Clause, consistent with its history and purpose, is that it does not prohibit inquiry into activities which are casually or incidentally related to legislative affairs but not a part of the legislative process itself. Under this indictment and these statutes no such proof is needed.

We hold that under this statute and this indictment, prosecution of appellee is not prohibited by the Speech or Debate Clause. Accordingly the judgment of the District Court is reversed and the case is remanded for further proceedings consistent with this opinion.

MR. JUSTICE BRENNAN, with whom MR. JUSTICE DOUGLAS joins, dissenting. . . .

There can be no doubt . . . that Senator Brewster's vote on new postal rates constituted legislative activity within the meaning of the Clause. The Senator could not be prosecuted or called to answer for his vote in any judicial or executive proceeding. But the Senator's immunity, I submit, goes beyond the vote itself and precludes all extra congressional scrutiny as to how and why he cast, or would have cast, his vote a certain way. . . .

MR. JUSTICE WHITE, with whom MR. JUSTICE DOUGLAS and MR. JUSTICE BRENNAN join, dissenting.

The question presented by this case is not whether bribery or other offensive conduct on the part of Members of Congress must or should go unpunished. No one suggests that the Speech or Debate Clause insulates Senators and Congressmen from accountability for their misdeeds. . . . The sole issue here is in what forum the accounting must take place. . . . The Speech or Debate Clause . . . reserves the power to discipline in the Houses of Congress. I would insist that those Houses develop their own institutions and procedures for dealing with those in their midst who would prostitute the legislative process.

Chapter Eleven

CONGRESSIONAL POWERS

INTRODUCTION

The first words of the Constitution, following the Preamble, are, "All legislative powers herein granted shall be vested in a Congress of the United States. . . ." As the legislative organ of a government of delegated powers, Congress must be able to support any exercise of legislative authority as both authorized, and not forbidden, by the Constitution. There are two types of authorizations in Article I, section 8. The first 17 clauses specifically enumerate a series of powers, ranging all the way from punishment of counterfeiting to the declaration of war. Then clause 18 is a general authorization "to make all laws which shall be necessary and proper for carrying into execution the foregoing powers. . . ."

Implied Powers

The relationship of clause 18 to the enumerated powers preceding it quickly became the subject of controversy between Federalists and Jeffersonians—between broad and strict constructionists. The issue was joined over Hamilton's plan for a national bank, as presented to the First Congress. There was no authorization in the Constitution for Congress to create a bank; in fact, the Convention had specifically refused to grant

Congress even a restricted power to create corporations. On the invitation of President Washington, Hamilton and Jefferson submitted their respective views on whether he should sign the bill creating the bank. Jefferson emphasized the "necessary" in the necessary and proper clause. Since all the enumerated powers could be carried out without a bank, it was not necessary and consequently not authorized. Hamilton, on the other hand, argued that the powers granted to Congress included the right to employ "all the means requisite and fairly applicable to the attainment of the ends of such power," unless they were specifically forbidden or immoral or contrary to the "essential ends of political society." The Hamiltonian theory of a broad and liberal interpretation of congressional power was successful in persuading Washington to sign the bank bill, and it has generally predominated in subsequent constitutional development. In 1819 Marshall gave the definitive statement of this view in the great case of *McCulloch* v. *Maryland*, where congressional authority to create a bank—the Bank of the United States, incorporated by statute in 1816—was again the issue. The doctrine of implied power, based on the necessary and proper clause, has ever since been a source of great significance in equipping Congress with authority commensurate with its responsibilities.

Dual Federalism

The principal doctrinal challenge of a general character which congressional power has had to meet since *McCulloch* is the contention that the powers reserved to the states under the Tenth Amendment constitute a limitation on expressly granted congressional authority. This theory, commonly called "dual federalism," grew out of the states' rights views of the Supreme Court under Chief Justice Taney. Its basic assumption was that the two levels of government were co-equal sovereignties, each supreme in its own sphere.

The concept of dual federalism received its clearest statement in *Hammer* v. *Dagenhart* (1918), where the Court by a five to four vote invalidated a congressional statute restricting the transportation in interstate commerce of goods produced by child labor. Much of the struggle in the middle 1930s between the conservative members of the Supreme Court and President Roosevelt may be seen as a clash between Taney's dual federalism and the older national supremacy of Marshall. In the end it was the interpretation of Marshall and Roosevelt that prevailed. In a series of cases culminating in *United States* v. *Darby Lumber Co.* (1941), the reconstituted Court upheld a number of federal laws which directly affected local policies.

In the 1970s the Supreme Court manifested a renewed interest in dual federalism. *Oregon* v. *Mitchell* (1970) invalidated congressional legislation lowering the voting age to 18 in state elections on the ground that this was a uniquely state function preserved to the states by the Constitution. Although *Maryland* v. *Wirtz* (1968) and *Fry* v. *United States* (1975) had upheld extension of federal wage and salary controls to state and municipal employees, in *National League of Cities* v. *Usery* (1976) the Court held that a 1974 federal wage and overtime law violated state sovereignty. These decisions can be better understood, however, in the context of the subsequent discussion of federalism and the federal commerce power in Chapters 12 and 14.

Delegation of Legislative Power

In principle, Congress cannot delegate its legislative powers to the administration or to the courts. In practice, however, the Supreme Court has recognized that Congress cannot cover every detail or foresee every eventuality when it passes a law and so has tended to accept broad legislative standards. In *Wayman* v. *Southard* (1825) Marshall approved a statute delegating rule making power to the Supreme Court, and *Field* v. *Clark* (1892) upheld a statute permitting the President to revise customs duties under certain circumstances.

It was not until the Court's troubles with President Roosevelt that the delegation rule was actually invoked to strike down congressional legislation in three significant cases. *Panama Refining Co.* v. *Ryan* (1935) concerned a statute giving the President authority to exclude from interstate commerce oil produced in excess of state regulations. **Schechter Poultry Corp.** v. **United States** (1935) held that the National Industrial Recovery Act had gone too far in authorizing the President to promulgate codes of fair competition for the nation's businesses. *Carter* v. *Carter Coal Co.* (1936) held that Congress had unconstitutionally delegated power to the President to set up a code of mandatory regulations for the coal industry.

Since this flurry no congressional statutes have been invalidated on delegation grounds. A Court minority did attempt to apply the *Schechter* rationale in *United States* v. *Sharpnack* (1958), and in *National Cable Television Association* v. *United States* (1974) the Court construed narrowly a statutory grant of power to the Federal Communications Commission to impose fees for its services in order to avoid a delegation issue. The action of Presidents Nixon and Ford in imposing license fees on imported oil for security reasons, which they justified under the Trade Expansion Act of 1962, was upheld in *Federal Energy Administration* v. *Algonquin SNG Inc.* (1976).

Under a series of Reorganization Acts dating back to 1939, the President has been authorized to prepare reorganization plans affecting the government departments, which become effective automatically unless there is an adverse vote by either house of Congress. This arrangement reverses the usual relationship of President and Congress and may appear to be a delegation of legislative power to the executive. In fact, the charge of unconstitutionality was seriously considered in Congress before passage of the 1977 act giving President Carter this type of reorganization authority.

The Taxing Power

One of the major motives of the Founders was to assure adequate financial support for the new government. Article I, section 8, gave Congress the power "to lay and collect taxes, duties, imposts and excises. . . ." In almost every decision touching on the constitutionality of federal taxation, the Supreme Court has stressed not only the breadth of this language but also the limits of its own reviewing powers in this vital area of public finance. Nevertheless, some constitutional issues concerning the federal taxing power have been raised.

DIRECT TAXES. Article I, section 9, provides that "No capitation, or other direct, tax shall be laid, unless in proportion to the census or enumeration herein before directed to be taken." Unfortunately, there was no agreed definition of a "direct tax." In *Hylton* v. *United States* (1796) a specific tax on carriages was held *not* to be a direct tax, the Court expressing the view that the only direct taxes were capitation and land taxes.

Income taxes cannot be apportioned among the states, and an unapportioned Civil War income tax was held not to be a direct tax in *Springer* v. *United States* (1881). But in *Pollock* v. *Farmers' Loan & Trust Co.* (1895) the Supreme Court, yielding to the clamor from propertied interests, held that the income tax passed by Congress in 1894 was a direct tax and consequently unconstitutional. A campaign to override the Court's decision got under way immediately and was finally successful when the Sixteenth Amendment was adopted in 1913.

INTERGOVERNMENTAL TAX IMMUNITY. The immunity doctrine was first developed in *McCulloch* v. *Maryland* (1819) and was applied to protect the Bank of the United States from state taxation. Marshall's rationalization was that "the power to tax was the power to destroy," and it was unthinkable that a state should be in a position to "destroy" a federal activity. It was not until 1871, in *Collector* v. *Day,* that the immunity doctrine was applied in reverse to hold the salary of a state judge immune from the federal Civil War income tax.

Not only were federal and state activities and employees given reciprocal exemption from taxation, but in the 1920s a conservative Court carried the immunity principle into a number of new areas. For example, in *Long* v. *Rockwood* (1928) the Court ruled that a state could not tax royalties on a patent granted by the United States. Conversely, *Burnet* v. *Coronado Oil & Gas Co.* (1932) invalidated a federal tax on income which private persons derived from leasing state-owned oil lands.

Throughout this period there was a strong protest, led by Justices Holmes, Brandeis, and Stone, against the extension of the immunity principle, and by 1938 this view won control of the Court. *Helvering* v. *Mountain Producers Corp.* (1938) reversed the *Burnet* and other oil lands leasing cases. In *Helvering* v. *Gerhardt* (1938) and *Graves* v. *O'Keefe* (1939), the Court demolished intergovernmental tax immunity for salaries of state and federal employees, overruling *Collector* v. *Day* and the other cases in that line.

Thus the immunity doctrine is no longer a substantial limitation on congressional taxing power. Intergovernmental exemptions are confined to the possessions, institutions, and activities of the governments themselves. The principal exception is federal tax immunity granted to income from state and municipal bonds.

TAXATION FOR NONREVENUE PURPOSES. Constitutional questions have occasionally been raised by congressional use of the taxing power for purposes which are primarily regulatory and which raise comparatively little revenue—sometimes none at all. Does this mixture of motives invalidate a tax statute? The Supreme Court has not thought so, except in a few instances and under unusual circumstances.

The protective tariff is a clear case of using taxation for goals other than the raising of revenue, and it has been regarded as constitutional ever since 1789. *Veazie Bank* v. *Fenno* (1869) validated a 10 percent tax on the circulation of state bank notes which Congress had adopted to drive them out of use in favor of the notes of national banks. The Court considered that the taxing power was here being used only as an auxiliary means for enforcing the federal government's admitted power to provide a sound and uniform national currency.

But even when there was no discernible relationship between the regulatory tax and some specific authority of Congress, the Court seldom objected. The classic case is *McCray* v. *United States* (1904), where the Court upheld a punitive tax on oleomargarine colored to look like butter, saying that it would not look into "the motives or purposes of Congress" in considering its power to enact legislation. The principle of the *McCray* case was again endorsed in *United States* v. *Doremus* (1919), where Congress used a small tax requirement to compel the registration of persons engaged in the narcotics trade. But four justices dissented on the ground that the statute was a bold attempt to exercise police power reserved to the states.

The principal case in which a federal tax was invalidated on the ground that it was not truly a revenue measure was *Bailey* v. *Drexel Furniture Co.* (1922), involving the child labor tax act passed by Congress in 1919 after the 1916 act, based on the commerce clause, had been held unconstitutional in *Hammer* v. *Dagenhart.* The Court, while denying that it had any right or desire to inquire into congressional motives, concluded that this "so-called tax" revealed on its face that it was not a revenue measure but rather a penalty to regulate child labor. Similarly, in *United States* v. *Constantine* (1935) a grossly disproportionate federal excise tax, imposed only on liquor dealers carrying on business in violation of local law, was declared unconstitutional.

Such holdings require the Court to charge that Congress has been guilty of improper motives and has used a legislative subterfuge to accomplish ends which the Constitution forbids. Consequently, it is not surprising that the *Bailey* and *Constantine* precedents have not been followed in subsequent cases, even in situations such as *Sonzinsky* v. *United States* (1937) and **United States** v. **Kahriger** (1953), in both of which cases the motivation of tax statutes was clearly not revenue. The gambling tax statute upheld in *Kahriger* was later invalidated in *Marchetti* v. *United States* (1968) and *Grosso* v. *United States* (1968), but on self-incrimination, not taxation, grounds.

The Spending Power

The basic principle of legislative control over the purse, established by the English Parliament after a long struggle with the crown, is safeguarded by the provision in Article I, section 9, which provides that "no money shall be drawn from the Treasury, but in consequence of appropriations made by law. . . ." But are there any constitutional limits upon the purposes for which Congress may appropriate federal funds? Clearly Congress can spend money to achieve any of the purposes delegated to it by the Constitution, such as regulating commerce or taking the census. But can reliance also be placed upon the rather enigmatic language of the taxing clause which speaks of paying the debts and providing for "the common defense and general welfare"?

Madison asserted that the general welfare clause was nothing more than a reference to the specifically enumerated powers in the subsequent clauses of the same section. Hamilton, on the other hand, contended that the clause conferred a power separate and distinct from the enumerated powers, and that Congress consequently had a substantive power to tax and to appropriate, limited only by the requirement of furthering the general welfare of the United States.

Until 1936 the Supreme Court had never had an opportunity to settle this argument, principally because a suit attacking federal spending could be prosecuted only by a litigant who had a sufficient legal interest in federal expenditures to give him standing to sue. The ruling to that effect in *Frothingham* v. *Mellon* (1923) has already been noted. But the special circumstances in the case of **United States v. Butler** (1936) made it possible to secure a court test of congressional spending power.

The Agricultural Adjustment Act of 1933 had provided for federal payments to farmers who would cooperate in the government's program of price stabilization through production control. The money paid to farmers was to come from processing taxes on agricultural commodities which were authorized by the same statute. Butler resisted the collection of taxes on cotton processed at his mill. He was bound to lose on this issue, since the processing tax was clearly a bona fide exercise of the federal taxing power. It was how the tax money was being spent that Butler objected to, but under the *Frothingham* doctrine no taxpayer could be heard in court to challenge the constitutionality of federal spending. Butler solved this dilemma by challenging the tax, not as a tax but as a means of financing a program of agricultural production control which he alleged to be an unconstitutional invasion of the powers of the states. The Court agreed with him that the tax and the spending were, in fact, "parts of a single scheme."

Consequently, the Court was given an opportunity to settle the argument that Madison and Hamilton had begun. In an important victory for the spending power, the justices voted for Hamilton. But the Court immediately proceeded to make the victory a hollow one, as far as this case was concerned, by transferring the argument to an entirely new issue. The Court majority ruled that whether the spending was for national rather than local welfare was of no importance, since as a statutory plan to regulate and control agricultural production the act invaded the reserved rights of the states and was consequently invalid under the Tenth Amendment.

Actually, the *Butler* decision had little effect. As a barrier to federal agricultural regulation it was soon bypassed as the type of program it condemned was reenacted by Congress under the commerce power and upheld in *Mulford* v. *Smith* (1939) and *Wickard* v. *Filburn* (1942). As a general threat to the spending power, it was dispelled in 1937 when the Court upheld the tax provisions of the Social Security Act in *Steward Machine Co.* v. *Davis* and in *Helvering* v. *Davis.* As already noted, the *Frothingham* barrier to court tests of the spending power has been somewhat weakened by the ruling in *Flast* v. *Cohen* (1968), making it possible to challenge federal appropriations on establishment of religion grounds, but there has as yet been no wider application of the *Flast* doctrine.

Because the legislative power to appropriate is so broad and so difficult to question, Congress has sometimes been tempted to use it to achieve purposes which it lacks more direct constitutional power to accomplish. In *United States* v. *Lovett* (1946) a rider to an appropriation act forbade the use of any funds appropriated by the act to pay the salaries of three named federal officials who had been "fingered" by the House Un-American Activities Committee. The Court declared the rider unconstitutional as a bill of attainder.

MC CULLOCH V. MARYLAND

4 Wheat. 316, 4 L. Ed. 579 (1819)

Congress created the Bank of the United States in 1791. Though the Constitution gave Congress no power to create corporations, the constitutionality of the bank was not tested in the courts before its charter expired in 1811. A second bank was chartered by Congress in 1816. It was politically unpopular, partly because of its competition with state banks. Maryland passed legislation imposing a heavy tax on bank notes issued by the Bank of the United States. McCulloch, cashier of the Baltimore branch, issued notes without paying the required tax.

MR. CHIEF JUSTICE MARSHALL delivered the opinion of the Court. . . .

In the case now to be determined, the defendant, a sovereign State, denies the obligation of a law enacted by the legislature of the Union, and the plaintiff, on his part, contests the validity of an act which has been passed by the legislature of that State. The constitution of our country, in its most interesting and vital parts, is to be considered; the conflicting powers of the government of the Union and of its members, as marked in that constitution, are to be discussed; and an opinion given, which may essentially influence the great operations of the government. . . .

If any one proposition could command the universal assent of mankind, we might expect it would be this—that the government of the Union, though limited in its powers, is supreme within its sphere of action. This would seem to result necessarily from its nature. It is the government of all; its powers are delegated by all; it represents all, and acts for all. Though any one State may be willing to control its operations, no State is willing to allow others to control them. The nation, on those subjects on which it can act, must necessarily bind its component parts. But this question is not left to mere reason: the people have, in express terms, decided it, by saying, "this constitution, and the laws of the United States, which shall be made in pursuance thereof," "shall be the supreme law of the land," and by requiring that the members of the State legislatures, and the officers of the executive and judicial departments of the States, shall take the oath of fidelity to it.

The government of the United States, then, though limited in its powers, is supreme; and its laws, when made in pursuance of the constitution, form the supreme law of the land, "any thing in the constitution or laws of any State to the contrary notwithstanding."

Among the enumerated powers, we do not find that of establishing a bank or creating a corporation. But there is no phrase in the instrument which, like the articles of confederation, excludes incidental or implied powers; and which requires that everything granted shall be expressly and minutely described. Even the 10th amendment, which was framed for the purpose of quieting the excessive jealousies which had been excited, omits the word "expressly," and declares only that the powers "not delegated to the United States, nor prohibited to the States, are reserved to the States or to the people"; thus leaving the question, whether the particular power which may become the subject of contest has been delegated to the one government, or prohibited to the other, to depend on a fair construction of the whole instrument. The men who drew and adopted this amendment had experienced the embarrassments resulting from the insertion of this word in the articles of confederation, and probably omitted it to avoid those embarrassments. A constitution, to contain an accurate detail of all the subdivisions of which its great powers will admit, and of all the means by which they may be carried into execution, would partake of the prolixity of a legal code, and could scarcely be embraced by the human mind. It would probably never be understood by the public. Its nature, therefore, requires, that only its great outlines should be marked, its important objects designated, and the minor ingredients which compose those objects be deduced from the nature of the objects themselves. That this idea was entertained by the framers of the American constitution, is not only to be inferred from the nature of the instrument, but from the language. Why else were some of the limitations, found in the ninth section of the 1st article, introduced? It is also, in some degree, warranted by their having omitted to use any restrictive term which might prevent its receiving a fair and just interpretation. In considering this question, then, we must never forget, that it is *a constitution* we are expounding.

Although, among the enumerated powers of government, we do not find the word "bank" or "incorporation," we find the great powers to lay and collect taxes; to borrow money; to regulate commerce; to declare and conduct a war; and to raise and support armies and navies. The sword and the purse, all the external relations, and no inconsiderable portion of the industry of the nation, are entrusted to its government. It can never be pretended that these vast powers draw after them others of inferior importance, merely because they are inferior. Such an idea can never be advanced. But it may with great reason be contended, that a government, entrusted with such ample powers, on the due execution of which the happiness and prosperity of the nation so vitally depends, must also be entrusted with ample means for their execution. The power being given, it is the interest of the nation to facilitate its execution. It can never be their interest, and cannot be presumed to have been their intention, to clog and embarrass its execution by withholding the most appropriate means. Throughout this vast republic, from the St. Croix to the Gulph of Mexico, from the Atlantic to the Pacific, revenue is to be collected and expended, armies are to be marched and supported. The exigencies of the nation may require that the treasure raised in the north should be transported to the south, that raised in the east conveyed to the west, or that this order should be reversed. Is that construction of the constitution to be preferred which would render these operations difficult, hazardous, and expensive? Can we adopt that construction, (unless the words imperiously require it,) which would impute to the framers of that instrument, when granting these powers for the public good, the intention of impeding their exercise by withholding a choice of means? If, indeed, such be the mandate of the constitution, we have only to obey; but that instrument does not profess to enumerate the means by which the powers it confers may be executed; nor does it prohibit the creation of a corporation, if the existence of such a being be essential to the beneficial exercise of those powers. It is, then, the subject of fair inquiry, how far such means may be employed. . . .

But the constitution of the United States has not left the right of Congress to employ the necessary means, for the execution of the powers conferred on the government, to general reasoning. To its enumeration of powers is added that of making "all laws which shall be necessary and proper, for carrying into execution the foregoing powers, and all other powers vested by this constitution, in the government of the United States, or in any department thereof."

The counsel for the State of Maryland have urged various arguments, to prove that this clause, though in terms a grant of power, is not so in effect; but is really restrictive of the general right, which might otherwise be implied, of selecting means for executing the enumerated powers.

In support of this proposition, they have found it necessary to contend, that this clause was inserted for the purpose of conferring on Congress the power of making laws. That, without it, doubts might be entertained, whether Congress could exercise its powers in the form of legislation.

But could this be the object for which it was inserted? . . . That a legislature, endowed with legislative powers, can legislate, is a proposition too self-evident to have been questioned.

But the argument on which most reliance is placed, is drawn from the peculiar language of this clause. Congress is not empowered by it to make all laws, which may have relation to the powers conferred on the government, but such only as may be *"necessary and proper"* for carrying them into execution. The word *"necessary,"* is considered as controlling the whole sentence, and as limiting the right to pass laws for the execution of the granted powers, to such as are indispensable, and without which the power would be nugatory. That it excludes the choice of means, and leaves to Congress, in each case, that only which is most direct and simple. . . . This clause, as construed by the State of Maryland, would abridge, and almost annihilate this useful and necessary right of the legislature to select its means. That this could not be intended, is, we should think, had it not been already controverted, too apparent for controversy. We think so for the following reasons:

1ST. The clause is placed among the powers of Congress, not among the limitations on those powers.

2ND. Its terms purport to enlarge, not to diminish the powers vested in the government. It purports to be an additional power, not a restriction on those already granted. . . . Had the intention been to make this clause restrictive, it would unquestionably have been so in form as well as in effect.

The result of the most careful and attentive consideration bestowed upon this clause is, that if it does not enlarge, it cannot be construed to restrain the powers of Congress, or to impair the right of the legislature to exercise its best judgment in the selection of measures to carry into execution the constitutional powers of the government. If no other motive for its insertion can be suggested, a sufficient one is found in the desire to remove all doubts respecting the right to legislate on that vast mass of incidental powers which must be involved in the constitution, if that instrument be not a splendid bauble.

We admit, as all must admit, that the powers of the government are limited, and that its limits are not to be transcended. But we think the sound construction of the constitution must allow to the national legislature that discretion, with respect to the means by which the powers it confers are to be carried into execution, which will enable that body to perform the high duties assigned to it, in the manner most beneficial to the people. Let the end be legitimate, let it be within the scope of the constitution, and all means which are appropriate, which are plainly adapted to that end, which are not prohibited, but consist with the letter and spirit of the constitution, are constitutional. . . .

After the most deliberate consideration, it is the unanimous and decided opinion of this Court, that the act to incorporate the Bank of the United States is a law made in pursuance of the constitution, and is a part of the supreme law of the land. . . .

SCHECHTER POULTRY CORPORATION V. UNITED STATES

295 U.S. 495, 55 S. Ct. 87, 7 L. Ed. 2d 1570 (1935)

The National Industrial Recovery Act was adopted by Congress as a major part of President Roosevelt's program to end the economic depression of the 1930s. Its purpose was to promote industry-wide agreements on wages, hours, and trade practices to prevent ruinous competition. Codes of fair practice were to be proposed by trade associations and made mandatory by presidential approval. The only standards for the exercise of executive discretion were that the trade associations must be representative and that the codes should not tend to promote monopolies.

MR. CHIEF JUSTICE HUGHES delivered the opinion of the Court. . . .

SECOND. *The question of the delegation of legislative power.* . . . The Congress is not permitted to abdicate or to transfer to others the essential legislative functions with which it is thus vested. We have repeatedly recognized the necessity of adapting legislation to complex conditions involving a host of details with which the national legislature cannot deal directly. We pointed out in the Panama Company case that the Constitution has never been regarded as denying to Congress the necessary resources of flexibility and practicality, which will enable it to perform its function in laying down policies and establishing standards, while leaving to selected instrumentalities the making of subordinate rules within prescribed limits and the determination of facts to which the policy as declared by the legislature is to apply. But we said that the constant recognition of the necessity and validity of such provisions, and the wide range of administrative authority which has been developed by means of them, cannot be allowed to obscure the limitations of the authority to delegate, if our constitutional system is to be maintained. . . .

. . . Section 3 of the Recovery Act is without precedent. It supplies no standards for any trade, industry or activity. It does not undertake to prescribe rules of conduct to be applied to particular states of fact determined by appropriate administrative procedure. Instead of prescribing rules of conduct, it authorizes the making of codes to prescribe them. For that legislative undertaking, section 3 sets up no standard, aside from the statement of the general aims of rehabilitation, correction and expansion described in section one. In view of the scope of that broad declaration, and of the nature of the few restrictions that are imposed, the discretion of the President in approving or prescribing codes, and thus enacting laws for the government of trade and industry throughout the country, is virtually unfettered. We think that the code-making authority thus conferred is an unconstitutional delegation of legislative power. . . .

MR. JUSTICE CARDOZO, concurring. . . .

The delegated power of legislation which has found expression in this code is not canalized within banks that keep it from overflowing. It is unconfined and vagrant, if I may borrow my own words in an earlier opinion. *Panama Refining Co.* v. *Ryan.* . . .

Here, in the case before us, is an attempted delegation not confined to any single act nor to any class or group of acts identified or described by reference or a standard. Here in effect is a roving commission to inquire into evils and upon discovery of them correct them.

I have said that there is no standard, definite or even approximate, to which legislation must conform. Let me make my meaning more precise. If codes of fair competition are codes eliminating "unfair" methods of competition ascertained upon inquiry to prevail in one industry or another, there is no unlawful delegation of legislative functions when the President is directed to inquire into such practices and denounce them when discovered. For many years a like power has been committed to the Federal Trade Commission with the approval of this court in a long series of decisions. . . .

But there is another conception of codes of fair competition, their significance and function, which leads to very different consequences, though it is one that is struggling now for recognition and acceptance. By this other conception a code is not to be restricted to the elimination of business practices that would be characterized by general acceptance as oppressive or unfair. It is to include whatever ordinances may be desirable or helpful for the wellbeing or prosperity of the industry affected. In that view, the function of its adoption is not merely negative, but positive; the planning of improvements as well as the extirpation of abuses. What is fair, as thus conceived, is not something to be contrasted with what is unfair or fraudulent or tricky. The extension becomes as wide as the field of industrial regulation. If that conception shall prevail, anything that Congress may do within the limits of the commerce clause for the betterment of business may be done by the President upon the recommendation of a trade association by calling it a code. This is delegation running riot. No such plenitude of power is susceptible of transfer. . . .

UNITED STATES V. KAHRIGER

345 U.S. 22, 73 S. Ct. 510, 97 L. Ed. 2d 754 (1952)

Following the televised hearings on gambling and organized crime conducted by Senator Estes Kefauver in 1950, Congress included in the Revenue Act of 1951 a tax on persons engaged in the business of accepting wagers, requiring them to register with the Collector of Internal Revenue. The tax was challenged on two grounds in this case—that it invaded the police power of the states under the guise of a tax measure and that the registration provisions violated the Fifth Amendment privilege against self-incrimination.

MR. JUSTICE REED delivered the opinion of the Court. . . .

It is conceded that a federal excise tax does not cease to be valid merely because it discourages or deters the activities taxed. Nor is the tax invalid because the revenue obtained is negligible. Appellee, however, argues that the sole purpose of the statute is to penalize only illegal gambling in the states through the guise of a tax measure. As with the . . . excise taxes which we have held to be valid, the instant tax has a regulatory effect. But regardless of its regulatory effect, the wagering tax produces revenue. As such it surpasses both the narcotics and firearms taxes which we have found valid.

It is axiomatic that the power of Congress to tax is extensive and sometimes falls with crushing effect on businesses deemed unessential or inimical to the public welfare, or where, as in dealings with narcotics, the collection of the tax also is difficult. As is well known, the constitutional restraints on taxing are few. . . . The remedy for excessive taxation is in the hands of Congress, not the courts. . . . It is hard to understand why the power to tax should raise more doubts because of indirect effects than other federal powers.

Penalty provisions in tax statutes added for breach of a regulation concerning activities in themselves subject only to state regulation have caused this Court to declare the enactments invalid. Unless there are provisions extraneous to any tax need, courts are without authority to limit the exercise of the taxing power. All the provisions of this excise are adapted to the collection of a valid tax.

Nor do we find the registration requirements of the wagering tax offensive. All that is required is the filing of names, addresses, and places of business. This is quite general in tax returns. Such data are directly and intimately related to the collection of the tax and are "obviously support-able as in aid of a revenue purpose." . . .

Since appellee failed to register for the wagering tax, it is difficult to see how he can now claim the privilege even assuming that the disclosure of violations of law is called for. . . .

Assuming that respondent can raise the self-incrimination issue, that privilege has relation only to past acts, not to future acts that may or may not be committed. . . . If respondent wishes to take wagers subject to excise taxes, . . . he must pay an occupational tax and register. Under the registration provisions of the wagering tax, appellee is not compelled to confess to acts already committed, he is merely informed by the statute that in order to engage in the business of wagering in the future he must fulfill certain conditions. . . .

MR. JUSTICE JACKSON, concurring. . . .

Here is a purported tax law which requires no reports and lays no tax except on specified gamblers whose calling in most states is illegal. It requires this group to step forward and identify themselves, not because they like others have income, but because of its source. This is difficult to regard as a rational or good-faith revenue measure, despite the defer-ence that is due Congress. On the contrary, it seems to be a plan to tax out of existence the professional gambler whom it has been found impos-sible to prosecute out of existence. . . .

It will be a sad day for the revenues if the good will of the people toward their taxing system is frittered away in efforts to accomplish by taxation moral reforms that cannot be accomplished by direct legislation. But the evil that can come from this statute will probably soon make itself manifest to Congress. The evil of a judicial decision impairing the legiti-mate taxing power by extreme constitutional interpretations might not be transient. Even though this statute approaches the fair limits of constitu-tionality, I join the decision of the Court. . . .

MR. JUSTICE FRANKFURTER, dissenting. . . .

Constitutional issues are likely to arise whenever Congress draws on the taxing power not to raise revenue but to regulate conduct. . . . When oblique use is made of the taxing power as to matters which substantively are not within the powers delegated to Congress, the Court cannot shut its eyes to what is obviously, because designedly, an attempt to control conduct which the Constitution left to the responsibility of the States, merely because Congress wrapped the legislation in the verbal cellophane of a revenue measure. . . . To allow what otherwise is excluded from congressional authority to be brought within it by casting legislation in the form of a revenue measure could, as so significantly expounded in the Child Labor Tax Case, . . . offer an easy way for the legislative imagination to control "any one of the great numbers of subjects of public interest, jurisdiction of which the States have never parted with . . ."

The context of the circumstances which brought forth this enactment . . . emphatically supports what was revealed on the floor of Congress, namely, that what was formally a means of raising revenue for the Federal Government was essentially an effort to check if not to stamp out professional gambling. . . .

The motive of congressional legislation is not for our scrutiny, provided only that the ulterior purpose is not expressed in ways which negative what the revenue words on their face express and which do not seek enforcement of the formal revenue purpose through means that offend those standards of decency in our civilization against which due process is a barrier.

Mr. Justice Black, with whom Mr. Justice Douglas concurs, dissenting. . . .

The Court . . . here sustains an Act which requires a man to register and confess that he is engaged in the business of gambling. . . . I would hold that this Act violates the Fifth Amendment. . . .

UNITED STATES V. BUTLER

297 U.S. 1, 56 S. Ct. 312, 80 L. Ed. 477 (1936)

The Agricultural Adjustment Act of 1933 provided for payment to farmers who would cooperate in the government's program of price stabilization through production control. The money paid the farmers was to come from processing taxes on agricultural commodities which were authorized by the same statute. Butler, as receiver for the Hoosac Mills, resisted the collection of taxes on cotton processed at that plant.

Mr. Justice Roberts delivered the opinion of the Court. . . .

In this case we must determine whether certain provisions of the Agricultural Adjustment Act, 1933, conflict with the Federal Constitution. . . .

First. At the outset the United States contends that the respondents have no standing to question the validity of the tax. . . . We conclude that the act is one regulating agricultural production; that the tax is a mere incident of such regulation and that the respondents have standing to challenge the legality of the exaction. . . .

SECOND. The Government asserts that even if the respondents may question the propriety of the appropriation . . . their attack must fail because Article I, section 8 of the Constitution authorizes the contemplated expenditure of the funds raised by the tax. This contention presents the great and the controlling question in the case. . . .

[T]he Government does not attempt to uphold the validity of the Act on the basis of the commerce clause, which, for the purpose of the present case, may be put aside as irrelevant.

The clause thought to authorize the legislation . . . confers upon the Congress power "to lay and collect Taxes, Duties, Imposts and Excises, to pay the Debts and provide for the common Defense and general Welfare of the United States. . . ." It is not contended that this provision grants power to regulate agricultural production upon the theory that such legislation would promote the general welfare. The government concedes that the phrase "to provide for the general welfare" qualifies the power "to lay and collect taxes." The view that the clause grants power to provide for the general welfare, independently of the taxing power, has never been authoritatively accepted. Mr. Justice Story points out that, if it were adopted, "it is obvious that under color of the generality of the words, to 'provide for the common defence and general welfare,' the government of the United States is, in reality, a government of general and unlimited powers, notwithstanding the subsequent enumeration of specific powers." The true construction undoubtedly is that the only thing granted is the power to tax for the purpose of providing funds for payment of the nation's debts and making provision for the general welfare.

Nevertheless, the Government asserts that warrant is found in this clause for the adoption of the Agricultural Adjustment Act. The argument is that Congress may appropriate and authorize the spending of moneys for the "general welfare"; that the phrase should be liberally construed to cover anything conducive to national welfare; that decision as to what will promote such welfare rests with Congress alone, and the courts may not review its determination; and, finally, that the appropriation under attack was in fact for the general welfare of the United States.

The Congress is expressly empowered to lay taxes to provide for the general welfare. Funds in the Treasury as a result of taxation may be expended only through appropriation. (Article 1, § 9, cl. 7.) They can never accomplish the objects for which they were collected, unless the power to appropriate is as broad as the power to tax. The necessary implication from the terms of the grant is that the public funds may be appropriated "to provide for the general welfare of the United States." These words cannot be meaningless, else they would not have been used. The conclusion must be that they were intended to limit and define the granted power to raise and to expend money. How shall they be construed to effectuate the intent of the instrument?

Since the foundation of the nation, sharp differences of opinion have persisted as to the true interpretation of the phrase. Madison asserted it amounted to no more than a reference to the other powers enumerated in the subsequent clauses of the same section; that, as the United States is a government of limited and enumerated powers, the grant of power to tax and spend for the general national welfare must be confined to the enumerated legislative fields committed to the Congress. In this view the phrase is mere tautology, for taxation and appropriation are or may be necessary incidents of the exercise of any of the enumerated legislative powers. Hamilton, on the other hand, maintained the clause confers a power separate and distinct from those later enumerated, is not restricted in meaning by the grant of them, and Congress consequently has a substantive power to tax and to appropriate, limited only by the requirement that it shall be exercised to provide for the general welfare of the United States. Each contention has had the support of those whose views are entitled to weight. This court has noticed the question, but has never found it necessary to decide which is the true construction. Mr. Justice Story, in his Commentaries, espouses the Hamiltonian position. We shall not review the writings of public men and commentators or discuss the legislative practice. Study of all these leads us to conclude that the reading advocated by Mr. Justice Story is the correct one. While, therefore, the power to tax is not unlimited, its confines are set in the clause which confers it, and not in those of Section 8 which bestow and define the legislative powers of the Congress. It results that the power of Congress to authorize expenditure of public moneys for public purposes is not limited by the direct grants of legislative power found in the Constitution.

But the adoption of the broader construction leaves the power to spend subject to limitations. . . .

Story says that if the tax be not proposed for the common defence or general welfare, but for other objects wholly extraneous, it would be wholly indefensible upon constitutional principles. And he makes it clear that the powers of taxation and appropriation extend only to matters of national, as distinguished from local welfare. . . .

We are not now required to ascertain the scope of the phrase "general welfare of the United States" or to determine whether an appropriation in aid of agriculture falls within it. Wholly apart from that question, another principle embedded in our Constitution prohibits the enforcement of the Agricultural Adjustment Act. The act invades the reserved rights of the states. It is a statutory plan to regulate and control agricultural production, a matter beyond the powers delegated to the federal government. The tax, the appropriation of the funds raised, and the direction for their disbursement, are but parts of the plan. They are but means to an unconstitutional end.

From the accepted doctrine that the United States is a government of delegated powers, it follows that those not expressly granted, or reasonably to be implied from such as are conferred, are reserved to the states or to the people. To forestall any suggestion to the contrary, the Tenth Amendment was adopted. The same proposition, otherwise stated, is that powers not granted are prohibited. None to regulate agricultural production is given, and therefore legislation by Congress for that purpose is forbidden. . . .

If the taxing power may not be used as the instrument to enforce a regulation of matters of state concern with respect to which the Congress has no authority to interfere, may it, as in the present case, be employed to raise the money necessary to purchase a compliance which the Congress is powerless to command? The Government asserts that whatever might be said against the validity of the plan, if compulsory, it is constitutionally sound because the end is accomplished by voluntary cooperation. There are two sufficient answers to the contention. The regulation is not in fact voluntary. The farmer, of course, may refuse to comply, but the price of such refusal is the loss of benefits. The amount offered is intended to be sufficient to exert pressure on him to agree to the proposed regulation. The power to confer or withhold unlimited benefits is the power to coerce or destroy. If the cotton grower elects not to accept the benefits, he will receive less for his crops; those who receive payments will be able to undersell him. The result may well be financial ruin. The coercive purpose and intent of the statute is not obscured by the fact that it has not been perfectly successful. It is pointed out that, because there still remained a minority whom the rental and benefit payments were insufficient to induce to surrender their independence of action, the Congress has gone further and, in the Bankhead Cotton Act, used the taxing power in more directly minatory fashion to compel submission. This progression only serves more fully to expose the coercive purpose of the so-called tax imposed by the present act. It is clear that the Department of Agriculture has properly described the plan as one to keep a non-cooperating minority in line. This is coercion by economic pressure. The asserted power of choice is illusory. . . .

Congress has no power to enforce its commands on the farmer to the ends sought by the Agricultural Adjustment Act. It must follow that it may not indirectly accomplish those ends by taxing and spending to purchase compliance. The Constitution and the entire plan of our government negative any such use of the power to tax and to spend as the act undertakes to authorize. It does not help to declare that local conditions throughout the nation have created a situation of national concern; for this is but to say that whenever there is a widespread similarity of local conditions, Congress may ignore constitutional limitations upon its own powers and usurp those reserved to the states. If, in lieu of compulsory regulation of subjects within the states' reserved jurisdiction, which is prohibited, the Congress could invoke the taxing and spending power as a means to accomplish the same end, clause 1 of § 8 of article 1 would become the instrument for total subversion of the governmental powers reserved to the individual states.

If the act before us is a proper exercise of the federal taxing power, evidently the regulation of all industry throughout the United States may be accomplished by similar exercises of the same power. . . .

Until recently no suggestion of the existence of any such power in the federal government has been advanced. The expressions of the framers of the Constitution, the decisions of this court interpreting that instrument and the writings of great commentators will be searched in vain for any suggestion that there exists in the clause under discussion or elsewhere in the Constitution, the authority whereby every provision and every fair implication from that instrument may be subverted, the independence of the individual states obliterated, and the United States converted into a central government exercising uncontrolled police power in every state of the Union, superseding all local control or regulation of the affairs or concerns of the states. . . .

Affirmed.

MR. JUSTICE STONE, dissenting. . . .
[Reprinted *supra*, Chapter Three]

Chapter Twelve

THE
COMMERCE
POWER

INTRODUCTION

The commerce clause is written in terms of a positive grant of power to Congress, and it does not say what power to regulate commerce, if any, is left to the states. In fact, Congress was slow to exercise its authority under the commerce clause, and for the first century of national existence, commerce power problems turned primarily on how far the states could go in regulating commerce without invading the congressional sphere.

This was the issue presented *Gibbons* v. *Ogden* (1824), the first commerce clause decision and one in which Chief Justice Marshall laid down principles that have affected all subsequent interpretations of its language. One major aspect of the ruling was the statement that congressional power over commerce "may very properly be restricted to that commerce which concerns more States than one." This language was soon translated into a distinction between "interstate" and "intrastate" commerce, with federal power limited to the former category and the crossing of a state line as the primary condition for congressional control.

Conversely, commercial operations which did not cross state lines had a prima facie claim to escape congressional regulation. This constitutional position came to be of great practical importance toward the end of the nineteenth century when Congress began to make greater use of its regulatory powers. Thus a prosecution of the sugar trust under the Sherman Act of 1890 was defeated in *United States* v. *E. C. Knight Co.* (1895) on the ground that the refining of sugar took place in one state and was a completely separate process from its distribution in interstate commerce.

Because of this production–distribution distinction, much litigation has been concerned with the precise point at which the local activity ends and interstate transportation begins. In general the rule is that local movement of goods preparatory to their delivery to a common carrier is not part of the interstate journey. The point at which commerce loses its interstate or foreign character and comes under state regulatory control has been an equally difficult problem. In *Brown* v. *Maryland* (1827) Marshall held that goods imported from abroad retained their character as imports as long as they remained unsold in the original package. The effect of the "original package" doctrine has been to prevent states from exerting their police power, but not their taxing power, on goods brought in from other states until after the first sale.

Congressional power to "regulate" commerce has been construed very broadly to cover not only protection and promotion but also restriction and even complete prohibition. Congress has on occasions used the commerce power as a kind of national police power. An 1895 statute making it unlawful to transport lottery tickets from state to state was upheld by the Court in *Champion* v. *Ames* (1903), and the same method of exclusion from interstate commerce was successfully used against impure food and drugs [*Hipolite Egg Co.* v. *United States* (1911)] and the white slave traffic [*Hoke* v. *United States* (1913)].

However, by a five to four vote in **Hammer v. Dagenhart** (1918) the Court declared the federal Child Labor Act of 1916 unconstitutional for its use of the same tactic. The Court sought to explain the inconsistency by arguing that lottery tickets and impure goods were harmful in and of themselves, while goods produced by child labor "are of themselves harmless." The weakness of this argument was obvious from the start, and eventually the *Hammer* decision was overruled in *United States* v. *Darby Lumber Co.* (1941).

Congressional power of regulation does not depend entirely upon the test of crossing a state line, however. In the *Gibbons* case Marshall recognized that commercial transactions within one state that "affected" other states might be subject to federal regulation. The Supreme Court has applied the "effect on commerce" doctrine in many situations. For example, where there is a "stream of commerce" moving across state lines, as in the raising of cattle and their transportation to stockyards for slaughter and processing, or in the growing, transportation, and marketing of grain, the sales in the stockyards or on the grain exchanges are integral parts of a stream of commerce which are subject to congressional regulation. The *Shreveport Rate Case* (1914) held that where intrastate freight rates have the effect of burdening commerce moving under interstate rates Congress can control the intrastate rates.

The Supreme Court, having once accepted "effect" on commerce as a justification for congressional regulation, was concerned that this test might be carried so far as to wipe out all areas of state control. Consequently, it endeavored to find some method for keeping the effect test within bounds. The device developed for this purpose was the "direct–indirect" distinction. A direct effect on commerce could be the basis for federal control but an indirect effect could not.

The two most famous cases in which the Court denied congressional power to regulate because of this test were ***Schechter Poultry Corp.* v. *United States*** (1935) and *Carter* v. *Carter Coal Co.* (1936). In both decisions the Court held unconstitutional legislation under which the President had promulgated codes of fair practice for most of the industries of the country, large and small, fixing minimum wages and maximum hours and regulating unfair or destructive competitive practices. The *Schechter* case involved the live poultry code, and the *Carter* case the bituminous coal code. In both cases the Court found that the activities were not transactions in interstate commerce, nor did they directly affect commerce. In the *Carter* case Justice Sutherland attempted to explain the difference between direct and indirect effects:

> The word "direct" implies that the activity or condition invoked or blamed shall operate proximately—not mediately, remotely, or collaterally—to produce the effect. It connotes the absence of an efficient intervening agency or condition. And the extent of the effect bears no logical relation to its character. . . . If the production by one man of a single ton of coal intended for interstate sale and shipment . . . affects interstate commerce indirectly, the effect does not become direct by multiplying the tonnage, or increasing the number of men employed, or adding to the expense or complexities of the business, or by all combined.

A constitutional doctrine that denied Congress the power to deal with national economic emergencies could not long be maintained. In 1937 the Court in ***National Labor Relations Board* v. *Jones & Laughlin Co.*** upheld the Wagner Act and in the process effectively liquidated directness of effect on commerce as a test of congressional power.

The *Jones & Laughlin* decision stated such a broad basis for the commerce power that few serious commerce clause cases subsequently arose. The Fair Labor Standards Act, legislating minimum wages and maximum hours as conditions for the shipment of goods in interstate commerce, was upheld in **United States v. Darby Lumber Co.** (1941). Drastic agricultural regulations were accepted by the Court in **Wickard v. Filburn** (1942). The Sherman Act was held applicable to the insurance business in *United States* v. *South-Eastern Underwriters Assn.* (1944), although Congress did take action to permit state regulation to continue. The Civil Rights Act of 1964, banning racial discrimination in public accommodations throughout the country, was upheld on the basis of the commerce power in **Heart of Atlanta Motel v. United States** (1964). The Civil Rights Act of 1968 prohibiting discrimination on the basis of race, color, religion, or national origin in the sale or rental of housing was based on the commerce clause, as was the Anti-Riot Act of 1968 which made it a federal crime to use the facilities of interstate commerce, or to cross state lines, for the purpose of inciting a riot or violence.

The only apparent limitation on the broad sweep of commerce power is the possible revival by the Burger Court of state sovereignty and the reserved powers of the states under the Tenth Amendment. In 1968 the Warren Court in *Maryland* v. *Wirtz* had predictably upheld an amendment to the Fair Labor Standards Act which extended minimum wage coverage to nonprofessional employees of state public schools, hospitals, and related institutions. Again, in *Fry* v. *United States* (1975) the federal wage and salary controls imposed under the Economic Stabilization Act of 1970 were held applicable to state employees. But in *National League of Cities* v. *Usery* (1976) a 1974 federal wages and overtime law was held to violate state sovereignty, and *Wirtz* was overruled. These cases will be discussed in Chapter Fourteen.

GIBBONS V. OGDEN

9 Wheat. 1, 6 L. Ed. 23 (1824)

Ogden had an exclusive license from the state of New York authorizing him to navigate its waters by steamboat. Gibbons had a license from the federal government under a 1795 act to engage in coastal navigation. Ogden sought to enjoin Gibbons from operating his vessels within New York waters. The injunction was issued, and Gibbons appealed.

MR. CHIEF JUSTICE MARSHALL delivered the opinion of the Court. . . .
The appellant contends that this decree is erroneous, because the [New York] laws which purport to give the exclusive privilege it sustains, are repugnant . . . to that clause in the Constitution which authorizes Congress to regulate commerce. . . .

As preliminary to the very able discussions of the constitution, which we have heard from the bar, and as having some influence on its construction, reference has been made to the political situation of these states, anterior to its formation. It has been said, that they were sovereign, were completely independent, and were connected with each other only by a league. This is true. But when these allied sovereigns converted their league into a government, when they converted their congress of ambassadors, deputed to deliberate on their common concerns, and to recommend measures of general utility, into a legislature, empowered to enact laws on the most interesting subjects, the whole character in which the states appear, underwent a change, the extent of which must be determined by a fair consideration of the instrument by which that change was effected.

This instrument contains an enumeration of powers expressly granted by the people to their government. It has been said, that these powers ought to be construed strictly. But why ought they to be so construed? Is there one sentence in the constitution which gives countenance to this rule? In the last of the enumerated powers, that which grants, expressly, the means for carrying all others into execution, congress is authorized "to make all laws which shall be necessary and proper" for the purpose. But this limitation on the means which may be used, is not extended to the powers which are conferred; nor is there one sentence in the constitution, which has been pointed out by the gentlemen of the bar, or which we have been able to discern, that prescribes this rule. We do not, therefore, think ourselves justified in adopting it. What do gentlemen mean, by a strict construction? If they contend only against that enlarged construction, which would extend words beyond their natural and obvious import, we might question the application of the term, but should not controvert the principle. If they contend for that narrow construction which, in support of some theory not to be found in the constitution, would deny to the government those powers which the words of the grant, as usually understood, import, and which are consistent with the general views and objects of the instrument—for that narrow construction, which would cripple the government, and render it unequal to the objects for which it is declared to be instituted, and to which the powers given, as fairly understood, render it competent—then we cannot perceive the propriety of this strict construction, nor adopt it as the rule by which the constitution is to be expounded. As men whose intentions require no concealment, generally employ the words which most directly and aptly express the ideas they intend to convey, the enlightened patriots who framed our constitution, and the people who adopted it, must be understood to have employed words in their natural sense, and to have intended what they have said. If, from the imperfection of human language, there should be serious doubts respecting the extent of any given power, it is a well settled rule, that the objects for which it was given, especially, when those objects are expressed in the instrument itself, should have great influence in the construction. . . . We know of no rule for construing the extent of such powers, other than is given by the language of the instrument which confers them, taken in connection with the purposes for which they were conferred.

The words are: "Congress shall have power to regulate commerce with foreign nations, and among the several states, and with the Indian tribes."

The subject to be regulated is commerce; and our constitution being, as was aptly said at the bar, one of enumeration, and not of definition, to ascertain the extent of the power, it becomes necessary to settle the meaning of the word. The counsel for the appellee would limit it to traffic, to buying and selling, or the interchange of commodities, and do not admit that it comprehends navigation. This would restrict a general term, applicable to many objects, to one of its significations. Commerce, undoubtedly, is traffic, but it is something more—it is intercourse. It describes the commercial intercourse between nations, and parts of nations, in all its branches, and is regulated by prescribing rules for carrying on that intercourse. The mind can scarcely conceive a system for regulating commerce between nations which shall exclude all laws concerning navigation, which shall be silent on the admission of the vessels of the one nation into the ports of the other, and be confined to prescribing rules for the conduct of individuals, in the actual employment of buying and selling or of barter.

If commerce does not include navigation, the government of the Union has no direct power over that subject, and can make no law prescribing what shall constitute American vessels, or requiring that they shall be navigated by American seamen. Yet this power has been exercised from the commencement of the government, has been exercised with the consent of all, and has been understood by all to be a commercial regulation. All America understands, and has uniformly understood, the word "commerce," to comprehend navigation. It was so understood, and must have been so understood, when the constitution was framed. The power over commerce, including navigation, was one of the primary objects for which the people of America adopted their government, and must have been contemplated in forming it. The convention must have used the word in that sense, because all have understood it in that sense, and the attempt to restrict it comes too late. . . .

The word used in the constitution, then, comprehends, and has been always understood to comprehend, navigation within its meaning; and a power to regulate navigation, is as expressly granted, as if that term had been added to the word "commerce." To what commerce does this power extend? The constitution informs us, to commerce "with foreign nations, and among the several states, and with the Indian tribes." It has, we believe, been universally admitted, that these words comprehend every species of commercial intercourse between the United States and foreign nations. No sort of trade can be carried on between this country and any other, to which this power does not extend. It has been truly said, that commerce, as the word is used in the constitution, is a unit, every part of which is indicated by the term.

If this be the admitted meaning of the word, in its application to foreign nations, it must carry the same meaning throughout the sentence, and remain a unit, unless there be some plain intelligible cause which alters it.

The subject to which the power is next applied, is to commerce, "among the several states." The word "among" means intermingled with. A thing which is among others, is intermingled with them. Commerce among the states, cannot stop at the external boundary line of each state, but may be introduced into the interior.

It is not intended to say, that these words comprehend that commerce, which is completely internal, which is carried on between man and man in a state, or between different parts of the same state, and which does not extend to or affect other states. Such a power would be inconvenient, and is certainly unnecessary.

Comprehensive as the word "among" is, it may very properly be restricted to that commerce which concerns more states than one. The phrase is not one which would probably have been selected to indicate the completely interior traffic of a state, because it is not an apt phrase for that purpose; and the enumeration of the particular classes of commerce to which the power was to be extended, would not have been made, had the intention been to extend the power to every description. The enumeration presupposes something not enumerated; and that something, if we regard the language or the subject of the sentence, must be the exclusively internal commerce of a state. The genius and character of the whole government seem to be, that its action is to be applied to all the external concerns of the nation, and to those internal concerns which affect the states generally; but not to those which are completely within a particular state, which do not affect other states, and with which it is not necessary to interfere, for the purpose of executing some of the general powers of the government. The completely internal commerce of a state, then, may be considered as reserved for the state itself.

But, in regulating commerce with foreign nations, the power of congress does not stop at the jurisdictional lines of the several states. It would be a very useless power, if it could not pass those lines. The commerce of the United States with foreign nations is that of the whole United States; every district has a right to participate in it. The deep streams which penetrate our country in every direction pass through the interior of almost every state in the Union, and furnish the means of exercising this right. If congress has the power to regulate it, that power must be exercised whenever the subject exists. If it exists within the states, if a foreign voyage may commence or terminate at a port within a state, then the power of congress may be exercised within a state.

This principle is, if possible, still more clear, when applied to commerce "among the several states." They either join each other, in which case they are separated by a mathematical line, or they are remote from each other, in which case other states lie between them. What is commerce "among" them; and how is it to be conducted? Can a trading expedition between two adjoining states, commence and terminate outside of each? And if the trading intercourse be between two states remote from each other, must it not commence in one, terminate in the other, and probably pass through a third? Commerce among the states must of necessity, be commerce with the states. In the regulation of trade with the Indian tribes, the action of the law, especially, when the constitution was made, was chiefly within a state. The power of congress, then, whatever it may be, must be exercised within the territorial jurisdiction of the several states. . . .

We are now arrived at the inquiry—what is this power? It is the power to regulate; that is, to prescribe the rule by which commerce is to be governed. This power, like all others vested in congress, is complete in itself, may be exercised to its utmost extent, and acknowledges no limitations, other than are prescribed in the constitution. These are expressed in plain terms, and do not affect the questions which arise in this case, or which have been discussed at the bar. . . .

But it has been urged, with great earnestness, that although the power of congress to regulate commerce with foreign nations, and among the several states, be co-extensive with the subject itself, and have no other limits than are prescribed in the constitution, yet the states may severally exercise the same power within their respective jurisdictions. In support of this argument, it is said that they possessed it as an inseparable attribute of sovereignty before the formation of the constitution, and still retain it, except so far as they have surrendered it by that instrument; that this principle results from the nature of the government, and is secured by the tenth amendment; that an affirmative grant of power is not exclusive, unless in its own nature it be such that the continued exercise of it by the former possessor is inconsistent with the grant, and that this is not of that description.

The appellant, conceding these postulates, except the last, contends that full power to regulate a particular subject implies the whole power, and leaves no residuum; that a grant of the whole is incompatible with the existence of a right in another to any part of it. Both parties have appealed to the constitution, to legislative acts, and judicial decisions; and have drawn arguments from all these sources to support and illustrate the propositions they respectively maintain.

The grant of the power to lay and collect taxes is, like the power to regulate commerce, made in general terms, and has never been understood to interfere with the exercise of the same power by the states; and hence has been drawn an argument which has been applied to the question under consideration. But the two grants are not, it is conceived, similar in their terms or their nature. Although many of the powers formerly exercised by the states are transferred to the government of the

Union, yet the state governments remain, and constitute a most important part of our system. The power of taxation is indispensable to their existence, and is a power which, in its own nature, is capable of residing in, and being exercised by, different authorities at the same time. We are accustomed to see it placed, for different purposes, in different hands. Taxation is the simple operation of taking small portions from a perpetually accumulating mass, susceptible of almost infinite division; and a power in one to take what is necessary for certain purposes, is not in its nature incompatible with a power in another to take what is necessary for other purposes. Congress is authorized to lay and collect taxes, etc., to pay the debts, and provide for the common defense and general welfare of the United States. This does not interfere with the power of the states to tax for the support of their own governments; nor is the exercise of that power by the states an exercise of any portion of the power that is granted to the United States. In imposing taxes for state purposes, they are not doing what congress is empowered to do. Congress is not empowered to tax for those purposes which are within the exclusive province of the States. When, then, each government exercises the power of taxation, neither is exercising the power of the other. But when a state proceeds to regulate commerce with foreign nations, or among the several states, it is exercising the very power that is granted to congress, and is doing the very thing which congress is authorized to do. There is no analogy, then, between the power of taxation and the power of regulating commerce.

In discussing the question whether this power is still in the states, in the case under consideration, we may dismiss from it the inquiry, whether it is surrendered by the mere grant to congress, or is retained until congress shall exercise the power. We may dismiss that inquiry because it has been exercised, and the regulations which congress deemed it proper to make are now in full operation. The sole question is, can a state regulate commerce with foreign nations and among the states while congress is regulating it? . . .

[MARSHALL'S conclusion was that] the laws of New York, as expounded by the highest tribunal of that state, have, in their application to this case, come into collision with an act of congress, and deprived a citizen of a right to which that act entitles him. . . .

The nullity of any act, inconsistent with the constitution, is produced by the declaration, that the constitution is the supreme law. The appropriate application of that part of the clause which confers the same supremacy on laws and treaties, is to such acts of the state legislatures as do not transcend their powers, but though enacted in the execution of acknowledged state powers, interfere with, or are contrary to, the laws of congress, made in pursuance of the constitution, or some treaty made under the authority of the United States. In every such case, the act of congress, or the treaty, is supreme; and the law of the state, though enacted in the exercise of powers not controverted, must yield to it. . . .

HAMMER V. DAGENHART

247 U.S. 251, 38 S. Ct. 529, 62 L. Ed. 1101 (1918)

The federal Child Labor Act of 1916 forbade the shipment in interstate commerce of goods produced by child labor. A lobbyist for Southern textile mills secured a constitutional challenge of the statute by arranging for the father of two children who worked in a North Carolina cotton mill to bring suit against enforcement of the act.[1]

MR. JUSTICE DAY delivered the opinion of the Court. . . .

The controlling question for decision is: Is it within the authority of Congress in regulating commerce among the States to prohibit the transportation in interstate commerce of manufactured goods, the product of a factory in which, within thirty days prior to their removal therefrom, children under the age of fourteen have been employed or permitted to work, or children between the ages of fourteen and sixteen years have been employed or permitted to work more than eight hours in any day, or more than six days in any week, or after the hour of 7 o'clock p.m. or before the hour of 6 o'clock a.m.?

The power essential to the passage of this act, the Government contends, is found in the commerce clause of the Constitution which authorizes Congress to regulate commerce with foreign nations and among the States.

In *Gibbons* v. *Ogden* . . . Chief Justice Marshall, speaking for this court, and defining the extent and nature of the commerce power, said, "It is the power to regulate, that is, to prescribe the rule by which commerce is to be governed." In other words, the power is one to control the means by which commerce is carried on, which is directly the contrary of the assumed right to forbid commerce from moving and thus destroy it as to particular commodities. But it is insisted that adjudged cases in this court establish the doctrine that the power to regulate given to Congress incidentally includes the authority to prohibit the movement of ordinary commodities and therefore that the subject is not open for discussion. The cases demonstrate the contrary. They rest upon the character of the particular subjects dealt with and the fact that the scope of governmental authority, state or national, possessed over them is such that the authority to prohibit is as to them but the exertion of the power to regulate.

The first of these cases is *Champion* v. *Ames,* . . . the so-called Lottery Case, in which it was held that Congress might pass a law having the effect to keep the channels of commerce free from use in the transportation of

[1]For the story of the development of this lawsuit, see Stephen B. Wood, *Constitutional Politics in the Progressive Era: Child Labor and the Law* (Chicago: The University of Chicago Press, 1968).

tickets used in the promotion of lottery schemes. In *Hipolite Egg Co.* v. *United States* . . . this court sustained the power of Congress to pass the Pure Food and Drug Act, which prohibited the introduction into the States by means of interstate commerce of impure foods and drugs. . . . In *Caminetti* v. *United States* . . . we held that Congress might prohibit the transportation of women in interstate commerce for the purpose of debauchery and kindred purposes. In *Clark Distilling Co.* v. *Western Maryland Railway Co.* . . . concluding the discussion which sustained the authority of the government to prohibit the transportation of liquor in interstate commerce, the court said: "The exceptional nature of the subject here regulated is the basis upon which the exceptional power exerted must rest and affords no ground for any fear that such power may be constitutionally extended to things which it may not, consistently with the guaranties of the Constitution, embrace."

In each of these instances the use of interstate transportation was necessary to accomplishment of harmful results. In other words, although the power over interstate transportation was to regulate, that could only be accomplished by prohibiting the use of the facilities of interstate commerce to effect the evil intended.

This element is wanting in the present case. The thing intended to be accomplished by this statute is the denial of the facilities of interstate commerce to those manufacturers in the States who employ children within the prohibited ages. The act in its effect does not regulate transportation among the States, but aims to standardize the ages at which children may be employed in mining and manufacturing within the States. The goods shipped are of themselves harmless. The act permits them to be freely shipped after thirty days from the time of their removal from the factory. When offered for shipment, and before transportation begins, the labor of their production is over, and the mere fact that they were intended for interstate commerce transportation does not make their production subject to federal control under the commerce power.

Commerce "consists of intercourse and traffic . . . and includes the transportation of persons and property, as well as the purchase, sale and exchange of commodities." The making of goods and the mining of coal are not commerce, nor does the fact that these things are to be afterwards shipped or used in interstate commerce, make their production a part thereof. . . .

The grant of power to Congress over the subject of interstate commerce was to enable it to regulate such commerce, and not to give it authority to control the States in the exercise of the police power over local trade and manufacture.

The grant of authority over a purely federal matter was not intended to destroy the local power always existing and carefully reserved to the States in the Tenth Amendment to the Constitution. . . .

That there should be limitations upon the right to employ children in mines and factories in the interest of their own and the public welfare, all will admit. That such employment is generally deemed to require regulation is shown by the fact that the brief of counsel states that every State in the Union has a law upon the subject, limiting the right to thus employ children. In North Carolina, the State wherein is located the factory in which the employment was had in the present case, no child under twelve years of age is permitted to work.

It may be desirable that such laws be uniform, but our Federal Government is one of enumerated powers. . . .

In interpreting the Constitution it must never be forgotten that the nation is made up of States to which are entrusted the powers of local government. And to them and to the people the powers not expressly [sic] delegated to the national government are reserved. . . . To sustain this statute would not be in our judgment a recognition of the lawful exertion of congressional authority over interstate commerce, but would sanction an invasion by the federal power of the control of a matter purely local in its character, and over which no authority has been delegated to Congress in conferring the power to regulate commerce among the States.

We have neither authority nor disposition to question the motives of Congress in enacting this legislation. The purposes intended must be attained consistently with constitutional limitations and not by an invasion of the powers of the States. This court has no more important function than that which devolves upon it the obligation to preserve inviolate the constitutional limitations upon the exercise of authority, federal and state, to the end that each may continue to discharge, harmoniously with the other, the duties entrusted to it by the Constitution.

In our view the necessary effect of this act is, by means of a prohibition against the movement in interstate commerce of ordinary commercial commodities, to regulate the hours of labor of children in factories and mines within the States, a purely state authority. Thus the act in a twofold sense is repugnant to the Constitution. It not only transcends the authority delegated to Congress over commerce but also exerts a power as to a purely local matter to which the federal authority does not extend. The far-reaching result of upholding the act cannot be more plainly indicated than by pointing out that if Congress can thus regulate matters entrusted to local authority by prohibition of the movement of commodities in interstate commerce, all freedom of commerce will be at an end, and the power of the State over local matters may be eliminated, and thus our system of government be practically destroyed.

For these reasons we hold that this law exceeds the constitutional authority of Congress. It follows that the decree of the District Court must be

Affirmed.

MR. JUSTICE HOLMES, dissenting. . . .

The first step in my argument is to make plain what no one is likely to dispute—that the statute in question is within the power expressly given to Congress if considered only as to its immediate effects and that if invalid it is so only upon some collateral ground. The statute confines itself to prohibiting the carriage of certain goods in interstate or foreign commerce. Congress is given power to regulate such commerce in unqualified terms. It would not be argued today that the power to regulate does not include the power to prohibit. Regulation means the prohibition of something, and when interstate commerce is the matter to be regulated I cannot doubt that the regulation may prohibit any part of such commerce that Congress sees fit to forbid. At all events it is established by the Lottery Case and others that have followed it that a law is not beyond the regulative power of Congress merely because it prohibits certain transportation out and out. . . . So I repeat that this statute in its immediate operation is clearly within the Congress' constitutional power.

The question then is narrowed to whether the exercise of its otherwise constitutional power by Congress can be pronounced unconstitutional because of its possible reaction upon the conduct of the States in a matter upon which I have admitted that they are free from direct control. I should have thought that that matter had been disposed of so fully as to leave no room for doubt. I should have thought that the most conspicuous decisions of this Court had made it clear that the power to regulate commerce and other constitutional powers could not be cut down or qualified by the fact that it might interfere with the carrying out of the domestic policy of any state. . . .

The notion that prohibition is any less prohibition when applied to things now thought evil I do not understand. But if there is any matter upon which civilized countries have agreed—far more unanimously than they have with regard to intoxicants and some other matters over which this country is now emotionally aroused—it is the evil of premature and excessive child labor. I should have thought that if we were to introduce our own moral conceptions where in my opinion they do not belong, this was pre-eminently a case for upholding the exercise of all its powers by the United States.

But I had thought that the propriety of the exercise of a power admitted to exist in some cases was for the consideration of Congress alone and that this Court always had disavowed the right to intrude its judgment upon questions of policy or morals. It is not for this Court to pronounce when prohibition is necessary to regulation if it ever may be necessary— to say that it is permissible as against strong drink but not as against the product of ruined lives.

The act does not meddle with anything belonging to the States. They may regulate their internal affairs and their domestic commerce as they like. But when they seek to send their products across the state line they are no longer within their rights. If there were no Constitution and no Congress their power to cross the line would depend upon their neighbors. Under the Constitution such commerce belongs not to the States but to Congress to regulate. It may carry out its views of public policy whatever indirect effect they may have upon the activities of the States. Instead of being encountered by a prohibitive tariff at her boundaries the State encounters the public policy of the United States which it is for

Congress to express. The public policy of the United States is shaped with a view to the benefit of the nation as a whole. If, as has been the case within the memory of men still living, a State should take a different view of the propriety of sustaining a lottery from that which generally prevails, I cannot believe that the fact would require a different decision from that reached in *Champion* v. *Ames.* Yet in that case it would be said with quite as much force as in this that Congress was attempting to intermeddle with the State's domestic affairs. The national welfare as understood by Congress may require a different attitude within its sphere from that of some self-seeking State. It seems to me entirely constitutional for Congress to enforce its understanding by all the means at its command.

MR. JUSTICE MCKENNA, MR. JUSTICE BRANDEIS and MR. JUSTICE CLARKE concur in this opinion.

SCHECHTER POULTRY CORPORATION V. UNITED STATES

295 U.S. 495, 55 S. Ct. 87, 7 L. Ed. 1570 (1935)

The National Industrial Recovery Act was a major reliance of the Roosevelt New Deal in its attack on the Depression. Under the statute, codes of fair practice, approved by the President, were adopted for most of the industries of the country, large and small, fixing minimum wages and maximum hours, and regulating unfair or deceptive competitive practices. The statute covered transactions "in or affecting interstate or foreign commerce." In this case a New York poultry dealer challenged his conviction for violating provisions of the Live Poultry Code.

MR. CHIEF JUSTICE HUGHES delivered the opinion of the Court. . . .

FIRST. Two preliminary points are stressed by the Government with respect to the appropriate approach to the important questions presented. We are told that the provision of the statute authorizing the adoption of codes must be viewed in the light of the grave national crisis with which Congress was confronted. Undoubtedly, the conditions to which power is addressed are always to be considered when the exercise of power is challenged. Extraordinary conditions may call for extraordinary remedies. But the argument necessarily stops short of an attempt to justify action which lies outside the sphere of constitutional authority. Extraordinary conditions do not create or enlarge constitutional power. The Constitution established a national government with powers deemed to be adequate, as they have proved to be both in war and peace, but these powers of the national government are limited by the constitutional grants. Those who act under these grants are not at liberty to transcend the imposed limits because they believe that more or different power is

necessary. Such assertions of extra-constitutional authority were anticipated and precluded by the explicit terms of the Tenth Amendment,—
"The powers not delegated to the United States by the Constitution, nor prohibited by it to the States, are reserved to the States respectively, or to the people."

The further point is urged that the national crisis demanded a broad and intensive cooperative effort by those engaged in trade and industry, and that this necessary cooperation was sought to be fostered by permitting them to initiate the adoption of codes. But the statutory plan is not simply one for voluntary effort. It does not seek merely to endow voluntary trade or industrial associations or groups with privileges or immunities. It involves the coercive exercise of the law-making power. The codes of fair competition, which the statute attempts to authorize, are codes of laws. If valid, they place all persons within their reach under the obligation of positive law, binding equally those who assent and those who do not assent. Violations of the provisions of the codes are punishable as crimes.

SECOND. *The question of the delegation of legislative power....*

THIRD. *The question of the application of the provisions of the Live Poultry Code to intrastate transactions.* Although the validity of the codes (apart from the question of delegation) rests upon the commerce clause of the Constitution, section 3(a) is not in terms limited to interstate and foreign commerce. From the generality of its terms, and from the argument of the government at the bar, it would appear that section 3(a) was designed to authorize codes without that limitation. But under section 3(f) penalties are confined to violations of a code provision "in any transaction in or affecting interstate or foreign commerce." This aspect of the case presents the question whether the particular provisions of the Live Poultry Code, which the defendants were convicted for violating and for having conspired to violate, were within the regulating power of Congress.

These provisions relate to the hours and wages of those employed by defendants in their slaughterhouses in Brooklyn and to the sales there made to retail dealers and butchers.

(1) Were these transactions *"in"* interstate commerce? Much is made of the fact that almost all the poultry coming to New York is sent there from other States. But the code provisions, as here applied, do not concern the transportation of the poultry from other States to New York, or the transactions of the commission men or others to whom it is consigned, or the sales made by such consignees to defendants. When defendants had made their purchases, whether at the West Washington Market in New York City or at the railroad terminals serving the City, or elsewhere, the poultry was trucked to their slaughterhouses in Brooklyn for local disposition. The interstate transactions in relation to that poultry then ended. Defendants held the poultry at their slaughterhouse markets for slaughter and local sale to retail dealers and butchers who in turn sold directly to consumers. Neither the slaughtering nor the sales by defendants were transactions in interstate commerce. *Brown* v. *Houston....*

The undisputed facts thus afford no warrant for the argument that the poultry handled by defendants at their slaughterhouse markets was in a *"current"* or *"flow"* of interstate commerce and was thus subject to congressional regulation. The mere fact that there may be a constant flow of commodities into a State does not mean that the flow continues after the property has arrived and has become commingled with the mass of property within the State and is there held solely for local disposition and use. So far as the poultry here in question is concerned, the flow in interstate commerce had ceased. The poultry had come to a permanent rest within the State. It was not held, used, or sold by defendants in relation to any further transactions in interstate commerce and was not destined for transportation to other States. Hence, decisions which deal with a stream of interstate commerce—where goods come to rest within a State temporarily and are later to go forward in interstate commerce—and with the regulations of transactions involved in that practical continuity of movement, are not applicable here. . . .

(2) Did the defendants' transactions directly *"affect"* interstate commerce so as to be subject to federal regulation? The power of Congress extends not only to the regulation of transactions which are part of interstate commerce, but to the protection of that commerce from injury. It matters not that the injury may be due to the conduct of those engaged in intrastate operations. Thus, Congress may protect the safety of those employed in interstate transportation "no matter what may be the source of the dangers which threaten it." *Southern Railway Company* v. *United States.* . . . We said in *Second Employers' Liability Cases* . . . that it is the "effect upon interstate commerce," not "the source of the injury," which is "the criterion of congressional power." We have held that, in dealing with common carriers engaged in both interstate and intrastate commerce, the dominant authority of Congress necessarily embraces the right to control their intrastate operations in all matters having such a close and substantial relation to interstate traffic that the control is essential or appropriate to secure the freedom of that traffic from interference or unjust discrimination and to promote the efficiency of the interstate service. *The Shreveport Case.* . . . And combinations and conspiracies to restrain interstate commerce, or to monopolize any part of it, are none the less within the reach of the Anti-Trust Act because the conspirators seek to attain their ends by means of intrastate activities. . . .

The instant case is not of that sort. This is not a prosecution for a conspiracy to restrain or monopolize interstate commerce in violation of the Anti-Trust Act. Defendants have been convicted, not upon direct charges of injury to interstate commerce or of interference with persons engaged in that commerce, but of violations of certain provisions of the Live Poultry Code and of conspiracy to commit these violations. Interstate commerce is brought in only upon the charge that violations of these provisions—as to hours and wages of employees and local sales— *"affected"* interstate commerce.

In determining how far the federal government may go in controlling intrastate transactions upon the ground that they "affect" interstate commerce, there is a necessary and well-established distinction between direct and indirect effects. The precise line can be drawn only as individual cases arise, but the distinction is clear in principle. Direct effects are illustrated by the railroad cases we have cited, as *e.g.,* the effect of failure to use prescribed safety appliances on railroads which are the highways of both interstate and intrastate commerce, injury to an employee engaged in an intrastate movement, the fixing of rates for intrastate transportation which unjustly discriminate against interstate commerce. But where the effect of intrastate transactions upon interstate commerce is merely indirect, such transactions remain within the domain of state power. If the commerce clause were construed to reach all enterprises and transactions which could be said to have an indirect effect upon interstate commerce, the federal authority would embrace practically all the activities of the people and the authority of the State over its domestic concerns would exist only by sufferance of the federal government. . . .

. . . The Government argues that hours and wages affect prices; that slaughterhouse men sell at a small margin above operating costs; that labor represents 50 to 60 per cent of these costs; that a slaughterhouse operator paying lower wages or reducing his cost by exacting long hours of work, translates his saving into lower prices; that this results in demands for a cheaper grade of goods; and that the cutting of prices brings about a demoralization of the price structure. Similar conditions may be adduced in relation to other businesses. The argument of the Government proves too much. If the federal government may determine the wages and hours of employees in the internal commerce of a State, because of their relation to cost and prices and their indirect effect upon interstate commerce, it would seem that a similar control might be exerted over other elements of cost, also affecting prices, such as the number of employees, rents, advertising, methods of doing business, etc. All the processes of production and distribution that enter into cost could likewise be controlled. If the cost of doing an intrastate business is in itself the permitted object of federal control, the extent of the regulation of cost would be a question of discretion and not of power.

The Government also makes the point that efforts to enact state legislation establishing high labor standards have been impeded by the belief that unless similar action is taken generally, commerce will be diverted from the States adopting such standards, and that this fear of diversion has led to demands for federal legislation on the subject of wages and hours. The apparent implication is that the federal authority under the commerce clause should be deemed to extend to the establishment of rules to govern wages and hours in intrastate trade and industry generally throughout the country, thus overriding the authority of the States to deal with domestic problems arising from labor conditions in their internal commerce.

It is not the province of the Court to consider the economic advantages or disadvantages of such a centralized system. It is sufficient to say that the Federal Constitution does not provide for it. Our growth and development have called for wide use of the commerce power of the federal government in its control over the expanded activities of interstate commerce, and in protecting that commerce from burdens, interferences, and conspiracies to restrain and monopolize it. But the authority of the federal government may not be pushed to such an extreme as to destroy the distinction, which the commerce clause itself establishes, between commerce "among the several States" and the internal concerns of a State. The same answer must be made to the contention that is based upon the serious economic situation which led to the passage of the Recovery Act, —the fall in prices, the decline in wages and employment, and the curtailment of the market for commodities. Stress is laid upon the great importance of maintaining wage distributions which would provide the necessary stimulus in starting "the cumulative forces making for expanding commercial activity." Without in any way disparaging this motive, it is enough to say that the recuperative efforts of the federal government must be made in a manner consistent with the authority granted by the Constitution. . . .

Mr. Justice Cardozo, concurring. . . .

NATIONAL LABOR RELATIONS BOARD V. JONES & LAUGHLIN STEEL CORP.

301 U.S. 1, 57 S. Ct. 615, 81 L. Ed. 893 (1937)

In 1935 Congress passed the National Labor Relations Act, also known as the Wagner Act, to protect the rights of employees to form unions and to bargain collectively. Certain types of interference with these rights were defined as unfair labor practices. The National Labor Relations Board was created by the statute to enforce its provisions. The NLRB charged the Jones & Laughlin Steel Corporation with various unfair and anti-union labor practices and ordered it to cease and desist and to take various remedial actions. The company refused to comply, and the Board sought enforcement of its order in court.

Mr. Chief Justice Hughes delivered the opinion of the Court. . . .

The Scope of the Act.—The Act is challenged in its entirety as an attempt to regulate all industry, thus invading the reserved powers of the States over their local concerns. It is asserted that the references in the Act to interstate and foreign commerce are colorable at best; that the Act is not a true regulation of such commerce or of matters which directly affect it but on the contrary has the fundamental object of placing under the compulsory supervision of the federal government all industrial labor relations within the nation. The argument seeks support in the broad words of the preamble (section one) and in the sweep of the provisions of the Act, and it is further insisted that its legislative history shows an essential universal purpose in the light of which its scope cannot be limited by either construction or by the application of the separability clause.

If this conception of terms, intent and consequent inseparability were sound, the Act would necessarily fall by reason of the limitation upon the federal power which inheres in the constitutional grant, as well as because of the explicit reservation of the Tenth Amendment. *Schechter Corp.* v. *United States.* . . . The authority of the federal government may not be pushed to such an extreme as to destroy the distinction, which the commerce clause itself establishes, between commerce "among the several States" and the internal concerns of a State. That distinction between what is national and what is local in the activities of commerce is vital to the maintenance of our federal system. . . .

We think it clear that the National Labor Relations Act may be construed so as to operate within the sphere of constitutional authority. The jurisdiction conferred upon the Board, and invoked in this instance, is found in § 10 (a), which provides:

"Sec. 10(a). The Board is empowered, as hereinafter provided, to prevent any person from engaging in any unfair labor practice (listed in § 8) affecting commerce."

The critical words of this provision, prescribing the limits of the Board's authority in dealing with the labor practices, are "affecting commerce." . . .

There can be no question that the commerce thus contemplated by the Act (aside from that within a Territory or the District of Columbia) is interstate and foreign commerce in the constitutional sense. The Act also defines the term "affecting commerce" (§ 2(6)):

"The term 'affecting commerce' means in commerce, or burdening or obstructing commerce or the free flow of commerce, or having led or tending to lead to a labor dispute burdening or obstructing commerce or the free flow of commerce."

This definition is one of exclusion as well as inclusion. The grant of authority to the Board does not purport to extend to the relationship between all industrial employees and employers. Its terms do not impose collective bargaining upon all industry regardless of effects upon interstate or foreign commerce. It purports to reach only what may be deemed to burden or obstruct that commerce and, thus qualified, it must be construed as contemplating the exercise of control within constitutional bounds. It is a familiar principle that acts which directly burden or obstruct interstate or foreign commerce, or its free flow, are within the reach of the congressional power. Acts having that effect are not rendered immune because they grow out of labor disputes. . . . Whether or not particular action does affect commerce in such a close and intimate fashion as to be subject to federal control, and hence to lie within the authority conferred upon the Board, is left by the statute to be determined as individual cases arise. . . .

THE APPLICATION OF THE ACT TO EMPLOYEES ENGAGED IN PRODUC-
TION.—THE PRINCIPLE INVOLVED.—Respondent says that whatever may
be said of employees engaged in interstate commerce, the industrial
relations and activities in the manufacturing department of respondent's
enterprise are not subject to federal regulation. The argument rests upon
the proposition that manufacturing in itself is not commerce. . . .

. . . Reference is made to our decision sustaining the Packers and
Stockyards Act. *Stafford* v. *Wallace.* . . . The Court found that the stockyards were but a "throat" through which the current of commerce flowed
and the transactions which there occurred could not be separated from
that movement. Hence the sales at the stockyards were not regarded as
merely local transactions, for while they created "a local change of title"
they did not "stop the flow," but merely changed the private interests in
the subject of the current. . . .

Respondent contends that the instant case presents material distinctions. Respondent says that the Aliquippa plant is extensive in size and
represents a large investment in buildings, machinery and equipment.
The raw materials which are brought to the plant are delayed for long
periods and, after being subjected to manufacturing processes "are
changed substantially as to character, utility and value." . . .

We do not find it necessary to determine whether these features of
defendant's business dispose of the asserted analogy to the "stream of
commerce" cases. The instances in which that metaphor has been used
are but particular, and not exclusive, illustrations of the protective power
which the Government invokes in support of the present Act. The congressional authority to protect interstate commerce from burdens and
obstructions is not limited to transactions which can be deemed to be an
essential part of a "flow" of interstate or foreign commerce. Burdens and
obstructions may be due to injurious action springing from other sources.
The fundamental principle is that the power to regulate commerce is the
power to enact "all appropriate legislation" for "its protection and advancement" . . . to adopt measures "to promote its growth and insure its
safety" . . . "to foster, protect, control and restrain." . . . That power is
plenary and may be exerted to protect interstate commerce "no matter
what the source of the dangers which threaten it." . . . Although activities
may be intrastate in character when separately considered, if they have
such a close and substantial relation to interstate commerce that their
control is essential or appropriate to protect that commerce from burdens and obstructions, Congress cannot be denied the power to exercise
that control. *Schechter Corporation* v. *United States.* Undoubtedly the scope
of this power must be considered in the light of our dual system of
government and may not be extended so as to embrace effects upon
interstate commerce so indirect and remote that to embrace them, in view
of our complex society, would effectually obliterate the distinction between what is national and what is local and create a completely centralized government. *Id.* The question is necessarily one of degree. As the
Court said in . . . *Stafford* v. *Wallace*: "Whatever amounts to more or less

constant practice, and threatens to obstruct or unduly to burden the freedom of interstate commerce is within the regulatory power of Congress under the commerce clause and it is primarily for Congress to consider and decide the fact of the danger and meet it."

That intrastate activities, by reason of close and intimate relation to interstate commerce, may fall within federal control is demonstrated in the case of carriers who are engaged in both interstate and intrastate transportation. There federal control has been found essential to secure the freedom of interstate traffic from interference or unjust discrimination and to promote the efficiency of the interstate service. . . .

The close and intimate effect which brings the subject within the reach of federal power may be due to activities in relation to productive industry although the industry when separately viewed is local. This has been abundantly illustrated in the application of the federal Anti-Trust Act. . . .

It is thus apparent that the fact that the employees here concerned were engaged in production is not determinative. The question remains as to the effect upon interstate commerce of the labor practice involved. In the Schechter case, we found that the effect there was so remote as to be beyond the federal power. To find "immediacy or directness" there was to find it "almost everywhere," a result inconsistent with the maintenance of our federal system. In the Carter case, the Court was of the opinion that the provisions of the statute relating to production were invalid upon several grounds,—that there was improper delegation of legislative power, and that the requirements not only went beyond any sustainable measure of protection of interstate commerce but were also inconsistent with due process. These cases are not controlling here.

EFFECTS OF THE UNFAIR LABOR PRACTICE IN RESPONDENT'S ENTERPRISE.—Giving full weight to respondent's contention with respect to a break in the complete continuity of the "stream of commerce" by reason of respondent's manufacturing operations, the fact remains that the stoppage of those operations by industrial strife would have a most serious effect upon interstate commerce. In view of respondent's far-flung activities, it is idle to say that the effect would be indirect or remote. It is obvious that it would be immediate and might be catastrophic. We are asked to shut our eyes to the plainest facts of our national life and to deal with the question of direct and indirect effects in an intellectual vacuum. Because there may be but indirect and remote effects upon interstate commerce in connection with a host of local enterprises throughout the country, it does not follow that other industrial activities do not have such a close and intimate relation to interstate commerce as to make the presence of industrial strife a matter of the most urgent national concern. When industries organize themselves on a national scale, making their relation to interstate commerce the dominant factor in their activities, how can it be maintained that their industrial labor relations constitute a forbidden field into which Congress may not enter when it is necessary to protect interstate commerce from the paralyzing consequences of industrial war? We have often said that interstate commerce itself is a practical conception. It is equally true that interferences with that commerce must be appraised by a judgment that does not ignore actual experience. . . .

Our conclusion is that the order of the Board was within its competency and that the Act is valid as here applied. The judgment of the Circuit Court of Appeals is reversed and the cause is remanded for further proceedings in conformity with this opinion.

Reversed.

MR. JUSTICE MCREYNOLDS delivered the following dissenting opinion. . . .

MR. JUSTICE VAN DEVANTER, MR. JUSTICE SUTHERLAND, MR. JUSTICE BUTLER and I are unable to agree with the decisions just announced. . . .

The Court as we think departs from well-established principles followed in *A. L. A. Schechter Poultry Corp.* v. *United States* . . . and *Carter* v. *Carter Coal Co.* . . . Every consideration brought forward to uphold the Act before us was applicable to support the Acts held unconstitutional in causes decided within two years. And the lower courts rightly deemed them controlling.

By its terms the Labor Act extends to employers—large and small—unless excluded by definition, and declares that if one of these interferes with, restrains, or coerces any employee regarding his labor affiliations, etc., this shall be regarded as unfair labor practice. . . .

The three respondents happen to be manufacturing concerns—one large, two relatively small. The Act is now applied to each upon grounds common to all. Obviously what is determined as to these concerns may gravely affect a multitude of employers who engage in a great variety of private enterprises—mercantile, manufacturing, publishing, stockraising, mining, etc. It puts into the hands of a Board control over purely local industry beyond anything heretofore deemed permissible. . . .

Any effect on interstate commerce by the discharge of employees shown here, would be indirect and remote in the highest degree, as consideration of the facts will show. In No. 419 [*National Labor Relations Board* v. *Jones & Laughlin Steel Corp.*] ten men out of ten thousand were discharged; in the other cases only a few. The immediate effect in the factory may be to create discontent among all those employed and a strike may follow, which, in turn, may result in reducing production, which ultimately may reduce the volume of goods moving in interstate commerce. By this chain of indirect and progressively remote events we finally reach the evil with which it is said the legislation under consideration undertakes to deal. A more remote and indirect interference with interstate commerce or a more definite invasion of the powers reserved to the States is difficult, if not impossible, to imagine.

The Constitution still recognizes the existence of States with indestructible powers; the Tenth Amendment was supposed to put them beyond controversy.

UNITED STATES V. DARBY LUMBER CO.

312 U.S. 100, 61 S. Ct. 451, 85 L. Ed. 609 (1941)

The Fair Labor Standards Act of 1938, also known as the Wages and Hours Act, provided for the fixing of minimum wages and maximum hours for employees "engaged in commerce or in the production of goods for commerce." The constitutional justification for the statute was that production of goods under substandard conditions constituted unfair competition, burdened commerce, and led to labor disputes.

MR. JUSTICE STONE delivered the opinion of the court. . . .

The two principal questions raised by the record in this case are, *first,* whether Congress has constitutional power to prohibit the shipment in interstate commerce of lumber manufactured by employees whose wages are less than a prescribed minimum or whose weekly hours of labor at that wage are greater than a prescribed maximum, and, *second,* whether it has power to prohibit the employment of workmen in the production of goods "for interstate commerce" at other than prescribed wages and hours.

The demurrer, so far as now relevant to the appeal, challenged the validity of the Fair Labor Standards Act under the Commerce Clause and the Fifth and Tenth Amendments. The district court quashed the indictment in its entirety upon the broad grounds that the Act, which it interpreted as a regulation of manufacture within the states, is unconstitutional. It declared that manufacture is not interstate commerce and that the regulation by the Fair Labor Standards Act of wages and hours of employment of those engaged in the manufacture of goods which it is intended at the time of production "may or will be" after production "sold in interstate commerce in part or in whole" is not within the congressional power to regulate interstate commerce.

The effect of the court's decision and judgment are thus to deny the power of Congress to prohibit shipment in interstate commerce of lumber produced for interstate commerce under the proscribed substandard labor conditions of wages and hours, its power to penalize the employer for his failure to conform to the wage and hour provisions in the case of employees engaged in the production of lumber which he intends thereafter to ship in interstate commerce in part or in whole according to the normal course of his business and its power to compel him to keep records of hours of employment as required by the statute and the regulations of the administrator. . . .

While manufacture is not of itself interstate commerce the shipment of manufactured goods interstate is such commerce and the prohibition of such shipment by Congress is indubitably a regulation of the commerce. The power to regulate commerce is the power "to prescribe the rule by which commerce is governed." *Gibbons* v. *Ogden*. . . . It extends not only to those regulations which aid, foster and protect the commerce, but embraces those which prohibit it. . . . It is conceded that the power of Congress to prohibit transportation in interstate commerce includes noxious articles, *Lottery Case; Hipolite Egg Co.* v. *United States* . . . cf. *Hoke* v. *United States;* . . . stolen articles, *Brooks* v. *United States* . . . kidnapped persons, *Gooch* v. *United States,* . . . and articles such as intoxicating liquor or convict made goods, traffic in which is forbidden or restricted by the laws of the state of destination. *Kentucky Whip & Collar Co.* v. *Illinois Central R. R. Co.* . . .

But it is said that the present prohibition falls within the scope of none of these categories; that while the prohibition is nominally a regulation of the commerce its motive or purpose is regulation of wages and hours of persons engaged in manufacture, the control of which has been reserved to the states and upon which Georgia and some of the states of destination have placed no restriction; that the effect of the present statute is not to exclude the prescribed articles from interstate commerce in aid of state regulation as in *Kentucky Whip & Collar Co.* v. *Illinois Central R. R. Co., supra,* but instead, under the guise of a regulation of interstate commerce, it undertakes to regulate wages and hours within the state contrary to the policy of the state which has elected to leave them unregulated. . . .

The motive and purpose of the present regulation is plainly to make effective the Congressional conception of public policy that interstate commerce should not be made the instrument of competition in the distribution of goods produced under substandard labor conditions, which competition is injurious to the commerce and to the states from and to which the commerce flows. The motive and purpose of a regulation of interstate commerce are matters for the legislative judgment upon the exercise of which the Constitution places no restriction and over which the courts are given no control. . . . Whatever their motive and purpose, regulations of commerce which do not infringe some constitutional prohibition are within the plenary power conferred on Congress by the Commerce Clause. Subject only to that limitation, . . . we conclude that the prohibition of the shipment interstate of goods produced under the forbidden substandard labor conditions is within the constitutional authority of Congress.

In the more than a century which has elapsed since the decision of *Gibbons* v. *Ogden,* these principles of constitutional interpretation have been so long and repeatedly recognized by this Court as applicable to the Commerce Clause, that there would be little occasion for repeating them now were it not for the decision of this Court twenty-two years ago in *Hammer* v. *Dagenhart.* . . . In that case it was held by a bare majority of the Court over the powerful and now classic dissent of Mr. Justice Holmes setting forth the fundamental issues involved, the Congress was without power to exclude the products of child labor from interstate commerce.

The reasoning and conclusion of the Court's opinion there cannot be reconciled with the conclusion which we have reached, that the power of Congress under the Commerce Clause is plenary to exclude any article from interstate commerce subject only to specific prohibitions of the Constitution.

Hammer v. *Dagenhart* has not been followed. The distinction on which the decision was rested that Congressional power to prohibit interstate commerce is limited to articles which in themselves have some harmful or deleterious property—a distinction which was novel when made and unsupported by any provision of the Constitution—has long since been abandoned. . . .

The conclusion is inescapable that *Hammer* v. *Dagenhart* was a departure from the principles which have prevailed in the interpretation of the commerce clause both before and since the decision and that such vitality, as a precedent, as it then had has long since been exhausted. It should be and now is overruled.

VALIDITY OF THE WAGE AND HOUR REQUIREMENTS. Section 15(a) (2) and §§ 6 and 7 require employers to conform to the wage and hour provisions with respect to all employees engaged in the production of goods for interstate commerce. As appellees' employees are not alleged to be "engaged in interstate commerce" the validity of the prohibition turns on the question whether the employment, under other than the prescribed labor standards, of employees engaged in the production of goods for interstate commerce is so related to the commerce and so affects it as to be within the reach of the power of Congress to regulate it. . . .

Congress, having by the present Act adopted the policy of excluding from interstate commerce all goods produced for the commerce which do not conform to the specified labor standards, it may choose the means reasonably adapted to the attainment of the permitted end, even though they involve control of intrastate activities. Such legislation has often been sustained with respect to powers, other than the commerce power granted to the national government, when the means chosen, although not themselves within the granted power, were nevertheless deemed appropriate aids to the accomplishment of some purpose within an admitted power of the national government. . . .

The Sherman Act and the National Labor Relations Act are familiar examples of the exertion of the commerce power to prohibit or control activities wholly intrastate because of their effect on interstate commerce. . . .

So far as *Carter* v. *Carter Coal Co.* . . . is inconsistent with this conclusion, its doctrine is limited in principle by the decisions under the Sherman Act and the National Labor Relations Act, which we have cited and which we follow. . . .

Our conclusion is unaffected by the Tenth Amendment which provides: "The powers not delegated to the United States by the Constitution nor prohibited by it to the states are reserved to the states respectively or to the people." The amendment states but a truism that all is retained which has not been surrendered. There is nothing in the history of its adoption to suggest that it was more than declaratory of the relationship between the national and state governments as it had been established by the Constitution before the amendment or that its purpose was other than to allay fears that the new national government might seek to exercise powers not granted, and that the states might not be able to exercise fully their reserved powers. . . .

The Act is sufficiently definite to meet constitutional demands. One who employs persons, without conforming to the prescribed wage and hour conditions, to work on goods which he ships or expects to ship across state lines, is warned that he may be subject to the criminal penalties of the Act. No more is required. . . .

We have considered, but find it unnecessary to discuss other contentions.

Reversed.

WICKARD V. FILBURN

317 U.S. 111, 63 S. Ct. 82, 87 L. Ed. 122 (1942)

The Agricultural Adjustment Act of 1938 authorized the Secretary of Agriculture to determine a national acreage for wheat, which was then apportioned to the states and to individual farmers in the form of production quotas. A farmer who produced wheat in excess of his quota was subject to penalties. Filburn produced wheat in excess of his quota but did not market it; instead he fed it to animals on his own farm. When action was brought against him by Secretary of Agriculture Wickard, Filburn sought an injunction to prevent imposition of the penalty for his excess production. In the Supreme Court opinion two other issues were discussed, but the excerpts which follow deal solely with the question whether the regulation was justified under the commerce power.

MR. JUSTICE JACKSON delivered the opinion of the Court. . . .

It is urged that under the Commerce Clause of the Constitution, Article I, § 8, clause 3, Congress does not possess the power it has in this instance sought to exercise. The question would merit little consideration since our decision in *United States* v. *Darby* . . . sustaining the federal power to regulate production of goods for commerce except for the fact that this Act extends federal regulation to production not intended in any part for commerce but wholly for consumption on the farm. The Act includes a definition of "market" and its derivatives so that as related to wheat in addition to its conventional meaning it also means to dispose of "by feeding (in any form) to poultry or livestock which, or the products of which, are sold, bartered, or exchanged, or to be so disposed of." Hence, marketing quotas not only embrace all that may be sold without penalty but also what may be consumed on the premises. Wheat produced on excess acreage is designated as "available for marketing" as so defined and the penalty is imposed thereon. Penalties do not depend upon whether any part of the wheat either within or without the quota is sold or intended to be sold. The sum of this is that the Federal Government fixes a quota including all that the farmer may harvest for sale or for his own farm needs, and declares that wheat produced on excess acreage may neither be disposed of nor used except upon payment of the penalty or except it is stored as required by the Act or delivered to the Secretary of Agriculture.

Appellee says that this is a regulation of production and consumption of wheat. Such activities are, he urges, beyond the reach of Congressional power under the Commerce Clause, since they are local in character, and their effects upon interstate commerce are at most "indirect." In answer the Government argues that the statute regulates neither production nor consumption, but only marketing; and, in the alternative, that if the Act does go beyond the regulation of marketing it is sustainable as a "necessary and proper" implementation of the power of Congress over interstate commerce.

The Government's concern lest the Act be held to be a regulation of production or consumption rather than of marketing is attributable to a few dicta and decisions of this Court which might be understood to lay it down that activities such as "production," "manufacturing," and "mining" are strictly "local" and, except in special circumstances which are not present here, cannot be regulated under the commerce power because their effects upon interstate commerce are, as matter of law, only "indirect." Even today, when this power has been held to have great latitude, there is no decision of this Court that such activities may be regulated where no part of the product is intended for interstate commerce or intermingled with the subjects thereof. We believe that a review of the course of decision under the Commerce Clause will make plain, however, that questions of the power of Congress are not to be decided by reference to any formula which would give controlling force to nomenclature such as "production" and "indirect" and foreclose consideration of the actual effects of the activity in question upon interstate commerce. . . .

The Court's recognition of the relevance of the economic effects in the application of the Commerce Clause . . . has made the mechanical application of legal formulas no longer feasible. Once an economic measure of the reach of the power granted to Congress in the Commerce Clause is accepted, questions of federal power cannot be decided simply by finding the activity in question to be "production" nor can consideration of its economic effects be foreclosed by calling them "indirect." The present Chief Justice has said in summary of the present state of the law: "The commerce power is not confined in its exercise to the regulation of commerce among the states. It extends to those activities intrastate which so affect interstate commerce, or the exertion of the power of Congress over it, as to make regulation of them appropriate means to the attainment of a legitimate end, the effective execution of the granted power to regulate interstate commerce. . . . The power of Congress over interstate commerce is plenary and complete in itself, may be exercised to its utmost extent, and acknowledges no limitations other than are prescribed in the Constitution. . . . It follows that no form of state activity can constitutionally thwart the regulatory power granted by the commerce clause to Congress. Hence the reach of that power extends to those intrastate activities which in a substantial way interfere with or obstruct the exercise of the granted power." *United States* v. *Wrightwood Dairy Co.* . . .

Whether the subject of the regulation in question was "production," consumption," or "marketing" is, therefore, not material for purposes of deciding the question of federal power before us. That an activity is of local character may help in a doubtful case to determine whether Congress intended to reach it. The same consideration might help in determining whether in the absence of Congressional action it would be permissible for the state to exert its power on the subject matter, even though in so doing it to some degree affected interstate commerce. But even if appellant's activity be local and though it may not be regarded as commerce, it may still, whatever its nature, be reached by Congress if it exerts a substantial economic effect on interstate commerce and this irrespective of whether such effect is what might at some earlier time have been defined as "direct" or "indirect." . . .

The effect of consumption of homegrown wheat on interstate commerce is due to the fact that it constitutes the most variable factor in the disappearance of the wheat crop. Consumption on the farm where grown appears to vary in an amount greater than 20 per cent of average production. The total amount of wheat consumed as food varies but relatively little, and use as seed is relatively constant. . . .

It is well established by decisions of this Court that the power to regulate commerce includes the power to regulate the prices at which commodities in that commerce are dealt in and practices affecting such prices. One of the primary purposes of the Act in question was to increase the market price of wheat and to that end to limit the volume thereof that could affect the market. It can hardly be denied that a factor of such volume and variability as home-consumed wheat would have a substantial influence on price and market conditions. This may arise because being in marketable condition such home-grown wheat overhangs the market and if induced by rising prices tends to flow into the market and check price increases. But if we assume that it is never marketed, it supplies a need of the man who grew it which would otherwise be reflected by purchases in the open market. Home-grown wheat in this sense competes with wheat in commerce. The stimulation of commerce is a use of a regulatory function quite as definitely as prohibitions or restrictions thereon. This record leaves us in no doubt that Congress may properly have considered that wheat consumed on the farm where grown if wholly outside the scheme of regulation would have a substantial effect in defeating and obstructing its purpose to stimulate trade therein at increased prices.

It is said, however, that this Act, forcing some farmers into the market to buy what they could provide for themselves, is an unfair promotion of the markets and prices of specializing wheat growers. It is of the essence of regulation that it lays a restraining hand on the self-interest of the regulated and that advantages from the regulation commonly fall to others. The conflicts of economic interest between the regulated and those who advantage by it are wisely left under our system to resolution by the Congress under its more flexible and responsible legislative process. Such conflicts rarely lend themselves to judicial determination. And with the wisdom, workability, or fairness, of the plan of regulation we have nothing to do. . . .

Reversed.

HEART OF ATLANTA MOTEL V. UNITED STATES

379 U.S. 241, 85 S. Ct. 348, 13 L. Ed. 2d 258 (1964)

KATZENBACH V. MC CLUNG

379 U.S. 294, 85 S. Ct. 377, 13 L. Ed. 2d 290 (1964)

Title II of the Civil Rights Act of 1964 guaranteed access to four classes of "public accommodation . . . without discrimination or segregation on the basis of race, color, religion, or national origin," provided that their operations "affect commerce." All hotels and motels "which provide lodging to transient guests" were declared by the statute to affect commerce *per se.* Restaurants and cafeterias were declared to affect commerce if they offered to serve interstate travelers or if a substantial portion of the food they served had "moved in commerce." In these two cases the act was applied against an Atlanta motel, 75 percent of whose guests came from out of state, and a restaurant where approximately half of the food served had moved in commerce.

Congress based its constitutional power to adopt this statute on both the equal protection clause of the Fourteenth Amendment and the commerce clause. However, Justice Clark, who wrote both opinions upholding the constitutionality of the act and its application in these cases, held that since the commerce power by itself amply supported the statute, there was no need to consider the equal protection ground. Justice Clark's opinions are omitted below, in favor of the concurring opinions of Justices Black and Douglas.

MR. JUSTICE BLACK, concurring. . . .

It requires no novel or strained interpretation of the Commerce Clause to sustain Title II as applied in either of these cases. At least since *Gibbons* v. *Ogden* . . . decided in 1824 in an opinion by Chief Justice John Marshall, it has been uniformly accepted that the power of Congress to regulate commerce among the States is plenary, "complete in itself, may be exercised to its utmost extent, and acknowledges no limitations, other than are prescribed in the constitution." . . . Nor is "Commerce" as used in the Commerce Clause to be limited to a narrow, technical concept. It includes not only, as Congress has enumerated in the Act, "travel, trade, traffic, commerce, transportation, or communication," but also all other unitary transactions and activities that take place in more States than one. That some parts or segments of such unitary transactions may take place only in one State cannot, of course, take from Congress its plenary power to regulate them in the national interest. The facilities and instrumentalities used to carry on this commerce, such as railroads, truck lines, ships, rivers, and even highways are also subject to congressional regulation, so far as is necessary to keep interstate traffic upon fair and equal terms. . . .

Furthermore, it has long been held that the Necessary and Proper Clause, Art 1, § 8, cl 18, adds to the commerce power of Congress the power to regulate local instrumentalities operating within a single state if their activities burden the flow of commerce among the States. Thus in the Shreveport Case . . . this Court recognized that Congress could not fully carry out its responsibility to protect interstate commerce were its constitutional power to regulate that commerce to be strictly limited to prescribing the rules for controlling the things actually moving in such commerce or the contracts, transactions, and other activities, immediately concerning them. Regulation of purely intrastate railroad rates is primarily a local problem for state rather than national control. But the Shreveport Case sustained the power of Congress under the Commerce Clause and the Necessary and Proper Clause to control purely intrastate rates, even though reasonable, where the effect of such rates was found to impose a discrimination injurious to interstate commerce. This holding that Congress had power under these clauses, not merely to enact laws governing interstate activities and transactions, but also to regulate even purely local activities and transactions where necessary to foster and protect interstate commerce, was amply supported by Mr. Justice (later Mr. Chief Justice) Hughes' reliance upon many prior holdings of this Court extending back to *Gibbons* v. *Ogden, supra.* And since the Shreveport Case this Court has steadfastly followed, and indeed has emphasized time and time again, that Congress has ample power to protect interstate commerce from activities adversely and injuriously affecting it, which but for this adverse effect on interstate commerce would be beyond the power of Congress to regulate. . . .

. . . I recognize that every remote possible, speculative effect on commerce should not be accepted as an adequate constitutional ground to uproot and throw into the discard all our traditional distinctions between what is purely local, and therefore controlled by state laws, and what affects the national interest and is therefore subject to control by federal laws. I recognize too that some isolated and remote lunch room which sells only to local people and buys almost all its supplies in the locality may possibly be beyond the reach of the power of Congress to regulate commerce, just as such an establishment is not covered by the present Act. But in deciding the constitutional power of Congress in cases like the two before us we do not consider the effect on interstate commerce of only one isolated, individual, local event, without regard to the fact that this single local event when added to many others of a similar nature may impose a burden on interstate commerce by reducing its volume or distorting its flow. . . .

Long ago this Court, again speaking through Mr. Chief Justice Marshall, said:

> Let the end be legitimate, let it be within the scope of the constitution, and all means which are appropriate, which are plainly adapted to that end, which are not prohibited, but consist with the letter and spirit of the constitution, are constitutional. (*McCulloch* v. *Maryland* . . . .)

By this standard Congress acted within its power here. In view of the Commerce Clause it is not possible to deny that the aim of protecting interstate commerce from undue burdens is a legitimate end. In view of the Thirteenth, Fourteenth and Fifteenth Amendments, it is not possible to deny that the aim of protecting Negroes from discrimination is also a legitimate end. The means adopted to achieve these ends are also appropriate, plainly adopted to achieve them and not prohibited by the Constitution but consistent with both its letter and spirit. . . .

Mr. Justice Douglas, concurring.

Though I join the Court's opinion, I am somewhat reluctant here, as I was in *Edwards* v. *California*, . . . to rest solely on the Commerce Clause. My reluctance is not due to any conviction that Congress lacks power to regulate commerce in the interests of human rights. It is rather my belief that the right of people to be free of state action that discriminates against them because of race, like the "right to persons to move freely from State to State" (*Edwards* v. *California* . . .) "occupies a more protected position in our constitutional system than does the movement of cattle, fruit, steel and coal across state lines." . . .

Hence I would prefer to rest on the assertion of legislative power contained in § 5 of the Fourteenth Amendment which states: "The Congress shall have power to enforce, by appropriate legislation, the provisions of this article"—a power which the Court concedes was exercised at least in part in this Act.

A decision based on the Fourteenth Amendment would have a more settling effect, making unnecessary litigation over whether a particular restaurant or inn is within the commerce definitions of the Act or whether a particular customer is an interstate traveler. Under my construction, the Act would apply to all customers in all the enumerated places of public accommodation. And that construction would put an end to all obstructionist strategies and finally close one door on a bitter chapter in American history.

Chapter Thirteen

THE
INVESTIGATORY
POWER

INTRODUCTION

The power of Congress to investigate is an implied power, supplementary to its specifically delegated powers to legislate, to appropriate, to pass on the elections and returns of members, and so on. The Supreme Court took a rather narrow view of the investigatory power when the issue was first raised. *Kilbourn* v. *Thompson* (1881) held invalid a House investigation into a bankrupt firm, of which the United States was one of the creditors. The Court held that the matter was not one on which Congress could validly legislate and that the controversy was already under adjudication in the courts. But in a later case, *In re Chapman* (1897), the Court upheld a Senate investigation of charges that senators were yielding to corrupt influences in considering a tariff bill.

These two nineteenth-century precedents were the principal guides for the Court when it came to decide **McGrain v. Daugherty** (1927), which grew out of the Senate's investigation of the role of the Department of Justice in the Teapot Dome scandal. The brother of the Attorney General resisted a Senate subpoena, and a federal district judge ruled that the Senate, exceeding its proper legislative powers, was really conducting a trial of the Attorney General. However, the Supreme Court ruled that the Senate was within its constitutional powers in investigating

the administration of the Justice Department, but it did state two important limitations on the investigatory power: that there was no "general"
power to inquire into private affairs and compel disclosures; and that a
witness "rightfully" might refuse to answer where the bounds of congressional power were exceeded or "the questions are not pertinent to the
matter under inquiry."

Serious questions as to the use of the investigatory power were raised
by the conduct of the House Committee on Un-American Activities,
established in 1938, and Senator Joseph McCarthy's activities in the
Committee on Government Operations between 1950 and 1954. Many
persons refused to answer inquiries by these committees on grounds of
self-incrimination under the Fifth Amendment. This course guaranteed
against a contempt citation, but laid the witness open to loss of employment and reputation. Other witnesses refused on the ground that their
First Amendment rights were being infringed.

For a considerable period the Supreme Court avoided passing on the
serious constitutional issues raised by these inquiries. Finally, in *Watkins*
v. United States (1957) the Court did uphold a witness who had declined
to testify before the Un-American Activities Committee, indicating some
intention to assume a measure of responsibility for determining whether
congressional committees were operating within their constitutional authority. However, while Chief Justice Warren's opinion invoked the First
Amendment rights of witnesses and warned that "there is no congressional power to expose for the sake of exposure," the actual holding was
a more limited one calling for closer control of committees by the parent
legislative body.

The *Watkins* decision was bitterly criticized by some members of Congress as interfering with legislative efforts to "expose communism," and
within two years the Court beat a retreat. **Barenblatt v. United States**
(1959) held that the House had adequately directed the work of the
Un-American Activities Committee, that First Amendment rights had to
be balanced against competing public interests, and that the courts could
not examine the motives of congressional inquisitors. Two 1961 decisions, *Wilkinson* v. *United States* and *Braden* v. *United States,* went even
further in upholding harassing techniques.

It thus appeared that the Court had recognized a practically unlimited
power of congressional inquiry, but, in fact, due partly to changes in the
Court's membership, *Braden* and *Wilkinson* marked the end of an era, and
the Court began to reverse almost every contempt conviction that came
before it. These reversals were accomplished for the most part without
challenging the scope of investigatory power or querying the motives of
the investigators. They were achieved primarily by strict judicial enforcement of the rules on pertinency, authorization, and procedure, plus strict

observance of the constitutional standards governing criminal prosecutions. First Amendment rights were invoked in one case, *Gibson* v. *Florida Legislative Investigation Committee* (1963), which involved a state legislative rather than a congressional committee.

McCarthy was censured by the Senate in 1954, and the Committee on Un-American Activities, after its name had been changed to the Committee on Internal Security in 1969, went out of existence in 1974. Responsibly used, the power to investigate is a vital safeguard against both governmental and private wrongdoings, as was so forcefully demonstrated by the Senate Select Committee on Watergate in 1973 and the House Judiciary Committee impeachment investigation in 1974.

MC GRAIN V. DAUGHERTY

273 U.S. 135, 47 S. Ct. 319, 71 L. Ed. 580 (1927)

In a post-Teapot Dome investigation of the Department of Justice and President Harding's Attorney General, Harry M. Daugherty, a Senate select committee subpoenaed his brother, Mally S. Daugherty. When he refused to comply, he was arrested by McGrain, Senate Sergeant-at-Arms. Daugherty obtained his release on habeas corpus, and McGrain appealed.

MR. JUSTICE VAN DEVANTER delivered the opinion of the court. . . .

The first of the principal questions, the one which the witness particularly presses on our attention, is . . . whether the Senate—or the House of Representatives, both being on the same plane in this regard—has power, through its own process, to compel a private individual to appear before it or one of its committees and give testimony needed to enable it efficiently to exercise a legislative function belonging to it under the Constitution.

The Constitution provides for a Congress consisting of a Senate and House of Representatives, and invests it with "all legislative powers" granted to the United States, and with power "to make all laws which shall be necessary and proper" for carrying into execution these powers and "all other powers" vested by the Constitution in the United States or in any department or office thereof. . . . But there is no provision expressly investing either house with power to make investigations and exact testimony, to the end that it may exercise its legislative function advisedly and effectively. So the question arises whether this power is so far incidental to the legislative function as to be implied.

In actual legislative practice, power to secure needed information by such means has long been treated as an attribute of the power to legislate.

It was so regarded in the British Parliament and in the colonial Legislatures before the American Revolution, and a like view has prevailed and been carried into effect in both houses of Congress and in most of the state Legislatures.

This power was both asserted and exerted by the House of Representatives in 1792, when it appointed a select committee to inquire into the St. Clair expedition and authorized the committee to send for necessary persons, papers and records. Mr. Madison, who had taken an important part in framing the Constitution only five years before, and four of his associates in that work, were members of the House of Representatives at the time, and all voted for the inquiry.... [T]he Senate ... inquiry ordered in 1859 respecting the raid by John Brown and his adherents on the armory and arsenal of the United States at Harper's Ferry is of special significance. The resolution directing the inquiry authorized the committee to send for persons and papers, to inquire into the facts pertaining to the raid and the means by which it was organized and supported, and to report what legislation, if any, was necessary to preserve the peace of the country and protect the public property. The resolution was briefly discussed and adopted without opposition. . . .

Four decisions of this Court are cited and more or less relied on, and we now turn to them.

The first decision was in *Anderson* v. *Dunn* . . . [1821]. The question there was whether, under the Constitution, the House of Representatives has power to attach and punish a person other than a member for contempt of its authority—in fact, an attempt to bribe one of its members. The Court regarded the powers as essential to the effective exertion of other powers expressly granted, and therefore as implied. . . .

The next decision was in *Kilbourn* v. *Thompson* . . . [1881]. The question there was whether the House of Representatives had exceeded its power in directing one of its committees to make a particular investigation. The decision was that it had. The principles announced and applied in the case are—that neither house of Congress possesses a "general power of making inquiry into the private affairs of the citizen"; that the power actually possessed is limited to inquiries relating to matters of which the particular house "has jurisdiction" and in respect of which it rightfully may take other action; that if the inquiry relates to "a matter wherein relief or redress could be had only by a judicial proceeding" it is not within the range of this power, but must be left to the courts, conformably to the constitutional separation of governmental powers; and that for the purpose of determining the essential character of the inquiry recourse may be had to the resolution or order under which it is made. . . .

Next in order is *In re Chapman* . . . [1896]. The inquiry there in question was conducted under a resolution of the Senate and related to charges, published in the press, that Senators were yielding to corrupt influences in considering a tariff bill then before the Senate and were speculating in stocks the value of which would be affected by pending amendments to the bill. Chapman appeared before the committee in response to a subpoena, but refused to answer questions pertinent to the inquiry, and was indicted and convicted under the act of 1857 for his refusal. The court sustained the constitutional validity of the act of 1857, and, after referring to the constitutional provision empowering either house to punish its members for disorderly behavior and by a vote of two-thirds to expel a member, held that the inquiry related to the integrity and fidelity of Senators in the discharge of their duties, and therefore to a matter "within the range of the constitutional powers of the Senate" and in respect of which it could compel witnesses to appear and testify. . . .

The latest case is *Marshall* v. *Gordon* . . . [1916]. The question there was whether the House of Representatives exceeded its power in punishing, as for a contempt of its authority, a person—not a member—who had written, published, and sent to the chairman of one of its committees an ill-tempered and irritating letter respecting the action and purposes of the committee. Power to make inquiries and obtain evidence by compulsory process was not involved. The court recognized distinctly that the House of Representatives has implied power to punish a person not a member for contempt, as was ruled in *Anderson* v. *Dunn, supra,* but held that its action in this instance was without constitutional justification.

While these cases are not decisive of the question we are considering, they definitely settle two propositions which we recognize as entirely sound and having a bearing on its solution: One, that the two houses of Congress, in their separate relations, possess, not only such powers as are expressly granted to them by the Constitution, but such auxiliary powers as are necessary and appropriate to make the express powers effective; and the other, that neither house is invested with "general" power to inquire into private affairs and compel disclosures, but only with such limited power of inquiry as is shown to exist when the rule of constitutional interpretation just stated is rightly applied. . . .

We are of opinion that the power of inquiry—with process to enforce it—is an essential and appropriate auxiliary to the legislative function. . . .

We come now to the question whether it sufficiently appears that the purpose for which the witness's testimony was sought was to obtain information in aid of the legislative function. The court below answered the question in the negative and put its decision largely on this ground. . . .

We are of opinion that the court's ruling on this question was wrong, and that it sufficiently appears, when the proceedings are rightly interpreted, that the object of the investigation and of the effort to secure the witness's testimony was to obtain information for legislative purposes.

It is quite true that the resolution directing the investigation does not in terms avow that it is intended to be in aid of legislation; but it does show that the subject to be investigated was the administration of the Department of Justice—whether its functions were being properly discharged or were being neglected or misdirected, and particularly whether the Attorney General and his assistants were performing or neglecting their duties in respect of the institution and prosecution of proceedings to punish crimes and enforce appropriate remedies against the wrongdoers; specific instances of alleged neglect being recited. Plainly the subject was one on which legislation could be had and would be materially aided by the information which the investigation was calculated to elicit. This becomes manifest when it is reflected that the functions of the Department of Justice, the powers and duties of the Attorney General, and the duties of his assistants are all subject to regulation by congressional legislation, and that the department is maintained and its activities are carried on under such appropriations as in the judgment of Congress are needed from year to year.

The only legitimate object the Senate could have in ordering the investigation was to aid it in legislating, and we think the subject-matter was such that the presumption should be indulged that this was the real object. An express avowal of the object would have been better; but in view of the particular subject-matter was not indispensable. . . .

We conclude that the investigation was ordered for a legitimate object; that the witness wrongfully refused to appear and testify before the committee and was lawfully attached; that the Senate is entitled to have him give testimony pertinent to the inquiry, either at its bar or before the committee; and that the district court erred in discharging him from custody under the attachment. . . .

What has been said requires that the final order in the district court discharging the witness from custody be reversed.

Final order reversed.

MR. JUSTICE STONE did not participate in the consideration or decision of the case.

WATKINS V. UNITED STATES

354 U.S. 178, 77 S. Ct. 1173, 1 L. Ed. 2d 1273 (1957)

Watkins was a labor union official who refused to answer questions before the House Un-American Activities Committee as to whether certain individuals were members of the Communist Party. He agreed to testify concerning persons whom he believed to be active current Communists but refused to answer questions about former members who to his best knowledge had long since removed themselves from the party. He contended that such questions were not authorized by law or relevant to the work of the committee and that answers would accomplish no purpose except exposure of past activities.

MR. CHIEF JUSTICE WARREN delivered the opinion of the Court. . . .

We start with several basic premises on which there is general agreement. The power of the Congress to conduct investigations is inherent in the legislative process. That power is broad. It encompasses inquiries concerning the administration of existing laws as well as proposed or possibly needed statutes. It includes surveys of defects in our social, economic or political system for the purpose of enabling the Congress to remedy them. It comprehends probes into departments of the Federal Government to expose corruption, inefficiency or waste. But broad as is this power of inquiry, it is not unlimited. There is no general authority to expose the private affairs of individuals without justification in terms of the functions of the Congress. This was freely conceded by the Solicitor General in his argument of this case. . . .

It is unquestionably the duty of all citizens to cooperate with the Congress in its efforts to obtain the facts needed for intelligent legislative action. It is their unremitting obligation to respond to subpoenas, to respect the dignity of the Congress and its committees and to testify fully with respect to matters within the province of proper investigation. This, of course, assumes that the constitutional rights of witnesses will be respected by the Congress as they are in a court of justice. . . .

In the decade following World War II, there appeared a new kind of congressional inquiry unknown in prior periods of American history. Principally this was the result of the various investigations into the threat of subversion of the United States Government, but other subjects of congressional interest also contributed to the changed scene. This new phase of legislative inquiry involved a broad-scale intrusion into the lives and affairs of private citizens. It brought before the courts novel questions of the appropriate limits of congressional inquiry. Prior cases, like *Kilbourn, McGrain* and *Sinclair,* had defined the scope of investigative power in terms of the inherent limitations of the sources of that power. In the more recent cases, the emphasis shifted to problems of accommodating the interest of the Government with the rights and privileges of individuals. The central theme was the application of the Bill of Rights as a restraint upon the assertion of governmental power in this form.

It was during this period that the Fifth Amendment privilege against self-incrimination was frequently invoked and recognized as a legal limit upon the authority of a committee to require that a witness answer its questions. Some early doubts as to the applicability of that privilege before a legislative committee never matured. When the matter reached this Court, the Government did not challenge in any way that the Fifth Amendment protection was available to the witness. . . .

A far more difficult task evolved from the claim by witnesses that the committees' interrogations were infringements upon the freedoms of the First Amendment. Clearly, an investigation is subject to the command that the Congress shall make no law abridging freedom of speech or press or assembly. While it is true that there is no statute to be reviewed and that an investigation is not a law, nevertheless an investigation is part of lawmaking. It is justified solely as an adjunct to the legislative process. The First Amendment may be invoked against infringement of the protected freedoms by law or by lawmaking.

Abuses of the investigative process may imperceptibly lead to abridgment of protected freedoms. The mere summoning of a witness and compelling him to testify, against his will, about his beliefs, expressions or associations is a measure of governmental interference. And when those forced revelations concern matters that are unorthodox, unpopular, or even hateful to the general public, the reaction in the life of the witness may be disastrous. This effect is even more harsh when it is past beliefs, expressions or associations that are disclosed and judged by current standards rather than those contemporary with the matters exposed. Nor does the witness alone suffer the consequences. Those who are identified by witnesses and thereby placed in the same glare of publicity are equally subject to public stigma, scorn and obloquy. Beyond that, there is the more subtle and immeasurable effect upon those who tend to adhere to the most orthodox and uncontroversial views and associations in order to avoid a similar fate at some future time. That this impact is partly the result of non-governmental activity by private persons cannot relieve the investigators of their responsibility for initiating the reaction. . . .

We have no doubt that there is no congressional power to expose for the sake of exposure. The public is, of course, entitled to be informed concerning the workings of its government. That cannot be inflated into a general power to expose where the predominant result can only be an invasion of the private rights of individuals. But a solution to our problem is not to be found in testing the motives of committee members for this purpose. Such is not our function. Their motives alone would not vitiate an investigation which had been instituted by a House of Congress if that assembly's legislative purpose is being served.

. . . It is the responsibility of the Congress, in the first instance, to insure that compulsory process is used only in furtherance of a legislative purpose. That requires that the instructions to an investigating committee spell out that group's jurisdiction and purpose with sufficient particularity. Those instructions are embodied in the authorizing resolution. That document is the committee's charter. Broadly drafted and loosely worded, however, such resolutions can leave trememdous latitude to the discretion of the investigators. The more vague the committee's charter is, the greater becomes the possibility that the committee's specific actions are not in conformity with the will of the parent House of Congress. . . .

The authorizing resolution of the Un-American Activities Committee was adopted in 1938 when a select committee, under the chairmanship of Representative Dies, was created. Several years later, the Committee was made a standing organ of the House with the same mandate. It defines the Committee's authority as follows:

The Committee on Un-American Activities, as a whole or by subcommittee, is authorized to make from time to time investigations of (i) the extent, character, and objects of un-American propaganda activities in the United States, (ii) the diffusion within the United

States of subversive and un-American propaganda that is instigated from foreign countries or of a domestic origin and attacks the principle of the forms of government as guaranteed by our Constitution, and (iii) all other questions in relation thereto that would aid Congress in any necessary remedial legislation.

It would be difficult to imagine a less explicit authorizing resolution. Who can define the meaning of "un-American"? What is that single, solitary "principle of the form of government as guaranteed by our constitution"? There is no need to dwell upon the language, however. At one time, perhaps, the resolution might have been read narrowly to confine the Committee to the subject of propaganda. The events that have transpired in the fifteen years before the interrogation of petitioner makes such a construction impossible at this date. . . .

Combining the language of the resolution with the construction it has been given, it is evident that the preliminary control of the Committee exercised by the House of Representatives is slight or non-existent. No one could reasonably deduce from the charter the kind of investigation that the Committee was directed to make. As a result, we are asked to engage in a process of retroactive rationalization. Looking backward from the events that transpired, we are asked to uphold the Committee's actions unless it appears that they were clearly not authorized by the charter. As a corollary to this inverse approach, the Government urges that we must view the matter hospitably to the power of the Congress—that if there is any legislative purpose which might have been furthered by the kind of disclosure sought, the witness must be punished for withholding it. No doubt every reasonable indulgence of legality must be accorded to the actions of a coordinate branch of our Government. But such deference cannot yield to an unnecessary and unreasonable dissipation of precious constitutional freedoms. . . .

It is, of course, not the function of this Court to prescribe rigid rules for the Congress to follow in drafting resolutions establishing investigating committees. That is a matter peculiarly within the realm of the legislature, and its decisions will be accepted by the courts up to the point where their own duty to enforce the constitutionally protected rights of individuals is affected.

. . . Plainly these committees are restricted to the missions delegated to them, i.e., to acquire certain data to be used by the House or the Senate in coping with a problem that falls within its legislative sphere. No witness can be compelled to make disclosures on matters outside that area. This is a jurisdictional concept of pertinency drawn from the nature of a congressional committee's source of authority. It is not wholly different from nor unrelated to the element of pertinency embodied in the criminal statute under which petitioner was prosecuted. When the definition of jurisdictional pertinency is as uncertain and wavering as in the case of the Un-American Activities Committee, it becomes extremely difficult for the Committee to limit its inquiries to statutory pertinency.

In fulfillment of their obligation under this statute, the courts must accord to the defendants every right which is guaranteed to defendants in all other criminal cases. Among these is the right to have available, through a sufficiently precise statute, information revealing the standard of criminality before the commission of the alleged offense. Applied to persons prosecuted under § 192, this raises a special problem in that the statute defines the crime as refusal to answer "any question pertinent to the question under inquiry." Part of the standard of criminality, therefore, is the pertinency of the questions propounded to the witness.

The problem attains proportion when viewed from the standpoint of the witness who appears before a congressional committee. He must decide at the time the questions are propounded whether or not to answer. . . .

It is obvious that a person compelled to make this choice is entitled to have knowledge of the subject to which the interrogation is deemed pertinent. That knowledge must be available with the same degree of explicitness and clarity that the Due Process Clause requires in the expression of any element of a criminal offense. The "vice of vagueness," must be avoided here as in all other crimes. There are several sources that can outline the "question under inquiry" in such a way that the rules against vagueness are satisfied. The authorizing resolution, the remarks of the chairman or members of the committee, or even the nature of the proceedings themselves might sometimes make the topic clear. This case demonstrates, however, that these sources often leave the matter in grave doubt.

The statement of the Committee Chairman in this case, in response to petitioner's protest, was woefully inadequate to convey sufficient information as to the pertinency of the questions to the subject under inquiry. Petitioner was thus not accorded a fair opportunity to determine whether he was within his rights in refusing to answer, and his conviction is necessarily invalid under the Due Process Clause of the Fifth Amendment.

. . . The conclusions which we have reached in this case will not prevent the Congress, through its committees, from obtaining any information it needs for the proper fulfillment of its role in our scheme of government. The legislature is free to determine the kinds of data that should be collected. It is only those investigations that are conducted by use of compulsory process that give rise to a need to protect the rights of individuals against illegal encroachment. That protection can be readily achieved through procedures which prevent the separation of power from responsibility and which provide the constitutional requisites of fairness for witnesses. A measure of added care on the part of the House and the Senate in authorizing the use of compulsory process and by their committees in exercising that power would suffice. That is a small price to pay if it serves to uphold the principles of limited, constitutional government without constricting the power of the Congress to inform itself.

The judgment of the Court of Appeals is reversed, and the case is remanded to the District Court with instructions to dismiss the indictment.

It is so ordered.

MR. JUSTICE BURTON and MR. JUSTICE WHITTAKER took no part in the consideration or decision of this case.

MR. JUSTICE FRANKFURTER, concurring. . . .

MR. JUSTICE CLARK, dissenting.

As I see it the chief fault in the majority opinion is its mischievous curbing of the informing function of the Congress. While I am not versed in its procedures, my experience in the executive branch of the Government leads me to believe that the requirements laid down in the opinion for the operation of the committee system of inquiry are both unnecessary and unworkable. . . .

It may be that at times the House Committee on Un-American Activities has, as the Court says, "conceived of its task in the grand view of its name." And, perhaps, as the Court indicates, the rules of conduct placed upon the Committee by the House admit of individual abuse and unfairness. But that is none of our affair. So long as the object of a legislative inquiry is legitimate and the questions propounded are pertinent thereto, it is not for the courts to interfere with the committee system of inquiry. To hold otherwise would be an infringement on the power given the Congress to inform itself, and thus a trespass upon the fundamental American principle of separation of powers. The majority has substituted the judiciary as the grand inquisitor and supervisor of congressional investigations. It has never been so. . . .

The Court condemns the long-established and long-recognized committee system of inquiry of the House because it raises serious questions concerning the protection it affords to constitutional rights. . . . In effect the Court honors Watkins' claim of a "right to silence" which brings all inquiries, as we know, to a "dead end." I do not see how any First Amendment rights were endangered here. There is nothing in the First Amendment that provides the guarantees Watkins claims. . . .

BARENBLATT V. UNITED STATES

360 U.S. 109, 79 S. Ct. 1081, 3 L. Ed. 2d 1115 (1959)

Lloyd Barenblatt, a college professor, was named by a witness before the House Committee on Un-American Activities in 1954 as having been a communist during his graduate student days from 1947 to 1950. The Committee called Barenblatt, but he refused to testify on the ground that the Committee was violating his First Amendment rights and conducting a legislative trial. His contempt conviction in federal district court was upheld by the court of appeals, and he appealed to the Supreme Court.

MR. JUSTICE HARLAN delivered the opinion of the Court. . . .

Our function, at this point, is purely one of constitutional adjudication in the particular case and upon the particular record before us, not to pass judgment upon the general wisdom or efficacy of the activities of this Committee in a vexing and complicated field.

The precise constitutional issue confronting us is whether the Subcommittee's inquiry into petitioner's past or present membership in the Communist Party transgressed the provisions of the First Amendment, which of course reach and limit congressional investigations. . . .

The Court's past cases establish sure guides to decision. Undeniably, the First Amendment in some circumstances protects an individual from being compelled to disclose his associational relationships. However, the protections of the First Amendment, unlike a proper claim of the privilege against self-incrimination under the Fifth Amendment, do not afford a witness the right to resist inquiry in all circumstances. Where First Amendment rights are asserted to bar governmental interrogation resolution of the issue always involves balancing by the courts of the competing private and public interests at stake in the particular circumstances shown. These principles were recognized in the Watkins case, where, in speaking of the First Amendment in relation to congressional inquiries, we said . . . "It is manifest that despite the adverse effects which follow upon compelled disclosure of private matters, not all such inquiries are barred. . . . The critical element is the existence of and the weight to be ascribed to, the interest of the Congress in demanding disclosures from an unwilling witness." . . . More recently in National Association for Advancement of Colored People v. State of Alabama . . . we applied the same principles in judging state action claimed to infringe rights of association assured by the Due Process Clause of the Fourteenth Amendment, and stated that the " 'subordinating interest of the State must be compelling' " in order to overcome the individual constitutional rights at stake. . . . In light of these principles we now consider petitioner's First Amendment claims.

The first question is whether this investigation was related to a valid legislative purpose, for Congress may not constitutionally require an individual to disclose his political relationships or other private affairs except in relation to such a purpose. . . .

That Congress has wide power to legislate in the field of Communist activity in this Country, and to conduct appropriate investigations in aid thereof, is hardly debatable. The existence of such power has never been questioned by this Court, and it is sufficient to say, without particularization, that Congress has enacted or considered in this field a wide range of legislative measures, not a few of which have stemmed from recommendations of the very Committee whose actions have been drawn in question here. In the last analysis this power rests on the right of self-preservation, "the ultimate value of any society," Dennis v. United States. . . . Justification for its exercise in turn rests on the long and widely accepted view that the tenets of the Communist Party include the ultimate overthrow of the Government of the United States by force and violence, a view which has been given formal expression by the Congress.

On these premises, this Court in its constitutional adjudications has consistently refused to view the Communist Party as an ordinary political party, and has upheld federal legislation aimed at the Communist problem which in a different context would certainly have raised constitutional issues of the gravest character. . . . On the same premises this Court has upheld under the Fourteenth Amendment state legislation requiring those occupying or seeking public office to disclaim knowing membership in any organization advocating overthrow of the Government by force and violence, which legislation none can avoid seeing was aimed at membership in the Communist Party. . . . Similarly, in other areas, this Court has recognized the close nexus between the Communist Party and violent overthrow of government. . . . To suggest that because the Communist Party may also sponsor peaceable political reforms the constitutional issues before us should now be judged as if that Party were just an ordinary political party from the standpoint of national security, is to ask this Court to blind itself to world affairs which have determined the whole course of our national policy since the close of World War II . . . and to the vast burdens which these conditions have entailed for the entire Nation. . . .

Nor can we accept the further contention that this investigation should not be deemed to have been in furtherance of a legislative purpose because the true objective of the Committee and of the Congress was purely "exposure." So long as Congress acts in pursuance of its constitutional power, the Judiciary lacks authority to intervene on the basis of the motives which spurred the exercise of that power. . . .

Finally, the record is barren of other factors which in themselves might sometimes lead to the conclusion that the individual interests at stake were not subordinate to those of the state. There is no indication in this record that the Subcommittee was attempting to pillory witnesses. Nor did petitioner's appearance as a witness follow from indiscriminate dragnet procedures, lacking in probable cause for belief that he possessed information which might be helpful to the Subcommittee. And the relevancy of the questions put to him by the Subcommittee is not open to doubt.

We conclude that the balance between the individual and the governmental interests here at stake must be struck in favor of the latter, and that therefore the provisions of the First Amendment have not been offended.

We hold that petitioner's conviction for contempt of Congress discloses no infirmity, and that the judgment of the Court of Appeals must be affirmed.

Affirmed.

MR. JUSTICE BLACK, with whom THE CHIEF JUSTICE [WARREN] and MR. JUSTICE DOUGLAS concur, dissenting. . . .

The First Amendment says in no equivocal language that Congress

shall pass no law abridging freedom of speech, press, assembly or petition. The activities of this Committee, authorized by Congress, do precisely that, through exposure, obloquy and public scorn. See Watkins v.
United States. . . . The Court does not really deny this fact but relies on
a combination of three reasons for permitting the infringement: (A) The
notion that despite the First Amendment's command Congress can
abridge speech and association if this Court decides that the governmental interest in abridging speech is greater than an individual's interest
in exercising that freedom, (B) the Government's right to "preserve
itself," (C) the fact that the Committee is only after Communists or
suspected Communists in this investigation. . . .

I do not agree that laws directly abridging First Amendment freedoms
can be justified by a congressional or judicial balancing process. . . . To
apply the Court's balancing test under such circumstances is to read the
First Amendment to say

> Congress shall pass no law abridging freedom of speech, press,
> assembly and petition, unless Congress and the Supreme Court
> reach the joint conclusion that on balance the interest of the Gov-
> ernment in stifling these freedoms is greater than the interest of the
> people in having them exercised.

This is closely akin to the notion that neither the First Amendment nor
any other provision of the Bill of Rights should be enforced unless the
Court believes it is *reasonable* to do so. Not only does this violate the
genius of our *written* Constitution, but it runs expressly counter to the
injunction to Court and Congress made by Madison when he introduced
the Bill of Rights.

> If they [the first ten amendments] are incorporated into the Consti-
> tution, independent tribunals of justice will consider themselves in
> a peculiar manner the guardians of those rights; they will be an
> impenetrable bulwark against *every* assumption of power in the Leg-
> islative or Executive: they will be naturally led to resist *every* en-
> croachment upon rights expressly stipulated for in the Constitution
> by the declaration of rights.

Unless we return to this view of our judicial function, unless we once
again accept the notion that the Bill of Rights means what it says and that
this Court must enforce that meaning, I am of the opinion that our great
charter of liberty will be more honored in the breach than in the observance.

But even assuming what I cannot assume, that some balancing is
proper in this case, I feel that the Court after stating the test ignores it
completely. At most it balances the right of the Government to preserve
itself, against Barenblatt's right to refrain from revealing Communist
affiliations. Such a balance, however, mistakes the factors to be weighed.

In the first place, it completely leaves out the real interest in Barenblatt's silence, the interest of the people as a whole in being able to join organizations, advocate causes and make political "mistakes" without later being subjected to governmental penalties for having dared to think for themselves. It is this right, the right to err politically, which keeps us strong as a Nation. For no number of laws against communism can have as much effect as the personal conviction which comes from having heard its arguments and rejected them, or from having once accepted its tenets and later recognized their worthlessness. Instead, the obloquy which results from investigations such as this not only stifles "mistakes" but prevents all but the most courageous from hazarding any views which might at some later time become disfavored. This result, whose importance cannot be overestimated, is doubly crucial when it affects the universities, on which we must largely rely for the experimentation and development of new ideas essential to our country's welfare. It is these interests of society, rather that Barenblatt's own right to silence, which I think the Court should put on the balance against the demands of the Government, if any balancing process is to be tolerated. Instead they are not mentioned, while on the other side the demands of the Government are vastly overstated and called "self-preservation." ... Such a result reduces "balancing" to a mere play on words and is completely inconsistent with the rules this Court has previously given for applying a "balancing test," where it is proper: "[T]he courts should be *astute* to examine the *effect* of the challenged legislation. Mere *legislative preferences or beliefs* ... may well support regulation directed at other personal activities, but be insufficient to justify such as diminishes the exercise of rights so vital to the maintenance of democratic institutions." Schneider v. State of New Jersey, Town of Irvington ... (Italics supplied.)

Part 2

THE
FEDERAL
SYSTEM

Chapter Fourteen

NATURE
OF
THE FEDERAL UNION

INTRODUCTION

The second organizing principle of the new government, federalism, was an invention of the Framers. Confronted with the New Jersey plan for a confederation and with the Virginia plan for a national government, they chose neither. Instead, the Convention developed a hitherto unknown governmental system in which the states delegated a portion of their soverign powers to a central government, while retaining all other powers and the guarantee of their continued existence and status (*The Federalist*, **Nos. 9 and 39**). This division of responsibilities and functions between two levels of government has come to be considered the true form of federalism.

The nature of the federal union created by the Constitution was a perennial matter of controversy until the issue was finally settled by the Civil War. The general political philosophy of the eighteenth century stressed contract as the basis of governmental authority. The Constitution was such a contract, but who were the parties to it—the states or the people of the United States? The language of the Constitution could be cited to support either view. Article VII provides that approval by conventions in nine states "shall be sufficient for the establishment of this Constitution between the states so ratifying the same." On the other hand, the Preamble declares that it is "the people of the United States" who "do ordain and establish this Constitution," and conventions rather than state legislatures were chosen as the instruments of ratification precisely to emphasize the popular basis of the contract.

State Resistance to Federal Power

In the pre-Civil War period there were three significant efforts to assert that state power could override national authority. The first took the form of the Kentucky and Virginia Resolutions, drafted by Jefferson and Madison as a protest against the Alien and Sedition Acts passed by the Federalist Congress in 1798. These resolutions developed the doctrines of nullification and interposition. They were circulated among the other states, and elicited responses from at least seven, mostly from the Federalist Northeast, upholding the concept of federal supremacy and denying the right of a state to nullify federal law. Jefferson's victory over the Federalists in the election of 1800, due in no small part to popular resentment against the Alien and Sedition Acts, terminated this episode.

The second attack on the theory of the Union saw an interesting reversal of roles. The New England states, suffering severe economic hardships resulting from President Jefferson's embargo policy, came to assert an extreme states' rights doctrine. This sectional disaffection was increased by the strains of the War of 1812, during which the New England states sometimes refused to cooperate with American military operations, and considerable trade with Britain was continued. The Hartford Convention of 1814–1815, in which the movement culminated, recommended to the legislatures of the states represented that they pass measures to protect their citizens from the operation of unconstitutional national acts. But before the resolutions even got to Washington, the war was over, the complaints were forgotten, and the only result of the Convention was to annihilate the Federalist Party.

The third and most clearly elaborated theory of nullification and resistance to national authority was stated in 1828 by John C. Calhoun, as a rationalization of Southern opposition to the continuous increase in tariff rates between 1816 and 1828. Calhoun was alarmed at the open talk of secession in the South, and offered the doctrine of nullification as a substitute, contending that his plan was a logical extension of the Virginia and Kentucky Resolutions.

Calhoun held that the Constitution was a compact formed by "sovereign and independent communities." The national government was not a party to the compact but an emanation from it, "a joint commission, appointed to superintend and administer the interests in which all are jointly concerned, but having, beyond its proper sphere, no more power than if it did not exist." In 1832 South Carolina carried this theory to the point of action by passing a statute purporting to nullify the Federal Tariff Acts of 1828 and 1832. President Jackson immediately challenged this action, saying that the power of nullification was "incompatible with the existence of the Union, contradicted expressly by the letter of the Constitution, unauthorized by its spirit, inconsistent with every principle on which it was founded, and destructive of the great object for which it was formed." He sent federal vessels into Charleston Harbor to enforce the tariff, but passage of a compromise tariff bill with lower rates made it possible for South Carolina to withdraw its nullification statute.

The final test remained. In the years preceding the Civil War, with the controversies over slavery and the tariff going on around them, Southern statesmen shifted their ground from the right of nullification to secession as a means to preserve their economic system and social institutions. For Calhoun, secession was justified as a final remedy to preserve states' rights. According to his theory, after a state had interposed its authority to prevent federal action, the federal government could appeal to the amending process. If three-fourths of the states upheld the federal claim, the matter was settled as far as those states were concerned. But the dissenting state was not obliged to acquiesce, if in its judgment the amending power had radically changed the character of the Constitution or the nature of the system.

Lincoln's decision to use force to keep the Southern states in the Union and the victory of the North in the Civil War closed the debate over the legality of secession. After the war the Supreme Court announced in **Texas** v. **White** (1869): "The Constitution, in all its provisions, looks to an indestructible Union, composed of indestructible States."

In 1956 the dust was blown off the doctrines of interposition and nullification, as they were invoked by several Southern states in protest against the Supreme Court's decision declaring racial segregation in the public schools unconstitutional. The Alabama legislature declared: "The decisions and orders of the Supreme Court of the United States relating to the separation of races in public schools are, as a matter of right, null, void, and of no effect; and . . . as a matter of right, this State is not bound to abide thereby." In the 1958 Little Rock case, **Cooper** v. **Aaron,** the Supreme Court disposed sharply and decisively of this contention, and in *Bush* v. *Orleans School Board* (1960) said: "If taken seriously, [interposition] is illegal defiance of constitutional authority."

Federal Supremacy

The federal system is based on the constitutional allocation of authority between the two levels of government. The powers of the federal government are only those delegated to it by that instrument, a prime example being the grants to Congress in Article I, section 8. Whether Congress in adopting any particular piece of legislation is acting within its constitutional powers is determined, of course, by the Supreme Court. *McCulloch* v. *Maryland* (1819) was the first great case in which the Court laid down rules for validating the exercise of congressional authority.

When Congress enters a field in which it is authorized to act, its legislation voids all incompatible state regulations, for Article VI provides that laws of the United States made in pursuance of the Constitution "shall be the supreme law of the land." Here again the Supreme Court has a key role to play. If Congress has indicated its intention to occupy a field entirely, then any state action impinging on that area is precluded; but federal statutes seldom specify whether their intention is to preempt the field. It falls ultimately to the Supreme Court to read the mind of Congress and to determine whether any room has been left for state action.

Most of the Court's preemption holdings have concerned state economic regulatory legislation challenged as in conflict with federal laws enacted under authority of the commerce clause, which will be considered in Chapter Sixteen. At this point two noncommerce clause cases may most usefully exemplify the Court's preemption reasoning.

In *Hines* v. *Davidowitz* (1941) the federal Alien Registration Act of 1940 (better known as the Smith Act) was held to supersede a Pennsylvania alien registration statute. The Court majority thought that the treatment of aliens, in whatever state they might be located, was "a matter of national moment." Moreover, for the states to assume responsibilities for the control of aliens might cause the national government embarrassment in relations with foreign powers. There were certain conflicting provisions in the two statutes which also supported the finding of conflict. For example, the state law required aliens to carry identification cards at all times, an obligation Congress had considered and rejected in passing the federal law.

The *Hines* decision supplied a precedent in the better-known case of **Pennsylvania** v. **Nelson** (1956), where the Court held that the same federal statute had preempted the task of protecting the United States against communist subversion, and so declared invalid a Pennsylvania anti-communist statute. Given the temper of the times in that Cold War period, the *Nelson* ruling was highly unpopular in many quarters, and an effort was made in Congress to pass a law forbidding the Court to strike down state laws on preemption grounds unless the congressional statute expressly declared that it had occupied the field, or unless there was "a direct and positive conflict" between the federal and state statutes. The bill was narrowly defeated in 1958 and 1959.

States may be denied the power to act, not only because Congress has preempted the field, but because state action is incompatible with the constitutional principles of federalism. In Chapter Sixteen we will see how states may be denied the right to adopt legislation affecting interstate commerce, even though there is no conflicting legislation, simply because a uniform national rule is thought to be required for the national welfare. Another example is provided by the Court's decisions on the right to travel.

Protection of the right to travel from state to state was originally derived from general principles of federalism. *Crandall* v. *Nevada* (1868) held that a tax of $1 per passenger on commercial vehicles leaving a state interfered with the government's need to call citizens to cross state lines in order to fill federal offices and to wage wars and with citizens' rights to carry on business among the states and to seek redress of grievances from the government. In *Edwards* v. *California* (1941) a statute making it a misdeameanor to bring indigents into the state was invalidated on the basis of the commerce clause.

More recently the right to travel has been related to individual freedoms. The right to travel abroad, which does not involve considerations of federalism, was upheld in *Kent* v. *Dulles* (1958) as an element of the liberty protected by the due process clause of the Fifth Amendment. In *United States* v. *Guest* (1966) the right to travel was characterized as "fundamental," without reference to any particular provision of the Constitution. The equal protection clause was invoked in *Shapiro* v. *Thompson* (1969) to strike down state and District of Columbia laws which denied welfare assistance to persons who had not been resident in the state or District for one year. *Dunn* v. *Blumstein* (1972) held residency requirement for voting an unconstitutional limitation on the "fundamental personal right . . . to travel." And *Memorial Hospital* v. *Maricopa County* (1974) ruled than an Arizona durational residency requirement for free medical care "penalizes indigents for exercising their right to migrate to and settle in that State." However, in **Sosna v. Iowa** (1975) the right to travel was subordinated to the right of the state to impose a one-year residency requirement for divorce proceedings.

State Power and the Tenth Amendment

In the Constitution, as originally drafted, no effort was made to state any general formula reserving to the states the powers not delegated to Congress. That nondelegated powers remained with the states was regarded as so obvious that it did not need to be spelled out. However, specific assurances were demanded during the ratification debates which were met by adding the Tenth Amendment: "The powers not delegated to the United States by the Constitution, nor prohibited by it to the States, are reserved to the States respectively, or to the people."

Clearly the Tenth Amendment was not intended to be a limitation on federal powers, for it excepts from its effect "powers . . . delegated to the United States." Nevertheless, as we saw in Chapter Eleven, advocates of states' rights have periodically attempted to create, out of the Amendment, barriers to federal action authorized elsewhere in the Constitution. This position has been characterized as "dual federalism," and its most noteworthy statement came in *Hammer* v. *Dagenhart* (1918), noted in Chapter Twelve for its limitation on the power of Congress to regulate commerce until it was overruled in *United States* v. *Darby Lumber Co.* (1941).

The illogic of dual federalism has often been asserted and demonstrated. Justice Harlan rejected it in *Champion* v. *Ames* (1903); in *Missouri* v. *Holland* (1920) Justice Holmes ridiculed the effort to decide a case on the basis of "some invisible radiation from the general terms of the Tenth Amendment." Chief Justice Stone in the *Darby* case said "the amendment states but a truism that all is retained which has not been surrendered."

But the death of the Tenth Amendment, like that of Mark Twain, turns out to have been somewhat exaggerated. In *United States* v. *Butler* (1936), Justice Roberts, having agreed that Congress could spend for the general welfare, made the concession meaningless by holding that the agriculture program for which funds were to be used invaded the rights reserved to the states by the Tenth Amendment. Unlike *Hammer, Butler* was never overruled, merely outflanked as Congress reenacted the agricultural control programs under the aegis of the commerce clause.

The letter or spirit of the Tenth Amendment has been invoked in other decisions. *New York* v. *United States* (1946), while upholding a federal tax on mineral water bottled by the state of New York, nevertheless warned that at least certain state activities were immune from federal taxation because it might "interfere unduly with the State's performance of its sovereign functions of government." Similarly, *Fry* v. *United States* (1975), though it upheld the application of federal wage-control legislation to state and local employees, added the caution that the Tenth Amendment was not without significance, saying, "The Amendment expressly declares the constitutional policy that Congress may not exercise power in a fashion that impairs the States' integrity or their ability to function effectively in a federal system."

Justice Black called on the mystique of "Our Federalism" in *Younger* v. *Harris* (1971) as a justification for protecting state court autonomy against federal court injunctions. Other decisions of the Burger Court, discussed in Chapter Fifteen, have limited the power of federal courts to remove civil rights cases from state to federal courts or to enforce federal civil rights laws against state infringement. But the most striking rehabilitation of the Tenth Amendment is that accomplished by Justice Rehnquist in *National League of Cities* v. *Usery* (1976). Challenging the plenary power of Congress to regulate commerce, which is as firmly established as any proposition in American constitutional law, this decision held a federal wages and overtime law covering state and local employees unconstitutional as a violation of state sovereignty.

THE FEDERALIST NO. 9

Alexander Hamilton

A firm Union will be of the utmost moment to the peace and liberty of the States as a barrier against domestic faction and insurrection. It is impossible to read the history of the petty republics of Greece and Italy without feeling sensations of horror and disgust at the distractions with which they were continually agitated, and at the rapid succession of revolutions by which they were kept in a state of perpetual vibration between the extremes of tyranny and anarchy. If they exhibit occasional calms, these only serve as short-lived contrasts to the furious storms that are to succeed. . . .

. . . The science of politics, however, like most other sciences, has received great improvement. The efficacy of various principles is now well understood, which were either not known at all, or imperfectly known to the ancients. The regular distribution of power into distinct departments; the introduction of legislative balances and checks; the institution of courts composed of judges holding their offices during good behavior; the representation of the people in the legislature by deputies of their own election: these are wholly new discoveries or have made their principal progress towards perfection in modern times. They are means, and powerful means, by which the excellencies of republican government may be retained and its imperfections lessened or avoided. To this catalogue of circumstances that tend to the amelioration of popular systems of civil government, I shall venture, however novel it may appear to some, to add one more, on a principle which has been made the foundation of an objection to the new Constitution; I mean the enlargement of the orbit within which such systems are to revolve, either in respect to the dimensions of a single State, or to the consolidation of several smaller States into one great Confederacy. . . .

The definition of a *confederate republic* seems simply to be "an assemblage of societies," or an association of two or more states into one state. The extent, modifications, and objects of the federal authority are mere matters of discretion. So long as the separate organization of the members be not abolished; so long as it exists, by a constitutional necessity, for local purposes; though it should be in perfect subordination to the general authority of the union, it would still be, in fact and in theory, an association of states, or a confederacy. The proposed Constitution, so far from implying an abolition of the State governments, makes them constituent parts of the national sovereignty, by allowing them a direct representation in the Senate, and leaves in their possession certain exclusive and very important portions of sovereign power. This fully corresponds, in every rational import of the terms, with the idea of a federal government. . . .

THE FEDERALIST NO. 39

James Madison

[The] adversaries of the proposed Constitution [say the Framers] "ought . . . to have preserved the *federal* form, which regards the Union as a *Confederacy* of sovereign states; instead of which they have framed a *national* government, which regards the Union as a *consolidation* of the States." . . .

The handle which has been made of this objection requires that it should be examined with some precision. . . .

FIRST.—In order to ascertain the real character of the government, it may be considered in relation to the foundation on which it is to be established; to the sources from which its ordinary powers are to be drawn; to the operation of those powers; to the extent of them; and to the authority by which future changes in the government are to be introduced.

On examining the first relation, it appears, on one hand, that the Constitution is to be founded on the assent and ratification of the people of America, given by deputies elected for the special purpose; but, on the other, that this assent and ratification is to be given by the people, not as individuals composing one entire nation, but as composing the distinct and independent States to which they respectively belong. It is to be the assent and ratification of the several States, derived from the supreme authority in each State—the authority of the people themselves. The act, therefore, establishing the Constitution will not be a *national* but a *federal* act. . . .

The next relation is to the sources from which the ordinary powers of government are to be derived. The House of Representatives will derive its powers from the people of America; and the people will be represented in the same proportion and on the same principle as they are in the legislature of a particular State. So far the government is *national*, not *federal.* The Senate, on the other hand, will derive its powers from the States as political and coequal societies; and these will be represented on the principle of equality in the Senate, as they now are in the existing Congress. So far the government is *federal,* not *national.* The executive power will be derived from a very compound source. The immediate election of the President is to be made by the States in their political characters. The votes allotted to them are in a compound ratio, which considers them partly as distinct and coequal societies, partly as unequal members of the same society. The eventual election, again, is to be made by that branch of the legislature which consists of the national representatives; but in this particular act they are to be thrown into the form of individual delegations from so many distinct and co-equal bodies politic. From this aspect of the government it appears to be of a mixed character, presenting at least as many *federal* as *national* features.

The difference between a federal and national government, as it relates to the *operation of the government,* is by the adversaries of the plan of the convention supposed to consist in this, that in the former the powers operate on the political bodies composing the Confederacy in their political capacities; in the latter, on the individual citizens composing the nation in their individual capacities. On trying the Constitution by this criterion, it falls under the *national* not the *federal* character. . . .

But if the government be national with regard to the *operation* of its powers, it changes its aspect again when we contemplate it in relation to the extent of its powers. The idea of a national government involves in it not only an authority over the individual citizens, but an indefinite supremacy over all persons and things, so far as they are objects of lawful government. Among a people consolidated into one nation, this supremacy is completely vested in the national legislature. Among communities united for particular purposes, it is vested partly in the general and partly in the municipal legislatures. In the former case, all local authorities are subordinate to the supreme; and may be controlled, directed, or abolished by it at pleasure. In the latter, the local or municipal authorities form distinct and independent portions of the supremacy, no more subject, within their respective spheres, to the general authority than the general authority is subject to them, within its own sphere. In this relation, then, the proposed government cannot be deemed a *national* one; since its jurisdiction extends to certain enumerated objects only, and leaves to the several States a residuary and inviolable sovereignty over all other subjects. . . .

If we try the Constitution by its last relation to the authority by which amendments are to be made, we find it neither wholly *national* nor wholly *federal.* Were it wholly national, the supreme and ultimate authority would reside in the *majority* of the people of the Union; and this authority would be competent at all times, like that of a majority of every national society to alter or abolish its established government. Were it wholly federal, on the other hand, the concurrence of each State in the Union would be essential to every alteration that would be binding on all. The mode provided by the plan of the convention is not founded on either of these principles. In requiring more than a majority, and particularly in computing the proportion by *States,* not by *citizens,* it departs from the national and advances towards the *federal* character; in rendering the concurrence of less than the whole number of States sufficient, it loses again the *federal* and partakes of the *national* character.

The proposed Constitution, therefore, even when tested by the rules laid down by its antagonists is, in strictness, neither a national nor a federal Constitution, but a composition of both. . . .

TEXAS V. WHITE

7 Wall. 700, 19 L. Ed. 227 (1869)

In 1866 Texas brought an action in the original jurisdiction of the Supreme Court to reclaim state bonds from private holders, including White. White's defense was that Texas was not at the time a state of the Union and consequently that the Supreme Court lacked jurisdiction to entertain the original action.

THE CHIEF JUSTICE [CHASE] delivered the opinion of the court. . . .

The first inquiries to which our attention was directed by counsel, arose upon the allegations of the answer of Chiles (1) that no sufficient authority is shown for the prosecution of the suit in the name and on the behalf of the State of Texas; and (2) that the State, having severed her relations with a majority of the States of the Union, and having by her ordinance of secession attempted to throw off her allegiance to the Constitution and government of the United States, has so far changed her status as to be disabled from prosecuting suits in the National courts. . . .

It [the word *state*] described sometimes a people or community of individuals united more or less closely in political relations, inhabiting temporarily or permanently in the same country; often it denotes only the country or territorial region, inhabited by such a community; not unfrequently it is applied to the government under which the people live; at other times it represents the combined idea of people, territory, and government. . . .

In the Constitution the term state most frequently expresses the combined idea just noticed, of people, territory, and government. A state, in the ordinary sense of the Constitution, is a political community of free citizens, occupying a territory of defined boundaries, and organized under a government sanctioned and limited by a written constitution, and established by the consent of the governed. It is the union of such states, under a common constitution, which forms the distinct and greater political unit, which that Constitution designates as the United States, and makes of the people and states which compose it one people and one country. . . .

Texas took part, with the other Confederate States, in the war of the rebellion, which these events made inevitable. During the whole of that war there was no governor, or judge, or any other State officer in Texas, who recognized the National authority. Nor was any officer of the United States permitted to exercise any authority whatever under the National government within the limits of the State, except under the immediate protection of the National military forces.

Did Texas, in consequence of these acts, cease to be a State? Or, if not, did the State cease to be a member of the Union?

It is needless to discuss, at length, the question whether the right of a State to withdraw from the Union for any cause, regarded by herself as sufficient, is consistent with the Constitution of the United States.

The Union of the States never was a purely artificial and arbitrary relation. It began among the Colonies, and grew out of common origin, mutual sympathies, kindred principles, similar interests, and geographical relations. It was confirmed and strengthened by the necessities of war, and received definite form, and character, and sanction from the Articles of Confederation. By these the Union was solemnly declared to "be perpetual." And when these Articles were found to be inadequate to the exigencies of the country, the Constitution was ordained "to form a more perfect Union." It is difficult to convey the idea of indissoluble unity more clearly than by these words. What can be indissoluble if a perpetual Union, made more perfect, is not?

But the perpetuity and indissolubility of the Union, by no means implies the loss of distinct and individual existence, or of the right of self-government by the States. Under the Articles of Confederation, each State retained its sovereignty, freedom, and independence, and every power, jurisdiction, and right not expressly delegated to the United States. Under the Constitution, though the powers of the States were much restricted, still, all powers not delegated to the United States, nor prohibited to the States, are reserved to the States respectively, or to the people. And we have already had occasion to remark at this term, that "the people of each State compose a State, having its own government, and endowed with all the functions essential to separate and independent existence," and that "without the States in union, there could be no such political body as the United States." *County of Lane* v. *Oregon.* . . . Not only therefore can there be no loss of separate and independent autonomy to the States, through their union under the Constitution, but it may be not unreasonably said that the preservation of the States, and the maintenance of their governments, are as much within the design and care of the Constitution as the preservation of the Union and the maintenance of the National government. The Constitution, in all of its provisions, looks to an indestructible Union, composed of indestructible States.

When, therefore, Texas became one of the United States, she entered into an indissoluble relation. All the obligations of perpetual union and all the guarantees of republican government in the Union, attached at once to the State. The act which consummated her admission into the Union was something more than a compact; it was the incorporation of a new member into the political body. And it was final. The union between Texas and the other States was as complete, as perpetual, and as indissoluble as the union between the original States. There was no place for reconsideration, or revocation, except through revolution, or through consent of the States.

Considered therefore as transactions under the Constitution, the ordinance of secession, adopted by the convention and ratified by a majority of the citizens of Texas, and all the acts of her legislature intended to give effect to that ordinance, were absolutely null. They were utterly without operation in law. The obligations of the State, as a member of the Union, and of every citizen of the State, as a citizen of the United States, remained perfect and unimpaired. It certainly follows that the State did not cease to be a State, nor her citizens to be citizens of the Union. If this were otherwise, the State must have become foreign, and her citizens foreigners. The war must have ceased to be a war for the suppression of rebellion, and must have become a war for conquest and subjugation.

Our conclusion therefore is, that Texas continued to be a State, and a State of the Union, notwithstanding the transactions to which we have referred. And this conclusion, in our judgment, is not in conflict with any act or declaration of any department of the National government, but entirely in accordance with the whole series of such acts and declarations since the first outbreak of the rebellion. . . .

[The right of Texas to bring suit was affirmed, and a decree issued enjoining White and others from setting up any claim to the bonds.]

Mr. Justice Grier, dissenting. . . .

The original jurisdiction of this court can be invoked only by one of the United States. The Territories have no such right conferred on them by the Constitution, nor have the Indian tribes who are under the protection of the military authorities of the government.

Is Texas one of these United States? Or was she such at the time the bill was filed, or since?

This is to be decided as *a political fact*, not as *a legal fiction*. This court is bound to know and notice the public history of the nation.

If I regard the truth of history for the last eight years, I cannot discover the State of Texas as one of these United States. . . .

[Justices Swayne and Miller agreed with Justice Grier in denying the capacity of Texas to bring suit.]

COOPER V. AARON

358 U.S. 1, 78 S. Ct. 1401, 3 L. Ed. 2d 5 (1958)

Following the Supreme Court's decision in *Brown* v. *Board of Education* (1954) the school board of Little Rock, Arkansas, prepared a program for desegregating the public school system, to begin in 1957 and to be completed in 1963. But the state legislature adopted legislation relieving school children from attendance at racially mixed schools, and in 1957 the governor sent units of the Arkansas National Guard to the high school to prevent black students from entering. A federal district judge enjoined state officials from interfering with the desegregation order, but violence then broke out, forcing President Eisenhower to send federal troops to effect admission of the black students.

In February, 1958, the school board, alleging that extreme public hostility toward attendance of the black students had made a sound educational program at the high school impossible, petitioned the federal district court to postpone the desegregation program for two and one-half years. The district judge granted the requested relief, but his ruling was reversed by the Court of Appeals in August, 1958. The Supreme Court unanimously affirmed the judgment of the Court of Appeals.

Opinion of the Court by the CHIEF JUSTICE, MR. JUSTICE BLACK, MR. JUSTICE FRANKFURTER, MR. JUSTICE DOUGLAS, MR. JUSTICE BURTON, MR. JUSTICE CLARK, MR. JUSTICE HARLAN, MR. JUSTICE BRENNAN, and MR. JUSTICE WHITTAKER. . . .

The controlling legal principles are plain. The command of the Fourteenth Amendment is that no "State" shall deny to any person within its jurisdiction the equal protection of the laws. "A State acts by its legislative, its executive, or its judicial authorities. It can act in no other way. The constitutional provision, therefore, must mean that no agency of the State, or of the officers or agents by whom its powers are exerted, shall deny to any person within its jurisdiction the equal protection of the laws. Whoever, by virtue of public position under a State government . . . denies or takes away the equal protection of the laws, violates the consitutional inhibition; and as he acts in the name of and for the State, and is clothed with the State's power, his act is that of the State. . . ."

. . . In short, the constitutional rights of children not to be discriminated against in school admission on grounds of race or color declared by this Court in the *Brown* case can neither be nullified openly and directly by state legislators or state executive or judicial officers, nor nullified indirectly by them through evasive schemes for segregation whether attempted "ingeniously or ingenuously." *Smith* v. *Texas* . . . [1940].

What has been said, in the light of the facts developed, is enough to dispose of the case. However, we should answer the premise of the actions of the Governor and Legislature that they are not bound by our holding in the *Brown* case. It is necessary only to recall some basic constitutional propositions which are settled doctrine.

Article 6 of the Constitution makes the Constitution the "supreme Law of the Land." In 1803, Chief Justice Marshall, speaking for a unanimous Court, referring to the Constitution as "the fundamental and paramount law of the nation," declared in the notable case of *Marbury* v. *Madison,* . . . that "It is emphatically the province and duty of the judicial department to say what the law is." This decision declared the basic principle that the federal judiciary is supreme in the exposition of the law of the Constitution, and that principle has ever since been respected by this Court and the Country as a permanent and indispensable feature of our constitutional system. It follows that the interpretation of the Fourteenth Amendment enunciated by this Court in the *Brown* Case is the supreme law of the land, and Art. 6 of the Constitution makes it of binding effect on the States "any Thing in the Constitution or Laws of any State to the Contrary notwithstanding." Every state legislator and executive and judicial officer is solemnly committed by oath taken pursuant to Art. 6, ¶3 "to support this Constitution." Chief Justice Taney, speaking for a unanimous Court in 1859, said that this requirement reflected the framers' "anxiety to preserve it [the Constitution] in full force, in all its powers, and to guard against resistance to or evasion of its authority, on the part of a State. . . ." *Ableman* v. *Booth.* . . .

No state legislator or executive or judicial officer can war against the Constitution without violating his undertaking to support it. Chief Justice Marshall spoke for a unanimous Court in saying that: "If the legislatures of the several states may, at will, annul the judgments of the courts of the United States, and destroy the rights acquired under those judgments, the constitution itself becomes a solemn mockery. . . ." *United States* v. *Peters.* . . . A Governor who asserts a power to nullify a federal court order is similarly restrained. If he had such power, said Chief Justice Hughes, in 1932, also for a unanimous Court, "it is manifest that the fiat of a state Governor, and not the Constitution of the United States, would be the supreme law of the land; that the restrictions of the Federal Constitution upon the exercise of state power would be but impotent phrases. . . ." *Sterling* v. *Constantine.* . . .

It is, of course, quite true that the responsibility for public education is primarily the concern of the States, but it is equally true that such responsibilities, like all other state activity, must be exercised consistently with federal constitutional requirements as they apply to state action. The Constitution created a government dedicated to equal justice under law. The Fourteenth Amendment embodied and emphasized that ideal. State support of segregated schools through any arrangement, management, funds, or property cannot be squared with the Amendment's command that no State shall deny to any person within its jurisdiction the equal protection of the laws. The right of a student not to be segregated on racial grounds in schools so maintained is indeed so fundamental and pervasive that it is embraced in the concept of due process of law. *Bolling*

v. *Sharpe.* . . . The basic decision in *Brown* was unanimously reached by this Court only after the case had been briefed and twice argued and the issues had been given the most serious consideration. Since the first *Brown* opinion three new Justices have come to the Court. They are at one with the Justices still on the Court who participated in the basic decision as to its correctness, and that decision is now unanimously reaffirmed. The principles announced in that decision and the obedience of the States to them, according to the command of the Constitution, are indispensable for the protection of the freedoms guaranteed by our fundamental charter for all of us. Our constitutional ideal of equal justice under law is thus made a living truth.

Affirmed.

PENNSYLVANIA V. NELSON

350 U.S. 497, 76 S. Ct. 477, 100 L. Ed. 640 (1956)

The Alien Registration Act of 1940, generally known as the Smith Act, among other provisions prohibited the knowing advocacy of the overthrow of the government of the United States by force and violence. The state of Pennsylvania also had a statute punishing seditious activities against the state and the United States. Nelson, already under federal sentence for violation of the Smith Act, was convicted in Pennsylvania of violating that state's sedition act. The Pennsylvania supreme court reversed the conviction on the ground that the Smith Act had preempted the state statute, and the state appealed to the Supreme Court.

MR. CHIEF JUSTICE WARREN delivered the opinion of the Court. . . .

It should be said at the outset that the decision in this case does not affect the right of States to enforce their sedition laws at times when the Federal Government has not occupied the field and is not protecting the entire country from seditious conduct. . . .

Where, as in the instant case, Congress has not stated specifically whether a federal statute has occupied a field in which the States are otherwise free to legislate, different criteria have furnished touchstones for decision. . . . In this case, we think that each of several tests of supersession is met.

First, "[t]he scheme of federal regulation [is] so pervasive as to make reasonable the inference that Congress left no room for the States to supplement it." The Congress determined in 1940 that it was necessary for it to re-enter the field of antisubversive legislation, which had been abandoned by it in 1921. In that year, it enacted the Smith Act which proscribes advocacy of the overthrow of any government—federal, state or local—by force and violence and organization of and knowing membership in a group which so advocates. Conspiracy to commit any of these acts is punishable under the general criminal conspiracy provisions. . . . The Internal Security Act of 1950 is aimed more directly at Communist organizations. It distinguishes between "Communist-action organizations" and "Communist-front organizations," requiring such organizations to register and to file annual reports with the Attorney General giving complete details as to their officers and funds. Members of Communist-action organizations who have not been registered by their organization must register as individuals. Failure to register . . . is punishable by a fine of not more than $10,000 for an offending organization and by a fine of not more than $10,000 or imprisonment for not more than five years or both for an individual offender—each day of failure to register constituting a separate offense. And the Act imposes certain sanctions upon both "action" and "front" organizations and their members. The Communist Control Act of 1954 declares "that the Communist Party of the United States, although purportedly a political party, is in fact an instrumentality of a conspiracy to overthrow the Government of the United States" and that "its role as the agency of a hostile foreign power renders its existence a clear present and continuing danger to the security of the United States." It also contains a legislative finding that the Communist Party is a "Communist-action organization" within the meaning of the Internal Security Act of 1950 and provides that "knowing" members of the Communist Party are "subject to all the provisions and penalties" of that Act. It furthermore sets up a new classification of "Communist-infiltrated organizations" and provides for the imposition of sanctions against them.

We examine these Acts only to determine the congressional plan. Looking to all of them in the aggregate, the conclusion is inescapable that Congress has intended to occupy the field of sedition. Taken as a whole, they evince a congressional plan which makes it reasonable to determine that no room has been left for the States to supplement it. Therefore, a state sedition statute is superseded regardless of whether it purports to supplement the federal law. . . .

Second, the federal statutes "touch a field in which the federal interest is so dominant that the federal system [must] be assumed to preclude enforcement of state laws on the same subject." . . . Congress has devised an all-embracing program for resistance to the various forms of totalitarian aggression. Our external defenses have been strengthened, and a plan to protect against internal subversion has been made by it. It has appropriated vast sums, not only for our own protection, but also to strengthen freedom throughout the world. It has charged the Federal Bureau of Investigation and the Central Intelligence Agency with responsibility for intelligence concerning Communist seditious activities against our Government, and has denominated such activities as part of a world conspiracy. It accordingly proscribed sedition against all government in the nation—national, state and local. Congress declared that these steps were taken "to provide for the common defense, to preserve the sovereignty of the United States as an independent nation, and to guarantee to each State a republican form of government." . . . Congress having thus treated seditious conduct as a matter of vital national concern, it is in no sense a local enforcement problem. . . .

Third, enforcement of state sedition acts presents a serious danger of conflict with the administration of the federal program. Since 1939, in order to avoid a hampering of uniform enforcement of its program by sporadic local prosecutions, the Federal Government has urged local authorities not to intervene in such matters, but to turn over to the federal authorities immediately and unevaluated all information concerning subversive activities. . . .

Moreover, the Pennsylvania Statute presents a peculiar danger of interference with the federal program. For, as the court below observed:

> "Unlike the Smith Act, which can be administered only by federal officers acting in their official capacities, indictment for sedition under the Pennsylvania statute can be initiated upon an information made by a private individual. The opportunity thus present for the indulgence of personal spite and hatred or for furthering some selfish advantage or ambition need only be mentioned to be appreciated. Defense of the Nation by law, no less than by arms, should be a public and not a private undertaking. It is important that punitive sanctions for sedition *against the United States* be such as have been promulgated by the central government authority and administered under the supervision and review of that authority's judiciary. If that be done, sedition will be detected and punished, no less, wherever it may be found, and the right of the individual to speak freely and without fear, even in criticism of the government, will at the same time be protected."

. . . [F]orty-two States plus Alaska and Hawaii have statutes which in some form prohibit advocacy of the violent overthrow of established government. These statutes are entitled anti-sedition statutes, criminal anarchy laws, criminal syndicalist laws, etc. Although all of them are primarily directed against the overthrow of the United States Government, they are in no sense uniform. And our attention has not been called to any case where the prosecution has been successfully directed against an attempt to destroy state or local government. Some of these Acts are studiously drawn and purport to protect fundamental rights by appropriate definitions, standards of proof and orderly procedures in keeping with the avowed congressional purpose "to protect freedom from those who would destroy it, without infringing upon the freedom of all our people." Others are vague and are almost wholly without such safeguards. Some even purport to punish mere membership in subversive organizations which the federal statutes do not punish where federal registration requirements have been fulfilled. . . .

Since we find that Congress has occupied the field to the exclusion of parallel state legislation, that the dominant interest of the Federal Government precludes state intervention, and that administration of state Acts would conflict with the operation of the federal plan, we are convinced that the decision of the Supreme Court of Pennsylvania is unassailable. . . .

The judgment of the Supreme Court of Pennsylvania is

Affirmed.

MR. JUSTICE REED, with whom MR. JUSTICE BURTON and MR. JUSTICE MINTON join, dissenting.

Congress has not, in any of its statutes relating to sedition, specifically barred the exercise of state power to punish the same Acts under state law. And, we read the majority opinion to assume for this case that, absent federal legislation, there is no constitutional bar to punishment of sedition against the United States by both a State and the Nation. The majority limits to the federal courts the power to try charges of sedition against the Federal Government. . . . [T]his Court should not void state legislation without a clear mandate from Congress.

We cannot agree that the federal criminal sanctions against sedition directed at the United States are of such a pervasive character as to indicate an intention to void state action. . . .

We are citizens of the United States and of the State wherein we reside and are dependent upon the strength of both to preserve our rights and liberties. Both may enact criminal statutes for mutual protection unless Congress has otherwise provided. . . . Congress was advised of the existing state sedition legislation when the Smith Act was enacted and has been kept current with its spread. No declaration of exclusiveness followed. . . .

The law stands against any advocacy of violence to change established governments. Freedom of speech allows full play to the processes of reason. The state and national legislative bodies have legislated within constitutional limits so as to allow the widest participation by the law enforcement officers of the respective governments. The individual States were not told that they are powerless to punish local acts of sedition, nominally directed against the United States. Courts should not interfere. We would reverse the judgment of the Supreme Court of Pennsylvania.

SOSNA V. IOWA

419 U.S. 393, 95 S. Ct. 553, 42 L. Ed. 2d 532 (1975)

A wife whose petition for divorce had been dismissed by an Iowa court because she failed to meet the state statutory requirement that a petitioner in a divorce action must be a resident of the state for one year preceding the filing of the petition brought a class action seeking to have the residency requirement declared unconstitutional.*

MR. JUSTICE REHNQUIST delivered the opinion of the Court. . . .

Appellant contends that the Iowa requirement of one year's residence is unconstitutional . . . because it establishes two classes of persons and discriminates against those who have recently exercised their right to travel to Iowa, thereby contravening the Court's holdings in Shapiro v. Thompson . . . (1969); Dunn v. Blumstein . . . (1972); and Memorial Hospital v. Maricopa County . . . (1974).

. . . State statutes imposing durational residency requirements were, of course, invalidated when imposed by States as a qualification for welfare payments, Shapiro . . .; for voting, Dunn . . .: and for medical care, Maricopa County. . . . But none of those cases intimated that the States might never impose durational residency requirements and such a proposition was in fact expressly disclaimed. What those cases had in common was that the durational residency requirements they struck down were justified on the basis of budgetary or recordkeeping considerations which were held insufficient to outweigh the constitutional claims of the individuals. But Iowa's divorce residency requirement is of a different stripe. Appellant was not irretrievably foreclosed from obtaining some part of what she sought, as was the case with the welfare recipients in Shapiro, the voters in Dunn, or the indigent patient in Maricopa County. She would eventually qualify for the same sort of adjudication which she demanded virtually upon her arrival in the State. Iowa's requirement delayed her access to the courts, but, by fulfilling it, she could ultimately have obtained the same opportunity for adjudication which she asserts ought to have been hers at an earlier point in time.

Iowa's residency requirement may reasonably be justified on grounds other than purely budgetary considerations or administrative convenience. . . . A decree of divorce is not a matter in which the only interested parties are the State as a sort of "grantor," and a divorce petitioner such as appellant in the role of "grantee." Both spouses are obviously interested in the proceedings, since it will affect their marital status and very likely their property rights. Where a married couple has minor children,

---

* By the time the case reached the Supreme Court the petitioner had met the one year residency requirement and secured a divorce. For this reason Justice White would have held the case moot.

a decree of divorce would usually include provisions for their custody and support. With consequences of such moment riding on a divorce decree issued by its courts Iowa may insist that one seeking to initiate such a proceeding have the modicum of attachment to the State required here.

Such a requirement additionally furthers the State's parallel interests both in avoiding officious intermeddling in matters in which another State has a paramount interest, and in minimizing the susceptibility of its own divorce decrees to collateral attack. A State such as Iowa may quite reasonably decide that it does not wish to become a divorce mill for unhappy spouses who have lived there as short a time as appellant had when she commenced her action in the state court after having long resided elsewhere. Until such time as Iowa is convinced that appellant intends to remain in the State, it lacks the "nexus between person and place of such permanence as to control the creation of legal relations and responsibilities of the utmost significance." Williams v. North Carolina . . . (1945). Perhaps even more important, Iowa's interests extend beyond its borders and include the recognition of its divorce decrees by other States under the Full Faith and Credit Clause of the Constitution, Art. IV, § 1. For that purpose, this Court has often stated that "judicial power to grant a divorce—jurisdiction, strictly speaking—is founded on domicil." . . . Where a divorce decree is entered after a finding of domicile in *ex parte* proceedings, this Court has held that the finding of domicile is not binding upon another State and may be disregarded in the face of "cogent evidence" to the contrary. . . . For that reason, the State asked to enter such a decree is entitled to insist that the putative divorce petitioner satisfy something more than the bare minimum of constitutional requirements before a divorce may be granted. The State's decision to exact a one-year residency requirement as a matter of policy is therefore buttressed by a quite permissible inference that this requirement not only effectuates state substantive policy but likewise provides a greater safeguard against successful collateral attack than would a requirement of bona fide residence alone. This is precisely the sort of determination that a State in the exercise of its domestic relations jurisdiction is entitled to make.

We therefore hold that the state interest in requiring that those who seek a divorce from its courts be genuinely attached to the State, as well as a desire to insulate divorce decrees from the likelihood of collateral attack, requires a different resolution of the constitutional issue presented than was the case in *Shapiro*, . . . *Dunn*, . . . and *Maricopa County*. . . .

MR. JUSTICE MARSHALL, with whom MR. JUSTICE BRENNAN joins, dissenting. . . .

The Court today departs sharply from the course we have followed in analyzing durational residency requirements since Shapiro v. Thompson . . . (1969). Because I think the principles set out in that case and its progeny compel reversal here, I respectfully dissent.

As we have made clear in *Shapiro* and subsequent cases, any classification that penalizes exercise of the constitutional right to travel is invalid unless it is justified by a compelling governmental interest. As recently as last Term we held that the right to travel requires that States provide the same vital governmental benefits and privileges to recent immigrants that they do to long-time residents. Memorial Hospital v. Maricopa County ... (1974). Although we recognized that not all durational residency requirements are penalties upon the exercise of the right to travel interstate, we held that free medical aid, like voting, see Dunn v. Blumstein ... (1972), and welfare assistance, see Shapiro v. Thompson, ... was of such fundamental importance that the State could not constitutionally condition its receipt upon long-term residence....

The Court omits altogether what should be the first inquiry: whether the right to obtain a divorce is of sufficient importance that its denial to recent immigrants constitutes a penalty on interstate travel. In my view, it clearly meets that standard. The previous decisions of this Court make it plain that the right of marital association is one of the most basic rights conferred on the individual by the State. The interests associated with marriage and divorce have repeatedly been accorded particular deference, and the right to marry has been termed "one of the vital personal rights essential to the orderly pursuit of happiness by free men." Loving v. Virginia, ... (1967). In Boddie v. Connecticut ... (1971), we recognized that the right to seek dissolution of the marital relationship was closely related to the right to marry, as both involve the voluntary adjustment of the same human relationship.... Without further laboring the point, I think it is clear beyond cavil that the right to seek dissolution of the marital relationship is of such fundamental importance that denial of this right to the class of recent interstate travelers penalizes interstate travel within the meaning of Shapiro, Dunn, and Maricopa County. ...

The Court proposes three defenses for the Iowa statute: first, the residency requirement merely delays receipt of the benefit in question— it does not deprive the applicant of the benefit altogether; second, since significant social consequences may follow from the conferral of a divorce, the State may legitimately regulate the divorce process; and third, the State has interests both in protecting itself from use as a "divorce mill" and in protecting its judgments from possible collateral attack in other States. In my view, the first two defenses provide no significant support for the statute in question here. Only the third has any real force.

With the first justification, the Court seeks to distinguish the Shapiro, Dunn, and Maricopa County cases. Yet the distinction the Court draws seems to me specious. Iowa's residency requirement, the Court says, merely forestalls access to the courts: applicants seeking welfare payments, medical aid, and the right to vote, on the other hand, suffer unrecoverable losses throughout the waiting period. This analysis, however, ignores the severity of the deprivation suffered by the divorce petitioner who is forced to wait a year for relief.... The injury accompanying that delay is not directly measurable in money terms like the loss of welfare benefits, but it cannot reasonably be argued that when the year has elapsed, the petitioner is made whole. The year's wait prevents re-marriage and locks both partners into what may be an intolerable, de-structive relationship. . . .

I find the majority's second argument no more persuasive. . . . To remark, as the Court does, that because of the consequences riding on a divorce decree "Iowa may insist that one seeking to initiate such a proceeding have the modicum of attachment to the State required here" is not to make an argument, but merely to state the result. . . .

The Court's third justification seems to me the only one that warrants close consideration. Iowa has a legitimate interest in protecting itself against invasion by those seeking quick divorces in a forum with relatively lax divorce laws. . . . If, as the majority assumes, Iowa is interested in assuring itself that its divorce petitioners are legitimately Iowa citizens, requiring petitioners to provide convincing evidence of bona fide domi-cile should be more than adequate to the task. . . .

NATIONAL LEAGUE OF CITIES V. USERY

426 U.S. 833, 96 S. Ct. 2465, 45 L. Ed. 2d 245 (1976)

The Fair Labor Standards Act of 1938, approved by the Supreme Court in *United States* v. *Darby Lumber Co.* (1941) as an exercise of the congressional power to regulate commerce, was amended in 1974 to make the provisions concerning minimum wages and maximum hours applicable to employees of the states and their political subdivisions. In *Maryland* v. *Wirtz* (1968) the Court had upheld an amendment to the Act which extended minimum wage coverage to nonprofessional and nonadministrative employees of state public schools, hospi-tals, and related institutions. *Fry* v. *United States* (1975) held federal wage and salary controls imposed under the Economic Stabilization Act of 1970 applicable to state employees.

MR. JUSTICE REHNQUIST delivered the opinion for the Court. . . .

It is established beyond peradventure that the Commerce Clause of Art. I of the Constitution is a grant of plenary authority to Congress. That authority is, in the words of Chief Justice Marshall in Gibbons v. Ogden, . . . ". . . the power to regulate; that is to prescribe the rule by which commerce is to be governed." . . .

Congressional power over areas of private endeavor, even when its exercise may pre-empt state law determinations contrary to the result which has commended itself to collective wisdom of Congress, has been held to be limited only by the requirement that "the means chosen by [Congress] must be reasonably adapted to the end permitted by the Constitution." Heart of Atlanta Motel, Inc. v. United States . . . (1964).

Appellants in no way challenge these decisions establishing the breadth of authority granted Congress under the commerce power. Their contention, on the contrary, is that when Congress seeks to regulate directly the activities of States as public employers, it transgresses an affirmative limitation on the exercise of its power akin to other commerce power affirmative limitations contained in the Constitution. Congressional enactments which may be fully within the grant of legislative authority contained in the Commerce Clause may nonetheless be invalid because found to offend against the right to trial by jury contained in the Sixth Amendment, United States v. Jackson . . . (1968), or the Due Process Clause of the Fifth Amendment, Leary v. United States . . . (1969). Appellants' essential contention is that the 1974 amendments to the Act, while undoubtedly within the scope of the Commerce Clause, encounter a similar constitutional barrier because they are to be applied directly to the States and subdivisions of States as employers.

This Court has never doubted that there are limits upon the power of Congress to override state sovereignty, even when exercising its otherwise plenary powers to tax or to regulate commerce which are conferred by Art. I of the Constitution. . . . In *Fry, supra,* the Court recognized that an express declaration of this limitation is found in the Tenth Amendment:

> "While the Tenth Amendment has been characterized as a 'truism,' stating merely that 'all is retained which has not been surrendered,' United States v. Darby . . . (1941), it is not without significance. The Amendment expressly declares the constitutional policy that Congress may not exercise power in a fashion that impairs the States' integrity or their ability to function effectively in a federal system. . . ."

. . . It is one thing to recognize the authority of Congress to enact laws regulating individual businesses necessarily subject to the dual sovereignty of the government of the Nation and of the State in which they reside. It is quite another to uphold a similar exercise of congressional authority directed not to private citizens, but to the States as States. We have repeatedly recognized that there are attributes of sovereignty attaching to every state government which may not be impaired by Congress not because Congress may lack an affirmative grant of legislative authority to reach the matter, but because the Constitution prohibits it from exercising the authority in that manner. . . .

One undoubted attribute of state sovereignty is the States' power to determine the wages which shall be paid to those whom they employ in order to carry out their governmental functions, what hours those persons will work, and what compensation will be provided where these employees may be called upon to work overtime. The question we must resolve in this case, then, is whether these determinations are "functions essential to separate and independent existence," . . . so that Congress may not abrogate the States' otherwise plenary authority to make them. . . .

Our examination of the effect of the 1974 amendments, as sought to be extended to the States and their political subdivisions, satisfies us that both the minimum wage and the maximum hour provisions will impermissibly interfere with the integral governmental functions of these bodies. We earlier noted some disagreement between the parties regarding the precise effect the amendments will have in application. We do not believe particularized assessments of actual impact are crucial to resolution of the issue presented, however. For even if we accept appellee's assessments concerning the impact of the amendments, their application will nonetheless significantly alter or displace the States' abilities to structure employer-employee relationships in such areas as fire prevention, police protection, sanitation, public health, and parks and recreation. These activities are typical of those performed by state and local governments in discharging their dual functions of administering the public law and furnishing public services. Indeed, it is functions such as these which governments are created to provide, services such as these which the States have traditionally afforded their citizens. If Congress may withdraw from the States the authority to make those fundamental employment decisions upon which their systems for performance of these functions must rest, we think there would be little left of the States' "separate and independent existence." . . . Thus, even if appellants may have overestimated the effect which the Act will have upon their current levels and patterns of governmental activity, the dispositive factor is that Congress has attempted to exercise its Commerce Clause authority to prescribe minimum wages and maximum hours to be paid by the States in their capacities as sovereign governments. In so doing, Congress has sought to wield its power in a fashion that would impair the States' "ability to function effectively within a federal system." . . . This exercise of congressional authority does not comport with the federal system of government embodied in the Constitution. We hold that insofar as the challenged amendments operate to directly displace the States' freedom to structure integral operations in areas of traditional governmental functions, they are not within the authority granted Congress by Art. I, § 8, cl. 3.

MR. JUSTICE BRENNAN, with whom MR. JUSTICE WHITE and MR. JUSTICE MARSHALL join, dissenting. . . .

The Court concedes, as of course it must, that Congress enacted the 1974 amendments pursuant to its exclusive power under Art. I, § 8, cl. 3, of the Constitution "To regulate Commerce . . . among the several States." It must therefore be surprising that my Brethren should choose this Bicentennial year of our independence to repudiate principles governing judicial interpretation of our Constitution settled since the time of Chief Justice John Marshall, discarding his postulate that the Constitution contemplates that restraints upon exercise by Congress of its plenary commerce power lie in the political process and not in the judicial process. For 152 years ago Chief Justice Marshall enunciated that principle to which, until today, his successors on this Court have been faithful.

"[T]he power over commerce . . . is vested in Congress as absolutely as it would be in a single government, having in its constitution the same restrictions on the exercise of the power as are found in the constitution of the United States. *The wisdom and the discretion of Congress, their identity with the people, and the influence which their constituents possess at elections, are . . . the sole restraints on which they have relied, to secure them from its abuse. They are the restraints on which the people must often rely solely, in all representative governments."* Gibbons v. Ogden (1824) (emphasis added). Only 34 years ago, Wickard v. Filburn . . . (1942), reaffirmed that "[a]t the beginning Chief Justice Marshall . . . made emphatic the embracing and penetrating nature of [Congress' commerce] power by warning that effective restraints on its exercise must proceed from political rather than from judicial processes." . . .

My Brethren thus have today manufactured an abstraction without substance, founded neither in the words of the Constitution nor on precedent. An abstraction having such profoundly pernicious consequences is not made less so by characterizing the 1974 amendments as legislation directed against the "States *qua* States.' . . . Of course, regulations that this Court can say are not regulations of "commerce" cannot stand. Santa Cruz Fruit Packing Co. v. NLRB. . . . (1938), and in this sense "[t]he Court has ample power to prevent . . . the utter destruction of the State as a sovereign political entity.' " *Maryland* v. *Wirtz* . . . (1968). But my Brethren make no claim that the 1974 amendments are not regulations of "commerce"; rather they overrule *Wirtz* in disagreement with historic principles that *United States* v. *California, supra,* reaffirmed: "[W]hile the commerce power has limits, valid general regulations of commerce do not cease to be regulations of commerce because a State is involved. If a state is engaging in economic activities that are validly regulated by the federal government when engaged in by private persons, the State too may be forced to conform its activities to federal regulation." . . . Clearly, therefore, my Brethren are also repudiating the long line of our precedents holding that a judicial finding that Congress has not unreasonably regulated a subject matter of "commerce" brings to an end the judicial role. . . .

The reliance of my Brethren upon the Tenth Amendment as "an express declaration of [a state sovereignty] limitation," . . . not only suggests that they overrule governing decisions of this Court that address this question but must astound scholars of the Constitution. For not only early decisions, *Gibbons* v. *Ogden,* . . . *McCulloch* v. *Maryland,* . . . and *Martin* v. *Hunter's Lessee* . . . (1816), hold that nothing in the Tenth Amendment constitutes a limitation on congressional exercise of powers delegated by the Constitution to Congress. . . . Rather, as the Tenth Amendment's significance was more recently summarized:

"The amendment states but a truism that all is retained which has not been surrendered. *There is nothing in the history of its adoption to suggest that it was more than declaratory of the relationship between the national and state governments as it had been established by the Constitution before the amendment* or that its purpose was other than to allay fears that the new national government might seek to exercise powers not granted, and that the states might not be able to exercise fully their reserved powers. . . .

"From the beginning and for many years the amendment has been construed as not depriving the national government of authority to resort to all means for the exercise of a granted power which are appropriate and plainly adapted to the permitted end." *United States v. Darby* . . . (emphasis added). . . .

Today's repudiation of this unbroken line of precedents that firmly reject my Brethren's ill-conceived abstraction can only be regarded as a transparent cover for invalidating a congressional judgment with which they disagree. . . .

My Brethren do more than turn aside longstanding constitutional jurisprudence that emphatically rejects today's conclusion. More alarming is the startling restructuring of our federal system, and the role they create therein for the federal judiciary. This Court is simply not at liberty to erect a mirror of its own conception of a desirable governmental structure. . . .

It is unacceptable that the judicial process should be thought superior to the political process in this area. Under the Constitution the judiciary has no role to play beyond finding that Congress has not made an unreasonable legislative judgment respecting what is "commerce." My Brother BLACKMUN suggests that controlling judicial supervision of the relationship between the States and our National Government by use of a balancing approach diminishes the ominous implications of today's decision. Such an approach, however, is a thinly veiled rationalization for judicial supervision of a policy judgment that our system of government reserves to Congress.

Judicial restraint in this area merely recognizes that the political branches of our Government are structured to protect the interests of the States, as well as the Nation as a whole, and that the States are fully able to protect their own interests in the premises. . . .

MR. JUSTICE STEVENS, dissenting. . . .

The Court holds that the Federal Government may not interfere with a sovereign state's inherent right to pay a substandard wage to a janitor at the state capitol. The principle on which the holding rests is difficult to perceive.

The Federal Government may, I believe, require the State to act impartially when it hires or fires the janitor, to withhold taxes from his pay check, to observe safety regulations when he is performing his job, to forbid him from burning too much soft coal in the capitol furnace, from dumping untreated refuse in an adjacent waterway, from overloading a state-owned garbage truck or from driving either the truck or the governor's limousine over 55 miles an hour. Even though these and many other activities of the capitol janitor are activities of the state *qua* state, I have no doubt that they are subject to federal regulation.

I agree that it is otherwise for the Federal Government to exercise its power in the ways described in the Court's opinion. For the proposition that regulation of the minimum price of a commodity—even labor—will increase the quantity consumed is not one that I can really understand. That concern, however, applies with even greater force to the private sector of the economy where the exclusion of the marginally employable does the greatest harm and, in all events, merely reflects my views on a policy issue which has been firmly resolved by the branches of government having power to decide such questions. As far as the complexities of adjusting police and fire departments to this sort of federal control are concerned, I presume that appropriate tailor-made regulations would soon solve their most pressing problems. After all, the interests adversely affected by this legislation are not without political power.

My disagreement with the wisdom of this legislation may not, of course, affect my judgment with respect to its validity. On this issue there is no dissent from the proposition that the Federal Government's power over the labor market is adequate to embrace these employees. Since I am unable to identify a limitation on that federal power that would not also invalidate federal regulation of state activities that I consider unquestionably permissible, I am persuaded that this statute is valid. Accordingly, with respect and a great deal of sympathy for the views expressed by the Court, I dissent from its constitutional holding.

Chapter Fifteen

JUDICIAL
FEDERALISM

INTRODUCTION

As we have seen, the Judiciary Act of 1789 set up a complete system of federal trial and appellate courts, thereby creating two systems of courts throughout the United States. The complication of a dual court system is one which other leading federal governments, such as Australia, Canada, and India, have avoided. In those countries there is only one federal court, superimposed on a complete system of state courts. By contrast the American system may seem cumbersome, making possible conflicts between the two judiciaries and requiring diplomacy in their relationships.

State Courts and Federal Jurisdiction

The first problem to be noted concerns jurisdiction. The Judiciary Act of 1789 defined federal jurisdiction, but it failed to bestow on federal courts all the jurisdiction to which the Constitution entitled them. At that time Congress was prepared to allow the state courts to handle a considerable part of what could have been federal court business. In particular, "federal question" suits were left to the state courts, and it was not until after the Civil War, in 1875, that the federal courts were authorized by

Congress to exercise all the heads of federal jurisdiction specified in the Constitution.

Even today suits falling under federal jurisdiction can be, and often are, brought in state courts, except in those areas, such as federal criminal, admiralty, patent, and bankruptcy cases, where Congress has given the federal courts exclusive jurisdiction. Federal jurisdiction suits begun in state courts can be removed to federal courts by appropriate action of the defendant. Where state courts do exercise federal jurisdiction, they are bound by the "supremacy clause" of the Constitution, Article VI, which, after making the Constitution, laws, and treaties of the United States "the supreme law of the land," continues: " . . . and the judges in every state shall be bound thereby, any thing in the Constitution or laws of any state to the contrary notwithstanding."

Cases decided in state court which involve a "federal question" are subject to review by the Supreme Court after they have progressed through the highest state court to which appeal is possible. Initially there was some resistance by state supreme courts to having their decisions reviewed by the U.S. Supreme Court, but in *Martin* v. *Hunter's Lessee* (1816) and *Cohens* v. *Virginia* (1821), federal judicial supremacy was firmly established.

Federal legislation provides a right of appeal to the Supreme Court from any decision of a state court of last resort declaring a federal law or treaty unconstitutional, and also from any state court decision upholding a state law or constitutional provision against a substantial challenge that it conflicts with a federal law, treaty, or constitutional provision. While in theory the Supreme Court must accept such appeals, in practice most of them are rejected "for want of a substantial federal question" or on other jurisdictional grounds.

While obedience of state courts to the Supreme Court's rulings is generally expected, it is by no means automatic. For example, when the Supreme Court reverses a state court decision, it generally returns (remands) the case to the state court for proceedings "not inconsistent with this opinion." These directions give considerable leeway to the state court; and not infrequently a party who wins on appeal to the Supreme Court still winds up losing on return to the state court. *Williams* v. *Georgia* (1955) is a classic case of this sort. The NAACP had to go to the Supreme Court four times between 1958 and 1964 before the Alabama supreme court would honor the Supreme Court's order protecting the membership lists of the organization [*NAACP* v. *Alabama* (1964)].

Apart from evasion of Supreme Court orders, there is room for conflict when state courts sense a shift in Supreme Court policy. Such a shift occurred when the Burger Court modified or reversed a number of constitutional positions taken by the more liberal Warren Court. Throughout the country state judges (as well as lower federal court judges) were placed in something of a quandary as to whether they should follow the Warren Court precedents or attempt to guess the directions in which the Burger Court was moving.

In this situation the supreme courts of several states endeavored to insulate themselves from the new, more conservative positions by basing their decisions on state constitutional provisions, which they were free to interpret, rather than on the similar language of the federal Constitution as interpreted by the Burger Court. The supreme courts of California, New Jersey, and Hawaii in particular adopted these tactics. Illustrative of the California court's position is the case of **People v. Brisendine** (1975). Another example is *State* v. *Johnson* (1975), where the New Jersey supreme court gave the search and seizure clause of the New Jersey constitution, which reads exactly the same as the Fourth Amendment, a more protective interpretation than that provided by the Burger Court, saying, ". . . we have the right to construe our State constitutional provision in accordance with what we conceive to be its plain meaning."[1]

Removal of Suits from State to Federal Courts

In 1866 the post-Civil War Congress, fearing that Southern judges would not enforce the civil rights statutes adopted to protect the newly freed blacks, authorized the removal of civil rights prosecutions from state to federal courts under certain circumstances. Denial of such removal petitions was made subject to appeal to the Supreme Court by the Civil Rights Act of 1964. Under this authority the Supreme Court has interpreted the right of removal rather narrowly.

In *Georgia* v. *Rachel* (1966) the Court did hold that the federal district court must grant a hearing to determine whether defendants under prosecution in state court for a restaurant sit-in had been ordered to leave solely for racial reasons. But in **City of Greenwood v. Peacock** (1966), decided on the same day, the Court held that removal would not be ordered on allegations by the defendants that they had been arrested and charged only because they were blacks or were engaged in helping blacks assert their civil rights. The *Peacock* decision was followed by the Burger Court in *Johnson* v. *Mississippi* (1975).

Federal Injunctions and Equitable Abstention

A statute of 1793 forbade federal courts to grant injunctions to stay proceedings in a state court "except as expressly authorized by Act of

---

[1]See William J. Brennan, Jr., "State Constitutions and the Protection of Individual Rights," *Harvard Law Review*, 90, 489 (1977).

Congress, or where necessary in aid of its jurisdiction, or to protect or effectuate its judgments." In addition to these exceptions, the Court in *Osborn* v. *Bank of the United States* (1824) asserted the right to restrain state officials from bringing proceedings in state courts to enforce an invalid state statute. However, under that decision a federal court injunction could be issued only after a finding of unconstitutionality in a lawsuit. In 1908 this requirement was abandoned in *Ex parte Young*, which held that the attorney general of a state could be enjoined from enforcing a state statute *pending* a determination of its constitutionality. Congressional displeasure with this expansion of federal court power led to the adoption in 1910 of the law requiring that a panel of three judges preside whenever the enforcement of a state statute was sought to be enjoined on the ground of unconstitutionality. As noted earlier, this requirement for three-judge courts was abolished in 1976.

In addition to injunctions under the principle of *Ex parte Young*, various federal civil rights statutes authorize litigants to protest state laws or proceedings in federal courts. Policy problems are thus created for federal judges. The principle of *comity* requires that they exercise self-restraint in order to avoid undue interference with proceedings in state courts. In *Railroad Commission of Texas* v. *Pullman Co.* (1941) the Supreme Court announced a rule of "equitable abstention," which required federal courts to suspend action on challenges to the constitutionality of state laws until the state courts had been accorded an opportunity authoritatively to interpret the statutory scheme being challenged. The state court construction might remove or modify the federal questions seemingly presented, thus avoiding unnecessary friction in federal–state relations.

The Warren Court, however, was reluctant to extend the abstention practice beyond the *Pullman* situation, and under the pressure of the civil rights problems of the 1960s the Court expanded federal judicial protection. Thus **Dombrowski** v. **Pfister** (1965) enjoined prosecution of civil rights activists under Louisiana anti-communist laws, the very existence of which the Court found to have a "chilling effect" upon the exercise of First Amendment rights.

The Burger Court, however, was less concerned about federal protection of civil rights and more concerned about the burden which these cases were imposing on the federal courts. In **Younger v. Harris** (1971) a federal district court had enjoined a criminal prosecution against a California socialist under a statute that was obviously unconstitutional, but the Supreme Court reversed, arguing that "a federal lawsuit to stop a prosecution in a state court is a serious matter." This attitude continued in *Huffman* v. *Pursue, Ltd.* (1975), which held that the *Younger* ban on federal injunctions extended to state civil as well as criminal proceedings.

Again, *Juidice* v. *Vail* (1977) ruled that a federal court could not intervene to halt contempt of court action against debtors under New York law.

The Burger Court followed the same policy of abstention in closing the federal courts to civil rights suits. The Civil Rights Act of 1871 provides for civil suit in federal court against any person acting under "color of any statute, ordinance, regulation, custom, or usage" who deprives a person of his constitutional rights (42 U. S. Code sec. 1983). Two 1976 decisions dramatically illustrate the recent Court's hostility to section 1983 lawsuits. In *Paul* v. *Davis* (1976) a man who had been wrongly listed in a police publication as an active shoplifter was denied the right to bring a federal civil rights damage suit, and **Rizzo** v. **Goode** (1976) held that "principles of federalism" forbade federal judicial interference in the internal disciplinary affairs of the Philadelphia police department.

State Courts and Federal Habeas Corpus

Under the 1867 habeas corpus statute previously mentioned, persons who have been convicted of crimes in state courts in alleged violation of their constitutional rights may, after their petition for certiorari to the U.S. Supreme Court has failed, secure a second opportunity for federal judicial review by filing for habeas corpus in the federal court for the district in which they are imprisoned. Appeal to a U.S. Court of Appeals and to the Supreme Court for a second time is then possible.

Since the 1940s resort to federal habeas corpus by state prisoners has escalated tremendously—from 127 petitions in 1941 to 7,626 in 1974. In 1953 Justice Jackson made reference in *Brown* v. *Allen* to this multiplicity of petitions, "so frivolous, so meaningless, and often so unintelligible that this worthlessness of the class discredits each individual application." In *Schneckloth* v. *Bustamonte* (1973) Justice Powell, with the support of three colleagues, attacked "the escalating use, over the past two decades, of federal habeas corpus to reopen and readjudicate state criminal judgment." He contended that the Court had extended habeas corpus "far beyond its historic bounds and in disregard of the writ's central purpose," resulting in unwise use of limited judicial resources, repetitive criminal litigation, and friction between federal and state systems of justice.

This position won the support of the Court majority in **Stone** v. **Powell** (1976), which held that attacks on state convictions through federal habeas corpus would no longer be permitted where the only challenge to the conviction was that evidence had been secured in violation of the Fourth Amendment, provided the defendant had been given a "full and fair" opportunity to make the Fourth Amendment claim in state court.

MARTIN V. HUNTER'S LESSEE

1 Wheaton 304, 4. L. Ed. 97 (1816)

In 1813 the Supreme Court reversed a decision of the Virginia Court of Appeals which involved an interpretation of the Jay Treaty covering land rights of British citizens in the United States. The Virginia court refused to enforce the Supreme Court's decision. While the state court recognized that Virginia was obliged to obey the Constitution, laws, and treaties of the United States, it contended that Virginia judges, as officials of a sovereign state, were entitled to make their own interpretations of federal law. The case then came back to the Supreme Court.

STORY, J., delivered the opinion of the court. . . .
This leads us to the consideration of the great question, as to the nature and extent of the appellate jurisdiction of the United States. We have already seen, that appellate jurisdiction is given by the constitution to the supreme court, in all cases where it has not original jurisdiction; subject, however, to such exceptions and regulations as congress may prescribe. It is, therefore, capable of embracing every case enumerated in the constitution, which is not exclusively to be decided by way of original jurisdiction. . . . The appellate power is not limited by the terms of the third article to any particular courts. The words are, "the judicial power (which includes appellate power) shall extend to all cases," &c., and "in all other cases before mentioned the supreme court shall have appellate jurisdiction." It is the case, then, and not the court, that gives the jurisdiction. If the judicial power extends to the case, it will be in vain to search in the letter of the constitution for any qualification as to the tribunal where it depends. . . .
If the constitution meant to limit the appellate jurisdiction to cases pending in the courts of the United States, it would necessarily follow, that the jurisdiction of these courts would, in all the cases enumerated in the constitution, be exclusive of state tribunals. . . .
But it is plain, that the framers of the constitution did contemplate that cases within the judicial cognisance of the United States, not only might, but would, arise in the state courts, in the exercise of their ordinary jurisdiction. With this view, the sixth article declares, that "this constitution, and the laws of the United States which shall be made in pursuance thereof, and all treaties made, or which shall be made, under the authority of the United States, shall be the supreme law of the land, and the judges in every state shall be bound thereby, anything in the constitution or laws of any state to the contrary notwithstanding." It is obvious, that this obligation is imperative upon the state judges, in their official, and not merely in their private, capacities. . . .
It must, therefore, be conceded, that the constitution not only contem-

plated, but meant to provide for cases within the scope of the judicial power of the United States, which might yet depend before state tribunals. It was foreseen, that in the exercise of their ordinary jurisdiction, state courts would incidentally take cognisance of cases arising under the constitution, the laws and treaties of the United States. Yet, to all these cases, the judicial power, by the very terms of the constitution, is to extend. . . .

It has been argued, that such an appellate jurisdiction over state courts is inconsistent with the genius of our governments, and the spirit of the constitution. That the latter was never designed to act upon state sovereignties, but only upon the people, and that if the power exists, it will materially impair the sovereignty of the states, and the independence of their courts. We cannot yield to the force of this reasoning; it assumes principles which we cannot admit, and draws conclusions to which we do not yield our assent.

It is a mistake, that the constitution was not designed to operate upon states, in their corporate capacities. It is crowded with provisions which restrain or annul the sovereignty of the states, in some of the highest branches of their prerogatives. The tenth section of the first article contains a long list of disabilities and prohibitions imposed upon the states. Surely, when such essential portions of state sovereignty are taken away, or prohibited to be exercised, it cannot be correctly asserted, that the constitution does not act upon the states. . . .

Nor can such a right be deemed to impair the independence of state judges. It is assuming the very ground in controversy, to assert that they possess an absolute independence of the United States. In respect to the powers granted to the United States, they are not independent; they are expressly bound to obedience, by the letter of the constitution; and if they should unintentionally transcend their authority, or misconstrue the constitution, there is no more reason for giving their judgments an absolute and irresistible force, than for giving it to the acts of the other co-ordinate departments of state sovereignty. . . .

This is not all. A motive of another kind, perfectly compatible with the most sincere respect for state tribunals, might induce the grant of appellate power over their decisions. That motive is the importance, and even necessity of uniformity of decisions throughout the whole United States, upon all subjects within the purview of the constitution. Judges of equal learning and integrity, in different states, might differently interpret the statute, or a treaty of the United States, or even the constitution itself: if there was no revising authority to control these jarring and discordant judgments, and harmonize them into uniformity, the laws, the treaties and the constitution of the United States would be different, in different states, and might, perhaps, never have precisely the same construction, obligation or efficiency, in any two states. The public mischiefs that would attend such a state of things would be truly deplorable. . . .

It is the opinion of the whole court, that the judgment of the court of appeals of Virginia, rendered on the mandate in this cause, be reversed, and the judgment of the district court, held at Winchester, be, and the same is hereby affirmed.

WILLIAMS V. GEORGIA

349 U.S. 375, 75 S. Ct. 814, 99 L. Ed. 1161 (1955)

Aubrey Williams, a black, was convicted of murder in 1953, in a trial where the names of white and black prospective jurors were on different color cards, making possible racial discrimination in jury selection. Two months after Williams' conviction, the Supreme Court in *Avery* v. *Georgia* reversed the conviction of another black where the same method of jury selection had been used. Williams' attorney then appealed the conviction of his client on the basis of the *Avery* ruling, but lost in the Georgia courts. The Supreme Court granted certiorari.

Mr. Justice Frankfurter delivered the opinion of the Court. . . .

On oral argument here . . . the State, with commendable regard for its responsibility, agreed that the use of yellow and white tickets in this case was, in light of this Court's decision in Avery, a denial of equal protection, so that a new trial would be required but for the failure to challenge the array. We need only add that it was the system of selection and the resulting danger of abuse which was struck down in Avery and not an actual showing of discrimination on the basis of comparative numbers of Negroes and whites on the jury lists. The question now before us, in view of the State's concession, is whether the ruling of the Georgia Supreme Court rests upon an adequate nonfederal ground, so that this Court is without jurisdiction to review the Georgia court.

A state procedural rule which forbids the raising of federal questions at late stages in the case, or by any other than a prescribed method, has been recognized as a valid exercise of state power. The principle is clear enough. But the unique aspects of the never-ending new cases that arise require its individual application to particular circumstances. Thus, we would have a different question from that before us if the trial court had no power to consider Williams' constitutional objection at the belated time he raised it. But, where a State allows questions of this sort to be raised at a late stage and be determined by its courts as a matter of discretion, we are not concluded from assuming jurisdiction and deciding whether the state court action in the particular circumstances is, in effect, an avoidance of the federal right. A state court may not, in the exercise of its discretion, decline to entertain a constitutional claim while passing upon kindred issues raised in the same manner.

The Georgia courts have indicated many times that motions for new trial after verdict are not favored, and that extraordinary motions for new trial after final judgment are favored even less. But the Georgia statute provides for such motion, and it has been granted in "exceptional" or "extraordinary" cases. The general rule is that the granting or denying of an extraordinary motion for new trial rests primarily in the discretion of the trial court, and the appellate court will not reverse except for a clear abuse of discretion. In practice, however, the Georgia appellate courts have not hesitated to reverse and grant a new trial in exceptional cases. . . .

We conclude that the trial court and the State Supreme Court declined to grant Williams' motion though possessed of power to do so under state law. Since his motion was based upon a constitutional objection, and one the validity of which has in principle been sustained here, the discretionary decision to deny the motion does not deprive this Court of jurisdiction to find that the substantive issue is properly before us.

But the fact that we have jurisdiction does not compel us to exercise it. . . . In the instant case, there is an important factor which has intervened since the affirmance by the Georgia Supreme Court which impels us to remand for that court's further consideration. This is the acknowledgment by the State before this Court that, as a matter of substantive law, Williams has been deprived of his constitutional rights. . . . We think that orderly procedure requires a remand to the State Supreme Court for reconsideration of the case. Fair regard for the principles which the Georgia courts have enforced in numerous cases and for the constitutional commands binding on all courts compels us to reject the assumption that the courts of Georgia would allow this man to go to his death as the result of a conviction secured from a jury which the State admits was unconstitutionally impaneled. . . .

Mr. Justice Clark, with whom Mr. Justice Reed and Mr. Justice Minton join, dissenting. . . .

WILLIAMS V. STATE

88 S. E. 2d 376 (1955)

Duckworth, Chief Justice.

"The powers not delegated to the United States by the Constitution, nor prohibited by it to the States, are reserved to the States respectively, or to the people." Constitution of the United States, 10th Amendment.

. . . Even though executives and legislators, not being constitutional lawyers, might often overstep the foregoing unambiguous constitutional prohibition of federal invasion of State jurisdiction, there can never be an acceptable excuse for judicial failure to strictly observe it. This court bows to the Supreme Court on all federal questions of law but we will not supinely surrender sovereign powers of this State. In this case the opinion of the majority of that court recognizes that this court decided the case according to established rules of law, and that no federal jurisdiction existed which would authorize that court to render a judgment either affirming or reversing the judgment of this court, which are the only judgments by that court that this court can constitutionally recognize.

The Supreme Court . . . undertakes to remand the case for further consideration, and in their opinion has pointed to Georgia law vesting in the trial judge discretion in ruling upon an extraordinary motion for new trial and apparently concluded therefrom that this court should reverse the trial court because that discretion was not exercised in the way the Supreme Court would have exercised it. We know and respect the universally recognized rule that the exercise of discretion never authorizes a violation or defiance of law. In this case, as pointed out by us, that law is that the question sought to be raised must be raised before trial and not otherwise.

Not in recognition of any jurisdiction of the Supreme Court to influence or in any manner to interfere with the functioning of this court on strictly State questions, but solely for the purpose of completing the record in this court in a case that was decided by us in 1953, and to avoid further delay, we state that our opinion in *Williams* v. *State* . . . is supported by sound and unchallenged law, conforms with the State and federal constitutions, and stands as the judgment of all seven of the Justices of this Court.

Judgment of affirmance rendered May 10, 1954, adhered to. All the Justices concur.[2]

NATIONAL ASSOCIATION FOR THE ADVANCEMENT OF COLORED PEOPLE V. ALABAMA

377 U.S. 288, 84 S. Ct. 1302, 12 L. Ed. 2d 325 (1964)

Like other states, Alabama requires out-of-state corporations to register and to meet certain requirements before doing business in the state. The NAACP, organized under the laws of New York, had a regional office in Alabama, but considered itself exempt from the statute and did not comply. After 1954 the organization became active in the state in seeking compliance with the Supreme Court's decision against racial segregation in the public schools. Alabama officials in 1956 brought action to enjoin the association from doing business in the state until it registered and met other requirements, including supplying a list of its members.

[2] After this rebuff by the Georgia Supreme Court, Williams' attorneys again petitioned the Supreme Court for review, which was denied on January 16, 1956. Williams died in the electric chair on March 30, 1956.

MR. JUSTICE HARLAN delivered the opinion of the Court.

This case, involving the right of the petitioner, the National Association for the Advancement of Colored People, to carry on activities in Alabama, reaches this Court for the fourth time. In 1956 the Attorney General of Alabama brought a suit in equity to oust the association, a New York "membership" corporation, from the State. The basis of the proceeding was the Association's alleged failure to comply with Alabama statutes requiring foreign corporations to register with the Alabama Secretary of State and perform other acts in order to qualify to do business in the State; the complaint alleged also that certain of the petitioner's activities in Alabama, detailed below, were inimical to the well-being of citizens of the State.

On the day the complaint was filed, the Attorney General obtained an *ex parte* restraining order barring the Association, *pendente lite*, from conducting any business within the State and from taking any steps to qualify to do business under state law. Before the case was heard on the merits, the Association was adjudged in contempt for failing to comply with a court order directing it to produce various records, including membership lists. The Supreme Court of Alabama dismissed the petition for certiorari to review the final judgment of contempt on procedural grounds . . . which this Court, on review, found inadequate to bar consideration of the Association's constitutional claims. . . . Upholding those claims, we reversed the judgment of contempt without reaching the question of the validity of the underlying restraining order.

In the second round of these proceedings the Supreme Court of Alabama, on remand "for proceedings not inconsistent" with this Court's opinion . . . again affirmed the judgment of contempt which this Court had overturned. . . . This decision was grounded on belief that this Court's judgment had rested on a "mistaken premise." . . . Observing that the premise of our prior decision had been one which the State had "plainly accepted" throughout the prior proceedings here, this Court ruled that the State could not for the first time on remand, change its stance. . . . We noted that the Supreme Court of Alabama "evidently was not acquainted with the detailed basis of the proceedings here" when it reaffirmed the judgment of contempt . . . and again remanded without considering the validity of the restraining order. In so doing, the Court said: "We assume that the State Supreme Court . . . will not fail to proceed promptly with the disposition of the matters left open under our mandate for further proceedings . . ." rendered in the prior case. . . .

Our second decision was announced on June 8, 1959. Unable to obtain a hearing on the merits in the Alabama courts, the Association, in June 1960, commenced proceedings in the United States District Court to obtain a hearing there. Alleging that the restraining order and the failure of the Alabama courts to afford it a hearing on the validity of the order were depriving it of constitutional rights, the Association sought to enjoin enforcement of the order. Without passing on the merits, the District Court dismissed the action, because it would not assume that the executive and judicial officers of Alabama involved in the litigation would fail to protect "the constitutional rights of all citizens." . . . The Court of Appeals agreed that the matter "should be litigated initially in the courts of the State." . . . It, however, vacated the judgment below and remanded the case to the District Court, with instructions "to permit the issues presented to be determined with expedition in the State courts," but to retain jurisdiction and take steps necessary to protect the Association's right to be heard on its constitutional claims. . . .

The jurisdiction of this Court was invoked a third time. On October 23, 1961, we entered an order as follows:

> . . . The judgment below is vacated, and the case is remanded to the Court of Appeals with instructions to direct the District Court to proceed with the trial of the issues in this action unless within a reasonable time, no later than January 2, 1962, the State of Alabama shall have accorded to petitioner an opportunity to be heard on its motion to dissolve the state restraining order of June 1, 1956, and upon the merits of the action in which such order was issued. Pending the final determination of all proceedings in the state action, the District Court is authorized to retain jurisdiction over the federal action and to take such steps as may appear necessary and appropriate to assure a prompt disposition of all issues involved in, or connected with, the state action. . . .

In December 1961, more than five years after it was "temporarily" ousted from Alabama, the Association obtained a hearing on the merits in the Circuit Court of Montgomery County, the court which had issued the restraining order in 1956. On December 29, 1961, the Circuit Court entered a final decree in which the court found that the Association had continued to do business in Alabama "in violation of the Constitution and laws of the state relating to foreign corporations" and that the Association's activities in the State were "in violation of other laws of the State of Alabama and are and have been a usurpation and abuse of its corporate functions and detrimental to the State of Alabama. . . ." The decree permanently enjoined the Association and those affiliated with it from doing "any further business of any description or kind" in Alabama and from attempting to qualify to do business there. The Association appealed to the Supreme Court of Alabama, which, on February 28, 1963, affirmed the judgment below without considering the merits. . . . This Court again granted certiorari. . . .

In the first proceedings in this case, we held that the compelled disclosure of the names of the petitioner's members would entail "the likelihood of a substantial restraint upon the exercise by petitioner's members of their right to freedom of association." . . . It is obvious that the complete suppression of the Association's activities in Alabama which was accomplished by the order below is an even more serious abridgment of that right. The allegations of illegal conduct contained in the . . . charge against the petitioner suggest no legitimate governmental objective which requires such restraint. . . .

There is no occasion in this case for us to consider how much survives of the principle that a State can impose such conditions as it chooses on the right of a foreign corporation to do business within the State, or can exclude it from the State altogether. . . . This case, in truth, involves not the privilege of a corporation to do business in a State, but rather the freedom of individuals to associate for the collective advocacy of ideas. "Freedoms such as . . . [this] are protected not only against heavy-handed frontal attack, but also from being stifled by more subtle governmental interference." Bates v. City of Little Rock. . . .

The judgment below must be reversed. In view of the history of this case, we are asked to formulate a decree for entry in the state courts which will assure the Association's right to conduct activities in Alabama without further delay. While such a course undoubtedly lies within this Court's power, Martin v. Hunter's Lessee . . . we prefer to follow our usual practice and remand the case to the Supreme Court of Alabama for further proceedings not inconsistent with this opinion. Such proceedings should include the prompt entry of a decree, in accordance with state procedures, vacating in all respects the permanent injunction order issued by the Circuit Court of Montgomery County, Alabama, and permitting the Association to take all steps necessary to qualify it to do business in Alabama. Should we unhappily be mistaken in our belief that the Supreme Court of Alabama will promptly implement this disposition, leave is given the Association to apply to this Court for further appropriate relief.

Reversed and remanded.[3]

PEOPLE V. BRISENDINE

Supreme Court of California 119 Cal. Rptr. 315 (1975)

In this case California officers conducted a warrantless stop-and-frisk-type search of suspects. In the subsequent prosecution the state defended the search as justified by the Supreme Court's decisions in *United States* v. *Robinson* (1973) and *Gustafson* v. *Florida* (1973).

MOSK, JUSTICE. . . .

Our vicarious exclusionary rule . . . has been a continuing feature of California law under our ability to impose higher standards for searches and seizures than compelled by the federal Constitution. . . .

[3]Faced with this ultimatum, the Alabama judges dissolved the injunction several months later.

. . . the California Constitution is, and always has been, a document of independent force. Any other result would contradict not only the most fundamental principles of federalism but also the historic bases of state charters. It is a fiction too long accepted that provisions in state constitutions textually identical to the Bill of Rights were intended to mirror their federal counterpart. The lesson of history is otherwise: the Bill of Rights was based upon the corresponding provisions of the first state constitutions, rather than the reverse. "By the end of the Revolutionary period, the concept of a Bill of Rights had been fully developed in the American system. Eleven of the 13 states (and Vermont as well) had enacted Constitutions to fill in the political gap caused by the overthrow of British authority. . . . Eight of the Revolutionary Constitutions were prefaced by Bills of Rights, while four contained guarantees of many of the most important individual rights in the body of their texts. Included in these Revolutionary constitutional provisions were *all of the rights that were to be protected in the federal Bill of Rights.* By the time of the Treaty of Paris (1783) then, the American inventory of individual rights had been virtually completed and included in the different state Constitutions whether in separate Bills of Rights or the organic texts themselves." (Italics added.) (1 Schwartz, The Bill of Rights: A Documentary History (1971) p. 383) . . . In particular, the Rights of the Colonists (Boston, 1772) declared for the first time "the right against unreasonable searches and seizures that was to ripen into the Fourth Amendment" . . . and that protection was embodied in every one of the eight state constitutions adopted prior to 1789 which contained a separate bill of rights. . . .

. . . We need not further extend this opinion to trace to their remote origins the historical roots of state constitutional provisions. Yet we have no doubt that such inquiry would confirm our view of the matter. The federal Constitution was designed to guard the states as sovereignties against potential abuses of centralized government; state charters, however, were conceived as the first and at one time the only line of protection of the individual against the excesses of local officials. Thus in determining that California citizens are entitled to greater protection under the California Constitution against unreasonable searches and seizures than that required by the United States Constitution, we are embarking on no revolutionary course. Rather we are simply reaffirming a basic principle of federalism—that the nation as a whole is composed of distinct geographical and political entities bound together by a fundamental federal law but nonetheless independently responsible for safeguarding the rights of their citizens.

The ultimate confirmation of our conclusion occurred, finally, when the people adopted article I, section 24, of the California Constitution at the November 1974 election, declaring that "Rights guaranteed by this Constitution are not dependent on those guaranteed by the United States Constitution." Of course this declaration of constitutional independence did not originate at that recent election; indeed the voters were told the provision was a mere reaffirmation of existing law.

Principles comparable to the foregoing were recently invoked by the Hawaii Supreme Court to invalidate under the Hawaii Constitution a search which would have been permissible under *Robinson.* [State v. Kaluna (Hawaii 1974)]. . . .

"However, as the ultimate judicial tribunal in this state, this court has final, unreviewable authority to interpret and enforce the Hawaii Constitution. We have not hesitated in the past to extend the protections of the Hawaii Bill of Rights beyond those of textually parallel provisions of the Federal Bill of Rights when logic and a sound regard for the purposes of those protections have so warranted. . . . In our view, the right to be free of 'unreasonable' searches and seizures under article I, section 5 of the Hawaii Constitution is enforceable by a rule of reason which requires that governmental intrusions into the personal privacy of citizens of this State be no greater in intensity than absolutely necessary under the circumstances." . . . The court further explained that although its holding "results in a divergence of meaning between words which are the same in both the federal and state constitutions, the system of federalism envisaged by the United States Constitution tolerates such divergence where the result is *greater* protection of individual rights under state law than under federal law. . . . In this respect, the opinion of the United States Supreme Court on the meaning of the phrase 'unreasonable searches and seizures' is merely another source of authority, admittedly to be afforded respectful consideration, but which we are free to accept or reject in establishing the outer limits of protection afforded by article I, section 5, of the Hawaii Constitution." . . .

For all the foregoing reasons Robinson is not controlling here. Rather, we reaffirm and follow the decisions . . . which impose a higher standard of reasonableness under article I, section 13, of the California Constitution.

WRIGHT, C. J., and TOBRINER and SULLIVAN, J. J., concur. . . .

BURKE, JUSTICE PRO TEM. (dissenting). MCCOMB and CLARK, J. J., concur.

CITY OF GREENWOOD V. PEACOCK

384 U.S. 808, 86 S. Ct. 1800, 16 L. Ed. 2d 944 (1966)

Black civil rights demonstrators engaged in a voter registration drive in Mississippi, having been arrested and prosecuted for obstructing the public streets and other offenses, filed petitions for removal of their cases to federal district court under provisions of the Civil Rights Act of 1866, 28 USC sec. 1443(1), which authorizes defendants "who are denied or cannot enforce in the courts . . . of the State or locality where they may be any of the rights secured to them by . . . this act" to seek such removal.

MR. JUSTICE STEWART delivered the opinion of the Court. . . .

In *State of Georgia* v. *Rachel* . . . decided today, we have held that removal of a state court trespass prosecution can be had under sec. 1443(1) upon a petition alleging that the prosecution stems exclusively from the petitioners' peaceful exercise of their right to equal accommodation in establishments covered by the Civil Rights Act of 1964. . . . Since that Act itself . . . specifically and uniquely guarantees that the conduct alleged in the removal petition in *Rachel* may "not be the subject of trespass prosecutions," the defendants inevitably are "denied or cannot enforce in the courts of [the] State a right under any law providing for . . . equal civil rights," by merely being brought before a state court to defend such a prosecution. . . . The present case differs from *Rachel* in two significant respects. First, no federal law confers an absolute right on private citizens —on civil rights advocates, on Negroes, or on anybody else—to obstruct a public street, to contribute to the delinquency of a minor, to drive an automobile without a license, or to bite a policeman. Second, no federal law confers immunity from state prosecution on such charges.

To sustain removal of these prosecutions to a federal court upon the allegations of the petitions in this case would therefore mark a complete departure from the terms of the removal statute. . . . It is *not* enough to support removal under sec. 1443(1) to allege or show that the defendant's federal equal civil rights have been illegally or corruptly denied by state administrative officials in advance of trial, that the charges against the defendant are false, or that the defendant is unable to obtain a fair trial in a particular state court. The motives of the officers bringing the charges may be corrupt, but that does not show that the state trial court will find the defendant guilty if he is innocent, or that in any other manner the defendant will be "denied or cannot enforce in the courts" of the State any right under a federal law providing for equal civil rights. The civil rights removal statute does not require and does not permit the judges of the federal courts to put their brethren of the state judiciary on trial. Under sec. 1443(1), the vindication of the defendant's federal rights is left to the state courts except in the rare situations where it can be clearly predicted by reason of the operation of a pervasive and explicit state or federal law that those rights will inevitably be denied by the very act of bringing the defendant to trial in the state court. . . .

What we have said is not for one moment to suggest that the individual petitioners in this case have not alleged a denial of rights guaranteed to them under federal law. If, as they allege, they are being prosecuted on baseless charges solely because of their race, then there has been an outrageous denial of their federal rights, and the federal courts are far from powerless to redress the wrongs done to them. The most obvious remedy is the traditional one . . . vindication of their federal claims on direct review by this Court. . . .

But there are many other remedies available in the federal courts. . . . If the state prosecution or trial on the charge of obstructing a public street or on any other charge would itself clearly deny their rights protected by the First Amendment, they may under some circumstances obtain an injunction in the federal court. See *Dombrowski* v. *Pfister*. . . . If they go to trial and there is a complete absence of evidence against them, their convictions will be set aside because of a denial of due process of law. *Thompson* v. *City of Louisville*. . . . If at their trial they are in fact denied any federal constitutional rights, and these denials go uncorrected by any courts of the State, the remedy of federal habeas corpus is freely available to them. *Fay* v. *Noia*. . . .

. . . we have determined that the provisions of sec. 1443(1) do not operate to work a wholesale dislocation of the historic relationship between the state and the federal courts in the administration of the criminal law . . . [or] justify removal of these state criminal prosecutions to a federal court. . . .

Judgment reversed.

MR. JUSTICE DOUGLAS, with whom the CHIEF JUSTICE [WARREN], MR. JUSTICE BRENNAN and MR. JUSTICE FORTAS concur, dissenting. . . .

With the coming of the Civil War it became plain that some state courts might be instruments for the destruction through harassment of guaranteed federal civil rights. We have seen this demonstrated in the flow of cases coming this way. But the minorities who are the subject of repression are not only those who espouse the cause of racial equality. Jehovah's Witnesses in many parts of the country have likewise felt the brunt of majoritarian control through state criminal administration. Before them were the labor union organizers. Before them were the Orientals. It is in this setting that the removal jurisdiction must be considered.

The removal laws . . . have responded to two main concerns: First, a federal fact-finding forum is often indispensable to the effective enforcement of those guarantees against local action. The federal guarantee turns ordinarily upon contested issues of fact. Those rights, therefore, will be of only academic value in many areas of the country unless the facts are objectively found. Secondly, swift enforcement of the federal right is imperative if the guarantees are to survive and not be slowly strangled by long, drawn-out, costly, cumbersome proceedings which the Congress feared might result in some state courts. . . .

In my view, sec. 1443(1) required the federal court to decide whether the defendant's allegation (that the state court will not fairly enforce his equal rights) is true. If the defendant is unable to demonstrate this inability to enforce his rights, the case is remanded to the state court. But if the federal court is persuaded that the state court indeed will not make a good-faith effort to apply the paramount federal law pertaining to "equal civil rights," then the federal court must accept the removal and try the case on the merits. . . . These defendants' federal civil rights may, of course, ultimately be vindicated if they persevere, live long enough, and have the patience and the funds to carry their cases for some years through the state courts to this Court. But it was precisely that burden that Congress undertook to take off the backs of this persecuted minority and all who espouse the cause of their equality.

DOMBROWSKI V. PFISTER

380 U.S. 479, 85 S. Ct. 1116, 14 L. Ed. 2d 22 (1965)

Certain Louisiana residents active in civil rights organizations brought suit in federal court to enjoin the governor, police, and chairman of the state legislative committee on un-American activities from prosecuting or threatening to prosecute them under Louisiana anti-subversive laws. They alleged that these threats were intended to deter them from seeking to promote civil rights for blacks. A three-judge district court dismissed the complaint, and they appealed to the Supreme Court.

MR. JUSTICE BRENNAN delivered the opinion of the Court. . . .

In Ex parte Young . . . the fountainhead of federal injunctions against state prosecutions, the Court characterized the power and its proper exercise in broad terms: it would be justified where state officers ". . . threaten and are about to commence proceedings either of a civil or criminal nature, to enforce against parties affected an unconstitutional act, violating the Federal Constitution. . . ." . . . Since that decision, however, considerations of federalism have tempered the exercise of equitable power, for the Court has recognized that federal interference with a State's good-faith administration of its criminal laws is peculiarly inconsistent with our federal framework. It is generally to be assumed that state courts and prosecutors will observe constitutional limitations as expounded by this Court, and that the mere possibility of erroneous initial application of constitutional standards will usually not amount to the irreparable injury necessary to justify a disruption of orderly state proceedings. . . . But the allegations in this complaint depict a situation in which defense of the State's criminal prosecution will not assure adequate vindication of constitutional rights. They suggest that a substantial loss or impairment of freedoms of expression will occur if appellants must await the state court's disposition and ultimate review in this Court of any adverse determination. These allegations, if true, clearly show irreparable injury.

A criminal prosecution under a statute regulating expression usually involves imponderables and contingencies that themselves may inhibit the full exercise of First Amendment freedoms. . . . When the statutes also have an overbroad sweep, as is here alleged, the hazard of loss or substantial impairment of those precious rights may be critical. For in such cases, the statutes lend themselves too readily to denial of those rights. The assumption that defense of a criminal prosecution will generally assure ample vindication of constitutional rights in unfounded in such cases. . . . For "[t]he threat of sanctions may deter . . . almost as potently as the actual application of sanctions. . . ." NAACP v. Button. . . . Because of the sensitive nature of constitutionally protected expression, we have not required that all of those subject to overbroad regulations risk prosecution to test their rights. For free expression—of transcendent value to all society, and not merely to those exercising their rights—might be the loser.... For example, we have consistently allowed attacks on overly broad statutes with no requirement that the person making the attack demonstrate that his own conduct could not be regulated by a statute drawn with the requisite narrow specificity.... If the rule were otherwise, the contours of regulation would have to be hammered out case by case—and tested only by those hardy enough to risk criminal prosecution to determine the proper scope of regulation.... By permitting determination of the invalidity of these statutes without regard to the permissibility of some regulation on the facts of particular cases, we have, in effect, avoided making vindication of freedom of expression await the outcome of protracted litigation. Moreover, we have not thought that the improbability of successful prosecution makes the case different. The chilling effect upon the exercise of First Amendment rights may derive from the fact of the prosecution, unaffected by the prospects of its success or failure....

It follows that the District Court erred in holding that the complaint fails to allege sufficient irreparable injury to justify equitable relief.

MR. JUSTICE BLACK and MR. JUSTICE STEWART took no part in the consideration or decision of this case....

MR. JUSTICE HARLAN, whom MR. JUSTICE CLARK, joins, dissenting.

The basic holding in this case marks a significant departure from a wise procedural principle designed to spare our federal system from premature federal judicial interference with state statutes or proceedings challenged on federal constitutional grounds. This decision abolishes the doctrine of federal judicial abstention in all suits attacking state criminal statutes for vagueness on First-Fourteenth Amendment grounds. As one who considers that it is a prime responsibility of this Court to maintain federal-state court relationships in good working order, I cannot subscribe to a holding which displays such insensitivity to the legitimate demands of those relationships under our federal system. I see no such incompatibility between the abstention doctrine and the full vindication of constitutionally protected rights as the Court finds to exist in cases of this kind.

In practical effect the Court's decision means that a State may no longer carry on prosecutions under statutes challengeable for vagueness on "First Amendment" grounds without the prior approval of the federal courts. For if such a statute can be so questioned (and few, at least colorably, cannot) then a state prosecution, if instituted after the commencement of a federal action, must be halted until the prosecuting authorities obtain in some other state proceeding a narrowing construction, which in turn would presumably be subject to further monitoring by the federal courts before the state prosecution would be allowed to proceed.

For me such a paralyzing of state criminal processes cannot be justified by any of the considerations which the Court's opinion advances in its support. High as the premium placed on First Amendment rights may be, I do not think that the Federal Constitution prevents a State from testing their availability through the medium of criminal proceedings, subject of course to this Court's ultimate review.

Underlying the Court's major premise that criminal enforcement of an overly broad statute affecting rights of speech and association is in itself a deterrent to the free exercise thereof seems to be the unarticulated assumption that state courts will not be as prone as federal courts to vindicate constitutional rights promptly and effectively. Such an assumption should not be indulged in the absence of a showing that such is apt to be so in a given case. No showing of that kind has been made. On the contrary, the Louisiana courts in this very case have already refused to uphold the seizure of appellants' books. . . . We should not assume that those courts would not be equally diligent in construing the statutes here in question in accordance with the relevant decisions of this Court. . . .

YOUNGER V. HARRIS

401 U.S. 37, 91 S. Ct. 746, 27 L. Ed. 2d 669 (1971)

A California socialist, John Harris, was charged with violation of that state's criminal syndicalism act. The Supreme Court had once upheld that statute in *Whitney* v. *California* (1927) but had later overruled *Whitney* in *Brandenburg* v. *Ohio* (1969). Harris alleged that the very existence of the statute acted to inhibit his right to free speech. A three-judge district court held the statute void because of vagueness and overbreadth, and granted the injunction. The state appealed to the Supreme Court.

MR. JUSTICE BLACK delivered the opinion of the Court. . . .

A federal lawsuit to stop a prosecution in a state court is a serious matter. . . .

Since the beginning of this country's history Congress has, subject to few exceptions, manifested a desire to permit state courts to try state cases free from interference by federal courts. . . .

The precise reasons for this longstanding public policy against federal court interference with state court proceedings have never been specifically identified but the primary sources of the policy are plain. One is the basic doctrine of equity jurisprudence that courts of equity should not act, and particularly should not act to restrain a criminal prosecution, when the moving party has an adequate remedy at law and will not suffer irreparable injury if denied equitable relief. The doctrine may originally have grown out of circumstances peculiar to the English judicial system and not applicable in this country, but its fundamental purpose of restraining equity jurisdiction within narrow limits is equally important under our Constitution, in order to prevent erosion of the role of the jury and avoid a duplication of legal proceedings and legal sanctions where a single suit would be adequate to protect the rights asserted. This underlying reason for restraining courts of equity from interfering with criminal prosecutions is reinforced by an even more vital consideration, the notion of "comity," that is, a proper respect for state functions, a recognition of the fact that the entire country is made up of a Union of separate state governments, and a continuance of the belief that the National Government will fare best if the States and their institutions are left free to perform their separate functions in their separate ways. This, perhaps for lack of a better and clearer way to describe it, is referred to by many as "Our Federalism," and one familiar with the profound debates that ushered our Federal Constitution into existence is bound to respect those who remain loyal to the ideals and dreams of "Our Federalism." The concept does not mean blind deference to "States' Rights" any more than it means centralization of control over every important issue in our National Government and its courts. The framers rejected both these courses. What the concept does represent is a system in which there is sensitivity to the legitimate interests of both State and National Governments, and in which the National Government, anxious though it may be to vindicate and protect federal rights and federal interests, always endeavors to do so in ways that will not unduly interfere with the legitimate activities of the States. It should never be forgotten that this slogan, "Our Federalism," born in the early struggling days of our Union of States, occupies a highly important place in our Nation's history and its future. . . .

This is where the law stood when the Court decided Dombrowski v. Pfister . . . and held that an injunction against the enforcement of certain state criminal statutes could properly issue under the circumstances presented in that case. . . .

The District Court . . . thought that the *Dombrowski* decision substantially broadened the availability of injunctions against state criminal prosecutions and that under that decision the federal courts may give equitable relief, without regard to any showing of bad faith or harassment, whenever a state statute is found "on its face" to be vague or overly broad, in violation of the First Amendment. We recognize that there are some statements in the *Dombrowski* opinion that would seem to support this argument. But . . . such statements were unnecessary to the decision of that case, because the Court found that the plaintiffs had alleged a basis for equitable relief under the long-established standards. In addition, we do not regard the reasons adduced to support this position as sufficient to justify such a substantial departure from the established doctrines regarding the availability of injunctive relief. It is undoubtedly true, as the Court stated in *Dombrowski*, that "[a] criminal prosecution under a statute regulating expression usually involves imponderables and contingencies that themselves may inhibit the full exercise of First Amendment freedoms." . . . But this sort of "chilling effect," as the Court called it, should not by itself justify federal intervention. . . .

Beyond all this is another, more basic consideration. Procedures for testing the constitutionality of a statute "on its face" in the manner apparently contemplated by *Dombrowski*, and for then enjoining all action to enforce the statute until the State can obtain court approval for a modified version, are fundamentally at odds with the function of the federal courts in our constitutional plan. The power and duty of the judiciary to declare laws unconstitutional is in the final analysis derived from its responsibility for resolving concrete disputes brought before the courts for decision; a statute apparently governing a dispute cannot be applied by judges, consistently with their obligations under the Supremacy Clause, when such an application of the statute would conflict with the Constitution, Marbury v. Madison. . . . But this vital responsibility, broad as it is, does not amount to an unlimited power to survey the statute books and pass judgment on laws before the courts are called upon to enforce them. . . .

For these reasons fundamental not only to our federal system but also to the basic functions of the Judicial Branch of the National Government under our Constitution, we hold that the *Dombrowski* decision should not be regarded as having upset the settled doctrines that have always confined very narrowly the availability of injunctive relief against state criminal prosecutions. We do not think that opinion stands for the proposition that a federal court can properly enjoin enforcement of a statute solely on the basis of a showing that the statute "on its face" abridges First Amendment rights. . . .

The judgment of the District Court is reversed, and the case is remanded for further proceedings not inconsistent with this opinion.

Reversed.

MR. JUSTICE BRENNAN with whom MR. JUSTICE WHITE and MR. JUSTICE MARSHALL join, concurring in the result. . . .

MR. JUSTICE DOUGLAS, dissenting.

The fact that we are in a period of history when enormous extra judicial sanctions are imposed on those who assert their First Amendment rights in unpopular causes emphasizes the wisdom of Dombrowski v. Pfister. . . . There we recognized that in times of repression, when interests with powerful spokesmen generate symbolic programs against nonconformists, the federal judiciary, charged by Congress with special vigilance for protection of civil rights, has special responsibilities to prevent an erosion of the individual's constitutional rights.

Dombrowski represents an exception to the general rule that federal courts should not interfere with state criminal prosecutions. The exception does not arise merely because prosecutions are threatened to which the First Amendment will be the proffered defense. *Dombrowski* governs statutes which are a blunderbuss by themselves or when used *en masse*— those that have an "overbroad" sweep. . . .

The special circumstances when federal intervention in a state criminal proceeding is permissible are not restricted to bad faith on the part of state officials or the threat of multiple prosecutions. They also exist where for any reason the state statute being enforced is unconstitutional on its face. . . .

RIZZO V. GOODE

423 U.S. 362, 96 S. Ct. 598, 46 L. Ed. 2d 561 (1976)

Plaintiffs representing the residents of Philadelphia brought two class action suits under 42 U.S.C. sec. 1983 against the mayor and other city and police officials alleging that the defendants had approved or condoned systematic violation of the constitutional rights of minorities and the poor by the police. The district court made extensive findings of fact relating to some 40 incidents of police misconduct over a one-year period. The court found a "pattern of frequent police violations" of constitutional rights, particularly against poor blacks and persons protesting police actions. Holding existing grievance and discipline procedures inadequate, the court ordered defendants to draw up a detailed plan to improve them. The Court of Appeals for the Third Circuit affirmed.

Mr. Justice Rehnquist delivered the opinion of the Court. . . .

The central thrust of respondents' efforts in the two trials was to lay a foundation for equitable intervention, in one degree or another, because of an assertedly pervasive pattern of illegal and unconstitutional mistreatment by police officers. This mistreatment was said to have been directed against minority citizens in particular and against all Philadelphia residents in general. The named individual and group respondents (hereafter individual respondents) were certified to represent these two classes. The principal petitioners here—the Mayor, the City Managing Director, and the Police Commissioner—were charged with conduct ranging from express authorization or encouragement of this mistreatment to failure to act in a manner so as to assure that it would not recur in the future. . . .

These actions were brought, and the affirmative equitable relief fashioned, under the Civil Rights Act of 1871, 42 U.S.C. § 1983. It provides that "[e]very person who, under color of [law] subjects, or causes to be subjected, any . . . person [within the jurisdiction of the United States] to the deprivation of any rights . . . secured by the Constitution and laws, shall be liable to the party injured in an action at law [or] suit in equity. . . ." The plain words of the statute impose liability—whether in the form of payment of redressive damages or being placed under an injunction—only for conduct which "subjects or causes to be subjected" the complainant to a deprivation of a right secured by the Constitution.

The findings of fact made by the District Court at the conclusion of these two parallel trials—in sharp contrast to that which respondents sought to prove with respect to petitioners—disclose a central paradox which permeates that Court's legal conclusions. Individual police officers *not named as parties* to the action were found to have violated the constitutional rights of particular individuals, only a few of whom were parties plaintiff. As the facts developed, there was no affirmative link between the occurrence of the various incidents of police misconduct and the adoption of any plan or policy by petitioners—express or otherwise—showing their authorization or approval of such misconduct. Instead, the *sole* causal connection found by the District Court between petitioners and the individual respondents was that in the absence of a change in police disciplinary procedures, the incidents were likely to continue to occur, not with respect to them but as to the members of the classes they represented. In sum, the genesis of this lawsuit—a heated dispute between individual citizens and certain policemen—has evolved into an attempt by the federal judiciary to resolve a "controversy" between the entire citizenry of Philadelphia and the petitioning elected and appointed officials over what steps might, in the Court of Appeals' words, "appeared to have the potential for prevention of future police misconduct." . . . The lower courts have, we think, overlooked several significant decisions of this Court in validating this type of litigation and the relief ultimately granted.

. . . We first of all entertain serious doubts whether on the facts as found there was made out the requisite Art. III case or controversy between the individually named respondents and petitioners. . . .

. . . [F]or the individual respondents' claim to "real and immediate" injury rests not upon what the named petitioners might do to them in the future—such as set a bond on the basis of race—but upon what one of a small, unnamed minority of policemen might do to them in the future because of that unknown policeman's perception of departmental disciplinary procedures. . . .

. . . Going beyond considerations concerning the existence of a live controversy and threshold statutory liability, we must address an additional and novel claim advanced by respondent classes. They assert that given the citizenry's "right" to be protected from unconstitutional exercises of police power, and the "need for protection from such abuses," respondents have a right to mandatory equitable relief in some form when those in supervisory positions do not institute steps to reduce the incidence of unconstitutional police misconduct. The scope of federal equity power, it is proposed, should be extended to the fashioning of prophylactic procedures for a state agency designed to minimize this kind of misconduct on the part of a handful of its employees. But on the facts of this case, not only is this novel claim quite at odds with the settled rule that in federal equity cases "the nature of the violation determines the scope of the remedy," . . . important considerations of federalism are additional factors weighing against it. Where, as here, the exercise of authority by state officials is attacked, federal courts must be constantly mindful of the "special delicacy of the adjustment to be preserved between federal equitable power and State administration of its own law." . . .

When a plaintiff seeks to enjoin the activity of a government agency, even within a unitary court system, his case must contend with "the well-established rule that the Government has traditionally been granted the widest latitude in the 'dispatch of its own internal affairs,' *Cafeteria and Restaurant Workers Union Local 473 A.F.L.-C.I.O. v. McElroy.* . . ." The District Court's injunctive order here, significantly revising the internal procedures of the Philadelphia police department, was indisputably a sharp limitation on the department's "latitude in the 'dispatch of its own internal affairs.' "

. . . When the frame of reference moves from a unitary court system, governed by the principles just stated, to a system of federal courts representing the Nation, subsisting side by side with 50 state judicial, legislative, and executive branches, appropriate consideration must be given to principles of federalism in determining the availability and scope of equitable relief. . . .

. . . Thus the principles of federalism which play such an important part in governing the relationship between federal courts and state governments, though initially expounded and perhaps entitled to their greatest weight in cases where it was sought to enjoin a criminal prosecution in progress, have not been limited either to that situation or indeed to a criminal proceeding itself. We think these principles likewise have applicability where injunctive relief is sought not against the judicial branch of the state government, but against those in charge of an executive branch of an agency of state or local governments such as respondents here. . . .

. . .Contrary to the District Court's flat pronouncement that a federal court's legal power to "supervise the functioning of the police department . . . is firmly established," it is the foregoing cases and principles that must govern consideration of the type of injunctive relief granted here. When it injected itself by injunctive decree into the internal disciplinary affairs of this state agency, the District Court departed from these precepts.

For the foregoing reasons the judgment of the Court of Appeals which affirmed the decree of the District Court is

Reversed.

MR. JUSTICE STEVENS took no part in the consideration or decision of this case.

MR. JUSTICE BLACKMUN with whom MR. JUSTICE BRENNAN and MR. JUSTICE MARSHALL join, dissenting.

To be sure, federal court intervention in the daily operation of a large city's police department, as the Court intimates, is undesirable and to be avoided if at all possible. The Court appropriately observes, however, . . . that what the Federal District Court did here was to engage in a careful and conscientious resolution of often sharply conflicting testimony and to make detailed findings of fact, now accepted by both sides, that attack the problem that is the subject of the respondents' complaint. The remedy was one evolved with the defendant officials' assent, reluctant though that assent may have been, and it was one that the Police Department concededly could live with. Indeed, the District Court, in its memorandum of October 5, 1973, stated that "the resolution of all the disputed items was more nearly in accord with the defendants' position than with the plaintiffs' position," and that the relief contemplated by the earlier order of March 14, 1973, . . . "did not go beyond what the defendants had always been willing to accept." . . . No one, not even this Court's majority, disputes the apparent efficacy of the relief or the fact that it effectuated a betterment in the system and should serve to lessen the number of instances of deprival of constitutional rights of members of the respondent classes. What is worrisome to the Court is abstract principle, and, of course, the Court has a right to be concerned with abstract principle that, when extended to the limits of logic, may produce untoward results in other circumstances on a future day. . . .

But the District Court here, with detailed, careful and sympathetic findings, ascertained the existence of violations of citizens' *constitutional* rights, of a pattern of that type of activity, of its likely continuance and recurrence, and of an official indifference as to doing anything about it. . . .

I would regard what was accomplished in this case as one of those rightly rare but nevertheless justified instances . . . of federal court "intervention" in a state or municipal executive area. The facts, the deprival of constitutional rights, and the pattern are all proved in sufficient degree. And the remedy is carefully delineated, worked out within the administrative structure rather then superimposed by edict upon it, and essentially, and concededly, "livable." In the City of Brotherly Love—or in any other American city—no less should be expected. It is a matter of regret that the Court sees fit to nullify what so meticulously and thoughtfully has been evolved to satisfy an existing need relating to constitutional rights that we cherish and hold dear.

STONE V. POWELL

428 U.S. 465, 96 S. Ct. 3037, 49 L. Ed. 2d 1067 (1976)

Powell was convicted of second-degree murder, and the California supreme court denied review. Instead of petitioning the Supreme Court on writ of certiorari, Powell filed a writ of federal habeas corpus, contending that evidence used to convict him had been secured by a search in connection with an illegal arrest and should have been excluded at the trial under the rule announced in *Mapp v. Ohio* (1961). The district judge denied this claim, but it was upheld by the federal Court of Appeals. Members of the Supreme Court, particularly Chief Justice Burger and Justice Powell, had been increasingly critical of the exclusionary rule, which Justice Cardozo had once criticized as requiring courts to let the criminal go free because the constable had blundered. The Court majority took this opportunity to restrict the application of the exclusionary rule when state convictions were subjected to Fourth Amendment challenges on federal habeas corpus. The decision was featured by a bitter attack on the ruling by Brennan and a rebuttal by Powell, principally in footnotes to his opinion for the Court.

MR. JUSTICE POWELL delivered the opinion of the Court. . . .

FOOTNOTE 37. The dissent characterizes the Court's opinion as laying the groundwork for a "drastic withdrawal of federal habeas jurisdiction, if not for all grounds . . . then at least [for many]. . . ." It refers variously to our opinion as a "novel reinterpretation of the habeas statutes," . . . as a "harbinger of future eviscerations of the habeas statutes," . . . as "rewriting Congress' jurisdictional statutes . . . and [barring] access to federal courts by state prisoners with constitutional claims distasteful to a majority" of the Court . . . and as a "denigration of constitutional guarantees [that] must appall citizens taught to expect judicial respect" of constitutional rights. . . .

With all respect, the hyperbole of the dissenting opinion is misdirected. Our decision today is *not* concerned with the scope of the habeas corpus statute as authority for litigating constitutional claims generally. We do reaffirm that the exclusionary rule is a judicially created remedy rather than a personal constitutional right, . . . and we emphasize the minimal utility of the rule when sought to be applied to Fourth Amendment claims in a habeas corpus proceeding. . . . In sum, we hold only that a federal court need not apply the exclusionary rule on habeas review of a Fourth Amendment claim absent a showing that the state prisoner was denied an opportunity for a full and fair litigation of that claim at trial and on direct review. Our decision does not mean that the federal court lacks jurisdiction over such a claim, but only that the application of the rule is limited to cases in which there has been both such a showing and a Fourth Amendment violation.

FOOTNOTE 35. The policy arguments . . . in support of the view that federal habeas corpus review is necessary to effectuate the Fourth Amendment stem from a basic mistrust of the state courts as fair and competent forums for the adjudication of federal constitutional rights. The argument is that state courts cannot be trusted to effectuate Fourth Amendment values through fair application of the rule, and the oversight jurisdiction of this Court on certiorari is an inadequate safeguard. The principal rationale for this view emphasizes the broad differences in the respective institutional setting within which federal judges and state judges operate. Despite differences in institutional environment and the unsympathetic attitude to federal constitutional claims of some state judges in years past, we are unwilling to assume that there now exists a general lack of appropriate sensitivity to constitutional rights in the trial and appellate courts of the several States. State courts, like federal courts, have a constitutional obligation to safeguard personal liberties and to uphold federal law. *Martin* v. *Hunter's Lessee.* . . . Moreover, the argument that federal judges are more expert in applying federal constitutional law is especially unpersuasive in the context of search-and-seizure claims, since they are dealt with on a daily basis by trial level judges in both systems. In sum, there is "no intrinsic reason why the fact that a man is a federal judge should make him more competent, or conscientious, or learned with respect to the [consideration of Fourth Amendment claims] than his neighbor in the state courthouse."

MR. JUSTICE BRENNAN, with whom MR. JUSTICE MARSHALL concurs, dissenting. . . .

The Court . . . argues that habeas relief for non-"guilt-related" constitutional claims is not mandated because such claims do not affect the "basic justice" of a defendant's detention . . .; this is presumably because the "ultimate goal" of the criminal justice system is "truth and justice." . . . This denigration of constitutional guarantees and *constitutionally mandated procedures,* relegated by the Court to the status of mere utilitarian tools, must appall citizens taught to expect judicial respect and support for their constitutional rights. Even if punishment of the "guilty" were society's highest value—and procedural safeguards denigrated to this end—in a constitution that a majority of the members of this Court would prefer, that is not the ordering of priorities under the Constitution forged by the Framers, and this Court's sworn duty is to uphold that Constitution and not frame its own. The procedural safeguards mandated in the Framers' Constitution are not admonitions to be tolerated only to the extent they serve functional purposes that ensure that the "guilty" are punished and the "innocent" freed; rather, every guarantee enshrined in the Constitution . . . is by it endowed with an independent vitality and value, and this Court is not free to curtail those constitutional guarantees even to punish the most obviously guilty. Particular constitutional rights that do not affect the fairness of fact-finding procedures cannot for that reason be denied at the trial itself. What possible justification then can there be for denying vindication of such rights on federal habeas when state courts do deny those rights at trial? To sanction disrespect and disregard for the Constitution in the name of protecting society from law-breakers is to make the government itself lawless. . . .

Enforcement of *federal* constitutional rights that redress constitutional violations directed against the "guilty" is a particular function of *federal* habeas review, lest judges trying the "morally unworthy" be tempted not to execute the supreme law of the land. State judges popularly elected may have difficulty resisting popular pressures not experienced by federal judges given lifetime tenure designed to immunize them from such influences, and the federal habeas statutes reflect the Congressional judgment that such detached federal review is a salutary safeguard against *any* detention of an individual "in violation of the Constitution or laws of the United States."

Federal courts have the duty to carry out the congressionally assigned responsibility to shoulder the ultimate burden of adjudging whether detentions violate federal law, and today's decision substantially abnegates that duty. The Court does not, because it cannot, dispute that institutional constraints totally preclude any possibility that this Court can adequately oversee whether state courts have properly applied federal law, and does not controvert the fact that federal habeas jurisdiction is partially designed to ameliorate that inadequacy. Thus, though I fully agree that state courts "have a constitutional obligation to safeguard personal liberties and to uphold federal law," and that there is no "general lack of appropriate sensitivity to constitutional rights in the trial and appellate courts of the several States," . . . I cannot agree that it follows that, as the Court holds today, federal court determinations of almost all Fourth Amendment claims of state prisoners should be barred and that state court resolution of those issues should be insulated from the federal review Congress intended. . . .

Chapter Sixteen

THE
STATES
AND COMMERCE

INTRODUCTION

State legislatures are continually passing statutes which, intentionally or not, assert regulatory powers over commerce among the states. Ever since *Gibbons* v. *Ogden* (1824) the Supreme Court has been deciding whether such state laws are in unconstitutional conflict with the congressional commerce power. These decisions require the Court to protect interstate commerce from discriminatory or burdening state regulations, while at the same time allowing states to defend their legitimate interests and the special needs of their citizens. In seeking some general rules to guide it in this balancing process, the Court has considered several alternatives.

In *Gibbons* v. *Ogden* the New York State steamboat monopoly law was defended on a theory of "concurrent power," i.e., that both federal and state governments had the right to regulate commerce. But Marshall quickly disposed of this notion as completely impractical, for dual regulations of the same commerce were bound to conflict.

A second theory proposed in *Gibbons* was the "dormant power" interpretation, which held that the mere grant of the commerce power to Congress, even though unexercised in a particular case and dormant, prevented the states from any regulation of commerce. Marshall avoided any consideration of this drastic position in *Gibbons* as pointless, since in fact federal coasting regulations on navigation *had* been adopted.

The position that Marshall seemed to adopt in *Gibbons* was "mutual exclusiveness." In this view, Congress and the states each had areas where they could regulate and from which the other was excluded. The states, for example, had responsibility for inspection, quarantine, or health laws; and over turnpikes, ferries, and "internal commerce" generally. But in *Gibbons* Marshall failed to make this division in any rigorous way, and his decision did not actually turn on this distinction.

It was not until 1852, in **Cooley v. Board of Wardens,** that the Court was able to settle on a viable theoretical foundation for deciding these conflicts by adopting the rule of "selective exclusiveness." Because of the almost infinite variety of commercial situations, Justice Curtis held, some subjects of regulation demanded "a single uniform rule," while others "as imperatively demand . . . that diversity which alone can meet the local necessities." In other words, whether congressional power over commerce was exclusive or not would depend upon the circumstances.

The pragmatism of the *Cooley* decision has characterized most subsequent judicial thinking in this field. The decisions are complicated and often seem contradictory, due partly to the welter of factual situations presented and the diversity of judicial views on the essential operating requirements of a viable federal commercial system.

Understanding of the cases may be facilitated by dividing them into two categories. First are those in which state legislation impinged on commerce and in which there is no relevant federal legislation. Here the conflict, if it exists, is directly with the commerce clause, and the Court must decide whether state regulation is consistent with the command for the maintenance of free trade that comes from the Constitution itself.

In such situations the Court may conclude that the state regulation is either valid or invalid. A holding of validity will rest on the *Cooley* grounds that the problem is essentially one where there is no necessity for a uniform national rule. The Court must also be convinced that no burden on interstate commerce results. Thus the *South Carolina Highway Department v. Barnwell Brothers* (1938) decision upheld fairly rigorous state regulations on the width and weight of motor trucks, since "few subjects of state regulation are so peculiarly of local concern as is the use of state highways," and the regulations fell equally on local and interstate commerce.

But where the Court *does* find that a single national rule is needed, or that a heavy or discriminatory burden on interstate commerce will result from state regulation, then it will invalidate the state law. The case of **Southern Pacific Co. v. Arizona** (1945) saw the Court majority reach such a result, which is in interesting contrast with the *Barnwell* case.

Other decisions reaching the same conclusion were *Morgan* v. *Virginia* (1946) and *Bibb* v. *Navajo Freight Lines* (1959). In *Morgan* the Virginia law requiring separation of white and colored passengers on all motor carriers was invalidated so far as it affected buses in interstate travel, for a "single, uniform rule to promote and protect national travel" was held essential.

Where a state regulation amounts to a complete obstruction to commerce, the case against it is very strong indeed. In *Edwards* v. *California* (1941) the Court held unconstitutional a state statute forbidding anyone knowingly to bring into the state a nonresident "indigent" person.

In the second situation, where state action is alleged to conflict with federal legislation, the Court's problem is simpler. The issue to be decided is whether Congress has completely occupied (preempted) the field, or whether it has left some room for nonconflicting state legislation. In a great many cases state laws regulating labor relations or commercial transportation have been attacked as in conflict with federal laws. Two cases illustrate the alternative positions which the Court may take. In *Huron Portland Cement Co.* v. *Detroit* (1960) a municipal smoke abatement ordinance was upheld even though its enforcement overrode federal steamship licensing and inspection laws. But in *City of Burbank* v. *Lockheed Air Terminal* (1973) the Court held that congressional legislation had preempted state and local control over aircraft noise. In 1977 the federal government approved landing rights for the noisy supersonic Concorde at thirteen major cities, and two lower federal courts ordered the New York Kennedy Airport to permit Concordes to land, but resistance there and in other cities left the issue unsettled.

COOLEY V. BOARD OF WARDENS

12 How. 299, 13 L. Ed. 996 (1852)

A state law of 1803 required vessels using the port of Philadelphia to engage a local pilot, or to pay one-half of the pilot fee into a pilot welfare fund. A federal law of 1789 permitted state pilotage acts to continue in effect. Cooley refused to pay the fee.

MR. JUSTICE CURTIS delivered the opinion of the court. . . .

It remains to consider the objection that it [the state act] is repugnant to the third clause of the eighth section of the first article. "The Congress shall have power to regulate commerce with foreign nations and among the several states, and with the Indian tribes."

That the power to regulate commerce includes the regulation of navigation, we consider settled. And when we look to the nature of the service performed by pilots, to the relations which that service and its compensations bear to navigation between the several states, and between the ports of the United States and foreign countries, we are brought to the conclusion, that the regulation of the qualifications of pilots, of the modes and times of offering and rendering their services, of the responsibilities which shall rest upon them, of the powers they shall possess, of the compensation they may demand, and of the penalties by which their rights and duties may be enforced, do constitute regulations of navigation, and consequently of commerce, within the just meaning of this clause of the Constitution.

The power to regulate navigation is the power to prescribe rules in conformity with which navigation must be carried on. It extends to the persons who conduct it, as well as to the instruments used. Accordingly, the first Congress assembled under the Constitution passed laws requiring the masters of ships and vessels of the United States to be citizens of the United States, and established many rules for the government and regulation of officers and seamen. . . . These have been from time to time added to and changed, and we are not aware that their validity has been questioned. . . .

The act of 1789 . . . already referred to, contains a clear legislative exposition of the Constitution by the first Congress, to the effect that the power to regulate pilots was conferred on Congress by the Constitution; as does also the act of March the 2d, 1837, the terms of which have just been given. The weight to be allowed to this contemporaneous construction, and the practice of Congress under it, has, in another connection, been adverted to. And a majority of the court are of opinion that a regulation of pilots is a regulation of commerce, within the grant to Congress of commercial power, contained in the third clause of the eighth section of the first article of the Constitution.

It becomes necessary, therefore, to consider whether this law of Pennsylvania, being a regulation of commerce, is valid.

The act of Congress of the 7th of August, 1789, sec. 4, is as follows:

> That all pilots in the bays, inlets, rivers, harbors, and ports of the United States shall continue to be regulated in conformity with the existing laws of the states, respectively, wherein such pilots may be, or with such laws as the states may respectively hereafter enact for the purpose, until further legislative provision shall be made by Congress.

If the law of Pennsylvania, now in question, had been in existence at the date of this act of Congress, we might hold it to have been adopted by Congress, and thus made a law of the United States, and so valid. Because this act does, in effect, give the force of an act of Congress, to the then existing state laws on this subject, so long as they should continue unrepealed by the state which enacted them.

But the law on which these actions are founded was not enacted till 1803. What effect then can be attributed to so much of the act of 1789, as declares, that pilots shall continue to be regulated in conformity "with such laws as the states may respectively hereafter enact for the purpose, until further legislative provision shall be made by Congress"?

If the states were divested of the power to legislate on this subject by the grant of the commercial power to Congress, it is plain this act could not confer upon them power thus to legislate. If the Constitution excluded the states from making any law regulating commerce, certainly Congress cannot regrant, or in any manner reconvey to the states that power. . . . [W]e are brought directly and unavoidably to the consideration of the question, whether the grant of the commercial power to Congress, did *per se* deprive the states of all power to regulate pilots. This question has never been decided by this court, nor, in our judgment, has any case depending upon all the considerations which must govern this one, come before this court. The grant of commercial power to Congress does not contain any terms which expressly exclude the states from exercising an authority over its subject-matter. If they are excluded, it must be because the nature of the power, thus granted to Congress, requires that a similar authority should not exist in the states. If it were conceded on the one side, that the nature of this power, like that to legislate for the District of Columbia, is absolutely and totally repugnant to the existence of similar power in the states, probably no one would deny that the grant of the power to Congress, as effectually and perfectly excludes the states from all future legislation on the subject, as if express words had been used to exclude them. And on the other hand, if it were admitted that the existence of this power in Congress, like the power of taxation, is compatible with the existence of a similar power in the states, then it would be in conformity with the contemporary exposition of the Constitution (Federalist, No. 32), and with the judicial construction, given from time to time by this court, after the most deliberate consideration, to hold that the mere grant of such a power to Congress, did not imply a prohibition on the states to exercise the same power; that it is not the mere existence of such a power, but its exercise by Congress, which may be incompatible with the exercise of the same power by the states, and that the states may legislate in the absence of congressional regulations. . . .

The diversities of opinion, therefore, which have existed on this subject, have arisen from the different views taken of the nature of this power. But when the nature of a power like this is spoken of, when it is said that the nature of the power requires that it should be exercised exclusively by Congress, it must be intended to refer to the subjects of that power, and to say they are of such a nature as to require exclusive legislation by Congress. Now the power to regulate commerce, embraces a vast field, containing not only many, but exceedingly various subjects, quite unlike in their nature; some imperatively demanding a single uniform rule, operating equally on the commerce of the United States in every port; and some, like the subject now in question, as imperatively demanding that diversity which alone can meet the local necessities of navigation.

Either absolutely to affirm, or deny that the nature of this power requires exclusive legislation by Congress, is to lose sight of the nature of the subjects of this power, and to assert concerning all of them, what is really applicable but to a part. Whatever subjects of this power are in their nature national, or admit only of one uniform system, or plan of regulation, may justly be said to be of such a nature as to require exclusive legislation by Congress. That this cannot be affirmed of laws for the regulation of pilots and pilotage is plain. The act of 1789 contains a clear and authoritative declaration by the first Congress, that the nature of this subject is such that until Congress should find it necessary to exert its power, it should be left to the legislation of the states; that it is local and not national; that it is likely to be the best provided for, not by one system, or plan or regulation, but by as many as the legislative discretion of the several states should deem applicable to the local peculiarities of the ports within their limits.

Viewed in this light, so much of this act of 1789 as declares that pilots shall continue to be regulated "by such laws as the states may respectively hereafter enact for that purpose," instead of being held to be inoperative, as an attempt to confer on the states a power to legislate, of which the Constitution had deprived them, is allowed an appropriate and important signification. It manifests the understanding of Congress, at the outset of the government, that the nature of this subject is not such as to require its exclusive legislation. The practice of the states, and of the national government, has been in conformity with this declaration, from the origin of the national government to this time; and the nature of the subject when examined is such as to leave no doubt of the superior fitness and propriety, not to say the absolute necessity, of different systems of regulation, drawn from local knowledge and experience, and conformed to local wants. How, then, can we say that, by the mere grant of power to regulate commerce, the states are deprived of all the power to legislate on this subject, because from the nature of the power the legislation of Congress must be exclusive? This would be to affirm that the nature of the power is, in this case, something different from the nature of the subject to which, in such case, the power extends, and that the nature of the power necessarily demands, in all cases, exclusive legislation by Congress, while the nature of one of the subjects of that power, not only does not require such exclusive legislation but may be best provided for by many different systems enacted by the states, in conformity with the circumstances of the ports within their limits. In construing an instrument designed for the formation of a government, and in determining the extent of one of its important grants of power to legislate, we can make no such distinction between the nature of the power and the nature of the subject on which that power was intended practically to operate, nor consider the grant more extensive by affirming of the power, what is not true of its subject now in question.

It is the opinion of a majority of the court that the mere grant to Congress of the power to regulate commerce did not deprive the states of power to regulate pilots, and that although Congress has legislated on this subject, its legislation manifests an intention, with a single exception, not to regulate this subject, but to leave its regulation to the several states. To these precise questions, which are all we are called on to decide, this opinion must be understood to be confined. It does not extend to the question what other subjects, under the commercial power, are within the exclusive control of Congress, or may be regulated by the states in the absence of all congressional legislation; nor to the general question, how far any regulation of a subject by Congress, may be deemed to operate as an exclusion of all legislation by the states upon the same subject. We decide the precise questions before us, upon what we deem sound principles, applicable to this particular subject in the state in which the legislation of Congress has left it. We go no further. . . .

We are of opinion that this state law . . . is therefore valid, and the judgment of the Supreme Court of Pennsylvania in each case must be affirmed.

[MR. JUSTICE DANIEL held that the right to establish pilotage laws was "an original and inherent power in the States, and not one to be . . . held subject to the sanction of the federal government." MR. JUSTICE McLEAN dissented on the ground that a state has no power to regulate foreign commerce.]

SOUTHERN PACIFIC CO. V. ARIZONA

325 U.S. 761, 65 S. Ct. 1515, 89 L. Ed. 1915 (1945)

An Arizona statute of 1912 limited the length of trains traveling in the state to 14 passenger or 70 freight cars. Against a contention by the Southern Pacific that the law was a burden on interstate commerce, the state supreme court upheld the statute as a safety measure adopted by the state under its police power to reduce the number of accidents.

MR. JUSTICE STONE delivered the opinion of the Court. . . .
. . . We are . . . brought to appellant's principal contention, that the state statute contravenes the commerce clause of the Federal Constitution.

Although the commerce clause conferred on the national government power to regulate commerce, its possession of the power does not exclude all state power of regulation. Ever since . . . *Cooley* v. *Board of Wardens* . . . it has been recognized that, in the absence of conflicting legislation by Congress, there is a residuum of power in the state to make laws governing matters of local concern which nevertheless in some measure affect interstate commerce or even, to some extent, regulate it. . . . Thus the states may regulate matters which, because of their number and diversity, may never be adequately dealt with by Congress. . . . When the regulation of matters of local concern is local in character and effect, and its impact on the national commerce does not seriously interfere with its operation, and the consequent incentive to deal with them nationally is slight, such regulation has been generally held to be within state authority. . . .

But ever since *Gibbons* v. *Ogden* . . . the states have not been deemed to have authority to impede substantially the free flow of commerce from state to state, or to regulate those phases of the national commerce which, because of the need of national uniformity, demand that their regulation, if any, be prescribed by a single authority. . . .

In the application of these principles some enactments may be found to be plainly within and others plainly without state power. But between these extremes lie the infinite variety of cases, in which regulation of local matters may also operate as a regulation of commerce, in which reconciliation of the conflicting claims of state and national power is to be attained only by some appraisal and accommodation of the competing demands of the state and national interests involved. . . .

For a hundred years it has been accepted constitutional doctrine that the commerce clause, without the aid of Congressional legislation, thus affords some protection from state legislation inimical to the national commerce, and that in such cases, where Congress has not acted, this Court, and not the state legislature, is under the commerce clause the final arbiter of the competing demands of state and national interests. . . .

Congress has undoubted power to redefine the distribution of power over interstate commerce. It may either permit the states to regulate the commerce in a manner which would otherwise not be permissible . . . or exclude state regulation even of matters of peculiarly local concern which nevertheless affect interstate commerce. . . .

But in general Congress has left it to the courts to formulate the rules thus interpreting the commerce clause in its application, doubtless because it has appreciated the destructive consequences to the commerce of the nation if their protection were withdrawn and has been aware that in their application state laws will not be invalidated without the support of relevant factual material which will "afford a sure basis" for an informed judgment. . . . Meanwhile, Congress has accommodated its legislation, as have the states, to these rules as an established feature of our constitutional system. There has thus been left to the state wide scope for the regulation of matters of local state concern, even though it in some measure affects the commerce, provided it does not materially restrict the free flow of commerce across state lines, or interfere with it in matters with respect to which uniformity of regulation is of predominant national concern.

Hence the matters for ultimate determination here are the nature and extent of the burden which the state regulation of interstate trains, adopted as a safety measure, imposes on interstate commerce, and whether the relative weights of the state and national interests involved are such as to make inapplicable the rule, generally observed, that the free flow of interstate commerce and its freedom from local restraints in matters requiring uniformity of regulation are interests safeguarded by the commerce clause from state interference. . . .

The findings show that the operation of long trains, that is trains of more than fourteen passengers and more than seventy freight cars, is standard practice over the main lines of the railroads of the United States, and that, if the length of trains is to be regulated at all, national uniformity in the regulation adopted, such as only Congress can prescribe, is practically indispensable to the operation of an efficient and economical national railway system. . . .

The unchallenged findings leave no doubt that the Arizona Train Limit Law imposes a serious burden on the interstate commerce conducted by appellant. It materially impedes the movement of appellant's interstate trains through that state and interposes a substantial obstruction to the national policy proclaimed by Congress, to promote adequate, economical and efficient railway transportation service. . . . Enforcement of the law in Arizona, while train lengths remain unregulated or are regulated by varying standards in other states, must inevitably result in an impairment of uniformity of efficient railroad operation because the railroads are subjected to regulation which is not uniform in its application. Compliance with a state statute limiting train lengths requires interstate trains of a length lawful in other states to be broken up and reconstituted as they enter each state according as it may impose varying limitations upon train lengths. The alternative is for the carrier to conform to the lowest train limit restriction of any of the states through which its trains pass, whose laws thus control the carriers' operations both within and without the regulating state. . . .

If one state may regulate train lengths, so may all the others, and they need not prescribe the same maximum limitation. The practical effect of such regulation is to control train operations beyond the boundaries of the state exacting it because of the necessity of breaking up and reassembling long trains at the nearest terminal points before entering and after leaving the regulating state. The serious impediment to the free flow of commerce by the local regulation of train lengths and the practical necessity that such regulation, if any, must be prescribed by a single body having a nationwide authority are apparent.

The trial court found that the Arizona law had no reasonable relation to safety, and made train operation more dangerous. Examination of the evidence and the detailed findings makes it clear that this conclusion was rested on facts found which indicate that such increased danger of accident and personal injury as may result from the greater length of trains is more than offset by the increase in the number of accidents resulting from the larger number of trains when train lengths are reduced. In considering the effect of the statute as a safety measure, therefore, the factor of controlling significance for present purposes is not whether there is basis for the conclusion of the Arizona Supreme Court that the increase in length of trains beyond the statutory maximum has an adverse effect upon safety of operation. The decisive question is whether in the circumstances the total effect of the law as a safety measure in reducing accidents and casualties is so slight or problematical as not to outweigh the national interest in keeping interstate commerce free from interferences which seriously impede it and subject it to local regulation which does not have a uniform effect on the interstate train journey which it interrupts. . . .

We think, as the trial court found, that the Arizona Train Limit Law, viewed as a safety measure, affords at most slight and dubious advantage, if any, over unregulated train lengths. . . . Its undoubted effect on the commerce is the regulation, without securing uniformity, of the length of trains operated in interstate commerce, which lack is itself a primary cause of preventing the free flow of commerce by delaying it and by substantially increasing its cost and impairing its efficiency. In these respects, the case differs from those where a state, by regulatory measures affecting the commerce, has removed or reduced safety hazards without substantial interference with the interstate movement of trains. . . .

The principle that, without controlling Congressional action, a state may not regulate interstate commerce so as substantially to affect its flow or deprive it of needed uniformity in its regulation is not to be avoided by "simply invoking the convenient apologetics of the police power." . . .

Appellees especially rely on . . . *South Carolina Highway Dept.* v. *Barnwell Bros.* . . . as supporting the state's authority to regulate the length of interstate trains. . . . [But that case] was concerned with the power of the state to regulate the weight and width of motor cars passing interstate over its highways, a legislative field over which the state has a far more extensive control than over interstate railroads. In that case . . . we were at pains to point out that there are few subjects of state regulation affecting interstate commerce which are so peculiarly of local concern as is the use of the state's highways. Unlike the railroads local highways are built, owned and maintained by the state or its municipal subdivisions. The state is responsible for their safe and economical administration. Regulations affecting the safety of their use must be applied alike to intrastate and interstate traffic. The fact that they affect alike shippers in interstate and intrastate commerce in great numbers, within as well as without the state, is a safeguard against regulatory abuses. Their regulation is akin to quarantine measures, game laws, and like local regulations of rivers, harbors, piers, and docks, with respect to which the state has exceptional scope for the exercise of its regulatory power, and which, Congress not acting, have been sustained even though they materially interfere with interstate commerce. . . .

The contrast between the present regulation and the full train crew laws in point of their effects on the commerce, and the like contrast with the highway safety regulations, in point of the nature of the subject of regulation and the state's interest in it, illustrate and emphasize the considerations which enter into a determination of the relative weights of state and national interests where state regulation affecting interstate commerce is attempted. Here examination of all the relevant factors makes it plain that the state interest is outweighed by the interest of the nation in an adequate, economical and efficient railway transportation service, which must prevail.

Reversed.

MR. JUSTICE RUTLEDGE concurs in the result.

MR. JUSTICE BLACK, dissenting.

The determination of whether it is in the interest of society for the length of trains to be governmentally regulated is a matter of public policy. Someone must fix that policy—either the Congress, or the state, or the courts. A century and a half of constitutional history and government admonishes this Court to leave that choice to the elected legislative representatives of the people themselves, where it properly belongs both on democratic principles and the requirements of efficient government.

I think that legislatures, to the exclusion of courts, have the constitutional power to enact laws limiting train lengths, for the purpose of reducing injuries brought about by "slack movements." Their power is not less because a requirement of short trains might increase grade crossing accidents. This latter fact raises an entirely different element of danger which is itself subject to legislative regulation. For legislatures may, if necessary, require railroads to take appropriate steps to reduce the likelihood of injuries at grade crossings. . . . And the fact that grade-crossing improvements may be expensive is no sufficient reason to say that an unconstitutional "burden" is put upon a railroad even though it be an interstate road. . . .

There have been many sharp divisions of this Court concerning its authority, in the absence of congressional enactment, to invalidate state laws as violating the Commerce Clause. . . . That discussion need not be renewed here, because even the broadest exponents of judicial power in this field have not heretofore expressed doubt as to a state's power, absent a paramount congressional declaration, to regulate interstate trains in the interest of safety. . . .

This record in its entirety leaves me with no doubt whatever that many employees have been seriously injured and killed in the past, and that many more are likely to be so in the future, because of "slack movement" in trains. Everyday knowledge as well as direct evidence presented at the various hearings, substantiates the report of the Senate Committee that danger from slack movement is greater in long trains than in short trains. It may be that offsetting dangers are possible in the operation of short trains. The balancing of these probabilities, however, is not in my judgment a matter for judicial determination, but one which calls for legislative consideration. Representatives elected by the people to make their laws, rather than judges appointed to interpret those laws, can best determine the policies which govern the people. That at least is the basic principle on which our democratic society rests. I would affirm the judgment of the Supreme Court of Arizona.

MR. JUSTICE DOUGLAS, dissenting. . . .

BIBB V. NAVAJO FREIGHT LINES, INC.

359 U.S. 520, 79 S. Ct. 962, 3 L. Ed. 2d 1003 (1959)

MR. JUSTICE DOUGLAS delivered the opinion of the Court.

We are asked in this case to hold that an Illinois statute requiring the use of a certain type of rear fender mudguard on trucks and trailers operated on the highways of that State conflicts with the Commerce Clause of the Constitution. The statutory specification for this type of mudguard provides that the guard shall contour the rear wheel, with the inside surface being relatively parallel to the top 90 degrees of the rear 180 degrees of the whole surface. The surface of the guard must extend downward to within 10 inches from the ground when the truck is loaded to its maximum legal capacity. The guards must be wide enough to cover the width of the protected tire, must be installed not more than 6 inches from the tire surface when the vehicle is loaded to maximum capacity, and must have a lip or flange on its outer edge of not less than 2 inches.

Appellees, interstate motor carriers holding certificates from the Interstate Commerce Commission, challenged the constitutionality of the Illinois Act. A specially constituted three-judge District Court concluded that it unduly and unreasonably burdened and obstructed interstate commerce, because it made the conventional or straight mudflap, which is legal in at least 45 States, illegal in Illinois, and because the statute, taken together with a Rule of the Arkansas Commerce Commission requiring straight mudflaps, rendered the use of the same motor vehicle equipment in both States impossible. The statute was declared to be violative of the Commerce Clause and appellants were enjoined from enforcing it. . . .

The power of the State to regulate the use of its highways is broad and pervasive. We have recognized the peculiarly local nature of this subject of safety, and have upheld state statutes applicable alike to interstate and intrastate commerce, despite the fact that they have an impact on interstate commerce. South Carolina State Highway Dept. v. Barnwell Bros. . . .

These safety measures carry a strong presumption of validity when challenged in court. If there are alternative ways of solving a problem, we do not sit to determine which of them is best suited to achieve a valid state objective. Policy decisions are for the state legislature, absent federal entry into the field. Unless we can conclude on the whole record that "the total effect of the law as a safety measure in reducing accidents and casualties is so slight or problematical as not to outweigh the national interest in keeping interstate commerce free from interferences which seriously impede it" (Southern Pacific Co. v. State of Arizona ...) we must uphold the statute.

The District Court found that "since it is impossible for a carrier operating in interstate commerce to determine which of its equipment will be used in a particular area, or on a particular day, or days, carriers operating into or through Illinois ... will be required to equip all their trailers in accordance with the requirements of the Illinois Splash Guard statute." With two possible exceptions the mudflaps required in those States which have mudguard regulations would not meet the standards required by the Illinois statute. The cost of installing the contour mudguards is $30 or more per vehicle. The District Court found that the initial cost of installing those mudguards on all the trucks owned by the appellees ranged from $4,500 to $45,840. There was also evidence in the record to indicate that the cost of maintenance and replacement of these guards is substantial.

Illinois introduced evidence seeking to establish that contour mudguards had a decided safety factor in that they prevented the throwing of debris into the faces of drivers of passing cars and into the windshields of a following vehicle. But the District Court in its opinion stated that it was "conclusively shown that the contour mud flap possesses no advantages over the conventional or straight mud flap previously required in Illinois and presently required in most of the states." ... and that "there is rather convincing testimony that use of the contour flap creates hazards previously unknown to those using the highways." ... These hazards were found to be occasioned by the fact that this new type of mudguard tended to cause an accumulation of heat in the brake drum, thus decreasing the effectiveness of brakes, and by the fact that they were susceptible of being hit and bumped when the trucks were backed up and of falling off on the highway.

These findings on cost and on safety are not the end of our problem. Local regulation of the weight of trucks using the highways upheld in Sproles v. Binford ... also involved increased financial burdens for interstate carriers. State control of the width and weight of motor trucks and trailers sustained in South Carolina State Highway Dept. v. Barnwell Bros. ... involved nice questions of judgment concerning the need of those regulations so far as the issue of safety was concerned. That case also presented the problem whether interstate motor carriers, who were required to replace all equipment or keep out of the State, suffered an unconstitutional restraint on interstate commerce. The matter of safety was said to be one essentially for the legislative judgment; and the burden of redesigning or replacing equipment was said to be a proper price to exact from interstate and intrastate motor carriers alike. And the same conclusion was reached in Maurer v. Hamilton ..., where a state law prohibited any motor carrier from carrying any other vehicle above the cab of the carrier vehicle or over the head of the operator of that vehicle.

Cost taken into consideration with other factors might be relevant in some cases to the issue of burden on commerce. But it has assumed no such proportions here. If we had here only a question whether the cost of adjusting an interstate operation to these new local safety regulations prescribed by Illinois unduly burdened interstate commerce, we would have to sustain the law under the authority of the *Sproles, Barnwell,* and *Maurer* cases. The same result would obtain if we had to resolve the much discussed issues of safety presented in this case.

This case presents a different issue. The equipment in the *Sproles, Barnwell,* and *Maurer* cases could pass muster in any State, so far as the records in those cases reveal. We were not faced there with the question whether one State could prescribe standards for interstate carriers that would conflict with the standards of another State, making it necessary, say, for an interstate carrier to shift its cargo to different designed vehicles once another state line was reached. We had a related problem in Southern Pacific Co. v. Arizona, . . . where the Court invalidated a statute of Arizona prescribing a maximum length of 70 cars for freight trains moving through that State. More closely in point is Morgan v. Virginia . . . where a local law required a reseating of passengers on interstate busses entering Virginia in order to comply with a local segregation law. Diverse seating arrangements for people of different races imposed by several States interfered, we concluded, with "the need for national uniformity in the regulations for interstate travel." . . . Those cases indicate the dimensions of our present problem.

An order of the Arkansas Commerce Commission, already mentioned, requires that trailers operating in that State be equipped with straight or conventional mudflaps. Vehicles equipped to meet the standards of the Illinois statute would not comply with Arkansas standards, and vice versa. Thus if a trailer is to be operated in both States, mudguards would have to be interchanged, causing a significant delay in an operation where prompt movement may be of the essence. . . .

It was also found that the Illinois statute seriously interferes with the "interline" operations of motor carriers—that is to say, with the interchanging of trailers between an originating carrier and another carrier when the latter serves an area not served by the former. These "interline" operations provide a speedy through-service for the shipper. Interlining contemplates the physical transfer of the entire trailer; there is no unloading and reloading of the cargo. The interlining process is particularly vital in connection with shipment of perishables, which would spoil if unloaded before reaching their destination, or with the movement of explosives carried under seal. . . .

This in summary is the rather massive showing of burden on interstate commerce which appellees made at the hearing. . . .

This is one of those cases—few in number—where local safety measures that are nondiscriminatory place an unconstitutional burden on interstate commerce. This conclusion is especially underlined by the deleterious effect which the Illinois law will have on the "interline" operation of interstate motor carriers. The conflict between the Arkansas regulation and the Illinois regulation also suggests that this regulation of mudguards is not one of those matters "admitting of diversity of treatment, according to the special requirement of local conditions," to use the words of Chief Justice Hughes in Sproles v. Binford. . . . A State which insists on a design out of line with the requirements of almost all the other States may sometimes place a great burden of delay and inconvenience on those interstate motor carriers entering or crossing its territory. Such a new safety device—out of line with the requirements of the other States —may be so compelling that the innovating State need not be the one to give way. But the present showing—balanced against the clear burden on commerce—is far too inconclusive to make this mudguard meet that test.

We deal not with absolutes but with questions of degree. The state legislatures plainly have great leeway in providing safety regulations for all vehicles—interstate as well as local. Our decisions so hold. Yet the heavy burden which the Illinois mudguard law places on the interstate movement of trucks and trailers seems to us to pass the permissible limits even for safety regulations.

Affirmed.

MR. JUSTICE HARLAN, whom MR. JUSTICE STEWART joins, concurring. . . .

CITY OF BURBANK V. LOCKHEED AIR TERMINAL

411 U.S. 624, 93 S. Ct. 1854, 36 L. Ed. 2d 547 (1973)

MR. JUSTICE DOUGLAS delivered the opinion of the Court.

The court in Cooley v. Board of Wardens. . . . first stated the rule of pre-emption which is the critical issue in the present case. Speaking through Justice Curtis, it said:

"Now the power to regulate commerce, embraces a vast field, containing not only many, but exceedingly various subjects, quite unlike in their nature; some imperatively demanding a single uniform rule, operating equally on the commerce of the United States in every port; and some, like the subject now in question, as imperatively demanding that diversity, which alone can meet the local necessities of navigation. . . . Whatever subjects of this power are in their nature national, or admit only of one uniform system, or plan of regulation, may justly be said to be of such a nature as to require exclusive legislation by Congress."

This suit brought by appellees asked for an injunction against the enforcement of an ordinance adopted by the City Council of Burbank, California, which made it unlawful for a so-called pure jet aircraft to take off from the Hollywood-Burbank Airport between 11 P.M. of one day and

7 A.M. the next day, and making it unlawful for the operator of that airport to allow any such aircraft to take off from that airport during such periods. The only regularly scheduled flight affected by the ordinance was an intrastate flight of Pacific Southwest Airlines originating in Oakland, California, and departing from Hollywood-Burbank Airport for San Diego every Sunday night at 11:30 P.M.

The District Court found the ordinance to be unconstitutional on both Supremacy Clause and Commerce Clause grounds. . . . The Court of Appeals affirmed on the grounds of the Supremacy Clause both as respects pre-emption and as respects conflict. . . . We affirm the Court of Appeals.

The Federal Aviation Act of 1958, . . . as amended by the Noise Control Act of 1972, and the regulations under it . . . are central to the question of pre-emption.

Section 1508 provides in part, "The United States of America is declared to possess and exercise complete and exclusive national sovereignty in the airspace of the United States . . ." By § 1348 the Administrator of the Federal Aeronautics Act (FAA) has been given broad authority to regulate the use of the navigable airspace, "in order to insure the safety of aircraft and the efficient utilization of such air space . . ." and "for the protection of persons and property on the ground. . . ."

Curfews, such as Burbank has imposed, would according to the testimony at the trial and the District Court's findings increase congestion, cause a loss of efficiency, and aggravate the noise problem.

The Noise Control Act of 1972 . . . provides that the Administrator "after consultation with appropriate Federal, State, and local agencies and interested persons" shall conduct a study of various facets of the aircraft "noise" problems and report to the Congress within nine months, *i.e.*, by July 1973. The 1972 Act by amending § 611 of the Federal Aviation Act, also involves the Environmental Protection Agency (EPA) in the comprehensive scheme of federal control of the aircraft noise problem. . . .

There is to be sure no express provision of pre-emption in the 1972 Act. That, however, is not decisive. . . . It is the pervasive nature of the scheme of federal regulation of aircraft noise that leads us to conclude that there is pre-emption. . . .

If we were to uphold the Burbank ordinance and a significant number of municipalities followed suit, it is obvious that fractionalized control of the timing of take-offs and landings would severely limit the flexibility of the FAA in controlling air traffic flow. The difficulties of scheduling flights to avoid congestion and the concomitant decrease in safety would be compounded. In 1960 the FAA rejected a proposed restriction on jet operations at Los Angeles airport between 10 P.M. and 7 A.M. because such restrictions could "create critically serious problems to all air transportation patterns." . . .

This decision, announced in 1960, remains peculiarly within the competence of the FAA, supplemented now by the input of the EPA. We are not at liberty to diffuse the powers given by Congress to FAA and EPA by letting the States or municipalities in on the planning. If that change is to be made, Congress alone must do it.

Affirmed.

MR. JUSTICE REHNQUIST, with whom MR. JUSTICE STEWART, MR. JUSTICE WHITE, and MR. JUSTICE MARSHALL join, dissenting.

The Court concludes that congressional legislation dealing with aircraft noise has so "pervaded" that field that Congress has *impliedly* preempted it, and therefore the ordinance of the city of Burbank here challenged is invalid under the Supremacy Clause of the Constitution. The Court says that "we need not, however, dwell long on the earlier versions of the Federal Aviation Act, for a 1972 Act put the question completely at rest." . . . Yet the House and Senate committee reports explicitly state that the 1972 Act to which the Court refers was *not* intended to alter the balance between state and federal regulation which had been struck by earlier congressional legislation in this area. The House Report . . . in discussing the general pre-emptive effect of the entire bill, stated:

> "The authority of State and local government to regulate use, operation or movement of products is not affected at all by the bill. (The preemption provision discussed in this paragraph does not apply to aircraft. See discussion of aircraft noise below.)"

The report went on to state specifically:

> "No provision of the bill is intended to alter in any way the relationship between the authority of the Federal Government and that of State and local governments that existed with respect to matters covered by section 611 of the Federal Aviation Act of 1958 prior to the enactment of the bill."

. . . Appellees do not contend that the noise produced by jet engines could not reasonably be deemed to affect adversely the health and welfare of persons constantly exposed to it; control of noise, sufficiently loud to be classified as a public nuisance at common law, would be a type of regulation well within the traditional scope of the police power possessed by States and local governing bodies. Because noise regulation has traditionally been an area of local, not national, concern, in determining whether congressional legislation has, by implication, foreclosed remedial local enactments "we start with the assumption that the historic police powers of the States were not to be superseded by the Federal Act unless that was the clear and manifest purpose of Congress." Rice v. Santa Fe Elevator Corp. . . . (1947). This assumption derives from our basic constitutional division of legislative competence between the States and Congress; from "due regard for the presuppositions of our embracing federal system, *including the principle of diffusion of power not as a matter of doctrinaire localism but as a promoter of democracy.* . . ." San Diego Building

Trades Council v. Garmon . . . (1959) (emphasis added). Unless the requisite pre-emptive intent is abundantly clear, we should hesitate to invalidate state and local legislation for the added reason that "the State is powerless to remove the ill effects of our decision, while the national government, which has the ultimate power, remains free to remove the burden." . . .

The District Court found that the Burbank ordinance would impose an undue burden on interstate commerce, and held it invalid under the Commerce Clause for that reason. Neither the Court of Appeals nor this Court's opinion, in view of their determination as to pre-emption, reached that question. The District Court's conclusion appears to be based at least in part on a consideration of the effect on interstate commerce that would result if all municipal airports in the country enacted ordinances such as that of Burbank. Since the proper determination of the question turns on an evaluation of the facts of each case, see, e. g., Bibb v. Navajo Freight Lines, Inc. . . . and not on a predicted proliferation of possibilities, the District Court's conclusion is of doubtful validity. The Burbank ordinance did not affect emergency flights, and had the total effect of prohibiting one scheduled commercial flight each week and several additional private flights by corporate executives; such a result can hardly be held to be an unreasonable burden on commerce. . . .

Chapter Seventeen

THE
STATES
AND ELECTIONS

INTRODUCTION

The Constitution recognized the primacy of the states in setting qualifications for voting, by providing that electors for members of the House of Representatives should "have the qualifications requisite for electors of the most numerous branch of the state legislature." However, Article I, section 4, authorized Congress to "make or alter" regulations established by the states with respect to the "times, places and manner" of holding congressional elections. In addition, five constitutional amendments have a bearing on elections and the electorate. The equal protection clause of the Fourteenth Amendment has been applied to forbid discriminatory practices by state election officials. The Fifteenth Amendment specifically forbids denial of the right to vote "on account of race, color, or previous condition of servitude." The Nineteenth Amendment guarantees woman suffrage, the Twenty-fourth bans use of the poll tax in federal elections, and the Twenty-sixth extends the franchise to 18-year-olds.

The states thus exercise the power of fixing voting qualifications within a strict framework of federal constitutional and statutory requirements, and the Supreme Court has invalidated state restrictions on the franchise in a number of areas.

All states require a certain period of residence in the state and locality as a qualification for voting. But in *Dunn* v. *Blumstein* (1972) the Court held that a residency requirement of one year in the state was excessive. While the Court suggested that a 30-day period ought to be sufficient to complete the administrative tasks involved, subsequent decisions accepted a 50-day period.

The voting age set by the states was traditionally 21. In the Voting Rights Act of 1970 Congress, influenced by the slogan that if 18-year-olds were old enough to fight in Vietnam, they were old enough to vote, fixed the voting age at 18 for all federal and state elections. A badly divided Court in *Oregon* v. *Mitchell* (1970) held that, while Congress could control the voting age in federal elections, the states were guaranteed that right for state and local elections. Congress immediately adopted the Twenty-sixth Amendment to reverse the Court's ruling on the latter point.

Many qualified voters are unable to vote because, though not convicted of any crime, thay are in prison awaiting trial on nonbailable offenses or because they are unable to post bail. In *O'Brien* v. *Skinner* (1974) the Court held that failure to provide absentee ballots or any alternative method of voting for such persons was a denial of equal protection.

State statutes generally deny the right to vote to convicted felons, this disqualification continuing even after they have served their sentences. The supreme court of California held in 1973 that this lifetime exclusion from the franchise served no compelling state interest, but in *Richardson* v. *Ramirez* (1974) the Supreme Court found a justification for the disqualification in the almost forgotten section 2 of the Fourteenth Amendment, which impliedly recognizes the right of states to deny the franchise "for participation in rebellion or other crime."

After adoption of the Twenty-fourth Amendment, which forbade the poll tax test only in federal elections, four states still enforced the tax for state elections. In **Harper v. Virginia State Board of Elections** (1966) the Court declared state poll taxes unconstitutional as an "invidious discrimination" and a denial of equal protection.

A much more significant barrier to the franchise were state literacy tests for voting, which were often combined with obligations to understand or interpret provisions of the state or federal constitutions. These tests were brazenly manipulated in some Southern states to prevent blacks from voting. The Voting Rights Act of 1965 largely terminated such abuses by suspending literacy and other "qualification" tests in all states and counties where less than 50 percent of persons of voting age were registered or had voted in the 1964 presidential election. This admittedly inexact test of voting discrimination affected six Southern states and certain counties in some other states. Also, appointment of federal voting examiners was provided for in any areas where the Attorney General certified they were needed to enforce the Fifteenth Amendment.

The Supreme Court upheld the Voting Rights Act in *South Carolina* v. *Katzenbach* (1966), and the law had a dramatic effect in increasing black registration. The statute, which had a five-year limitation, was extended in 1970 and the suspension of literacy tests made nationwide (upheld in *Oregon* v. *Mitchell*); it was again extended in 1975 for seven years, with the ban on literacy tests made permanent. Bilingual voting information was also required in areas where there were substantial numbers of non-English speaking voters.

The Supreme Court's principle of "one person, one vote," already discussed in Chapter Ten insofar as it affected representation in Congress, had its major impact on state legislatures. The rule of population equality in election districts was first announced in the Georgia county-unit case, *Gray* v. *Sanders* (1963), and it was immediately clear that it would also be applied against the widespread population inequalities among state legislative electoral districts. However, in view of the traditional practice in many states of basing representation in one house on local government units rather than on population, it was anticipated that the Court might accept some compromise in the one-person, one-vote formula. But *Reynolds* v. *Sims* (1964) enforced the rule of population equality for electoral districts for both houses, thereby initiating a wholesale revision in state election districts.

As already noted, the Court initially tended to insist on a very close approximation of population equality in voting districts, for example, in *Kirkpatrick* v. *Preisler* (1969) and *Wells* v. *Rockefeller* (1969). But subsequently the Court permitted greater variations, as in *Mahan* v. *Howell* (1973), where a spread of 16.4 percent between the most and least populous districts was accepted to permit conformity to county and city boundaries. Likewise, *Gaffney* v. *Cummings* (1973) upheld a Connecticut reapportionment plan which sought to achieve fair representation between the major political parties.

The authority of the Constitution and Congress over primary elections in the states was seriously questioned by the Court's decision in *Newberry* v. *United States* (1921). Some Southern states interpreted the ruling to mean that no constitutional protections covered primary elections and began openly to exclude black voters from primaries. However, a 1923 Texas law prohibiting blacks from voting in the state's Democratic primaries was declared unconstitutional by the Supreme Court in *Nixon* v. *Herndon* (1927) as a denial of equal protection by state action under the Fourteenth Amendment. The legislature then sought to avoid the state action issue by simply authorizing party executive committees to prescribe the qualifications for voting in primaries. But this tactic also failed; the Court in *Nixon* v. *Condon* (1932) held that the party committee was acting as agent of the state.

In neither of these decisions did the Court question the *Newberry* assumption that primaries were outside the protection of the Constitution. Taking advantage of this situation, the Texas Democratic party, on its own authority and with no state authorization, adopted a resolution confining party membership to white citizens. In *Grovey* v. *Townsend* (1935) the Supreme Court agreed that this was not state action and so did not violate the Fourteenth Amendment.

The *Grovey* notion that parties are private clubs and that primaries are not part of the election process was so clearly contrary to fact that it could not be long maintained. In *United States* v. *Classic* (1941) the federal corrupt practices act was held applicable to a congressional primary election in Louisiana. This ruling prepared the way for *Smith* v. *Allwright* (1944), which held that parties are agents of the state and that discrimination against blacks was state action in violation of the Fifteenth Amendment.

HARPER V. VIRGINIA STATE BOARD OF ELECTIONS

383 U.S. 663, 86 S. Ct. 1079, 16 L. Ed. 2d 169 (1966)

The Virginia constitution required all residents of the state 21 years of age or older to pay an annual poll tax. Failure to pay resulted in the loss of the right to vote.

MR. JUSTICE DOUGLAS delivered the opinion of the Court. . . .

We conclude that a State violates the Equal Protection Clause of the Fourteenth Amendment whenever it makes the affluence of the voter or payment of any fee an electoral standard. Voter qualifications have no relation to wealth nor to paying or not paying this or any other tax. Our cases demonstrate that the Equal Protection Clause of the Fourteenth Amendment restrains the States from fixing voter qualifications which invidiously discriminate. . . . Previously we had said that neither homesite nor occupation "affords a permissible basis for distinguishing between qualified voters within the State." Gray v. Sanders. . . . We think the same must be true of requirements of wealth or affluence or payment of a fee.

. . . Recently in Reynolds v. Sims, . . . we said, "Undoubtedly, the right of suffrage is a fundamental matter in a free and democratic society. Especially since the right to exercise the franchise in a free and unimpaired manner is preservative of other basic civil and political rights, any alleged infringement of the right of citizens to vote must be carefully and meticulously scrutinized." . . .

We say the same whether the citizen, otherwise qualified to vote, has $1.50 in his pocket or nothing at all, pays the fee or fails to pay it. The principle that denies the State the right to dilute a citizen's vote on account of his economic status or other such factors by analogy bars a system which excludes those unable to pay a fee to vote or who fail to pay. . . .

We agree, of course, with Mr. Justice Holmes that the Due Process Clause of the Fourteenth Amendment "does not enact Mr. Herbert Spencer's Social Statics" (Lochner v. People of State of New York . . .). Likewise, the Equal Protection Clause is not shackled to the political theory of a particular era. In determining what lines are unconstitutionally discriminatory, we have never been confined to historic notions of equality, any more than we have restricted due process to a fixed catalogue of what was at a given time deemed to be the limits of fundamental rights. . . . Notions of what constitutes equal treatment for purposes of the Equal Protection Clause *do* change. . . .

We have long been mindful that where fundamental rights and liberties are asserted under the Equal Protection Clause, classifications which might invade or restrain them must be closely scrutinized and carefully confined. . . .

Those principles apply here. For to repeat, wealth or fee paying has, in our view, no relation to voting qualifications; the right to vote is too precious, too fundamental to be so burdened or conditioned.

Reversed.

MR. JUSTICE BLACK, dissenting. . . .

A study of our cases shows that this Court has refused to use the general language of the Equal Protection Clause as though it provided a handy instrument to strike down state laws which the Court feels are based on bad governmental policy. The equal protection cases carefully analyzed boil down to the principle that distinctions drawn and even discriminations imposed by state laws do not violate the Equal Protection Clause so long as these distinctions and discriminations are not "irrational," "irrelevant," "unreasonable," "arbitrary," or "invidious." These vague and indefinite terms do not, of course, provide a precise formula or an automatic mechanism for deciding cases arising under the Equal Protection Clause. The restrictive connotations of these terms, however . . . are a plain recognition of the fact that under a proper interpretation of the Equal Protection Clause States are to have the broadest kind of leeway in areas where they have a general constitutional competence to act. . . .

MR. JUSTICE HARLAN, whom MR. JUSTICE STEWART joins, dissenting. . . .

The final demise of state poll taxes, already totally proscribed by the Twenty-Fourth Amendment with respect to federal elections and abolished by the States themselves in all but four States with respect to state elections, is perhaps in itself not of great moment. But the fact that the *coup de grace* has been administered by this Court instead of being left to the affected States or to the federal political process should be a matter of continuing concern to all interested in maintaining the proper role of this tribunal under our scheme of government. . . .

SOUTH CAROLINA V. KATZENBACH

383 U.S. 301, 86 S. Ct. 803, 15 L. Ed. 2d 769 (1966)

The state of South Carolina filed a complaint in the original jurisdiction of the Supreme Court seeking to enjoin the U.S. Attorney General from enforcement of the provisions of the Voting Rights Act of 1965, which are summarized in the Court's opinion.

MR. CHIEF JUSTICE WARREN delivered the opinion of the Court. . . .

The Voting Rights Act was designed by Congress to banish the blight of racial discrimination in voting, which has infected the electoral process in parts of our country for nearly a century. The Act creates stringent new remedies for voting discrimination where it persists on a pervasive scale, and in addition the statute strengthens existing remedies for pockets of voting discrimination elsewhere in the country. Congress assumed the power to prescribe these remedies from § 2 of the Fifteenth Amendment, which authorizes the National Legislature to effectuate by "appropriate" measures the constitutional prohibition against racial discrimination in voting. We hold that the sections of the Act which are properly before us are an appropriate means for carrying out Congress' constitutional responsibilities and are consonant with all other provisions of the Constitution. We therefore deny South Carolina's request that enforcement of these sections of the Act be enjoined.

The constitutional propriety of the Voting Rights Act of 1965 must be judged with reference to the historical experience which it reflects. Before enacting the measure, Congress explored with great care the problem of racial discrimination in voting. The House and Senate Committees on the Judiciary each held hearings for nine days and received testimony from a total of 67 witnesses. More than three full days were consumed discussing the bill on the floor of the House, while the debate in the Senate covered 26 days in all. At the close of these deliberations, the verdict of both chambers was overwhelming. The House approved the bill by a vote of 328–74, and the measure passed the Senate by a margin of 79–18.

Two points emerge vividly from the voluminous legislative history of the Act contained in the committee hearings and floor debates. First:

Congress felt itself confronted by an insidious and pervasive evil which had been perpetuated in certain parts of our country through unremitting and ingenious defiance of the Constitution. Second: Congress concluded that the unsuccessful remedies which it had prescribed in the past would have to be replaced by sterner and more elaborate measures in order to satisfy the clear commands of the Fifteenth Amendment. We pause here to summarize the majority reports of the House and Senate Committees, which document in considerable detail the factual basis for these reactions by Congress.

The Fifteenth Amendment to the Constitution was ratified in 1870. Promptly thereafter Congress passed the Enforcement Act of 1870, which made it a crime for public officers and private persons to obstruct exercise of the right to vote. The statute was amended in the following year to provide for detailed federal supervision of the electoral process, from registration to the certification of returns. As the years passed and fervor for racial equality waned, enforcement of the laws became spotty and ineffective, and most of their provisions were repealed in 1894. The remnants have had little significance in the recently renewed battle against voting discrimination.

Meanwhile, beginning in 1890, the States of Alabama, Georgia, Louisiana, Mississippi, North Carolina, South Carolina, and Virginia enacted tests still in use which were specifically designed to prevent Negroes from voting. Typically, they made the ability to read and write a registration qualification and also required completion of a registration form. These laws were based on the fact that as of 1890 in each of the named States, more than two-thirds of the adult Negroes were illiterate while less than one quarter of the adult whites were unable to read or write. At the same time, alternate tests were prescribed in all of the named States to assure that white illiterates would not be deprived of the franchise. These included grandfather clauses, property qualifications, "good character" tests, and the requirement that registrants "understand" or "interpret" certain matter.

The course of subsequent Fifteenth Amendment litigation in this Court demonstrates the variety and persistence of these and similar institutions designed to deprive Negroes of the right to vote. Grandfather clauses were invalidated in Guinn v. United States. . . . Procedural hurdles were struck down in Lane v. Wilson. . . . The white primary was outlawed in Smith v. Allwright . . . and Terry v. Adams. . . . Improper challenges were nullified in United States v. Thomas. . . . Racial gerrymandering was forbidden by Gomillion v. Lightfoot. . . . Finally, discriminatory application of voting tests was condemned in . . . Louisiana v. United States. . . .

According to the evidence in recent Justice Department voting suits, the latter stratagem is now the principal method used to bar Negroes from the polls. Discriminatory administration of voting qualifications has been found in all eight Alabama cases, in all nine Louisiana cases, and in all nine Mississippi cases which have gone to final judgment. Moreover, in almost all of these cases, the courts have held that the discrimination was pursuant to a widespread "pattern or practice." White applicants for registration have often been excused altogether from the literacy and understanding tests or have been given easy versions, have received extensive help from voting officials, and have been registered despite serious errors in their answers. Negroes, on the other hand, have typically been required to pass difficult versions of all the tests, without any outside assistance and without the slightest error. The good-morals requirement is so vague and subjective that it has constituted an open invitation to abuse at the hands of voting officials. Negroes obliged to obtain vouchers from registered voters have found it virtually impossible to comply in areas where almost no Negroes are on the rolls.

In recent years, Congress has repeatedly tried to cope with the problem by facilitating case-by-case litigation against voting discrimination. The Civil Rights Act of 1957 authorized the Attorney General to seek injunctions against public and private interference with the right to vote on racial grounds. Perfecting amendments in the Civil Rights Act of 1960 permitted the joinder of States as parties defendant, gave the Attorney General access to local voting records, and authorized courts to register voters in areas of systematic discrimination. Title I of the Civil Rights Act of 1964 expedited the hearing of voting cases before three-judge courts and outlawed some of the tactics used to disqualify Negroes from voting in federal elections.

Despite the earnest efforts of the Justice Department and of many federal judges, these new laws have done little to cure the problem of voting discrimination. According to estimates by the Attorney General during hearings on the Act, registration of voting-age Negroes in Alabama rose only from 14.2% to 19.4% between 1958 and 1964; in Louisiana it barely inched ahead from 31.7% to 31.8% between 1956 and 1965; and in Mississippi it increased only from 4.4% to 6.4% between 1954 and 1964. In each instance, registration of voting age whites ran roughly 50 percentage points or more ahead of Negro registration.

The previous legislation has proved ineffective for a number of reasons. Voting suits are unusually onerous to prepare, sometimes requiring as many as 6,000 man-hours spent combing through registration records in preparation for trial. Litigation has been exceedingly slow, in part because of the ample opportunities for delay afforded voting officials and others involved in the proceedings. Even when favorable decisions have finally been obtained, some of the States affected have merely switched to discriminatory devices not covered by the federal decrees or have enacted difficult new tests designed to prolong the existing disparity between white and Negro registration. Alternatively, certain local officials have defied and evaded court orders or have simply closed their registration offices to freeze the voting rolls. The provision of the 1960 law authorizing registration by federal officers has had little impact on local maladministration because of its procedural complexities. . . .

The Voting Rights Act of 1965 reflects Congress' firm intention to rid the country of racial discrimination in voting. The heart of the Act is a complex scheme of stringent remedies aimed at areas where voting discrimination has been most flagrant. Section 4(a)–(d) lays down a formula defining the States and political subdivisions to which these new remedies apply. The first of the remedies, contained in § 4(a), is the suspension of literacy tests and similar voting qualifications for a period of five years from the last occurrence of substantial voting discrimination. Section 5 prescribes a second remedy, the suspension of all new voting regulations pending review by federal authorities to determine whether their use would prepetuate voting discrimination. The third remedy, covered in §§ 6(b), 7, 9, and 13(a), is the assignment of federal examiners on certification by the Attorney General to list qualified applicants who are thereafter entitled to vote in all elections.

Other provisions of the Act prescribe subsidiary cures for persistent voting discrimination. Section 8 authorizes the appointment of federal poll-watchers in places to which federal examiners have already been assigned. Section 10(d) excuses those made eligible to vote in sections of the country covered by § 4(b) of the Act from paying accumulated past poll taxes for state and local elections. Section 12(e) provides for balloting by persons denied access to the polls in areas where federal examiners have been appointed. . . .

After enduring nearly a century of widespread resistance to the Fifteenth Amendment, Congress has marshalled an array of potent weapons against the evil, with authority in the Attorney General to employ them effectively. Many of the areas directly affected by this development have indicated their willingness to abide by any restraints legitimately imposed upon them. We here hold that the portions of the Voting Rights Act properly before us are a valid means for carrying out the commands of the Fifteenth Amendment. Hopefully, millions of non-white Americans will now be able to participate for the first time on an equal basis in the government under which they live. We may finally look forward to the day when truly "[t]he right of citizens of the United States to vote shall not be denied or abridged by the United States or by any State on account of race, color, or previous condition of servitude."

The bill of complaint is dismissed.

Bill dismissed.

MR. JUSTICE BLACK, concurring and dissenting.

I agree with substantially all of the Court's opinion sustaining the power of Congress under § 2 of the Fifteenth Amendment to suspend state literacy tests and similar voting qualifications and to authorize the Attorney General to secure the appointment of federal examiners to register qualified voters in various sections of the country. . . . I have no doubt whatever as to the power of Congress under § 2 to enact the provisions of the Voting Rights Act of 1965 dealing with the suspension of state voting tests that have been used as notorious means to deny and abridge voting rights on racial grounds. . . .

Though, as I have said, I agree with most of the Court's conclusions,

I dissent from its holding that every part of § 5 of the Act is constitutional. Section 4(a), to which § 5 is linked, suspends for five years all literacy tests and similar devices in those States coming within the formula of § 4(b). Section 5 goes on to provide that a State covered by § 4(b) can in no way amend its constitution or laws relating to voting without first trying to persuade the Attorney General of the United States or the Federal District Court for the District of Columbia that the new proposed laws do not have the purpose and will not have the effect of denying the right to vote to citizens on account of their race or color. I think this section is unconstitutional. . . . Section 5, by providing that some of the States cannot pass state laws or adopt state constitutional amendments without first being compelled to beg federal authorities to approve their policies, so distorts our constitutional structure of government as to render any distinction drawn in the Constitution between state and federal power almost meaningless.

REYNOLDS V. SIMS

377 U.S. 533, 84 S. Ct. 1362, 12 L. Ed. 2d 506 (1964)

The apportionment plan for the Alabama legislature had been drawn up after the census of 1900. By 1964 senate districts varied from 15,000 to 634,000 in population, and house districts from 6,700 to 104,000. After the decision in *Baker* v. *Carr* the legislature prepared a reapportionment plan, which was rejected by the federal district court. The court then drew up its own plan, which both sides, voters and state officials, appealed to the Supreme Court.

MR. CHIEF JUSTICE WARREN delivered the opinion of the Court. . . .

Undeniably the Constitution of the United States protects the right of all qualified citizens to vote, in state as well as in federal elections. A consistent line of decisions by this Court in cases involving attempts to deny or restrict the right of suffrage has made this indelibly clear. It has been repeatedly recognized that all qualified voters have a constitutionally protected right to vote, Ex parte Yarbrough . . . and to have their votes counted, United States v. Mosley. . . . The right to vote can neither be denied outright, Guinn v. United States . . . nor destroyed by alteration of ballots, see United States v. Classic . . ., nor diluted by ballot-box stuffing, Ex parte Siebold. . . . The right to vote freely for the candidate of one's choice is of the essence of a democratic society, and any restrictions on that right strike at the heart of representative government. And the right of suffrage can be denied by a debasement or dilution of the weight of a citizen's vote just as effectively as by wholly prohibiting the free exercise of the franchise.

In Baker v. Carr we held that a claim asserted under the Equal Protection Clause challenging the constitutionality of a State's apportionment of seats in its legislature, on the ground that the right to vote of certain citizens was effectively impaired since debased and diluted, in effect presented a justiciable controversy subject to adjudication by federal courts. . . .

In Gray v. Sanders . . ., we held that the Georgia county unit system, applicable in statewide primary elections was unconstitutional since it resulted in a dilution of the weight of the votes of certain Georgia voters merely because of where they resided. After indicating that the Fifteenth and Nineteenth Amendments prohibit a State from over-weighting or diluting votes on the basis of race or sex, we stated:

> How then can one person be given twice or ten times the voting power of another person in a statewide election merely because he lives in a rural area or because he lives in the smallest rural county? Once the geographical unit for which a representative is to be chosen is designated, all who participate in the election are to have an equal vote—whatever their race, whatever their sex, whatever their occupation, whatever their income, and wherever their home may be in that geographical unit. This is required by the Equal Protection Clause of the Fourteenth Amendment. The concept of "we the people" under the Constitution visualizes no preferred class of voters but equality among those who meet the basic qualifications. The idea that every voter is equal to every other voter in his State, when he casts his ballot in favor of one of several competing candidates, underlies many of our decisions.

In Wesberry v. Sanders . . ., we held that attacks on the constitutionality of congressional districting plans enacted by state legislatures do not present nonjusticiable questions and should not be dismissed generally for "want of equity." We determined that the constitutional test for the validity of congressional districting schemes was one of the substantial equality of population among the various districts established by a state legislature for the election of members of the Federal House of Representatives.

In that case we decided that an apportionment of congressional seats which "contracts the value of some votes and expands that of others" is unconstitutional, since "the Federal Constitution intends that when qualified voters elect members of Congress each vote be given as much weight as any other vote. . . ." We concluded that the constitutional prescription for election of members of the House of Representatives "by the People," construed in its historical context, "means that as nearly as is practicable one man's vote in a congressional election is to be worth as much as another's." We further stated: . . .

> No right is more precious in a free country than that of having a voice in the election of those who make the laws under which, as good citizens, we must live. Other rights, even the most basic, are illusory if the right to vote is undermined. Our Constitution leaves

no room for classification of people in a way that unnecessarily abridges this right. . . .

Legislators represent people, not trees or acres. Legislators are elected by voters, not farms or cities or economic interests. As long as ours is a representative form of government, and our legislatures are those instruments of government elected directly by and directly representative of the people, the right to elect legislators in a free and unimpaired fashion is a bedrock of our political system. It could hardly be gainsaid that a constitutional claim had been asserted by an allegation that certain otherwise qualified voters had been entirely prohibited from voting for members of their state legislature. And, if a State should provide that the votes of citizens in one part of the State should be given two times, or five times, or 10 times the weight of votes of citizens in another part of the State, it could hardly be contended that the right to vote of those residing in the disfavored areas had not been effectively diluted. . . . Of course, the effect of state legislative districting schemes which give the same number of representatives to unequal numbers of constituents is identical. . . . One must be ever aware that the Constitution forbids "sophisticated as well as simple-minded modes of discrimination." Lane v. Wilson. . . . As we stated in Wesberry v. Sanders . . .:

> We do not believe that the Framers of the Constitution intended to permit the same vote-diluting discrimination to be accomplished through the device of districts containing widely varied numbers of inhabitants. To say that a vote is worth more in one district than in another would . . . run counter to our fundamental ideas of democratic government. . . .

Logically, in a society ostensibly grounded on representative government, it would seem reasonable that a majority of the people of a State could elect a majority of that State's legislators. To conclude differently, and to sanction minority control of state legislative bodies, would appear to deny majority rights in a way that far surpasses any possible denial of minority rights that might otherwise be thought to result. Since legislatures are responsible for enacting laws by which all citizens are to be governed, they should be bodies which are collectively responsive to the popular will. And the concept of equal protection has been traditionally viewed as requiring the uniform treatment of persons standing in the same relation to the governmental action questioned or challenged. With respect to the allocation of legislative representation, all voters, as citizens of a State, stand in the same relation regardless of where they live. Any suggested criteria for the differentiation of citizens are insufficient to justify any discrimination, as to the weight of their votes, unless relevant to the permissible purposes of legislative apportionment. Since the achieving of fair and effective representation for all citizens is concededly the basic aim of legislative apportionment, we conclude that the Equal

Protection Clause guarantees the opportunity for equal participation by all voters in the election of state legislators. Diluting the weight of voters because of place of residence impairs basic constitutional rights under the Fourteenth Amendment just as much as invidious discriminations based upon factors such as race, Brown v. Board of Education ... or economic status, Griffin v. Illinois. ... Our constitutional system amply provides for the protection of minorities by means other than giving them majority control of state legislatures. And the democratic ideals of equality and majority rule, which have served this Nation so well in the past, are hardly of any less significance for the present and the future.

We are told that the matter of apportioning representation in a state legislature is a complex and many-faceted one. We are advised that States can rationally consider factors other than population in apportioning legislative representation. We are admonished not to restrict the power of the States to impose differing views as to political philosophy on their citizens. We are cautioned about the dangers of entering into political thickets and mathematical quagmires. Our answer is this: a denial of constitutionally protected rights demands judicial protection; our oath and our office require no less of us. ...

To the extent that a citizen's right to vote is debased, he is that much less a citizen. The fact that an individual lives here or there is not a legitimate reason for overweighting or diluting the efficacy of his vote. ...

We hold that, as a basic constitutional standard, the Equal Protection Clause requires that the seats in both houses of a bicameral state legislature must be apportioned on a population basis. ...

The system of representation in the two Houses of the Federal Congress is one ingrained in our Constitution, as part of the law of the land. It is one conceived out of compromise and concession indispensable to the establishment of our federal republic. Arising from unique historical circumstances, it is based on the consideration that in establishing our type of federalism a group of formerly independent States bound themselves together under one national government. Admittedly, the original 13 States surrendered some of their sovereignty in agreeing to join together "to form a more perfect Union." But at the heart of our constitutional system remains the concept of separate and distinct governmental entities which have delegated some, but not all, of their formerly held powers to the single national government. The fact that almost three-fourths of our present States were never in fact independently sovereign does not detract from our view that the so-called federal analogy is inapplicable as a sustaining precedent for state legislative apportionments. ...

Political subdivisions of States—counties, cities, or whatever—never were and never have been considered as sovereign entities. Rather, they have been traditionally regarded as subordinate governmental instrumentalities created by the State to assist in the carrying out of state governmental functions. ...

We do not believe that the concept of bicameralism is rendered anachronistic and meaningless when the predominant basis of representation in the two state legislative bodies is required to be the same—population. A prime reason for bicameralism, modernly considered, is to insure mature and deliberate consideration of, and to prevent precipitate action on, proposed legislative measures. Simply because the controlling criterion for apportioning representation is required to be the same in both houses does not mean that there will be no differences in the complexion of the two bodies. Different constituencies can be represented in the two houses. One body could be composed of single-member districts while the other could have at least some multimember districts. The length of terms of the legislators in the separate bodies could differ. The numerical size of the two bodies could be made to differ, even significantly, and the geographical size of districts from which legislators are elected could also be made to differ. And apportionment in one house could be arranged so as to balance off minor inequities in the representation of certain areas in the other house. . . .

By holding that as a federal constitutional requisite both houses of a state legislature must be apportioned on a population basis, we mean that the Equal Protection Clause requires that a State make an honest and good faith effort to construct districts, as nearly of equal population as is practicable. We realize that it is a practical impossibility to arrange legislative districts so that each one has an identical number of residents, or citizens, or voters. Mathematical exactness or precision is hardly a workable constitutional requirement.

We affirm the judgment below and remand the cases for further proceedings consistent with the views stated in this opinion.

It is so ordered.

Mr. Justice Clark, concurring in the affirmance.

The Court goes much beyond the necessities of this case in laying down a new "equal population" principle for state legislative apportionment. This principle seems to be an offshoot of Gray v. Sanders . . ., i.e., "one person, one vote," modified by the "nearly as is practicable" admonition of Wesberry v. Sanders. . . . Whether "nearly as is practicable" means "one person, one vote" qualified by "mathematical nicety" is not clear from the majority's use of these vague and meaningless phrases. But whatever the standard, the Court applies it to each house of the State Legislature.

It seems to me that all the Court need say in this case is that each plan considered by the trial court is "a crazy quilt," clearly revealing invidious discrimination in each house of the Legislature and therefore violative of the Equal Protection Clause. . . .

I, therefore, do not reach the question of the so-called "federal analogy." But in my view, if one house of the State Legislature meets the population standard, representation in the other house might include some departure from it so as to take into account, on a rational basis, other factors in order to afford some representation to the various elements of the State. . . .

MR. JUSTICE STEWART . . .

I would affirm the judgment of the District Court holding that this apportionment violated the Equal Protection Clause. . . .

MR. JUSTICE HARLAN, dissenting. . . .

The Court's elaboration of its new "constitutional" doctrine indicates how far—and how unwisely—it has strayed from the appropriate bounds of its authority. The consequence of today's decision is that in all but the handful of States which may already satisfy the new requirements the local District Court or, it may be, the state courts, are given blanket authority and the constitutional duty to supervise apportionment of the State Legislatures. It is difficult to imagine a more intolerable and inappropriate interference by the judiciary with the independent legislatures of the States. . . .

With these cases the Court approaches the end of the third round set in motion by the complaint filed in Baker v. Carr. What is done today deepens my conviction that judicial entry into this realm is profoundly ill-advised and constitutionally impermissible. As I have said before, Wesberry v. Sanders . . . I believe that the vitality of our political system, on which in the last analysis all else depends, is weakened by reliance on the judiciary for political reform; in time a complacent body politic may result.

These decisions also cut deeply into the fabric of our federalism. What must follow from them may eventually appear to be the product of state legislatures. Nevertheless, no thinking person can fail to recognize that the aftermath of these cases, however desirable it may be thought in itself, will have been achieved at the cost of a radical alteration in the relationship between the States and the Federal Government, more particularly the Federal Judiciary. Only one who has an overbearing impatience with the federal system and its political processes will believe that that cost was not too high or was inevitable.

Finally, these decisions give support to a current mistaken view of the Constitution and the constitutional function of this Court. This view, in a nutshell, is that every major social ill in this country can find its cure in some constitutional "principle," and that this Court should "take the lead" in promoting reform when other branches of government fail to act. The Constitution is not a panacea for every blot upon the public welfare, nor should this Court, ordained as a judicial body, be thought of as a general haven for reform movements. The Constitution is an instrument of government, fundamental to which is the premise that in a diffusion of governmental authority lies the greatest promise that this Nation will realize liberty for all its citizens. This Court, limited in function in accordance with that premise, does not serve its high purpose when it exceeds its authority, even to satisfy justified impatience with the slow workings of the political process. For when, in the name of constitutional interpretation, the Court adds something to the Constitution that was deliberately excluded from it, the Court in reality substitutes its view of what should be so for the amending process. . . .

GUIDE TO THE STUDY
OF SUPREME COURT
DECISIONS

Judicial decisions are identified by the names of the parties, as *Gibbons* v. *Ogden* or *Kent* v. *Dulles*. The "v." is an abbreviation of the Latin "versus," here translated as "against." Generally, the first name is that of the plaintiff, the one who started the proceedings, and the second is that of the defendant, of whom the plaintiff complains and against whom he seeks relief. On appeal, the party asking for review by a higher court is known as the appellant or petitioner, and his opponent as the appellee or respondent. If it is the defendant who appeals, the order of the names in the caption may be reversed and the defendant's, as appellant or petitioner, placed first.

The usual lawsuit has two parties of equal standing and opposed interests. In some proceedings, however, there will be only one party, at least in the initial stages. Anyone seeking a writ of habeas corpus directly from the Supreme Court must start by asking leave to file his petition. Since at this point no other party is or has been directly involved, the papers will be headed simply *Ex parte Jones*. "Ex parte" is lawyers' Latin meaning "on the part of" or "from the side of." The papers and decisions in many proceedings which do not necessarily have two adversary parties of the usual kind may also be entitled *In re Jones*, that is, "in the matter of Jones."

Supreme Court decisions can be identified by reference to the set of printed reports in which they are published. The citation for *Kent* v. *Dulles* is 357 U.S. 116. The first number indicates volume; the initials U.S. refer to the United States Reports, the official series published by the Government Printing Office; and the final number indicates the page where the decision begins.

Supreme Court decisions are also collected in two other sets of reports issued by commercial publishing houses. One is the Supreme Court Reporter, abbreviated S. Ct.; the citation for *Kent* v. *Dulles* in this source is 78 S. Ct. 1113. The other is known as Lawyers Edition, cited as L. Ed.; *Kent* v. *Dulles* is 2 L. Ed. 2d 1204.

Up to 1874, Supreme Court cases were identified not by the name of the series or set of volumes in which they were published, but by the name of the reporter who collected them. The citation for *Gibbons* v. *Ogden*, decided in 1824, is 9 Wheat. 1. "Wheat." is an abbreviation for Wheaton, whose twelve volumes of reports cover the years 1816–1827. The complete list of these early reporters, with the customary abbreviations, is as follows:

Dallas (Dall.)	1789–1800	U.S. 1–4
Cranch (Cr.)	1801–1815	5–13
Wheaton (Wheat.)	1816–1827	14–25
Peters (Pet.)	1828–1842	26–41
Howard (How.)	1843–1860	42–65
Black (Bl.)	1861–1862	66–67
Wallace (Wall.)	1863–1874	68–90

These volumes, ninety in all, have also been assigned numbers in the U.S. series, as indicated.

Decisions of the United States Courts of Appeals are published in the Federal Reporter, now in its second series (F. 2d). District court judges do not always file formal written opinions, but may do so, and these are collected in the Federal Supplement (F. Supp.).

The process of summarizing or abstracting a court decision is referred to as "briefing" the opinion. A sample brief is given below.

McCULLOCH v. MARYLAND

4 Wheat. 316 (1819)

(1) *Character of the action.* From decision against him in Court of Appeals of state of Maryland, McCulloch appealed on writ of error to United States Supreme Court under section 25, Judiciary Act of 1789.

(2) *Facts.* Congress in 1816 passed act incorporating the Second Bank of the United States. Maryland in 1818 passed an act taxing all banks or branches not chartered by the state at prohibitory rates. Tax was on all notes issued by such banks or in lieu thereof a flat tax of $15,000 per year, with $500 penalty for each violation. McCulloch, cashier of Maryland branch of the Bank of the United States, issued notes and refused to pay the tax. Maryland brought suit against him to recover the penalties and obtained decision against McCulloch.

(3) *Issues.* (*a*) Has Congress power to incorporate the Bank of the United States? Yes. (*b*) Has Maryland the right to levy this tax against the bank chartered by Congress? No.

(4) *Decision.* Judgment of Court of Appeals of Maryland is reversed and annulled.

(5) *Opinion or reasons for the decision.* Marshall, C.J.: Has Congress power to charter bank? Constitution is not a mere compact of sovereign states, but established a supreme national government. Admittedly Congress is not expressly given power to issue charters of incorporation. But Tenth Amendment does not limit Congress's powers to those *expressly* granted. Congress is expressly granted power to lay and collect taxes, borrow money, regulate commerce, declare war, raise and support armies. Congress must have means to accomplish these ends. Power of issuing charters of incorporation only an incidental power. Congress expressly given power "to make all laws necessary and proper for carrying foregoing powers into execution." This is a grant of power, not a restriction. "Necessary and proper" does not limit Congress to those means which are indispensable but entitles it to use all those which are convenient and appropriate. Charter of bank is appropriate.

Can Maryland lay tax against the bank? Bank an instrument of the national government, which having power to create it also has power to preserve it. But state power to tax involves power to destroy it. National constitution and laws supreme and state laws repugnant thereto are void. No argument to say that we should assume Maryland will not use tax power to destroy. Therefore tax is unconstitutional.

(6) *Concurring or dissenting opinions.* None.

(7) *Comments.* This decision stems from Hamilton's opinion on constitutionality of the First Bank of the United States; cf. also Jefferson's opinion. It is the classic statement of the doctrines of implied powers of the national government, national supremacy over the states, and the function of the Court as umpire of the federal system. Cf. the Virginia and Kentucky Resolutions. Its influence on later statesmen such as Webster and Lincoln is incalculable.

A GLOSSARY OF LEGAL WORDS

AND PHRASES

FREQUENTLY FOUND

IN SUPREME COURT CASES

Advisory Opinion: An opinion rendered in a hypothetical case.

Amicus Curiae: Friend of the court, a third party who presents a brief to a court on behalf of one or the other of the parties in a case.

Appeal: A request from the losing party in a case that the decision be reviewed by a higher court. Acceptance of the request and issuance of a writ of appeal is mandatory for the higher court.

Appellant: The party who appeals a decision from a lower to a higher court.

Appellee: The party against whom an appeal is taken.

Brief: The written or printed argument presented to the court by counsel.

Certification: A process whereby a lower court requests a higher court to decide certain questions present in a given case pending final decision by the lower court.

Certiorari: A request from the losing party in a case that the decision be reviewed by a higher court. Acceptance of the request and issuance of a writ of certiorari is discretionary with the higher court.

Declaratory Judgment: A decision of a court which declares the legal rights of the parties to the case before any injury has been suffered by either of the parties. A declaratory-judgment action differs from the normal decision in that the court renders its judgment without a specific order.

Defendant: The party against whom legal action is taken; particularly, a person accused or convicted of a criminal offense.

Demurrer: A response which challenges the sufficiency of a complaint. It says, "Even if everything you say in your complaint is true, you still have no right to obtain a judgment against me."

Diversity Jurisdiction: That aspect of the jurisdiction of the federal courts which applies to suits between citizens of different states.

Ejusdem Generis: Of the same kind. In an enumeration of certain things or conditions which also contains a catch-all phrase, the latter is limited to things or conditions of the same type as those enumerated. Thus, a listing of physical properties which contains the phrase, "and any other thing," would not be construed to apply to intangible matters.

Et Al.:   And another; and others.

Ex Parte: A hearing or examination in the presence of only one of the parties to a case, such as a writ of *habeas corpus* (q.v.).

Ex Rel.:   By or on the information of. Used in case titles to designate the person at whose insistence the government or a public official is acting.

Federal Question: A case which contains a major issue involving the United States Constitution or a provision of an Act of Congress or United States treaty. The jurisdiction of the federal courts is governed, in part, by the existence of a federal question.

Habeas Corpus: You have the body. A writ to an official having custody of another ordering him to produce the prisoner for the purpose of allowing the court to ascertain the legality of the prisoner's detention.

In Forma Pauperis: In the form of a pauper; as a poor person. Permission to bring legal action without the payment of required fees for counsel, writs, transcripts, subpoenas, and the like.

In Personam: Against a person. A legal proceeding instituted to obtain decrees or judgments against a person.

In Re: In the matter of; concerning.

In Rem: Against a thing. A legal proceeding instituted to obtain decrees or judgments against property.

Injunction: A writ prohibiting an individual or organization from performing some specified action.

Mandamus: A writ ordering an individual or organization to perform some specified action.

Miscellaneous Docket: The docket of the United States Supreme Court on which are listed all cases filed *in forma pauperis* (q.v.).

Moot Question: Where the result sought by the lawsuit has occurred, or conditions have so changed, as to make it impossible for the court to grant the relief sought.

Obiter Dicta: Occasionally referred to as either "obiter," "dicta," or "dictum." An assertion made in an opinion of a court which is not pertinent to the decision made in the case.

Per Curiam: By the court. An opinion of the court which is authored by the justices collectively.

Petitioner: The party who brings an action; the complainant.

Plaintiff: The party who brings an action; the complainant.

Political Question: Issues in a case which the Court believes should be decided by a nonjudicial unit of government.

Prima Facie: At first glance; without investigation or evaluation. That which, if not rebutted, is sufficient to establish a fact or case.

Probable Cause: The information a police officer must have in order to be entitled to obtain an arrest or search warrant from a judge, or be permitted to arrest or search without a warrant.

Ratio Decidendi: The basis of a decision. The grounds upon which a case has been decided.

Res Judicata: An adjudicated matter. A legal issue which has been decided by a court.

Respondent: The party against whom legal action is taken; the party against whom a writ of *certiorari* (q.v.) is sought.

Right: That which a person is entitled to keep and enjoy; to be protected by law in its enjoyment. A right constitutes a claim when it is not in one's possession. The word "right" also signifies an interest when used in regard to property. "Right" in this sense entitles a person to hold or convey his property at pleasure.

Standing: The qualifications needed to bring legal action. These qualifications relate to the existence of a controversy in which the plaintiff (q.v.) himself has suffered or is about to suffer an injury to or infringement upon a legally protected right (q.v.) which a court is competent to redress.

Stare Decisis: To stand on what has been decided; to adhere to the decision of previous cases. It is a rule, sometimes departed from, that a point settled in a previous case becomes a precedent which should be followed in subsequent cases decided by the same court.

Sub Silentio: Under silence; without notice being taken.

Summary Proceeding: A judicial action, usually a judgment or decision, which is taken without benefit of a formal hearing. Summary decisions of the Supreme Court are those made without the Court having heard oral argument.

Tort: A willful or negligent injury to a plaintiff's person, property, or reputation.

Ultra Vires: An action beyond the legal power or authority of a corporation, governmental agency, or official.

Venue: The jurisdiction where a case is to be heard. Normally a case is heard by the relevant court in whose district the crime or the cause of action occurred.

Writ: A formal order from a court enjoining an individual or organization to do, or to refrain from, some specified action.

Writ of Error: A request for review of a decision by a higher court. Acceptance of the request is mandatory for the higher court. Only matters of law and not of fact are subject to review under this writ. The writ of error was abolished in 1925 as a means of bringing cases to the United States Supreme Court.

CONSTITUTION
OF THE UNITED STATES
OF AMERICA

We the people of the United States, in Order to form a more perfect Union, establish Justice, insure domestic Tranquility, provide for the common defence, promote the general Welfare, and secure the Blessings of Liberty to ourselves and our Posterity, do ordain and establish this CONSTITUTION for the United States of America.

ARTICLE I

SECTION 1. All legislative Powers herein granted shall be vested in a Congress of the United States, which shall consist of a Senate and House of Representatives.

SECTION 2. *1* The House of Representatives shall be composed of Members chosen every second Year by the People of the several States, and the Electors in each State shall have the Qualifications requisite for Electors of the most numerous Branch of the State Legislature.

2 No Person shall be a Representative who shall not have attained to the Age of twenty five Years, and been seven Years a Citizen of the United States, and who shall not, when elected, be an Inhabitant of that State in which he shall be chosen.

3 Representatives and direct Taxes[1] shall be apportioned among the several States which may be included within this Union according to their

[1]Modified as to direct taxes by the Sixteenth Amendment.

respective Numbers, which shall be determined by adding to the whole Number of free Persons, including those bound to Service for a Term of Years, and excluding Indians not taxed, three fifths of all other Persons.[2] The actual Enumeration shall be made within three Years after the first Meeting of the Congress of the United States, and within every subsequent Term of ten Years, in such Manner as they shall by Law direct. The Number of Representatives shall not exceed one for every thirty Thousand, but each State shall have at Least one Representative; and until such enumeration shall be made, the State of New Hampshire shall be entitled to chuse three, Massachusetts eight, Rhode-Island and Providence Plantations one, Connecticut five, New-York six, New Jersey four, Pennsylvania eight, Delaware one, Maryland six, Virginia ten, North Carolina five, South Carolina, five, and Georgia three.

4 When vacancies happen in the Representation from any State, the Executive Authority thereof shall issue Writs of Election to fill such Vacancies.

5 The House of Representatives shall chuse their Speaker and other Officers; and shall have the sole Power of Impeachment.

SECTION 3. *1* The Senate of the United States shall be composed of two Senators from each State, chosen by the Legislature thereof,[3] for six Years; and each Senator shall have one Vote.

2 Immediately after they shall be assembled in Consequence of the first Election, they shall be divided as equally as may be into three Classes. The Seats of the Senators of the first Class shall be vacated at the Expiration of the second Year, of the second Class at the Expiration of the fourth Year, and of the third Class at the Expiration of the sixth Year, so that one third may be chosen every second Year; and if Vacancies happen by Resignation, or otherwise, during the Recess of the Legislature of any State, the Executive thereof may make temporary Appointments until the next Meeting of the Legislature, which shall then fill such Vacancies.

3 No Person shall be a Senator who shall not have attained to the Age of thirty Years, and been nine Years a Citizen of the United States, and who shall not, when elected, be an Inhabitant of that State for which he shall be chosen.

4 The Vice President of the United States shall be President of the Senate, but shall have no Vote, unless they be equally divided.

5 The Senate shall chuse their other Officers, and also a President pro tempore, in the Absence of the Vice President, or when he shall exercise the Office of President of the United States.

6 The Senate shall have the sole Power to try all Impeachments. When sitting for that Purpose, they shall be on Oath or Affirmation. When the President of the United States is tried, the Chief Justice shall preside: And no Person shall be convicted without the Concurrence of two thirds of the Members present.

[2]Replaced by the Fourteenth Amendment.
[3]Modified by the Seventeenth Amendment.

7 Judgment in Cases of Impeachment shall not extend further than to removal from office, and disqualification to hold and enjoy any Office of honor, Trust or Profit under the United States: but the Party convicted shall nevertheless be liable and subject to Indictment, Trial, Judgment and Punishment, according to Law.

Section 4. *1* The Times, Places and Manner of holding Elections for Senators and Representatives, shall be prescribed in each State by the Legislature thereof; but the Congress may at any time by Law make or alter such Regulations, except as to the Places of chusing Senators.

2 The Congress shall assemble at least once in every Year, and such Meeting shall be on the first Monday in December, unless they shall by Law appoint a different Day.[4]

Section 5. *1* Each House shall be the Judge of the Elections, Returns and Qualifications of its own Members, and a Majority of each shall constitute a Quorum to do Business; but a smaller Number may adjourn from day to day, and may be authorized to compel the attendance of absent Members, in such Manner, and under such Penalties as each House may provide.

2 Each House may determine the Rules of its Proceedings, punish its Members for Disorderly Behaviour, and, with the Concurrence of two thirds, expel a Member.

3 Each House shall keep a Journal of its Proceedings, and from time to time publish the same, excepting such Parts as may in their Judgment require Secrecy; and the Yeas and Nays of the Members of either House on any question shall, at the Desire of one fifth of those Present, be entered on the Journal.

4 Neither House, during the Session of Congress, shall, without the Consent of the other, adjourn for more than three days, nor to any other Place than that in which the two Houses shall be sitting.

Section 6. *1* The Senators and Representatives shall receive a Compensation for their Services, to be ascertained by Law, and paid out of the Treasury of the United States. They shall in all Cases, except Treason, Felony and Breach of the Peace, be privileged from Arrest during their Attendance at the Session of their respective Houses, and in going to and returning from the same; and for any Speech or Debate in either House, they shall not be questioned in any other Place.

2 No Senator or Representative shall, during the Time for which he was elected, be appointed to any civil Office under the Authority of the United States, which shall have been created, or the Emoluments whereof shall have been encreased during such time; and no Person holding any Office under the United States, shall be a member of either House during his Continuance in Office.

[4]Modified by the Twentieth Amendment.

SECTION 7. *1* All Bills for raising Revenue shall originate in the House of Representatives; but the Senate may propose or concur with Amendments as on other Bills.

2 Every Bill which shall have passed the House of Representatives and the Senate, shall, before it become a Law, be presented to the President of the United States; If he approve he shall sign it, but if not he shall return it, with his Objections to that House in which it shall have originated, who shall enter the Objections at large on their Journal, and proceed to reconsider it. If after such Reconsideration two thirds of that House shall agree to pass the Bill, it shall be sent, together with the Objections, to the other House, by which it shall likewise be reconsidered, and if approved by two thirds of that House, it shall become a Law. But in all such Cases the Votes of both Houses shall be determined by Yeas and Nays, and the Names of the Persons voting for and against the Bill shall be entered on the Journal of each House respectively. If any Bill shall not be returned by the President within ten Days (Sundays excepted) after it shall have been presented to him, the same shall be a Law, in like Manner as if he had signed it, unless the Congress by their Adjournment prevent its Return, in which Case it shall not be a Law.

3 Every Order, Resolution, or Vote to which the Concurrence of the Senate and House of Representatives may be necessary (except on a question of Adjournment) shall be presented to the President of the United States; and before the same shall take Effect, shall be approved by him, or being disapproved by him, shall be repassed by two thirds of the Senate and House of Representatives, according to the Rules and Limitations prescribed in the Case of a Bill.

SECTION 8. The Congress shall have Power *1* To lay and collect Taxes, Duties, Imposts and Excises, to pay the Debts and provide for the common Defence and general Welfare of the United States; but all Duties, Imposts and Excises shall be uniform throughout the United States;

2 To borrow Money on the credit of the United States;

3 To regulate Commerce with foreign Nations, and among the several States, and with the Indian Tribes;

4 To establish an uniform Rule of Naturalization, and uniform Laws on the subject of Bankruptcies throughout the United States;

5 To coin Money, regulate the Value thereof, and of foreign Coin, and fix the Standard of Weights and Measures;

6 To provide for the Punishment of counterfeiting the Securities and current Coin of the United States;

7 To establish Post Offices and post Roads;

8 To promote the Progress of Science and useful Arts, by securing for limited Times to Authors and Inventors the exclusive Right to their respective Writings and Discoveries;

9 To constitute Tribunals inferior to the supreme Court;

10 To define and punish Piracies and Felonies committed on the high Seas, and Offences against the Law of Nations;

11 To declare War, grant Letters of Marque and Reprisal, and make Rules concerning Captures on Land and Water;

12 To raise and support Armies, but no Appropriation of Money to that Use shall be for a longer Term than two Years;

13 To provide and maintain a Navy;

14 To make Rules for the Government and Regulation of the land and naval Forces;

15 To provide for calling forth the Militia to execute the Laws of the Union, suppress Insurrections and repel Invasions;

16 To provide for organizing, arming, and disciplining, the Militia, and for governing such Part of them as may be employed in the Service of the United States, reserving to the States respectively, the Appointment of the Officers, and the Authority of training the Militia according to the discipline prescribed by Congress;

17 To exercise exclusive Legislation in all Cases whatsoever, over such District (not exceeding ten Miles square) as may, by Cession of particular States, and the Acceptance of Congress, become the Seat of the Government of the United States, and to exercise like Authority over all Places purchased by the Consent of the Legislature of the State in which the same shall be, for the Erection of Forts, Magazines, Arsenals, dock-Yards, and other needful Buildings;—And

18 To make all Laws which shall be necessary and proper for carrying into Execution the foregoing Powers, and all other Powers vested by this Constitution in the Government of the United States, or in any Department or Officer thereof.

SECTION 9. *1* The Migration or Importation of such Persons as any of the States now existing shall think proper to admit, shall not be prohibited by the Congress prior to the Year one thousand eight hundred and eight, but a Tax or duty may be imposed on such Importation, not exceeding ten dollars for each Person.

2 The Privilege of the Writ of Habeas Corpus shall not be suspended, unless when in Cases of Rebellion or Invasion the public Safety may require it.

3 No Bill of Attainder or ex post facto Law shall be passed.

4 No Capitation, or other direct, Tax shall be laid, unless in Proportion to the Census or Enumeration herein before directed to be taken.[5]

5 No Tax or Duty shall be laid on Articles exported from any State.

6 No Preference shall be given by any Regulation of Commerce or Revenue to the Ports of one State over those of another: nor shall Vessels bound to, or from, one State, be obliged to enter, clear, or pay Duties in another.

---

[5]Modified by the Sixteenth Amendment.

7 No Money shall be drawn from the Treasury, but in Consequence of Appropriations made by Law; and a regular Statement and Account of the Receipts and Expenditures of all public Money shall be published from time to time.

8 No Title of Nobility shall be granted by the United States; And no Person holding any Office of Profit or Trust under them, shall, without the Consent of the Congress, accept of any present, Emolument, Office, or Title, of any kind whatever, from any King, Prince, or foreign State.

SECTION 10. *1* No State shall enter into any Treaty, Alliance, or Confederation; grant Letters of Marque and Reprisal; coin Money; emit Bills of Credit; make any Thing but gold and silver Coin a Tender in Payment of Debts; pass any Bill of Attainder, ex post facto Law, or Law impairing the Obligation of Contracts, or grant any Title of Nobility.

2 No State shall, without the Consent of the Congress, lay any Imposts or Duties on Imports or Exports, except what may be absolutely necessary for executing its inspection Laws; and the net Produce of all Duties and Imposts, laid by any State on Imports or Exports, shall be for the Use of the Treasury of the United States; and all such Laws shall be subject to the Revision and Controul of the Congress.

3 No State shall, without the Consent of Congress, lay any Duty of Tonnage, keep Troops, or Ships of War in time of Peace, enter into any Agreement or Compact with another State, or with a foreign Power, or engage in War, unless actually invaded, or in such imminent Danger as will not admit of delay.

ARTICLE II

SECTION 1. *1* The executive Power shall be vested in a President of the United States of America. He shall hold his office during the Term of four Years, and, together with the Vice President, chosen for the same Term, be elected, as follows.

2 Each State shall appoint, in such Manner as the Legislature thereof may direct, a Number of Electors, equal to the whole Number of Senators and Representatives to which the State may be entitled in the Congress: but no Senator or Representative, or Person holding an Office of Trust or Profit under the United States, shall be appointed an Elector.

3 The Electors shall meet in their respective States, and vote by Ballot for two Persons, of whom one at least shall not be an inhabitant of the same State with themselves. And they shall make a List of all the Persons voted for, and of the Number of Votes for each; which List they shall sign and certify, and transmit sealed to the Seat of Government of the United States, directed to the President of the Senate. The President of the Senate shall, in the Presence of the Senate and House of Representatives, open all the Certificates, and the Votes shall then be counted. The Person having the greatest Number of Votes shall be the President, if such

Number be a Majority of the whole Number of Electors appointed; and if there be more than one who have such Majority, and have an equal Number of Votes, then the House of Representatives shall immediately chuse by Ballot one of them for President; and if no Person have a Majority, then from the five highest on the List the said House shall in like Manner chuse the President. But in chusing the President, the Votes shall be taken by States, the Representation from each State having one Vote; A quorum for this Purpose shall consist of a Member or Members from two thirds of the States, and a Majority of all the States shall be necessary to a Choice. In every Case, after the Choice of the President, the Person having the greatest Number of Votes of the Electors shall be the Vice President. But if there should remain two or more who have equal Votes, the Senate shall chuse from them by Ballot the Vice President.[6]

4 The Congress may determine the Time of chusing the Electors, and the Day on which they shall give their Votes; which Day shall be the same throughout the United States.

5 No Person except a natural born Citizen, or a Citizen of the United States, at the time of the Adoption of this Constitution, shall be eligible to the Office of President; neither shall any Person be eligible to that Office who shall not have attained to the Age of thirty five Years, and been fourteen Years a Resident within the United States.

6 In Case of the Removal of the President from Office, or of his Death, Resignation, or Inability to discharge the Powers and Duties of the said Office, the Same shall devolve on the Vice President, and the Congress may by Law provide for the Case of Removal, Death, Resignation, or Inability, both of the President and Vice President, declaring what officer shall then act as President, and such Officer shall act accordingly, until the Disability be removed, or a President shall be elected.

7 The President shall, at stated Times, receive for his Services, a Compensation, which shall neither be encreased nor diminished during the Period for which he shall have been elected, and he shall not receive within that Period any other Emolument from the United States, or any of them.

8 Before he enter on the Execution of his Office, he shall take the following Oath or Affirmation:—"I do solemnly swear (or affirm) that I will faithfully execute the Office of President of the United States, and will to the best of my Ability, preserve, protect and defend the Constitution of the United States."

SECTION 2. *1* The President shall be Commander in Chief of the Army and Navy of the United States, and of the Militia of the several States, when called into the actual Service of the United States; he may require the Opinion, in writing, of the principal Officer in each of the

[6]This paragraph was replaced in 1804 by the Twelfth Amendment.

executive Departments, upon any Subject relating to the Duties of their respective Offices, and he shall have Power to grant Reprieves and Pardons for Offences against the United States, except in Cases of Impeachment.

2 He shall have Power, by and with the Advice and Consent of the Senate, to make Treaties, provided two thirds of the Senators present concur; and he shall nominate, and by and with the Advice and Consent of the Senate, shall appoint Ambassadors, other public Ministers and Consuls, Judges of the supreme Court, and all other Officers of the United States, whose Appointments are not herein otherwise provided for, and which shall be established by Law: but the Congress may by Law vest the Appointment of such inferior Officers, as they think proper, in the President alone, in the Courts of Law, or in the Heads of Departments.

3 The President shall have Power to fill up all Vacancies that may happen during the Recess of the Senate, by granting Commissions which shall expire at the End of their next Session.

SECTION 3. He shall from time to time give to the Congress Information of the State of the Union, and recommend to their Consideration such Measures as he shall judge necessary and expedient; he may, on extraordinary Occasions, convene both Houses, or either of them, and in Case of Disagreement between them, with Respect to the Time of Adjournment, he may adjourn them to such Time as he shall think proper; he shall receive Ambassadors and other public Ministers; he shall take Care that the Laws be faithfully executed, and shall Commission all the Officers of the United States.

SECTION 4. The President, Vice President and all civil Officers of the United States, shall be removed from Office on Impeachment for, and Conviction of, Treason, Bribery, or other high Crimes and Misdemeanors.

ARTICLE III

SECTION 1. The Judicial Power of the United States, shall be vested in one supreme Court, and in such inferior Courts as the Congress may from time to time ordain and establish. The Judges, both of the supreme and inferior Courts, shall hold their Offices during good Behaviour, and shall, at stated Times, receive for their Services, a Compensation, which shall not be diminished during their Continuance in Office.

SECTION 2. 1 The Judicial Power shall extend to all Cases, in Law and Equity, arising under this Constitution, the Laws of the United States, and Treaties made, or which shall be made, under their Authority;—to all

Cases affecting Ambassadors, other public Ministers and Consuls;—to all Cases of admiralty and maritime Jurisdiction;—to Controversies to which the United States shall be a Party;—to Controversies between two or more States;—between a State and Citizens of another State;[7]—between Citizens of different States;—between Citizens of the same State claiming Lands under Grants of different states, and between a State, or the Citizens thereof, and foreign States, Citizens or Subjects.

2 In all Cases affecting Ambassadors, other public Ministers and Consuls, and those in which a State shall be Party, the supreme Court shall have original Jurisdiction. In all the other Cases before mentioned, the Supreme Court shall have appellate Jurisdiction, both as to Law and Fact, with such Exceptions, and under such Regulations as the Congress shall make.

3 The Trial of all Crimes, except in Cases of Impeachment, shall be by Jury; and such Trial shall be held in the State where the said Crimes shall have been committed; but when not committed within any State, the Trial shall be at such Place or Places as the Congress may by Law have directed.

Section 3. *1* Treason against the United States, shall consist only in levying War against them, or in adhering to their Enemies, giving them Aid and Comfort. No Person shall be convicted of Treason unless on the Testimony of two Witnesses to the same overt Act, or on Confession in open Court.

2 The Congress shall have Power to declare the Punishment of Treason, but no Attainder of Treason shall work Corruption of Blood, or Forfeiture except during the Life of the Person attainted.

ARTICLE IV

Section 1. Full Faith and Credit shall be given in each State to the public Acts, Records, and judicial Proceedings of every other State. And the Congress may by general Laws prescribe the Manner in which such Acts, Records and Proceedings shall be proved, and the Effect thereof.

Section 2. *1* The Citizens of each State shall be entitled to all Privileges and Immunities of Citizens in the several States.

2 A Person charged in any State with Treason, Felony, or other Crime, who shall flee from Justice, and be found in another State, shall on Demand of the executive Authority of the State from which he fled, be delivered up, to be removed to the State having Jurisdiction of the Crime.

3 No Person held to Service or Labour in one State, under the Laws thereof, escaping into another, shall, in Consequence of any Law or

[7]Restricted by the Eleventh Amendment.

Regulation therein, be discharged from such Service or Labour, but shall be delivered up on Claim of the Party to whom such Service or Labour may be due.

SECTION 3. *1* New States may be admitted by the Congress into this Union; but no new State shall be formed or erected within the Jurisdiction of any other States; nor any State be formed by the Junction of two or more States, or Parts of States, without the Consent of the Legislatures of the States concerned as well as of the Congress.

2 The Congress shall have Power to dispose of and make all needful Rules and Regulations respecting the Territory or other Property belonging to the United States; and nothing in this Constitution shall be so construed as to Prejudice any Claims of the United States, or of any particular State.

SECTION 4. The United States shall guarantee to every State in this Union a Republican Form of Government, and shall protect each of them against Invasion; and on Application of the Legislature, or of the Executive (when the Legislature cannot be convened) against domestic Violence.

ARTICLE V

The Congress, whenever two thirds of both Houses shall deem it necessary, shall propose Amendments to this Constitution, or, on the Application of the Legislatures of two thirds of the several States, shall call a Convention for proposing Amendments, which, in either Case, shall be valid to all Intents and Purposes, as Part of this Constitution, when ratified by the Legislatures of three fourths of the several States, or by Conventions in three fourths thereof, as the one or the other Mode of Ratification may be proposed by the Congress; Provided that no Amendment which may be made prior to the Year One thousand eight hundred and eight shall in any Manner affect the first and fourth Clauses in the Ninth Section of the first Article; and that no State, without its Consent, shall be deprived of its equal Suffrage in the Senate.

ARTICLE VI

1 All Debts contracted and Engagements entered into, before the Adoption of this Constitution, shall be as valid against the United States under this Constitution, as under the Confederation.

2 This Constitution, and the Laws of the United States which shall be made in Pursuance thereof; and all Treaties made, or which shall be made, under the Authority of the United States, shall be the supreme Law of the Land; and the Judges in every State shall be bound thereby, any Thing in the Constitution or Laws of any State to the Contrary notwithstanding.

3 The Senators and Representatives before mentioned, and the Members of the several State Legislatures, and all executive and judicial Officers, both of the United States and of the several States, shall be bound by Oath or affirmation, to support this Constitution; but no religious Test shall ever be required as a Qualification to any Office or Public Trust under the United States.

ARTICLE VII

The Ratification of the Conventions of nine States, shall be sufficient for the Establishment of this Constitution between the States so ratifying the Same.

AMENDMENTS

Amendment I

Congress shall make no law respecting an establishment of religion, or prohibiting the free exercise thereof; or abridging the freedom of speech, or of the press; or the right of the people peaceably to assemble, and to petition the Government for a redress of grievances.

Amendment II

A well regulated Militia, being necessary to the security of a free State, the right of the people to keep and bear Arms, shall not be infringed.

Amendment III

No Soldier shall, in time of peace be quartered in any house, without the consent of the Owner, nor in time of war, but in a manner to be prescribed by law.

Amendment IV

The right of the people to be secure in their persons, houses, papers, and effects, against unreasonable searches and seizures, shall not be violated, and no Warrants shall issue, but upon probable cause, supported by Oath or affirmation, and particularly describing the place to be searched, and the persons or things to be seized.

Amendment V

No person shall be held to answer for a capital, or otherwise infamous crime, unless on a presentment or indictment of a Grand Jury, except in cases arising in the land or naval forces, or in the Militia, when in actual service in time of War or public danger; nor shall any person be subject for the same offence to be twice put in jeopardy of life or limb; nor shall be compelled in any criminal case to be a witness against himself; nor be deprived of life, liberty, or property, without due process of law; nor shall private property be taken for public use, without just compensation.

Amendment VI

In all criminal prosecutions the accused shall enjoy the right to a speedy and public trial, by an impartial jury of the State and district wherein the crime shall have been committed, which district shall have been previously ascertained by law, and to be informed of the nature and cause of the accusation; to be confronted with the witnesses against him: to have compulsory process for obtaining witnesses in his favor, and to have the Assistance of Counsel for his defence.

Amendment VII

In suits at common law, where the value in controversy shall exceed twenty dollars, the right of trial by jury shall be preserved, and no fact tried by a jury shall be otherwise re-examined in any Court of the United States, than according to the rules of the common law.

Amendment VIII

Excessive bail shall not be required, nor excessive fines imposed, nor cruel and unusual punishments inflicted.

Amendment IX

The enumeration in the Constitution, of certain rights, shall not be construed to deny or disparage others retained by the people.

Amendment X

The powers not delegated to the United States by the Constitution, nor prohibited by it to the States, are reserved to the States respectively, or to the people.

[The first ten Amendments were adopted in 1791.]

Amendment XI

The Judicial power of the United States shall not be construed to extend to any suit in law or equity, commenced or prosecuted against one of the United States by Citizens of another State, or by Citizens or Subjects of any Foreign State. [Adopted in 1798.]

Amendment XII

The Electors shall meet in their respective states, and vote by ballot for President and Vice-President, one of whom, at least, shall not be an inhabitant of the same state with themselves; they shall name in their ballots the person voted for as President, and in distinct ballots the person voted for as Vice-President, and they shall make distinct lists of all persons voted for as President, and of all persons voted for as Vice-President, and of the number of votes for each, which lists they shall sign and certify, and transmit sealed to the seat of the government of the United States, directed to the President of the Senate;—The President of the Senate shall, in the presence of the Senate and House of Representatives, open all the certificates and the votes shall then be counted;—The person having the greatest number of votes for President, shall be the President, if such number be a majority of the whole number of Electors appointed; and if no person have such majority, then from the persons having the highest numbers not exceeding three on the list of those voted for as President, the House of Representatives shall choose immediately, by ballot, the President. But in choosing the President, the votes shall be taken by states, the representation from each state having one vote; a quorum for this purpose shall consist of a member or members from two-thirds of the states, and a majority of all the states shall be necessary to a choice. And if the House of Representatives shall not choose a President whenever the right of choice shall devolve upon them, before the fourth day of March next following, then the Vice-President shall act as President, as in the case of the death or other constitutional disability of the President.—The person having the greatest number of votes as Vice-President, shall be the Vice-President, if such number be a majority of the whole number of Electors appointed, and if no person have a majority, then from the two highest numbers on the list, the Senate shall choose the Vice-President; a quorum for the purpose shall consist of two-thirds of the whole number of Senators, and a majority of the whole number shall be necessary to a choice. But no person constitutionally ineligible to the office of President shall be eligible to that of Vice-President of the United States. [Adopted in 1804.]

Amendment XIII

SECTION 1. Neither slavery nor involuntary servitude, except as a punishment for crime whereof the party shall have been duly convicted, shall exist within the United States, or any place subject to their jurisdiction.

SECTION 2. Congress shall have power to enforce this article by appropriate legislation. [Adopted in 1865.]

Amendment XIV

SECTION 1. All persons born or naturalized in the United States, and subject to the jurisdiction thereof, are citizens of the United States and of the State wherein they reside. No State shall make or enforce any law which shall abridge the privileges or immunities of citizens of the United States; nor shall any State deprive any person of life, liberty, or property, without due process of law; nor deny to any person within its jurisdiction the equal protection of the laws.

SECTION 2. Representatives shall be apportioned among the several States according to their respective numbers, counting the whole number of persons in each State, excluding Indians not taxed. But when the right to vote at any election for the choice of electors for President and Vice President of the United States, Representatives in Congress, the Executive and Judicial officers of a State, or the members of the Legislature thereof, is denied to any of the male inhabitants of such State, being twenty-one years of age, and citizens of the United States, or in any way abridged, except for participation in rebellion. or other crime, the basis of representation therein shall be reduced in the proportion which the number of such male citizens shall bear to the whole number of male citizens twenty-one years of age in such State.

SECTION 3. No person shall be a Senator or Representative in Congress, or elector of President and Vice President, or hold any office, civil or military, under the United States, or under any State, who, having previously taken an oath, as a member of Congress, or as an officer of the United States, or as a member of any State legislature, or as an executive or judicial officer of any State, to support the Constitution of the United States, shall have engaged in insurrection or rebellion against the same, or given aid or comfort to the enemies thereof. But Congress may by a vote of two-thirds of each House, remove such disability.

SECTION 4. The validity of the public debt of the United States, authorized by law, including debts incurred for payment of pensions and bounties for services in suppressing insurrection or rebellion, shall not be questioned. But neither the United States nor any State shall assume or pay any debt or obligation incurred in aid of insurrection or rebellion against the United States, or any claim for the loss or emancipation of any slave; but all such debts, obligations and claims shall be held illegal and void.

SECTION 5. The Congress shall have power to enforce, by appropriate legislation, the provisions of this article. [Adopted in 1868.]

Amendment XV

SECTION 1. The right of citizens of the United States to vote shall not be denied or abridged by the United States or by any State on account of race, color, or previous condition of servitude.

SECTION 2. The Congress shall have power to enforce this article by appropriate legislation. [Adopted in 1870.]

Amendment XVI

The Congress shall have power to lay and collect taxes on incomes, from whatever source derived, without apportionment among the several States, and without regard to any census or enumeration. [Adopted in 1913.]

Amendment XVII

The Senate of the United States shall be composed of two Senators from each State, elected by the people thereof, for six years; and each Senator shall have one vote. The electors in each State shall have the qualifications requisite for electors of the most numerous branch of the State legislatures.

When vacancies happen in the representation of any State in the Senate, the executive authority of such State shall issue writs of election to fill such vacancies: *Provided,* That the legislature of any State may empower the executive thereof to make temporary appointments until the people fill the vacancies by election as the legislature may direct.

This amendment shall not be so construed as to affect the election or term of any Senator chosen before it becomes valid as part of the Constitution. [Adopted in 1913.]

Amendment XVIII

SECTION 1. After one year from the ratification of this article the manufacture, sale, or transportation of intoxicating liquors within, the importation thereof into, or the exportation thereof from the United States and all territory subject to the jurisdiction thereof for beverage purposes is hereby prohibited.

SECTION 2. The Congress and the several States shall have concurrent power to enforce this article by appropriate legislation.

SECTION 3. This article shall be inoperative unless it shall have been ratified as an amendment to the Constitution by the legislatures of the several States, as provided in the Constitution, within seven years from the date of the submission hereof to the States by the Congress. [Adopted in 1919.]

Amendment XIX

The right of citizens of the United States to vote shall not be denied or abridged by the United States or by any State on account of sex.

Congress shall have power to enforce this article by appropriate legislation. [Adopted in 1920.]

Amendment XX

SECTION 1. The terms of the President and Vice President shall end at noon at the 20th day of January, and the terms of Senators and Representatives at noon on the 3d day of January, of the years in which such terms would have ended if this article had not been ratified; and terms of their successors shall then begin.

SECTION 2. The Congress shall assemble at least once in every year, and such meeting shall begin at noon on the 3d day of January, unless they shall by law appoint a different day.

SECTION 3. If, at the time fixed for the beginning of the term of the President, the President elect shall have died, the Vice President elect shall become President. If a President shall not have been chosen before the time fixed for the beginning of his term, or if the President elect shall have failed to qualify, then the Vice President elect shall act as President until a President shall have qualified; and the Congress may by law provide for the case wherein neither a President elect nor a Vice President elect shall have qualified, declaring who shall then act as President, or the manner in which one who is to act shall be selected, and such person shall act accordingly until a President or Vice President shall have qualified.

SECTION 4. The Congress may by law provide for the case of the death of any of the persons from whom the House of Representatives may choose a President whenever the right of choice shall have devolved upon them, and for the case of the death of any of the persons from whom the Senate may choose a Vice President whenever the right of choice shall have devolved upon them.

SECTION 5. Sections 1 and 2 shall take effect on the 15th day of October following the ratification of this article.

SECTION 6. This article shall be inoperative unless it shall have been ratified as an amendment to the Constitution by the legislatures of three-fourths of the several States within seven years from the date of its submission. [Adopted in 1933.]

Amendment XXI

SECTION 1. The eighteenth article of amendment to the Constitution of the United States is hereby repealed.

SECTION 2. The transportation or importation into any State, Territory, or possession of the United States for delivery or use therein of intoxicating liquors, in violation of the laws thereof, is hereby prohibited.

SECTION 3. This article shall be inoperative unless it shall have been ratified as an amendment to the Constitution by conventions in the several States, as provided in the Constitution, within seven years from the date of the submission hereof to the States by the Congress. [Adopted in 1933.]

Amendment XXII

SECTION 1. No person shall be elected to the office of the President more than twice, and no person who has held the office of President, or acted as President, for more than two years of a term to which some other person was elected President shall be elected to the office of the President more than once. But this Article shall not apply to any persons holding the office of President when this Article was proposed by the Congress, and shall not prevent any person who may be holding the office of President, or acting as President, during the term within which this Article becomes operative from holding the office of President or acting as President during the remainder of such term.

SECTION 2. This Article shall be inoperative unless it shall have been ratified as an amendment to the Constitution by the legislatures of three-fourths of the several States within seven years from the date of its submission to the states by the Congress. [Adopted in 1951.]

Amendment XXIII

SECTION 1. The District constituting the seat of Government of the United States shall appoint in such manner as the Congress may direct:

A number of electors of President and Vice President equal to the whole number of Senators and Representatives in Congress to which the District would be entitled if it were a State, but in no event more than the least populous states; they shall be in addition to those appointed by the States, but they shall be considered, for the purposes of the election of President and Vice President, to be electors appointed by a State; and they shall meet in the District and perform such duties as provided by the twelfth article of amendment.

SECTION 2. The Congress shall have power to enforce this article by appropriate legislation. [Adopted in 1961].

SECTION 1. The right of citizens of the United States to vote in any primary or other election for President or Vice President, for electors for President or Vice President, or for Senator or Representative in Congress, shall not be denied or abridged by the United States or any State by reason of failure to pay poll tax or other tax.

SECTION 2. The Congress shall have power to enforce this article by appropriate legislation. [Adopted in 1964.]

Amendment XXV

SECTION 1. In case of the removal of the President from office or of his death or resignation, the Vice President shall become President.

SECTION 2. Whenever there is a vacancy in the office of the Vice President, the President shall nominate a Vice President who shall take office upon confirmation by a majority vote of both Houses of Congress.

SECTION 3. Whenever the President transmits to the President pro tempore of the Senate and the Speaker of the House of Representatives his written declaration that he is unable to discharge the powers and duties of his office, and until he transmits to them a written declaration to the contrary, such powers and duties shall be discharged by the Vice President as Acting President.

SECTION 4. Whenever the Vice President and a majority of either the principal officers of the executive departments or of such other body as Congress may by law provide, transmit to the President pro tempore of the Senate and the Speaker of the House of Representatives their written declaration that the President is unable to discharge the powers and duties of his office, the Vice President shall immediately assume the powers and duties of the office as Acting President.

Thereafter, when the President transmits to the President pro tempore of the Senate and the Speaker of the House of Representatives his written declaration that no inability exists, he shall resume the powers and duties of his office unless the Vice President and a majority of either the principal officers of the executive departments or of such other body as Congress may by law provide, transmit within four days to the President pro tempore of the Senate and the Speaker of the House of Representatives their written declaration that the President is unable to discharge the powers and duties of his office. Thereupon Congress shall decide the issue, assembling within forty-eight hours for that purpose if not in session. If the Congress, within twenty-one days after receipt of the latter written declaration, or if Congress is not in session, within twenty-one days after Congress is required to assemble, determines by two-thirds vote of both Houses that the President is unable to discharge the powers and duties of his office, the Vice President shall continue to discharge the same as Acting President; otherwise, the President shall resume the powers and duties of his office. [Adopted in 1967.]

Amendment XXVI

SECTION 1. The rights of citizens of the United States, who are eighteen years of age or older, to vote shall not be denied or abridged by the United States or any state on account of age.

SECTION 2. The Congress shall have the power to enforce this article by appropriate legislation. [Adopted in 1971.]

Amendment XXVII (Proposed)[8]

SECTION 1. Equality of rights under the law shall not be denied or abridged by the United States or by any state on account of sex.

SECTION 2. The Congress shall have the power to enforce, by appropriate legislation, the provisions of this article.

SECTION 3. This amendment shall take effect two years after the date of ratification. [Proposed by Congress on March 22, 1972.]

---

[8]The Congressional Resolution proposing the Amendment provided that it must be ratified "within seven years from the date of its submission by the Congress" to become effective. By June, 1977, the Amendment had been ratified by 35 of the required 38 states.

SELECTED REFERENCES

THE COURT SYSTEM

ABRAHAM, HENRY J. *Justices and Presidents: A Political History of Appointments to the Supreme Court.* New York: Oxford University Press, 1974.

ABRAHAM, HENRY J. *The Judicial Process* (3rd ed.). New York: Oxford University Press, 1975.

BICKEL, ALEXANDER M. *The Least Dangerous Branch.* Indianapolis: Bobbs-Merrill, 1962.

BICKEL, ALEXANDER M. *The Supreme Court and the Idea of Progress.* New York: Harper & Row, 1970.

CHASE, HAROLD W. *Federal Judges: The Appointing Process.* Minneapolis: University of Minnesota Press, 1972.

FRANKFURTER, FELIX, and JAMES M. LANDIS. *The Business of the Supreme Court.* New York: Macmillan, 1928.

JACKSON, ROBERT H. *The Supreme Court in the American System of Government.* Cambridge, Mass.: Harvard University Press, 1955.

KURLAND, PHILIP B. *Politics, the Constitution, and the Warren Court.* Chicago: University of Chicago Press, 1970.

KURLAND, PHILIP B., ed. *The Supreme Court Review.* Chicago: University of Chicago Press, 1960–1976.

LEWIS, ANTHONY. *Gideon's Trumpet.* New York: Random House, 1964.

McCLOSKEY, ROBERT G. *The American Supreme Court.* Chicago: University of Chicago Press, 1960.

MURPHY, PAUL L. *The Constitution in Crisis Times: 1918–1969.* New York: Harper & Row, 1972.

MURPHY, WALTER F., and C. HERMAN PRITCHETT. *Courts, Judges, and Politics* (2d ed.). New York: Random House, 1974.

PRITCHETT, C. HERMAN. *The American Constitution* (3d ed.), Chaps. 6–8. New York: McGraw-Hill, 1977.

PRITCHETT, C. HERMAN. *The Roosevelt Court: A Study in Judicial Politics and Values, 1937–1947.* Chicago: Quadrangle Books, 1969.

ROHDE, DAVID W., and HAROLD J. SPAETH. *Supreme Court Decision Making.* San Francisco: Freeman, 1976.

SHOGAN, ROBERT. *A Question of Judgment: The Fortas Case.* Indianapolis: Bobbs-Merrill, 1972.

STEAMER, ROBERT J. *The Supreme Court in Crisis.* Amherst: University of Massachusetts Press, 1971.

SWINDLER, WILLIAM F. *Court and Constitution in the Twentieth Century: 1932–1968.* Indianapolis: Bobbs-Merrill, 1972.

WILKINSON, J. HARVIE. *Serving Justice: A Supreme Court Clerk's View.* New York: Charterhouse, 1974.

THE PRESIDENCY

BARBER, JAMES D. *Choosing the President.* Englewood Cliffs, N.J.: Prentice-Hall, 1974.

BERGER, RAOUL. *Executive Privilege: A Constitutional Myth.* Cambridge, Mass.: Harvard University Press, 1974.

BERGER, RAOUL. *Impeachment: The Constitutional Problems.* Cambridge, Mass.: Harvard University Press, 1973.

BICKEL, ALEXANDER M. *Reform and Continuity: The Electoral College, the Convention, and the Party System.* New York: Harper & Row, 1971.

CORWIN, EDWARD S. *The President: Office and Powers* (4th ed.). New York: New York University Press, 1957.

CRONIN, THOMAS E. *The State of the Presidency.* Boston: Little, Brown, 1975.

CRONIN, THOMAS E., and REXFORD G. TUGWELL. *The Presidency Reappraised* (2d ed.). New York: Praeger, 1977.

FISHER, LOUIS. *Presidential Spending Power.* Princeton: Princeton University Press, 1975.

HENKIN, LOUIS. *Foreign Affairs and the Constitution.* Mineola, N.Y.: Foundation, 1972.

KALLENBACH, JOSEPH. *The American Chief Executive.* New York: Harper & Row, 1966.

KOENIG, LOUIS W. *The Chief Executive* (3d ed.). New York: Harcourt Brace Jovanovich, 1975.

LONGLEY, LAWRENCE D., and ALAN G. BRAUN. *The Politics of Electoral College Reform* (2d ed.). New Haven: Yale University Press, 1975.

PEIRCE, NEAL R. *The People's President.* New York: Simon and Schuster, 1968.

SCHLESINGER, ARTHUR M., JR. *The Imperial Presidency.* Boston: Houghton, Mifflin, 1973.

SCIGLIANO, ROBERT. *The Supreme Court and the Presidency.* New York: Free Press, 1971.

CONGRESS

BAKER, GORDON E. *The Reapportionment Revolution.* New York: Random House, 1966.

CLAUDE, RICHARD. *The Supreme Court and the Electoral Process.* Baltimore: Johns Hopkins Press, 1970.

DIXON, ROBERT G. *Democratic Representation: Reapportionment in Law and Politics.* New York: Oxford University Press, 1968.

ELLIOTT, WARD E. Y. *The Rise of Guardian Democracy: The Supreme Court's Role in Voting Rights Disputes, 1845–1969.* Cambridge, Mass.: Harvard University Press, 1974.

FISHER, LOUIS. *President and Congress: Power and Policy.* New York: Free Press, 1972.

Impeachment and the United States Congress. Washington, D.C.: Congressional Quarterly, 1974.

MANSFIELD, HARVEY C., SR. *Congress Against the President.* New York: Praeger, 1975.

MURPHY, WALTER F. *Congress and the Court.* Chicago: University of Chicago Press, 1962.

POLSBY, NELSON W., ed. *Reapportionment in the 1970s.* Berkeley: University of California Press, 1971.

PRITCHETT, C. HERMAN. *The American Constitution* (3d ed.), Chaps. 9–13. New York: McGraw-Hill, 1977.

TAYLOR, TELFORD. *Grand Inquest.* New York: Simon and Schuster, 1955.

THE FEDERAL SYSTEM

ELAZAR, DANIEL J. *American Federalism: A View from the States* (2d ed.). New York: Crowell, 1972.

GOLDWIN, ROBERT A., ed. *A Nation of States: Essays on the American Federal System.* Chicago: Rand McNally, 1963.

GRODZINS, MORTON. *The American System.* Chicago: Rand McNally, 1966.

LEACH, RICHARD. *American Federalism.* New York: Norton, 1970.

REAGAN, MICHAEL D. *The New Federalism.* New York: Oxford University Press, 1972.

RIKER, WILLIAM. *Federalism: Origin, Operation, Significance.* Boston: Little, Brown, 1964.

SUNDQUIST, JAMES L. *Making Federalism Work.* Washington, D.C.: Brookings Institution, 1969.

WILDAVSKY, AARON. *American Federalism in Perspective.* Boston: Little, Brown, 1967.

INDEX OF CASES

Note: Decisions reprinted in this book are shown in boldface and appear on the italicized pages.